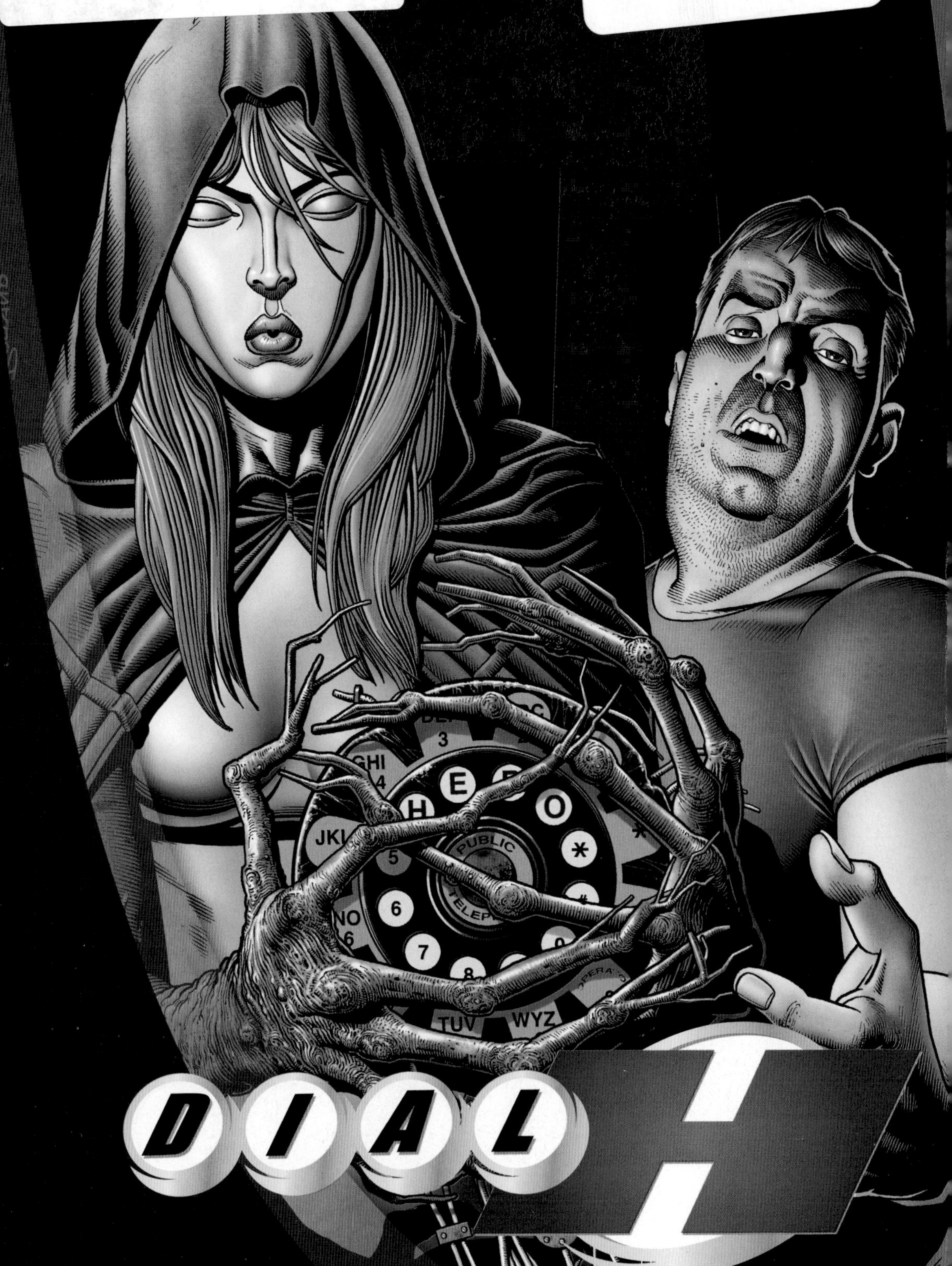

DIAL H

VOLUME 1 **INTO YOU**

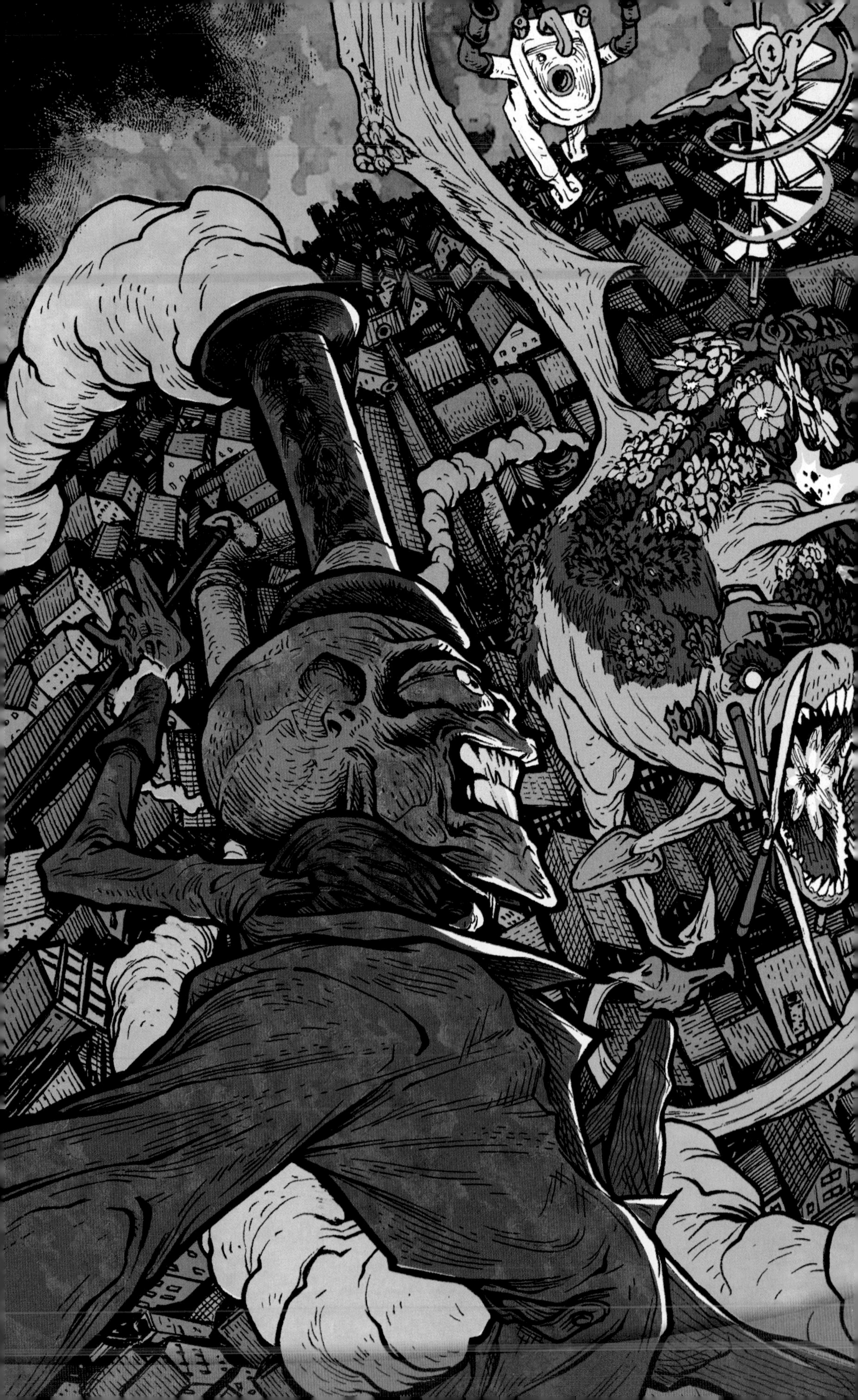

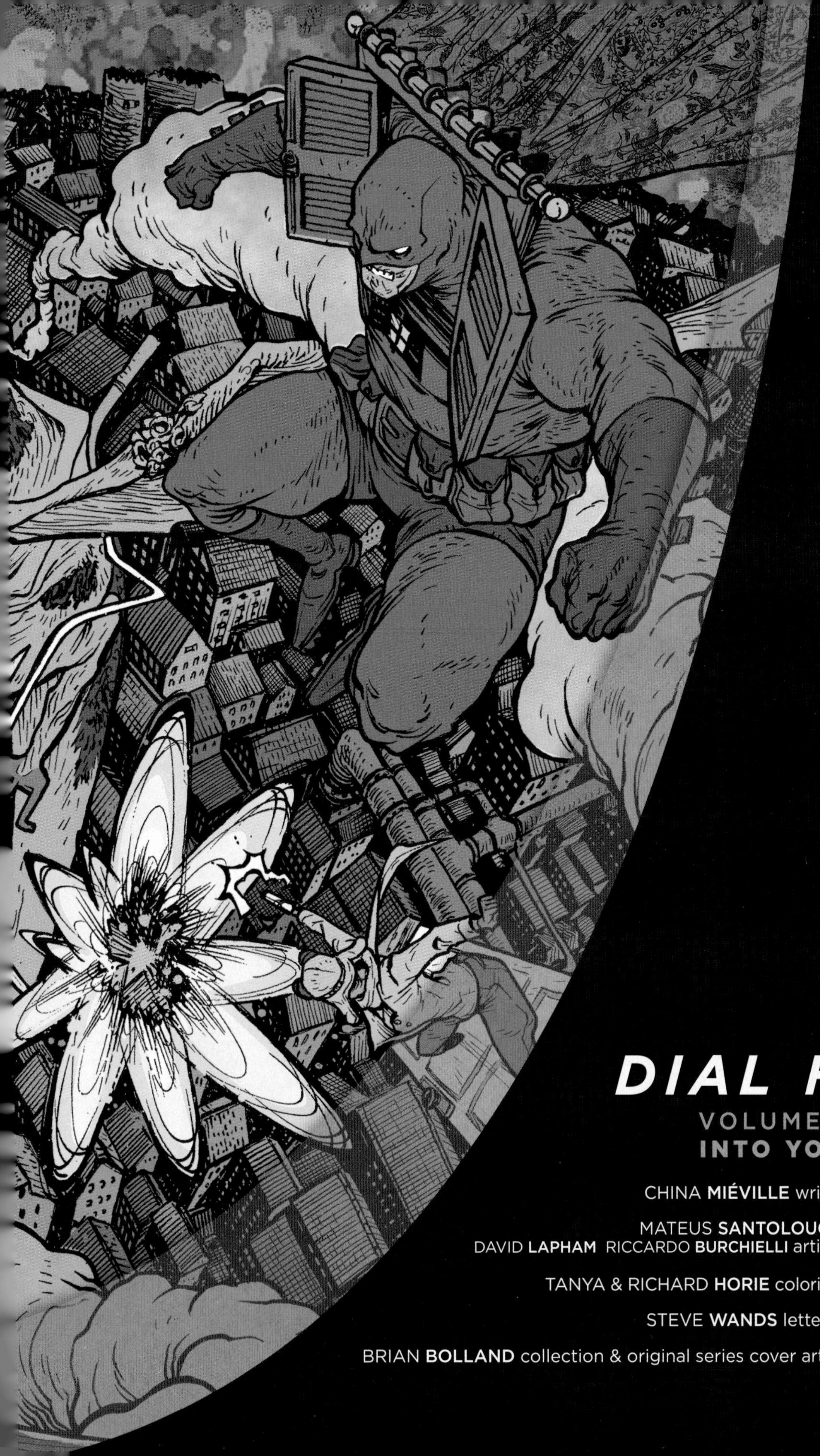

DIAL H

VOLUME 1
INTO YOU

CHINA **MIÉVILLE** writer

MATEUS **SANTOLOUCO**
DAVID **LAPHAM** RICCARDO **BURCHIELLI** artists

TANYA & RICHARD **HORIE** colorists

STEVE **WANDS** letterer

BRIAN **BOLLAND** collection & original series cover artist

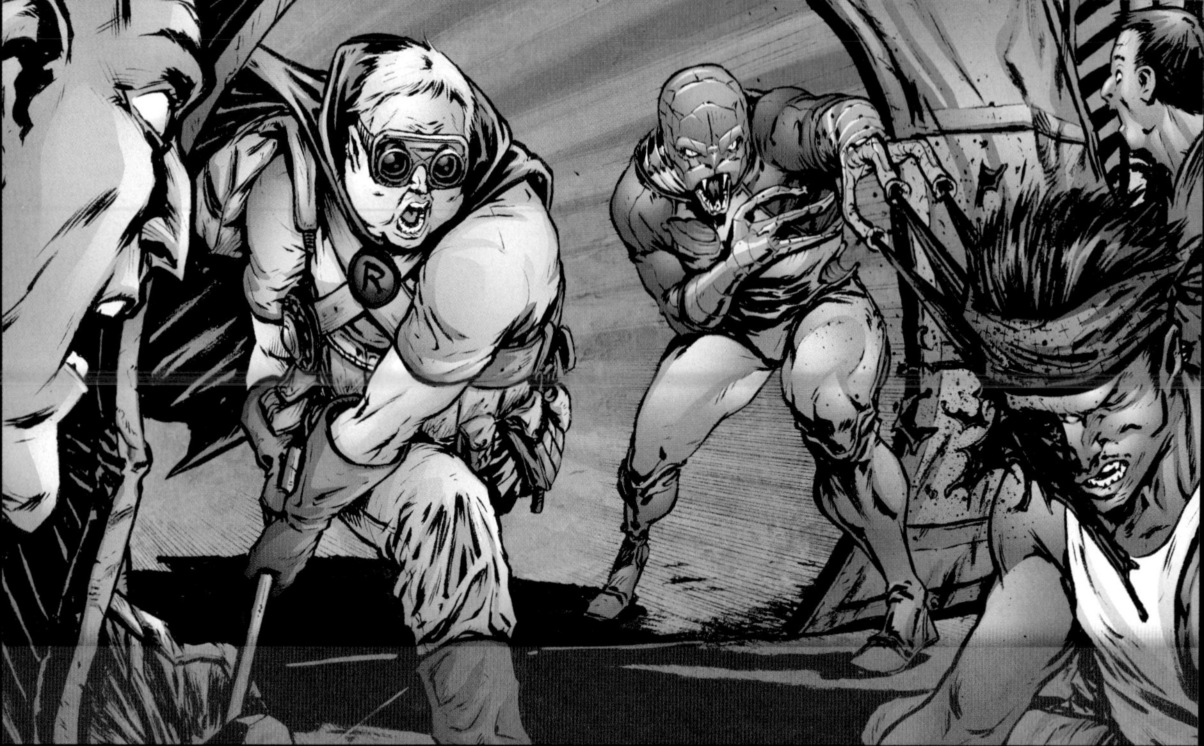

KAREN BERGER Editor – Original Series JOE HUGHES, GREGORY LOCKARD Assistant Editors – Original Series
JEFF BOISON Editor ROBBIN BROSTERMAN Design Director – Books
ROBBIE BIEDERMAN Publication Design

BOB HARRAS VP – Editor-in-Chief

DIANE NELSON President DAN DIDIO and JIM LEE Co-Publishers
GEOFF JOHNS Chief Creative Officer
JOHN ROOD Executive VP – Sales, Marketing and Business Development
AMY GENKINS Senior VP – Business and Legal Affairs NAIRI GARDINER Senior VP – Finance
JEFF BOISON VP – Publishing Operations MARK CHIARELLO VP – Art Direction and Design
JOHN CUNNINGHAM VP – Marketing TERRI CUNNINGHAM VP – Talent Relations and Services
ALISON GILL Senior VP – Manufacturing and Operations HANK KANALZ Senior VP – Digital

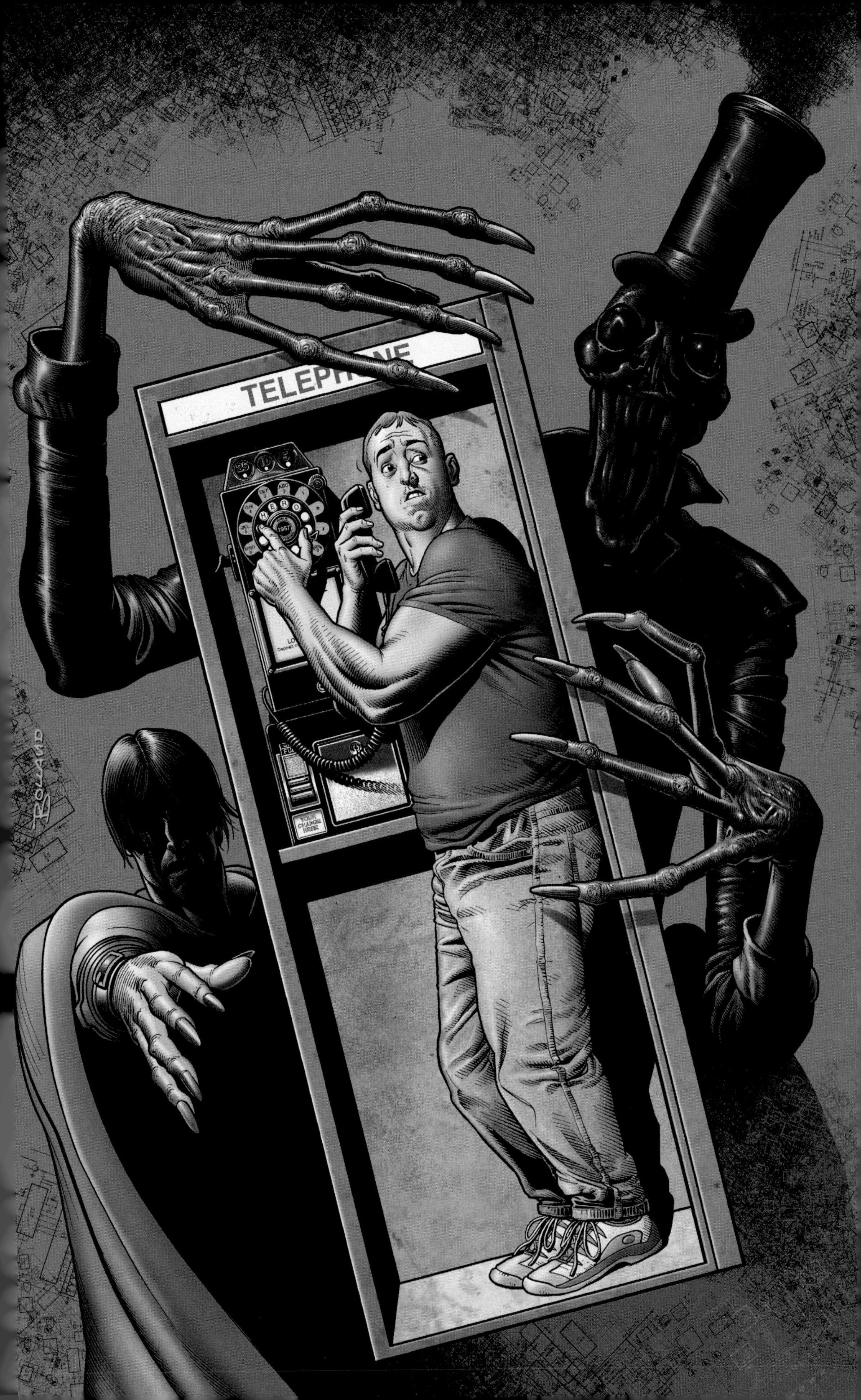
YOUR CHANGE HERE
BOLLAND

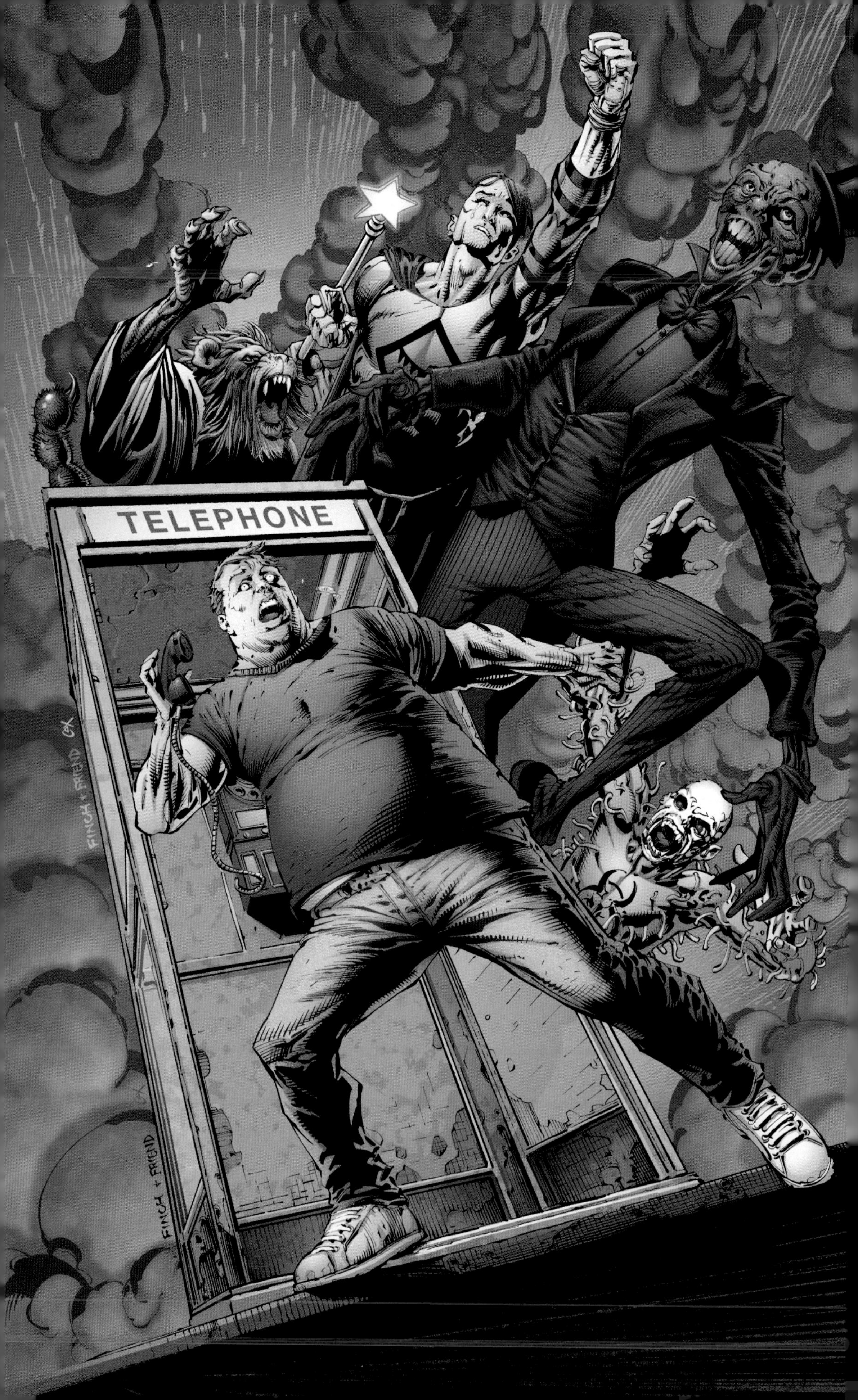
TELEPHONE

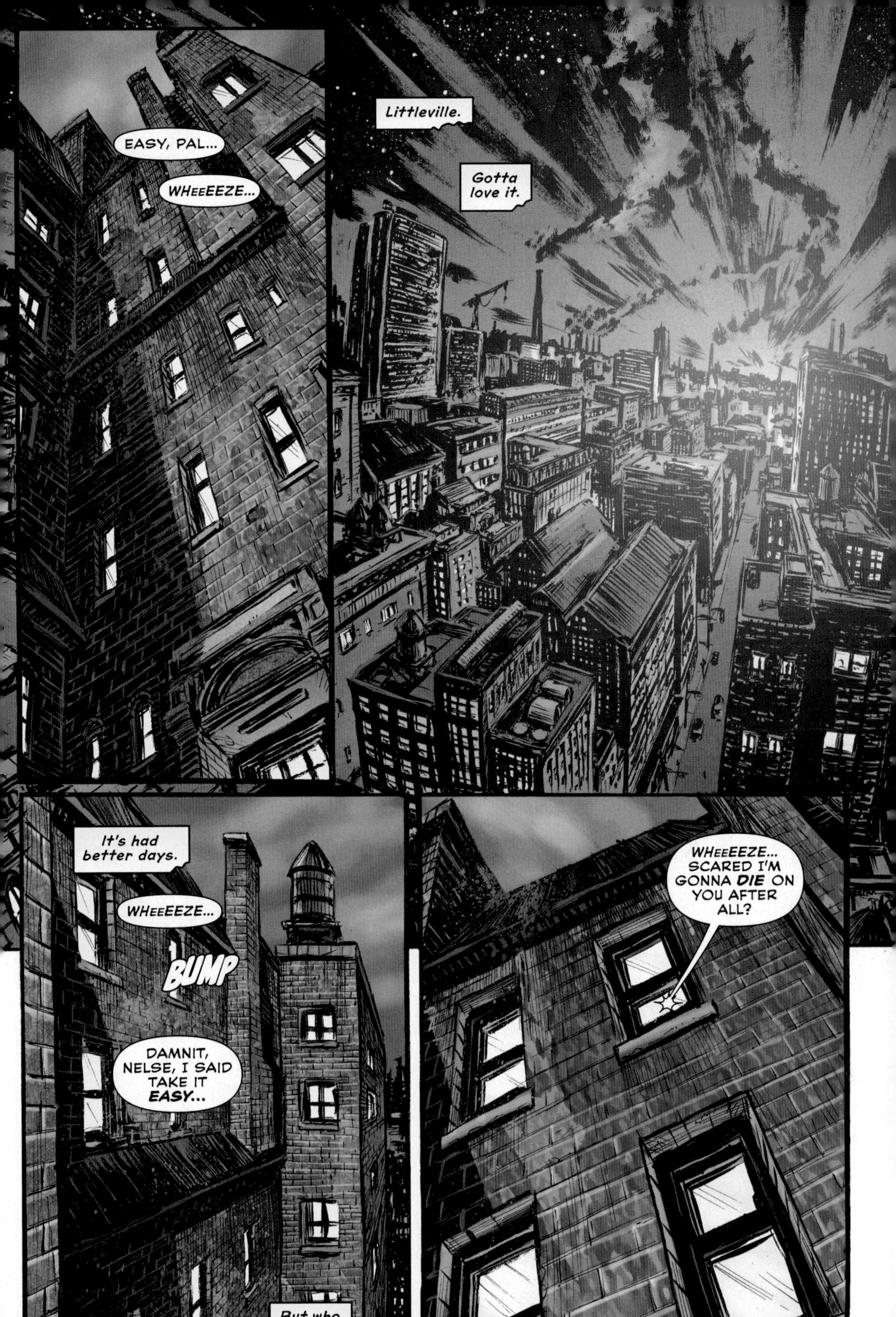
EASY, PAL...
WHEEEEZE...
Littleville.
Gotta love it.
It's had better days.
WHEEEEZE...
BUMP
DAMNIT, NELSE, I SAID TAKE IT EASY...
But who hasn't?
WHEEEEZE... SCARED I'M GONNA DIE ON YOU AFTER ALL?

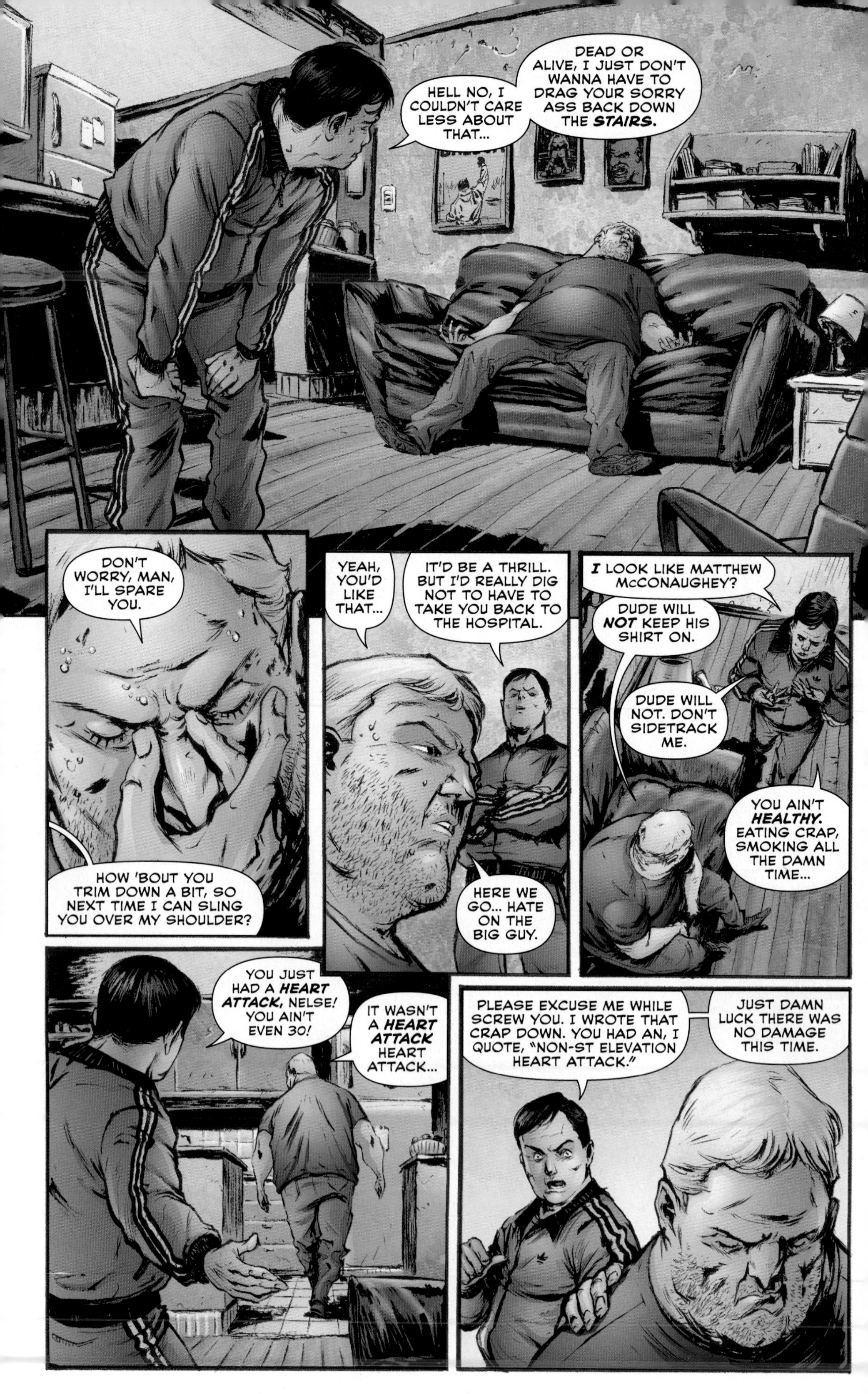
HELL NO, I COULDN'T CARE LESS ABOUT THAT...
DEAD OR ALIVE, I JUST DON'T WANNA HAVE TO DRAG YOUR SORRY ASS BACK DOWN THE **STAIRS.**
DON'T WORRY, MAN, I'LL SPARE YOU.
HOW 'BOUT YOU TRIM DOWN A BIT, SO NEXT TIME I CAN SLING YOU OVER MY SHOULDER?
YEAH, YOU'D LIKE THAT...
IT'D BE A THRILL. BUT I'D REALLY DIG NOT TO HAVE TO TAKE YOU BACK TO THE HOSPITAL.
HERE WE GO... HATE ON THE BIG GUY.
I LOOK LIKE MATTHEW McCONAUGHEY?
DUDE WILL ***NOT*** KEEP HIS SHIRT ON.
DUDE WILL NOT. DON'T SIDETRACK ME.
YOU AIN'T ***HEALTHY.*** EATING CRAP, SMOKING ALL THE DAMN TIME...
YOU JUST HAD A ***HEART ATTACK,*** NELSE! YOU AIN'T EVEN 30!
IT WASN'T A ***HEART ATTACK*** HEART ATTACK...
PLEASE EXCUSE ME WHILE SCREW YOU. I WROTE THAT CRAP DOWN. YOU HAD AN, I QUOTE, "NON-ST ELEVATION HEART ATTACK."
JUST DAMN LUCK THERE WAS NO DAMAGE THIS TIME.

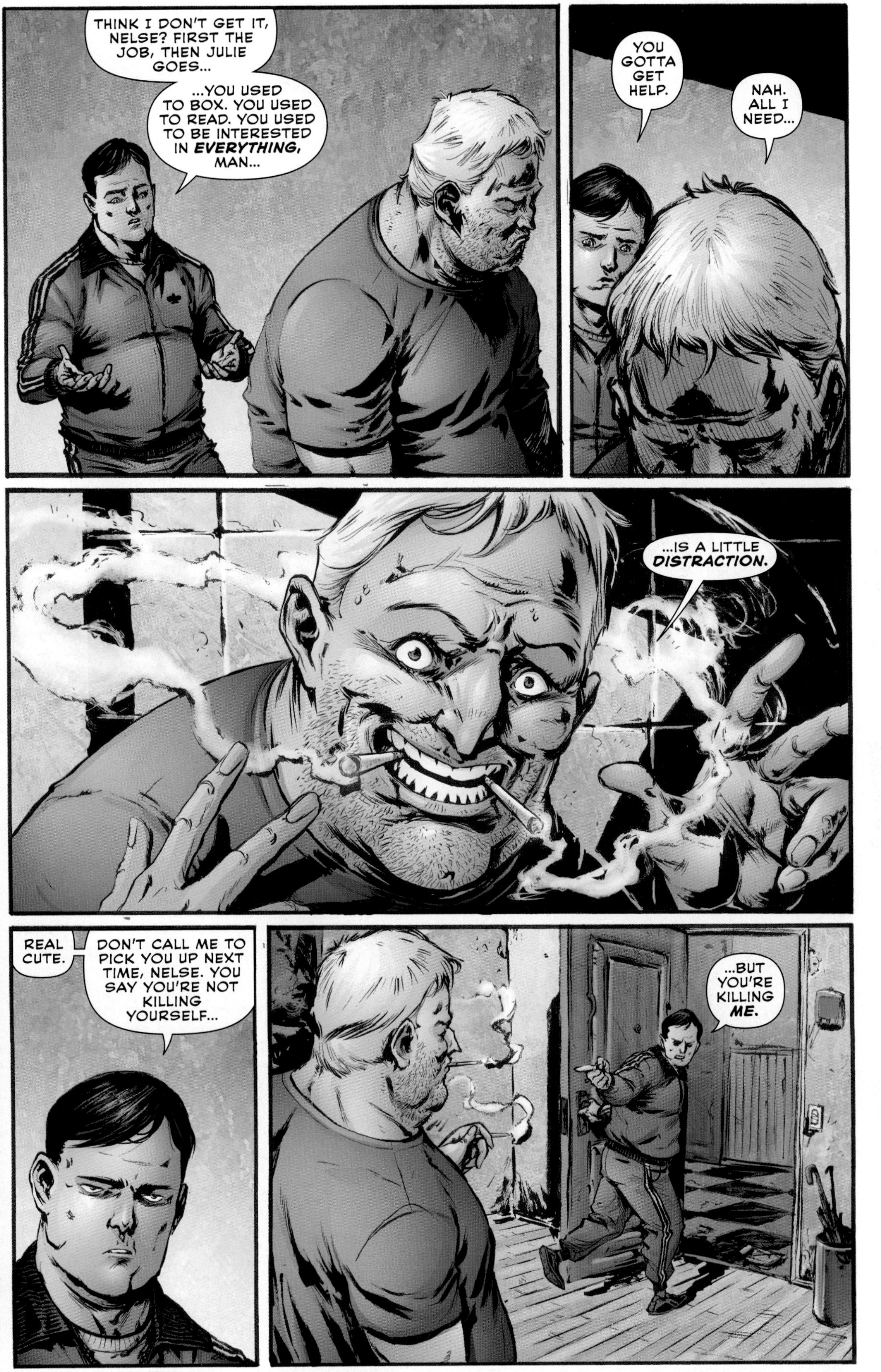
THINK I DON'T GET IT, NELSE? FIRST THE JOB, THEN JULIE GOES...
...YOU USED TO BOX. YOU USED TO READ. YOU USED TO BE INTERESTED IN EVERYTHING, MAN...
YOU GOTTA GET HELP.
NAH. ALL I NEED...
...IS A LITTLE DISTRACTION.
REAL CUTE.
DON'T CALL ME TO PICK YOU UP NEXT TIME, NELSE. YOU SAY YOU'RE NOT KILLING YOURSELF...
...BUT YOU'RE KILLING ME.

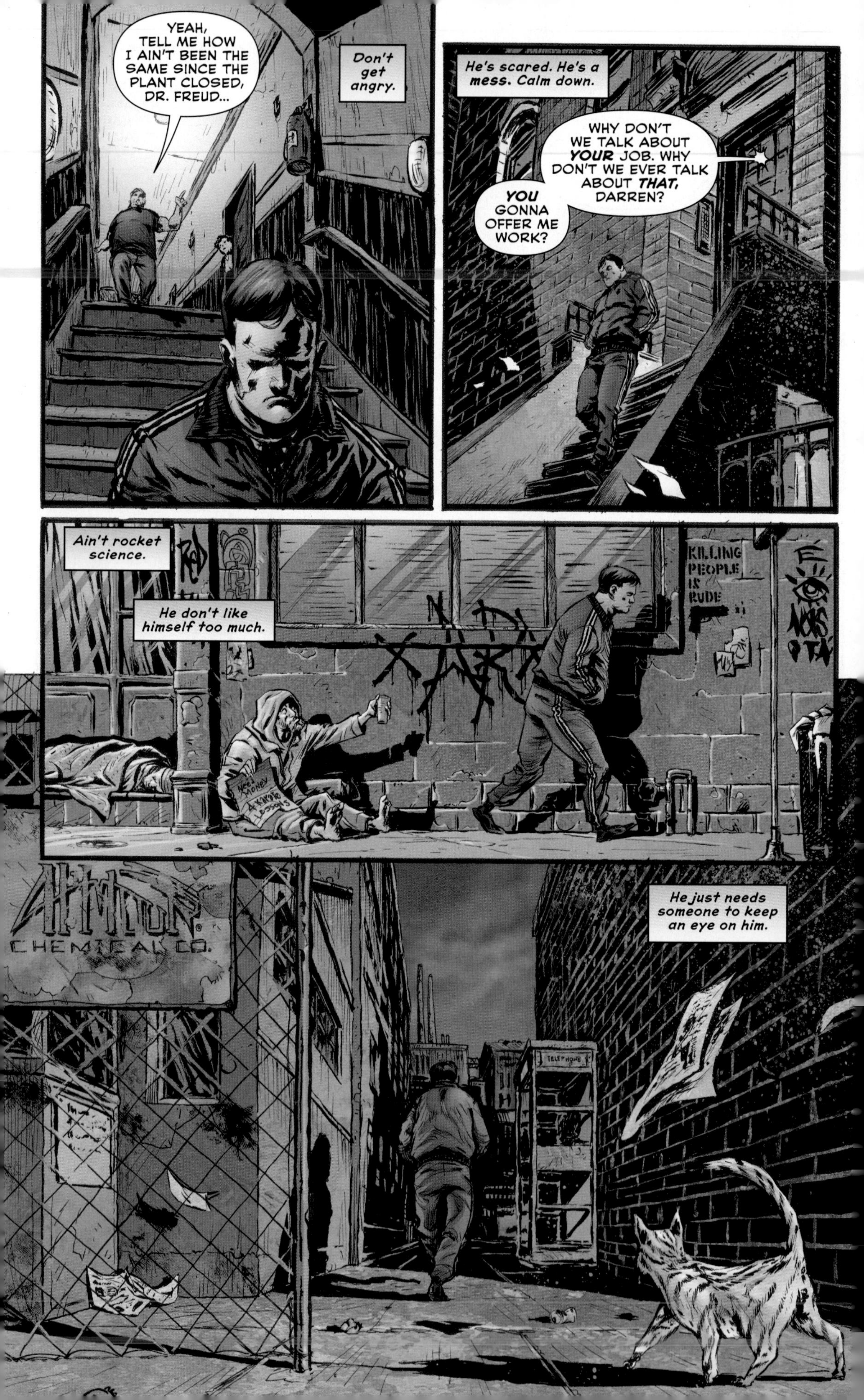

YEAH, TELL ME HOW I AIN'T BEEN THE SAME SINCE THE PLANT CLOSED, DR. FREUD...
Don't get angry.
He's scared. He's a mess. Calm down.
WHY DON'T WE TALK ABOUT YOUR JOB. WHY DON'T WE EVER TALK ABOUT THAT, DARREN?
YOU GONNA OFFER ME WORK?
Ain't rocket science.
He don't like himself too much.
KILLING PEOPLE IS RUDE
He just needs someone to keep an eye on him.
CHEMICAL CO.
TELEPHONE

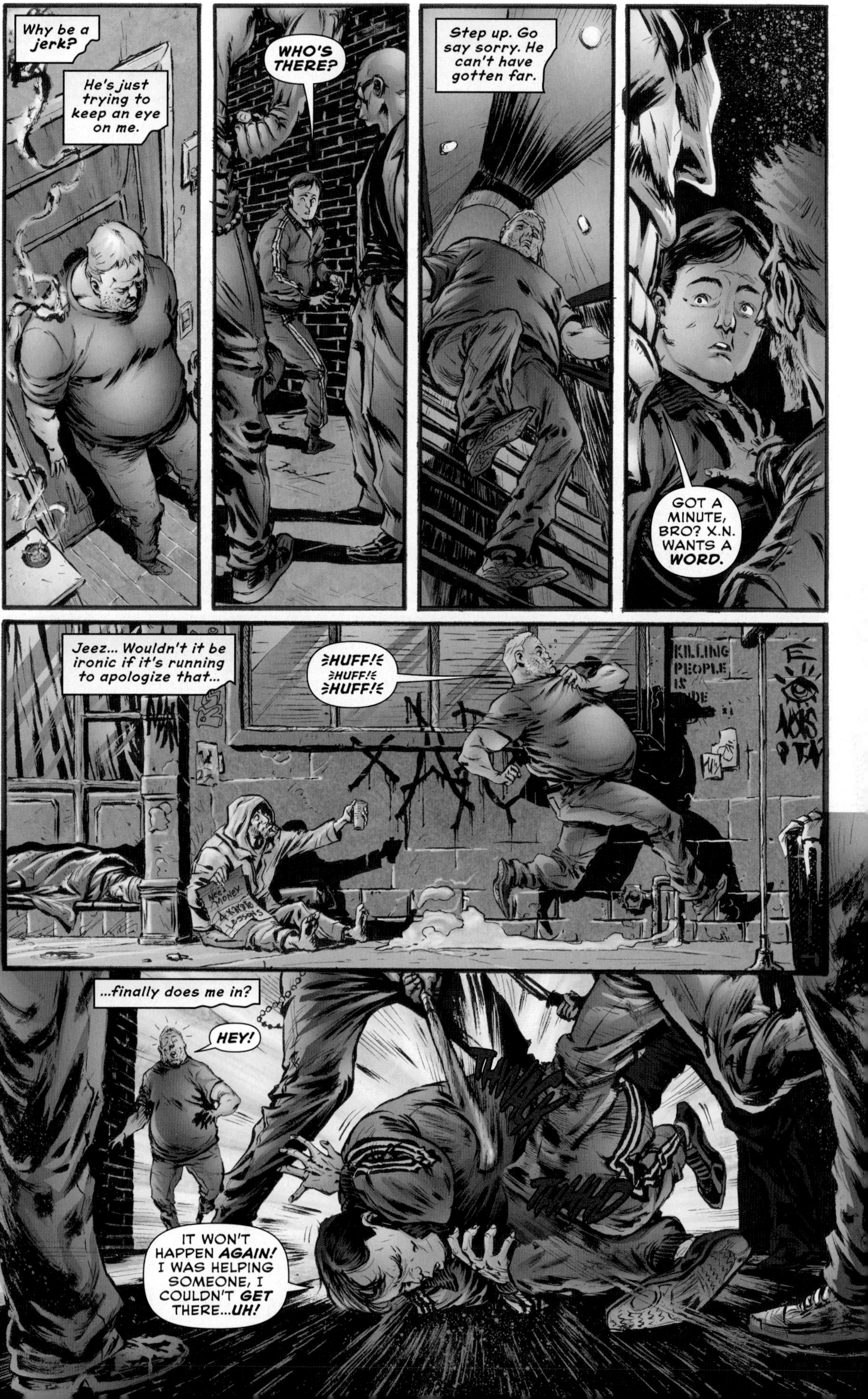
Why be a jerk?
He's just trying to keep an eye on me.
WHO'S THERE?
Step up. Go say sorry. He can't have gotten far.
GOT A MINUTE, BRO? X.N. WANTS A WORD.
Jeez... Wouldn't it be ironic if it's running to apologize that...
HUFF! HUFF! HUFF!
KILLING PEOPLE IS
...finally does me in?
HEY!
IT WON'T HAPPEN AGAIN! I WAS HELPING SOMEONE, I COULDN'T GET THERE...UH!

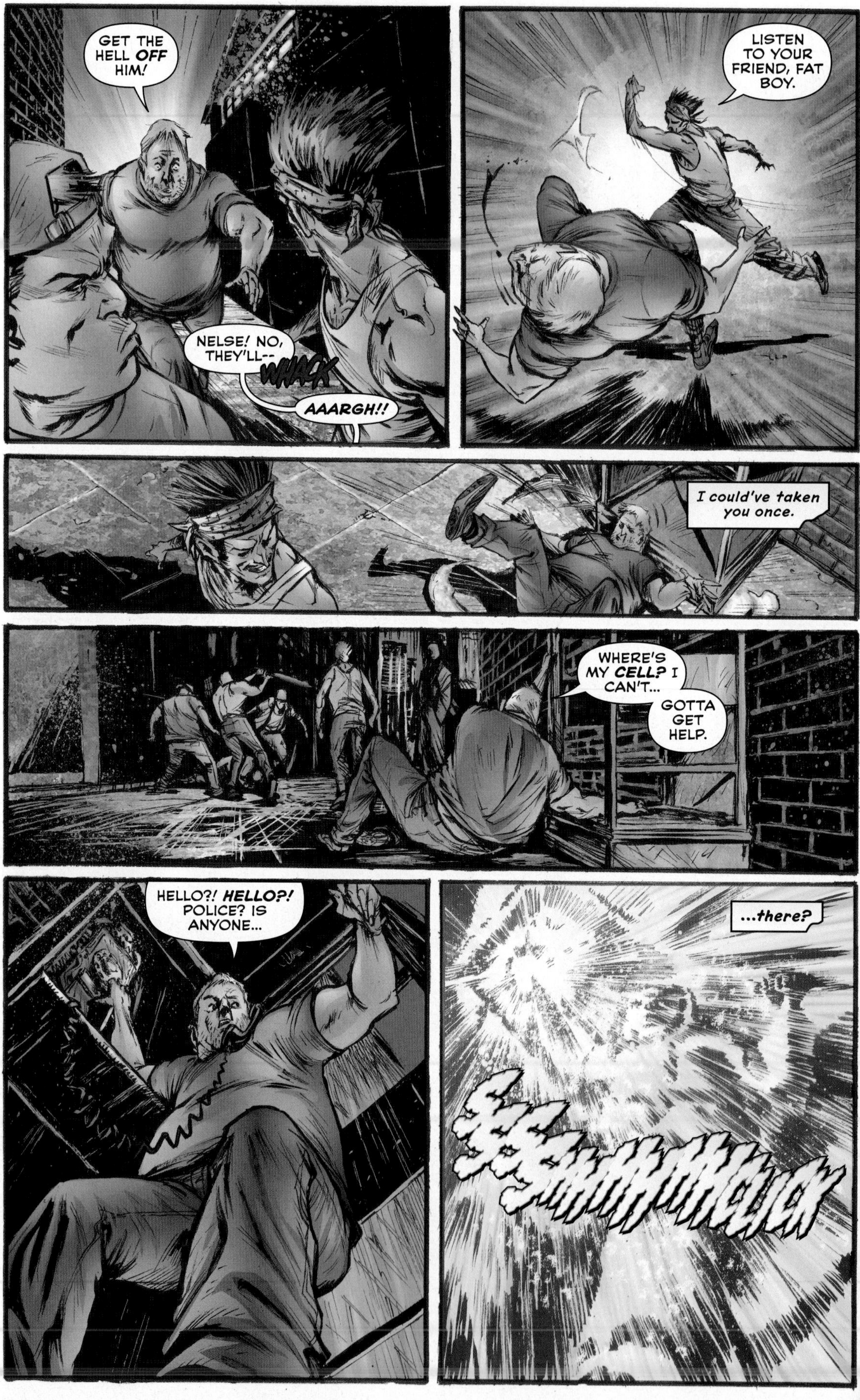
GET THE HELL OFF HIM!
NELSE! NO, THEY'LL--
WHACK
AAARGH!!
LISTEN TO YOUR FRIEND, FAT BOY.
I could've taken you once.
WHERE'S MY CELL? I CAN'T...
GOTTA GET HELP.
HELLO?! HELLO?! POLICE? IS ANYONE...
...there?

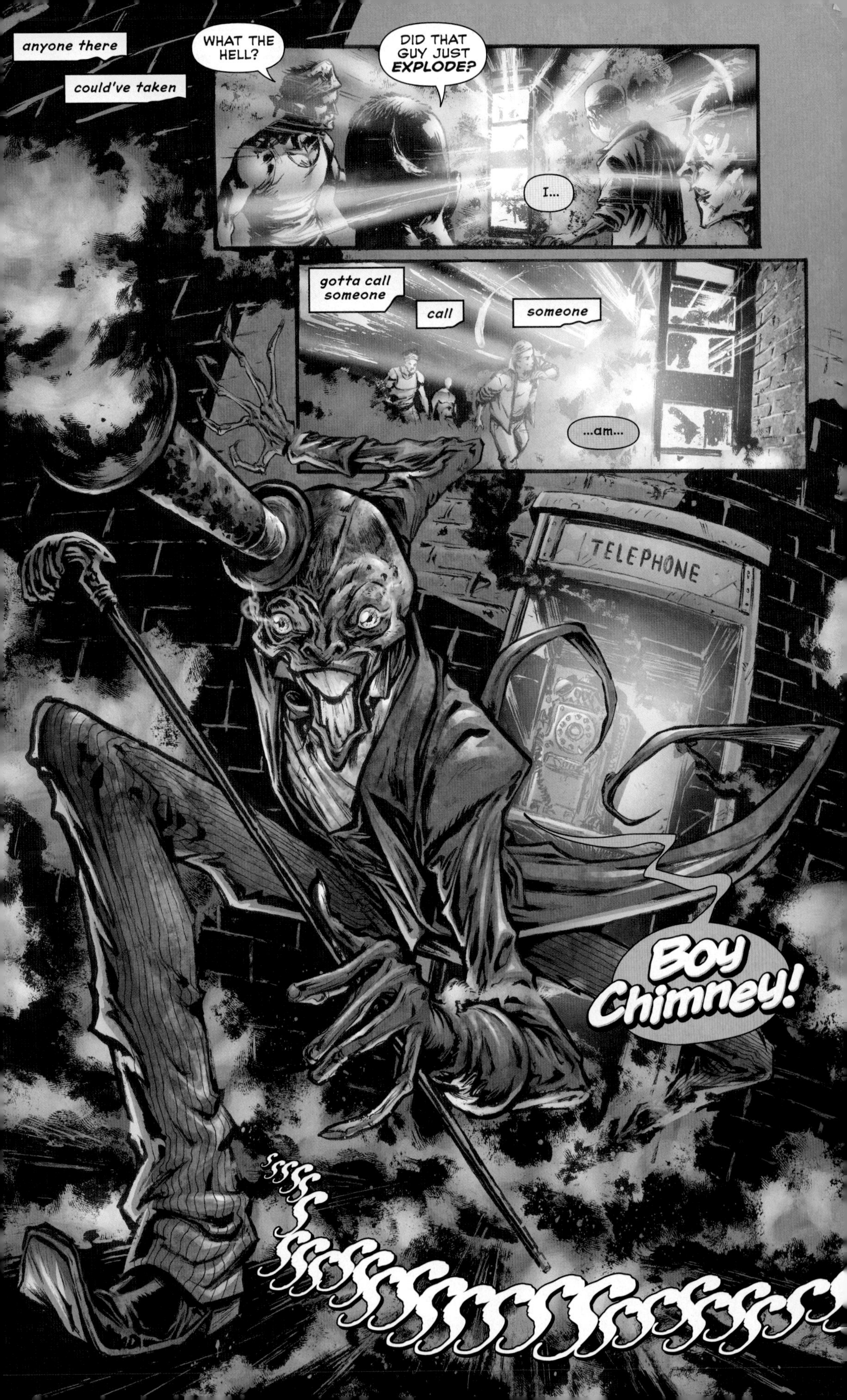
anyone there
could've taken
WHAT THE HELL?
DID THAT GUY JUST EXPLODE?
I...
gotta call someone
call
someone
...am...
TELEPHONE
Boy Chimney!
SSSSSSSSSSSSSSSSSSSSSSSSS

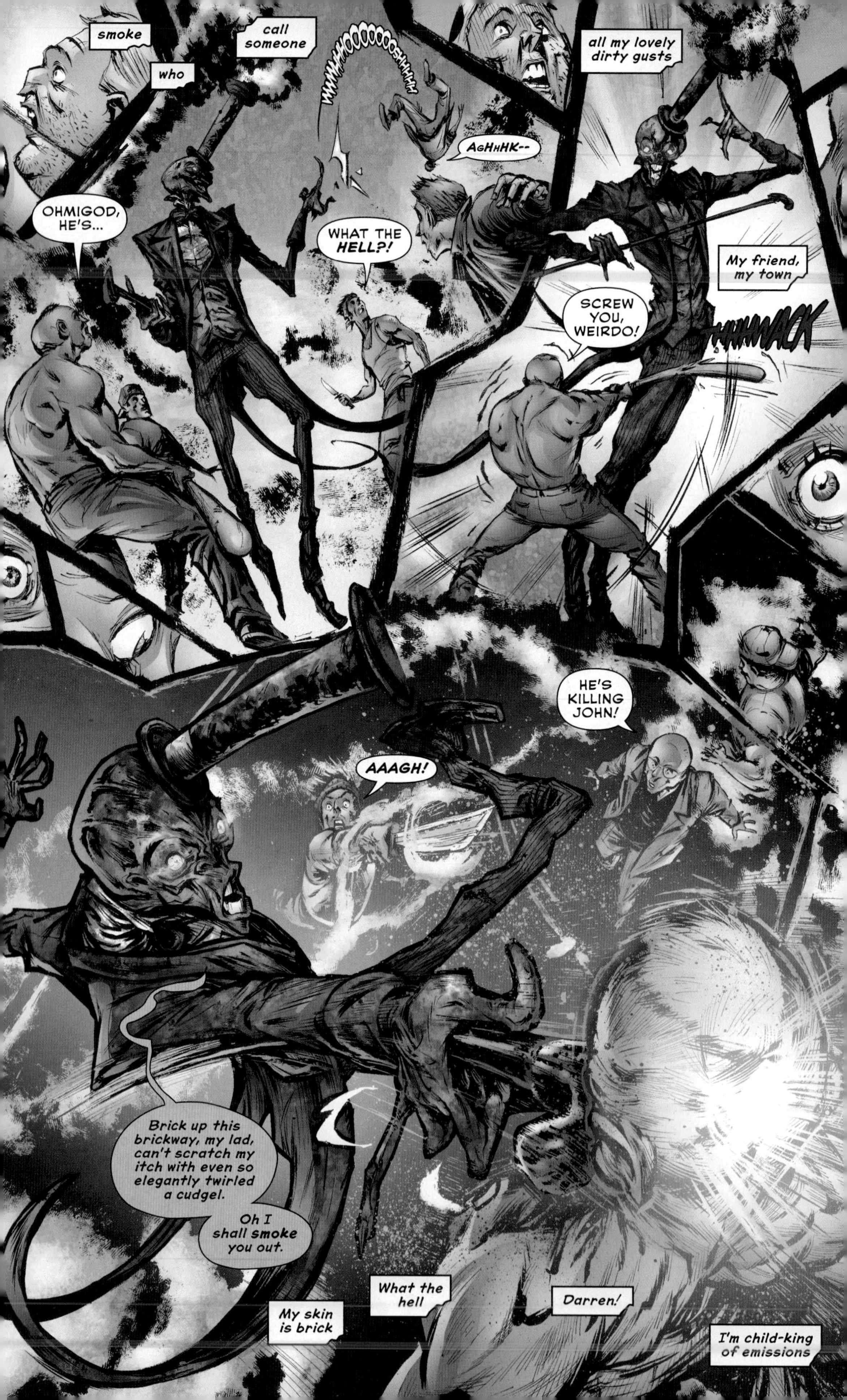
smoke
who
call someone
all my lovely dirty gusts
OHMIGOD, HE'S...
WHAT THE HELL?!
AGHHHK--
My friend, my town
SCREW YOU, WEIRDO!
HE'S KILLING JOHN!
AAAGH!
Brick up this brickway, my lad, can't scratch my itch with even so elegantly twirled a cudgel.
Oh I shall smoke you out.
My skin is brick
What the hell
Darren!
I'm child-king of emissions

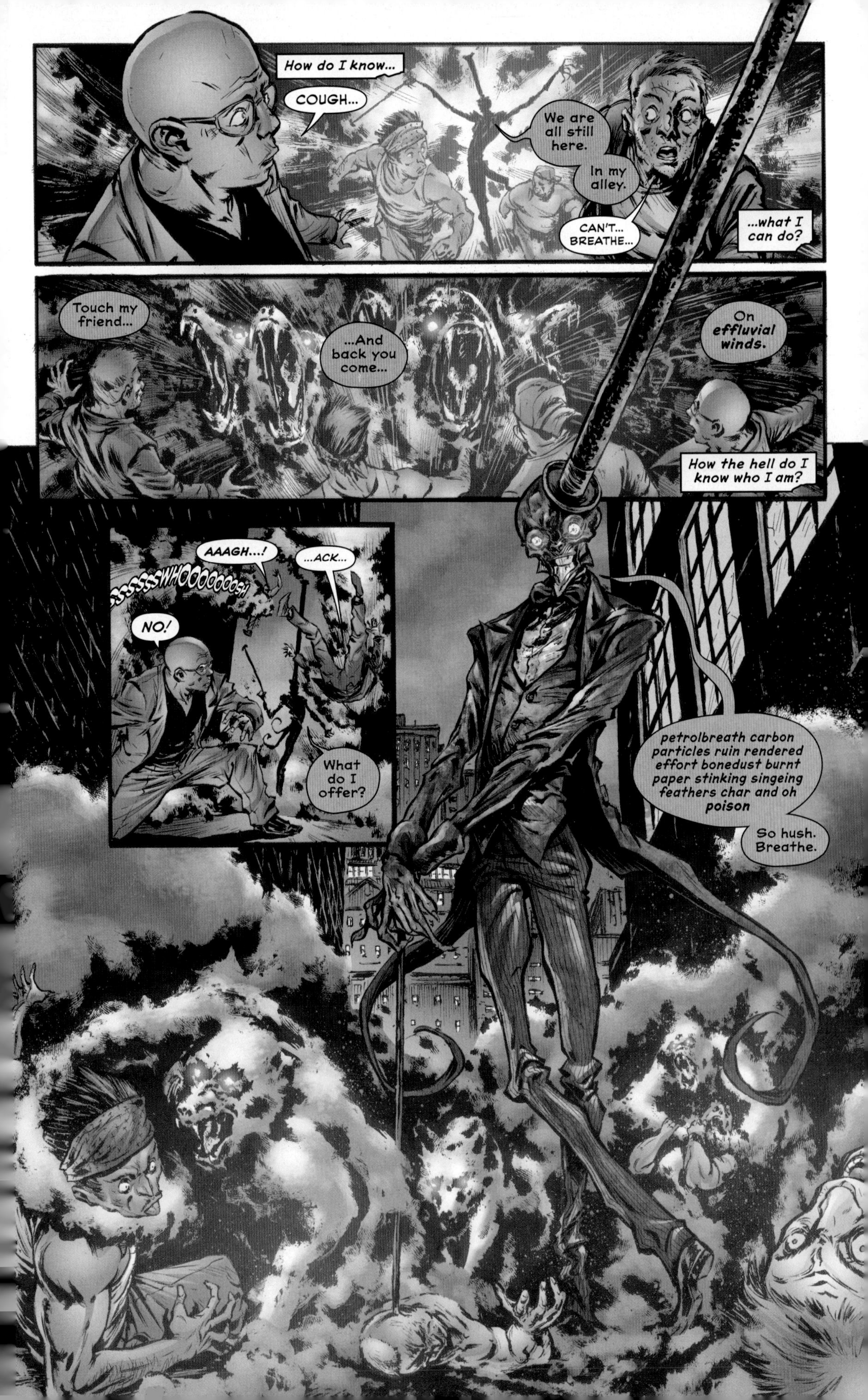
How do I know...
COUGH...
We are all still here.
In my alley.
CAN'T... BREATHE...
...what I can do?
Touch my friend...
...And back you come...
On effluvial winds.
How the hell do I know who I am?
SSSSSSWHOOOOOOOSH
AAAGH...!
...ACK...
NO!
What do I offer?
petrolbreath carbon particles ruin rendered effort bonedust burnt paper stinking singeing feathers char and oh poison
So hush. Breathe.

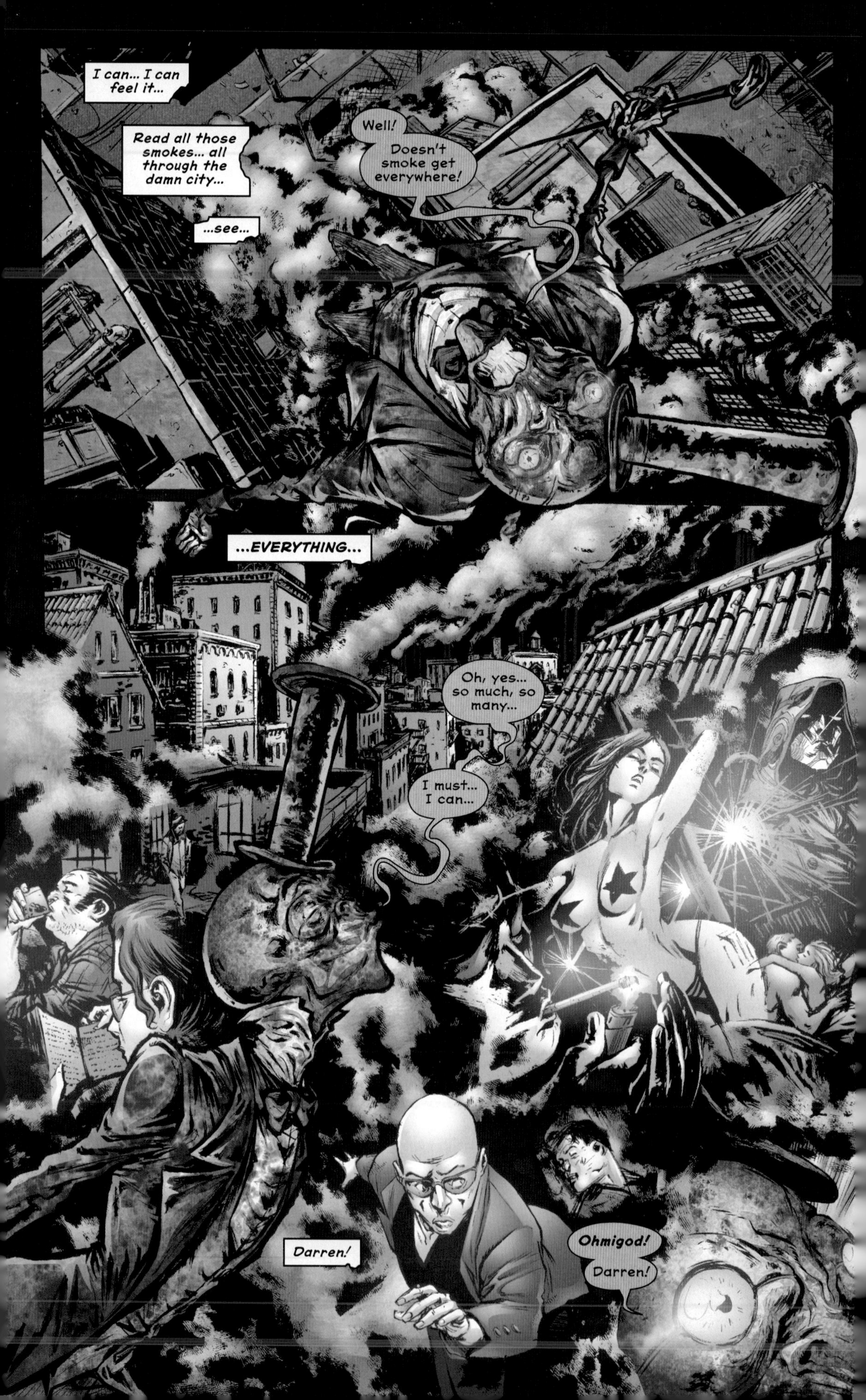
I can... I can feel it...
Read all those smokes... all through the damn city...
Well!
Doesn't smoke get everywhere!
...see...
...EVERYTHING...
Oh, yes... so much, so many...
I must... I can...
Darren!
Ohmigod!
Darren!

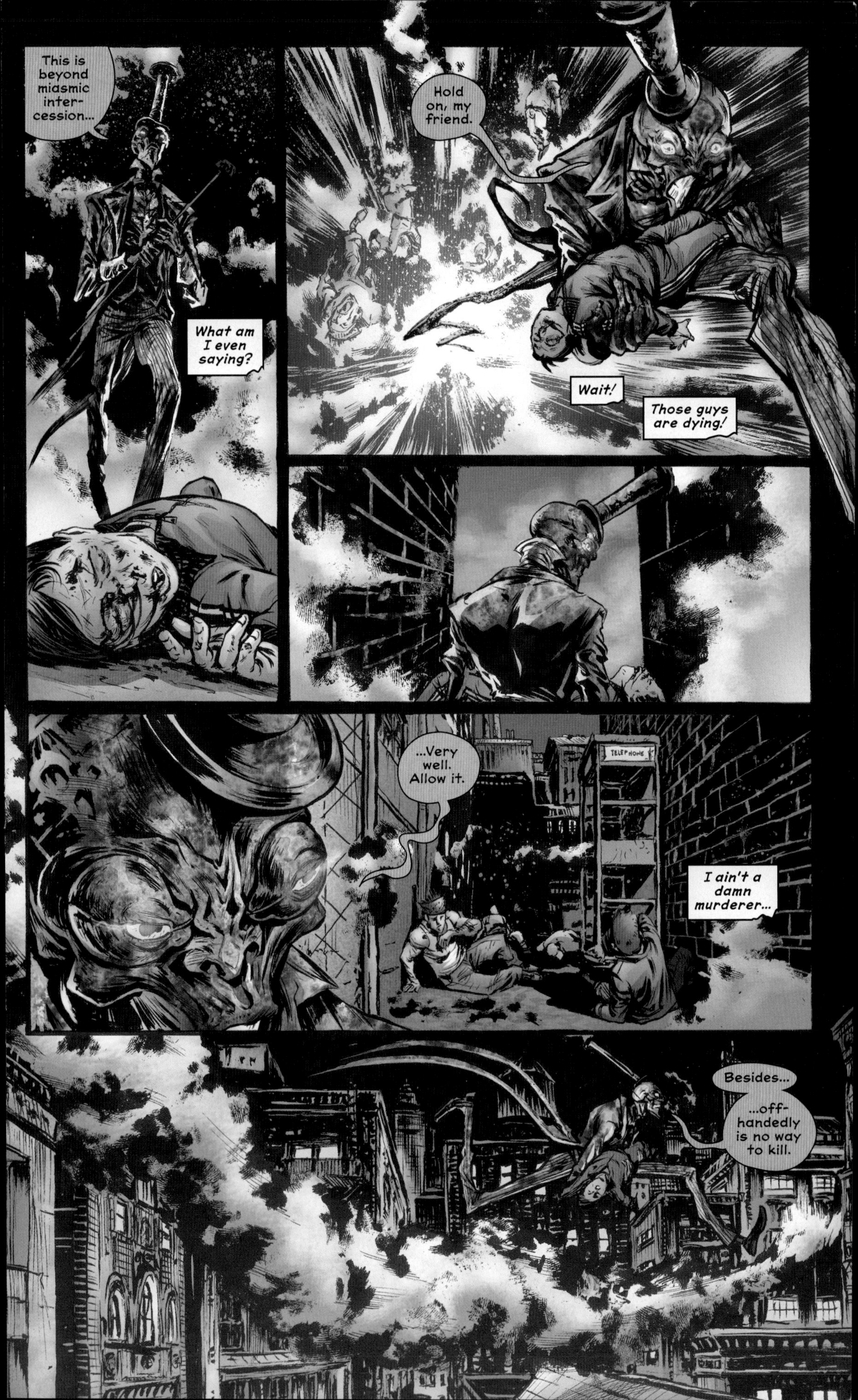
This is beyond miasmic inter-cession...
What am I even saying?
Hold on, my friend.
Wait!
Those guys are dying!
...Very well. Allow it.
I ain't a damn murderer...
Besides...
...off-handedly is no way to kill.

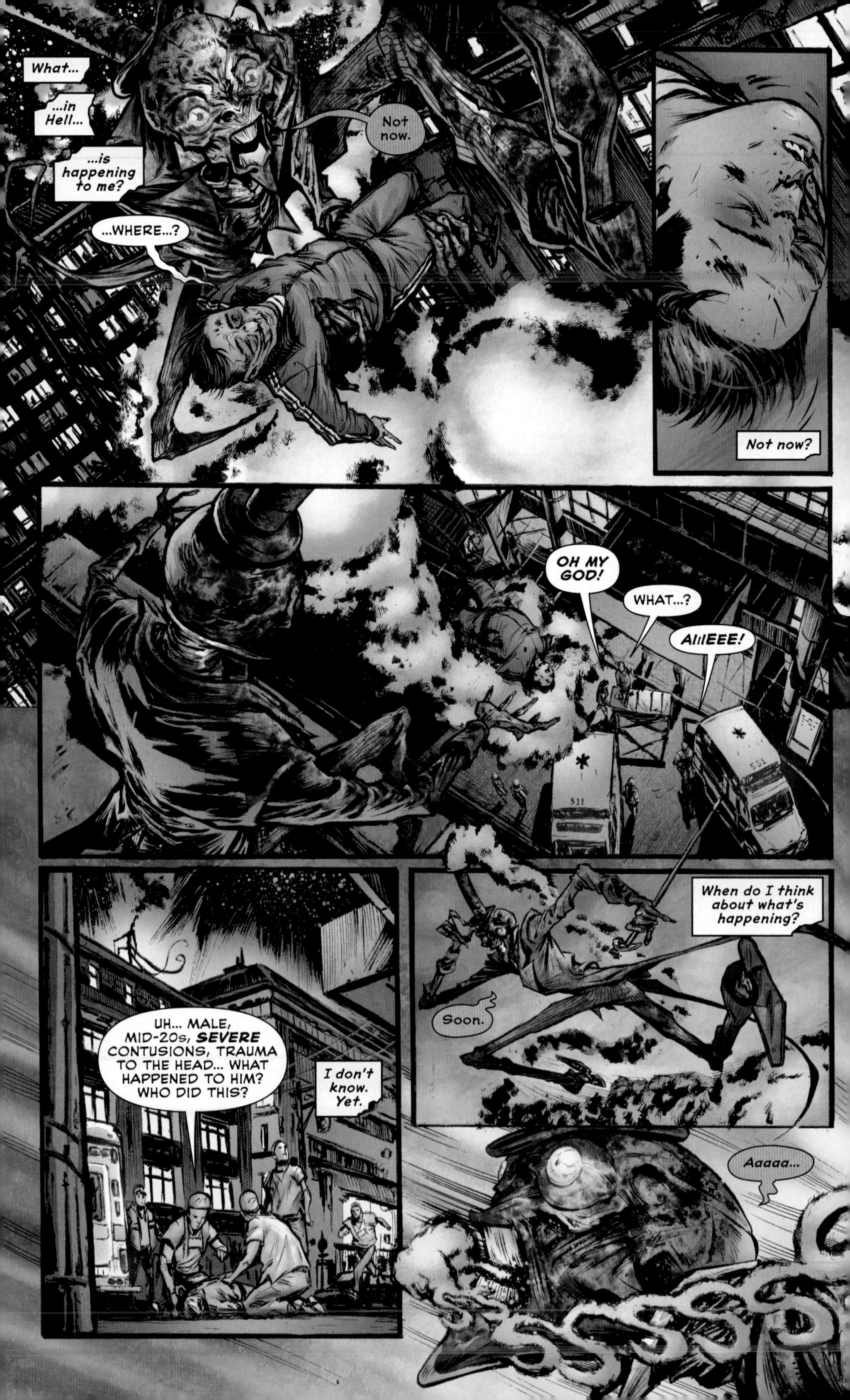
What...
...in Hell...
...is happening to me?
Not now.
...WHERE...?
Not now?
OH MY GOD!
WHAT...?
AIIIEEE!
When do I think about what's happening?
Soon.
UH... MALE, MID-20s, SEVERE CONTUSIONS, TRAUMA TO THE HEAD... WHAT HAPPENED TO HIM? WHO DID THIS?
I don't know. Yet.
Aaaaa...
SSSSS

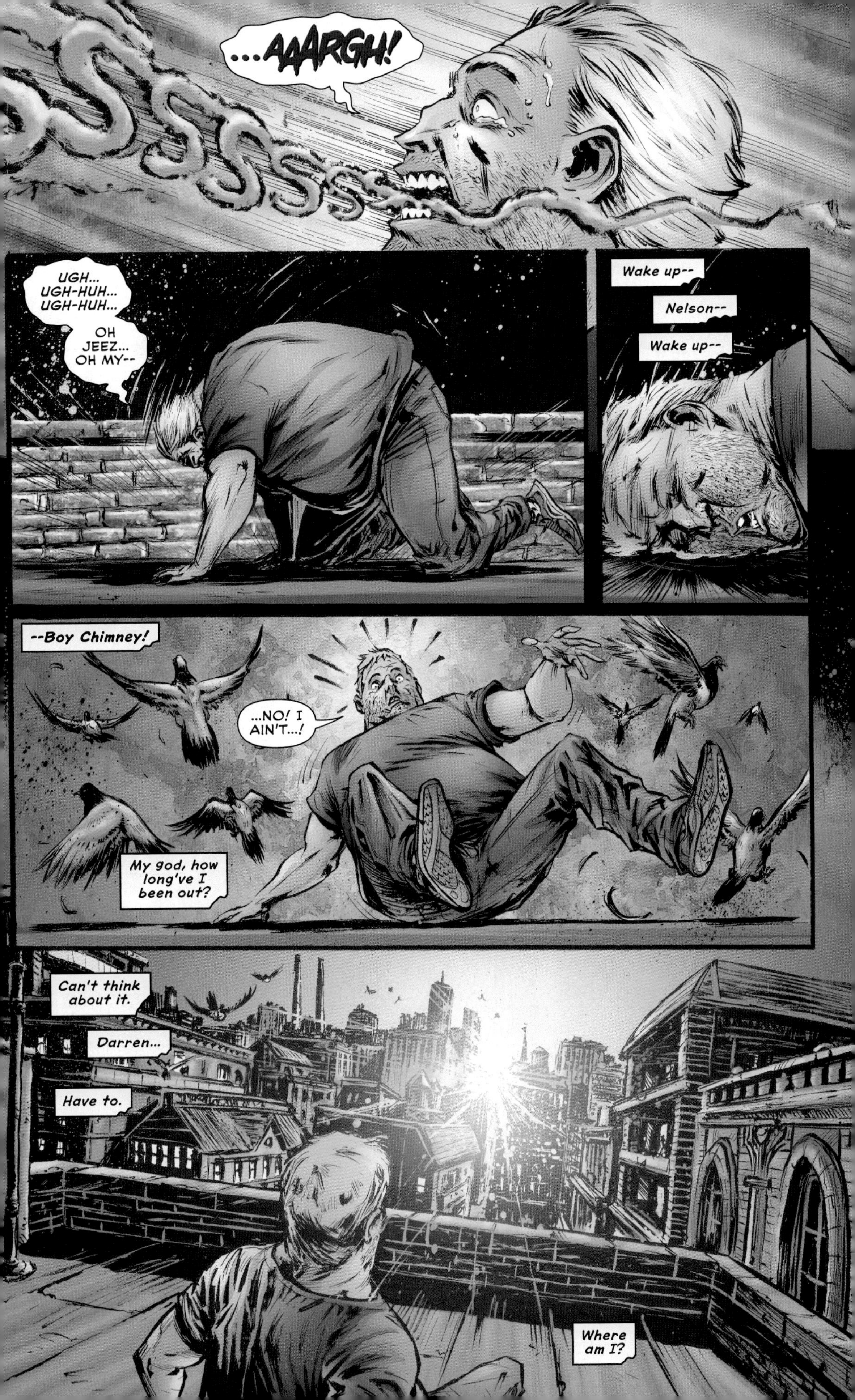
...AAARGH!
SSSSSSSS
UGH... UGH-HUH... UGH-HUH...
OH JEEZ... OH MY--
Wake up--
Nelson--
Wake up--
--Boy Chimney!
...NO! I AIN'T...!
My god, how long've I been out?
Can't think about it.
Darren...
Have to.
Where am I?

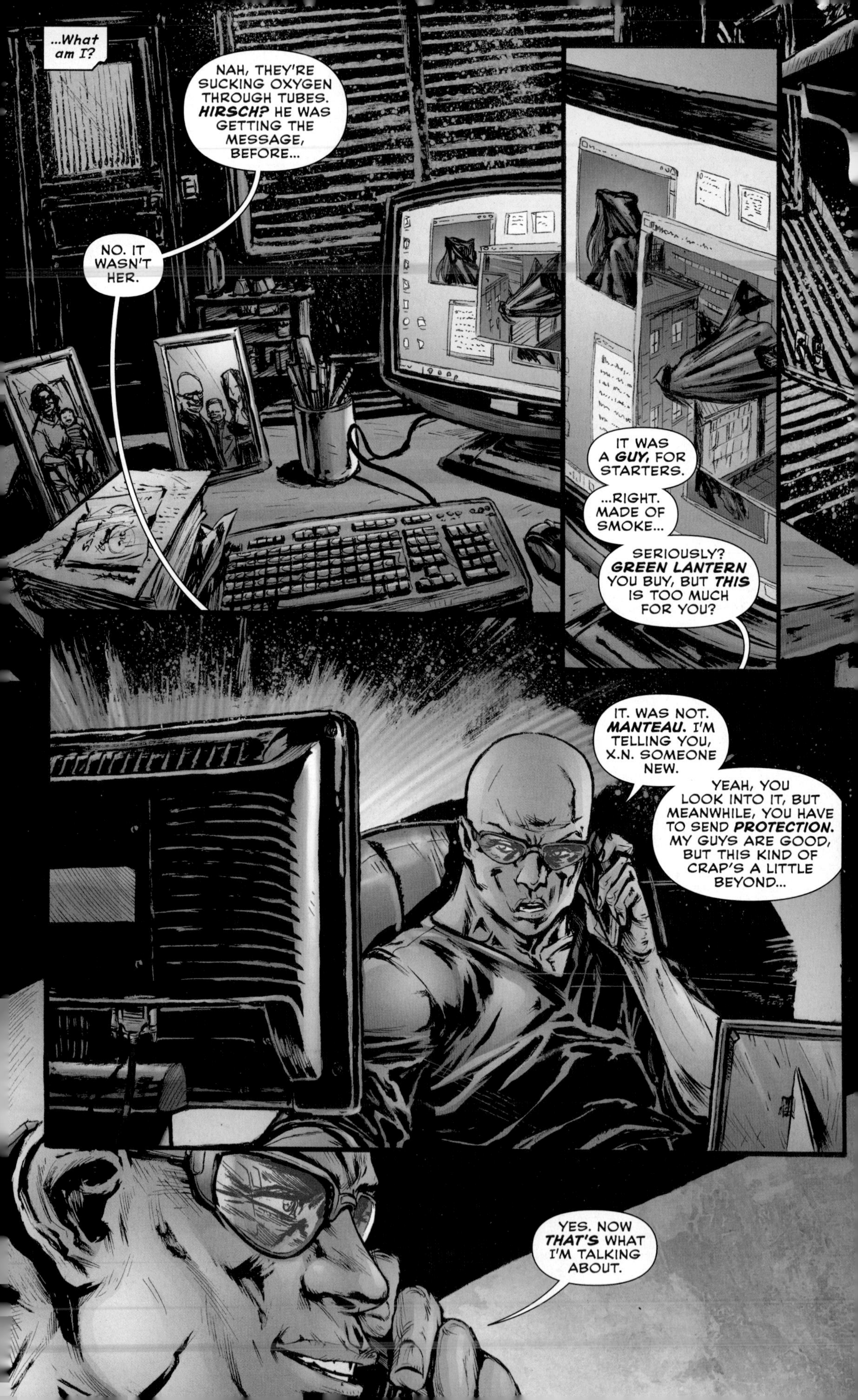

...What am I?
NAH, THEY'RE SUCKING OXYGEN THROUGH TUBES. HIRSCH? HE WAS GETTING THE MESSAGE, BEFORE...
NO. IT WASN'T HER.
IT WAS A GUY, FOR STARTERS.
...RIGHT. MADE OF SMOKE...
SERIOUSLY? GREEN LANTERN YOU BUY, BUT THIS IS TOO MUCH FOR YOU?
IT. WAS NOT. MANTEAU. I'M TELLING YOU, X.N. SOMEONE NEW.
YEAH, YOU LOOK INTO IT, BUT MEANWHILE, YOU HAVE TO SEND PROTECTION. MY GUYS ARE GOOD, BUT THIS KIND OF CRAP'S A LITTLE BEYOND...
YES. NOW THAT'S WHAT I'M TALKING ABOUT.

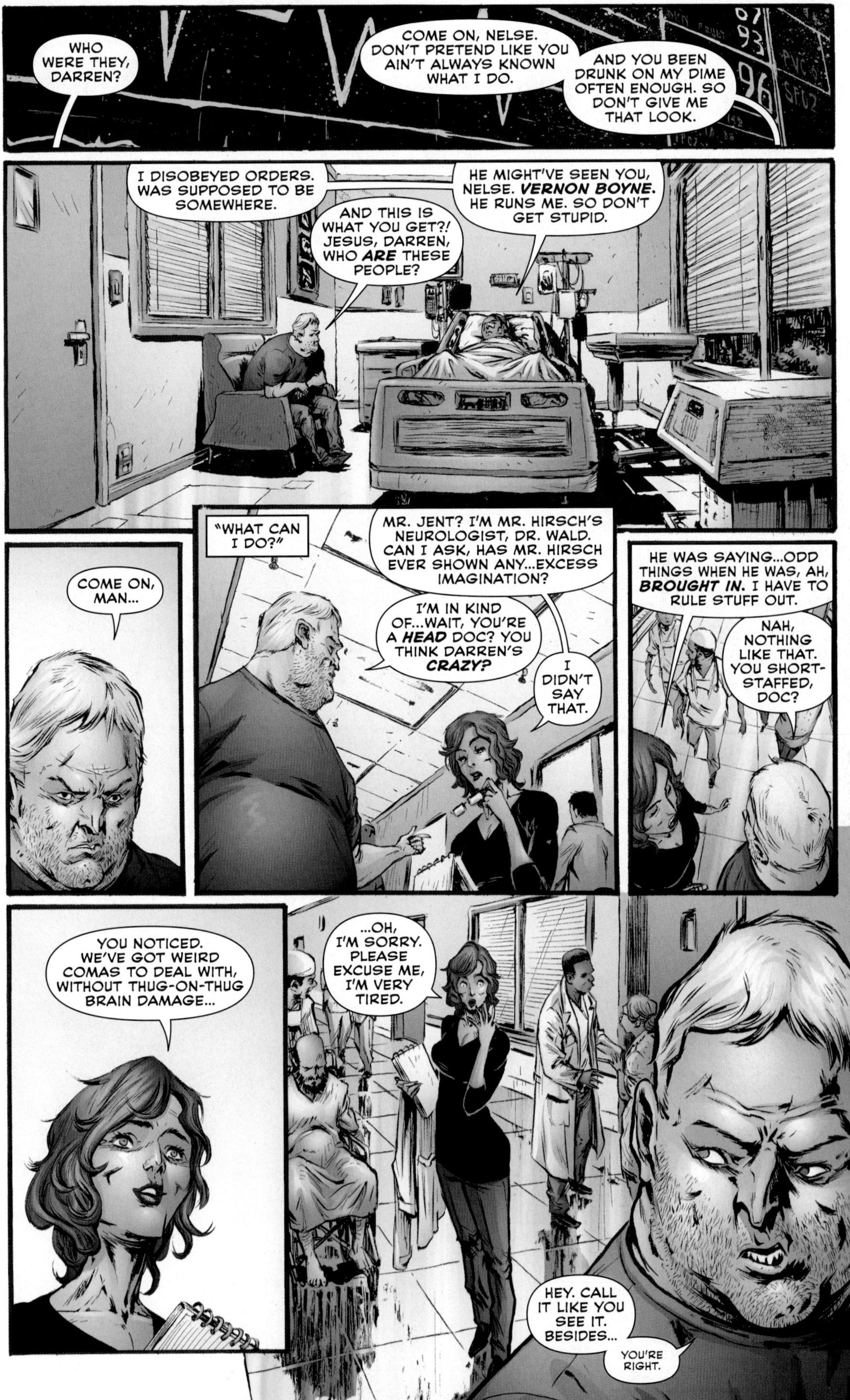

WHO WERE THEY, DARREN?
COME ON, NELSE. DON'T PRETEND LIKE YOU AIN'T ALWAYS KNOWN WHAT I DO.
AND YOU BEEN DRUNK ON MY DIME OFTEN ENOUGH. SO DON'T GIVE ME THAT LOOK.
I DISOBEYED ORDERS. WAS SUPPOSED TO BE SOMEWHERE.
AND THIS IS WHAT YOU GET?! JESUS, DARREN, WHO ARE THESE PEOPLE?
HE MIGHT'VE SEEN YOU, NELSE. VERNON BOYNE. HE RUNS ME. SO DON'T GET STUPID.
COME ON, MAN...
"WHAT CAN I DO?"
MR. JENT? I'M MR. HIRSCH'S NEUROLOGIST, DR. WALD. CAN I ASK, HAS MR. HIRSCH EVER SHOWN ANY...EXCESS IMAGINATION?
I'M IN KIND OF...WAIT, YOU'RE A HEAD DOC? YOU THINK DARREN'S CRAZY?
I DIDN'T SAY THAT.
HE WAS SAYING...ODD THINGS WHEN HE WAS, AH, BROUGHT IN. I HAVE TO RULE STUFF OUT.
NAH, NOTHING LIKE THAT. YOU SHORT-STAFFED, DOC?
YOU NOTICED. WE'VE GOT WEIRD COMAS TO DEAL WITH, WITHOUT THUG-ON-THUG BRAIN DAMAGE...
...OH, I'M SORRY. PLEASE EXCUSE ME, I'M VERY TIRED.
HEY. CALL IT LIKE YOU SEE IT. BESIDES...
YOU'RE RIGHT.

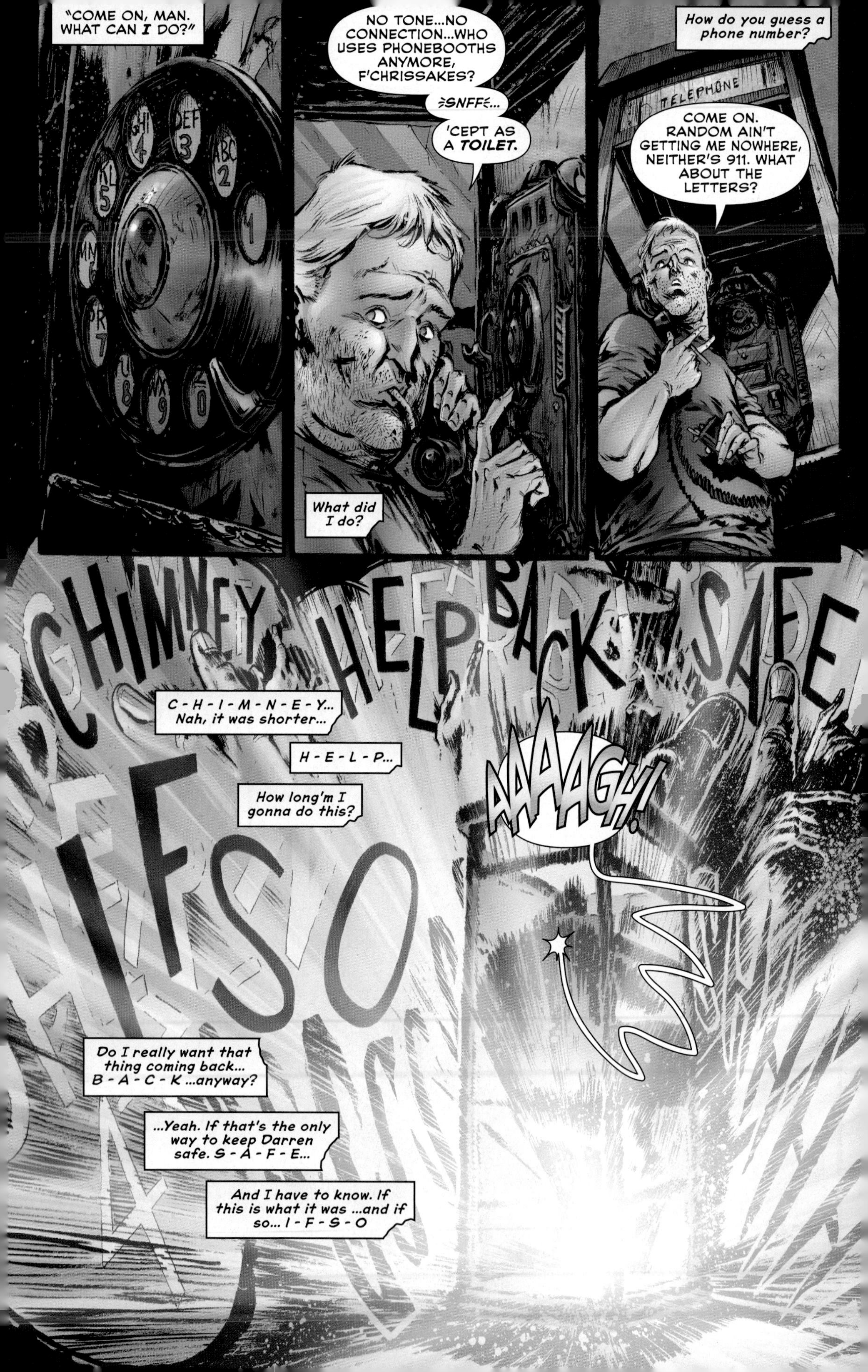
"COME ON, MAN. WHAT CAN I DO?"
NO TONE...NO CONNECTION...WHO USES PHONEBOOTHS ANYMORE, F'CHRISSAKES?
SNFF...
'CEPT AS A TOILET.
What did I do?
How do you guess a phone number?
TELEPHONE
COME ON. RANDOM AIN'T GETTING ME NOWHERE, NEITHER'S 911. WHAT ABOUT THE LETTERS?
CHIMNEY
HELP
BACK
SAFE
C-H-I-M-N-E-Y... Nah, it was shorter...
H-E-L-P...
How long'm I gonna do this?
AAAAGH!
IFSO
Do I really want that thing coming back... B-A-C-K ...anyway?
...Yeah. If that's the only way to keep Darren safe. S-A-F-E...
And I have to know. If this is what it was ...and if so... I-F-S-O

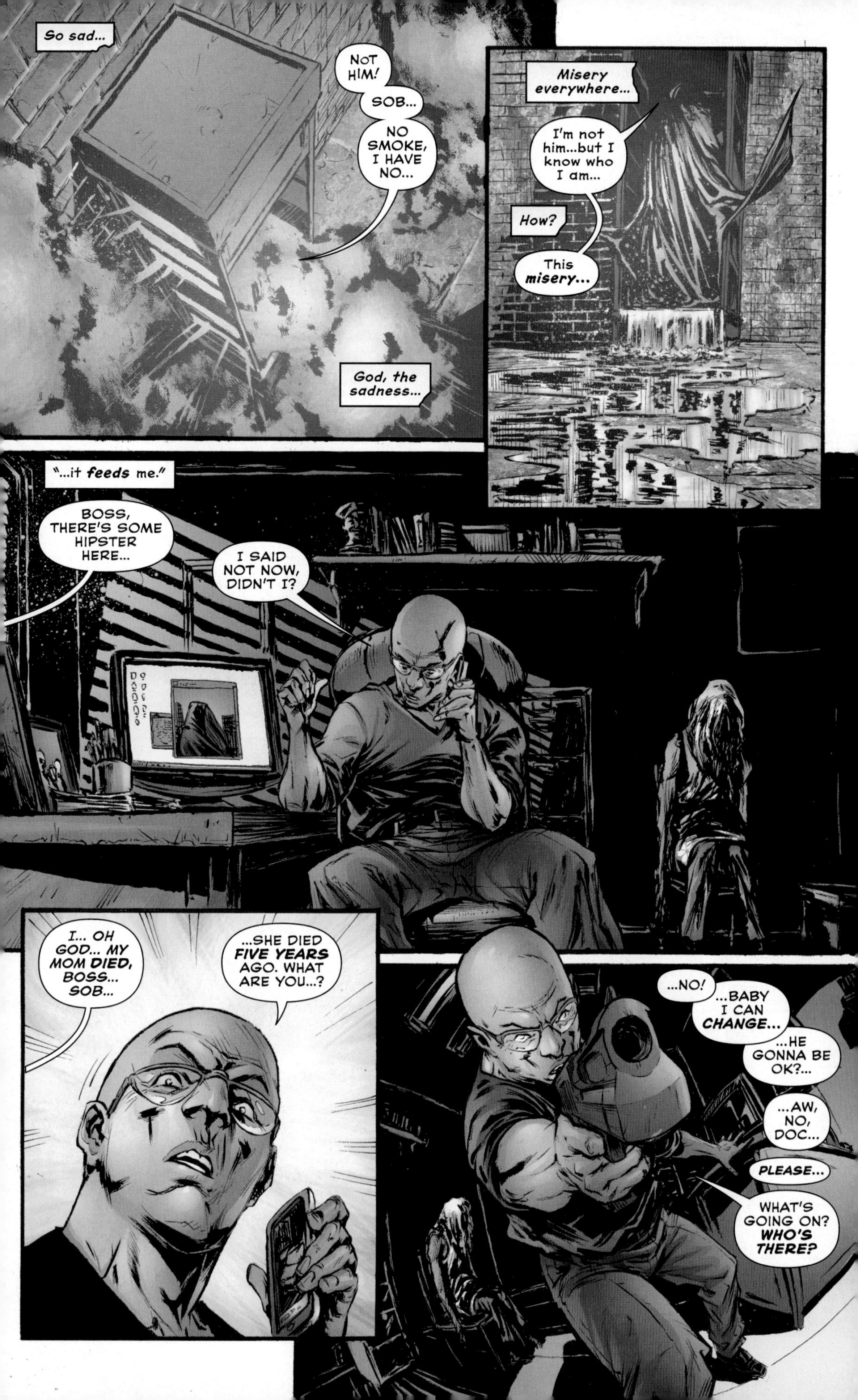

So sad...
NOT HIM!
SOB...
NO SMOKE, I HAVE NO...
God, the sadness...
Misery everywhere...
I'm not him...but I know who I am...
How?
This misery...
"...it feeds me."
BOSS, THERE'S SOME HIPSTER HERE...
I SAID NOT NOW, DIDN'T I?
I... OH GOD... MY MOM DIED, BOSS... SOB...
...SHE DIED FIVE YEARS AGO. WHAT ARE YOU...?
...NO!
...BABY I CAN CHANGE...
...HE GONNA BE OK?...
...AW, NO, DOC...
PLEASE...
WHAT'S GOING ON? WHO'S THERE?

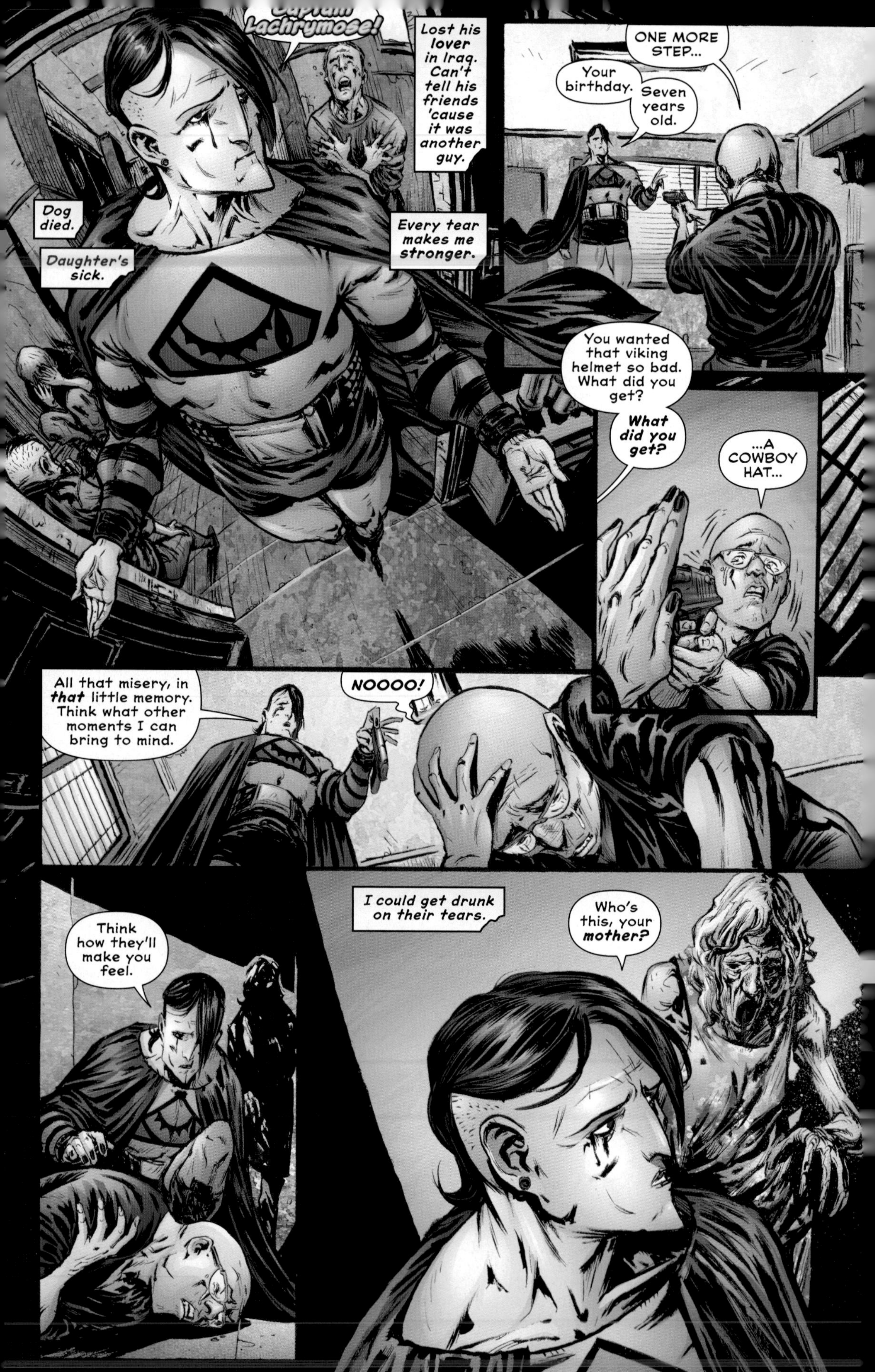
Lachrymose!
Lost his lover in Iraq. Can't tell his friends 'cause it was another guy.
Dog died.
Daughter's sick.
Every tear makes me stronger.
ONE MORE STEP...
Your birthday.
Seven years old.
You wanted that viking helmet so bad. What did you get?
What did you get?
...A COWBOY HAT...
All that misery, in that little memory. Think what other moments I can bring to mind.
NOOOO!
Think how they'll make you feel.
I could get drunk on their tears.
Who's this, your mother?

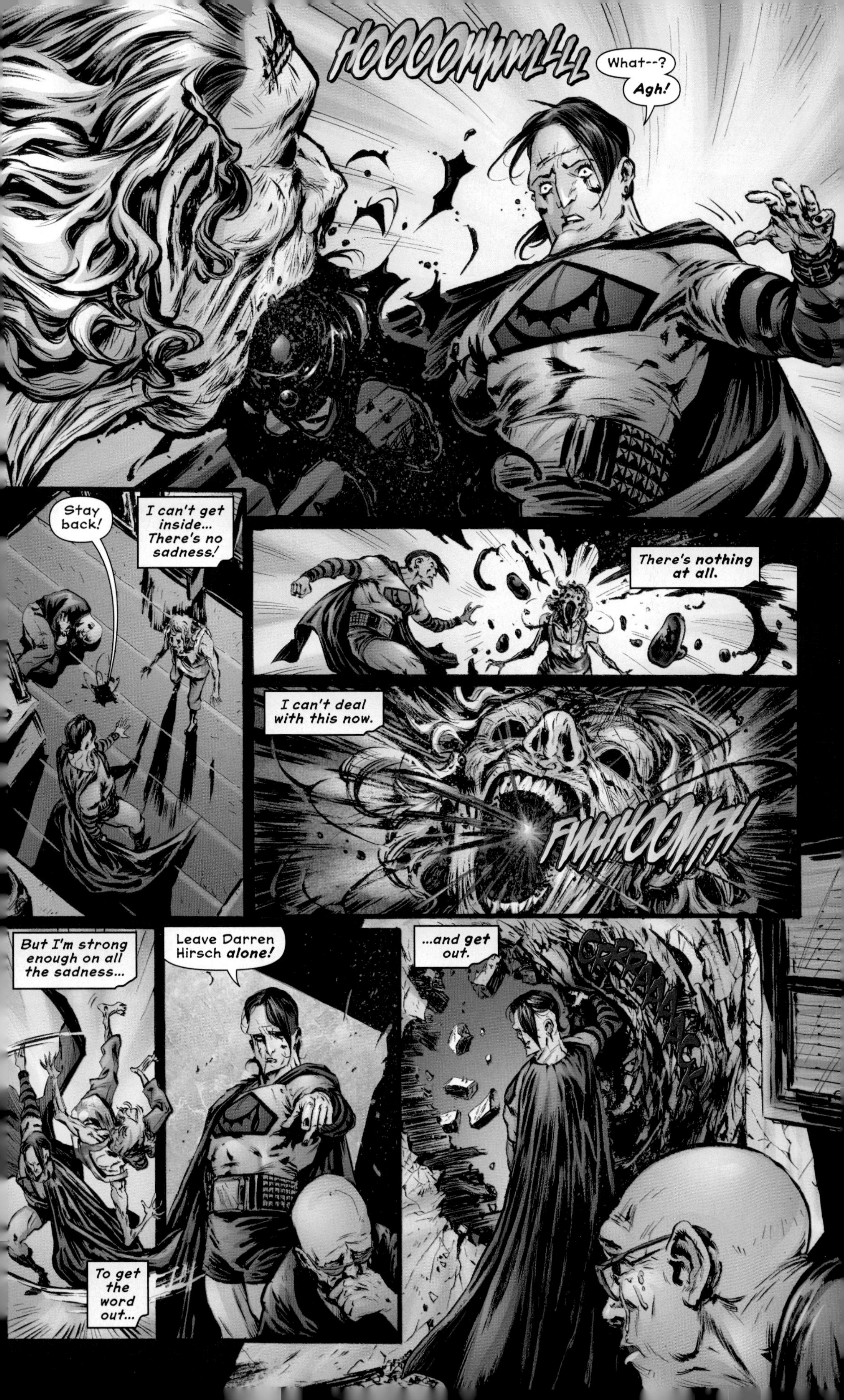
HOOOOMMMLLL
What--?
Agh!
Stay back!
I can't get inside... There's no sadness!
There's nothing at all.
I can't deal with this now.
FWAHOOMPH
But I'm strong enough on all the sadness...
To get the word out...
Leave Darren Hirsch alone!
...and get out.
CRRRAAAACK

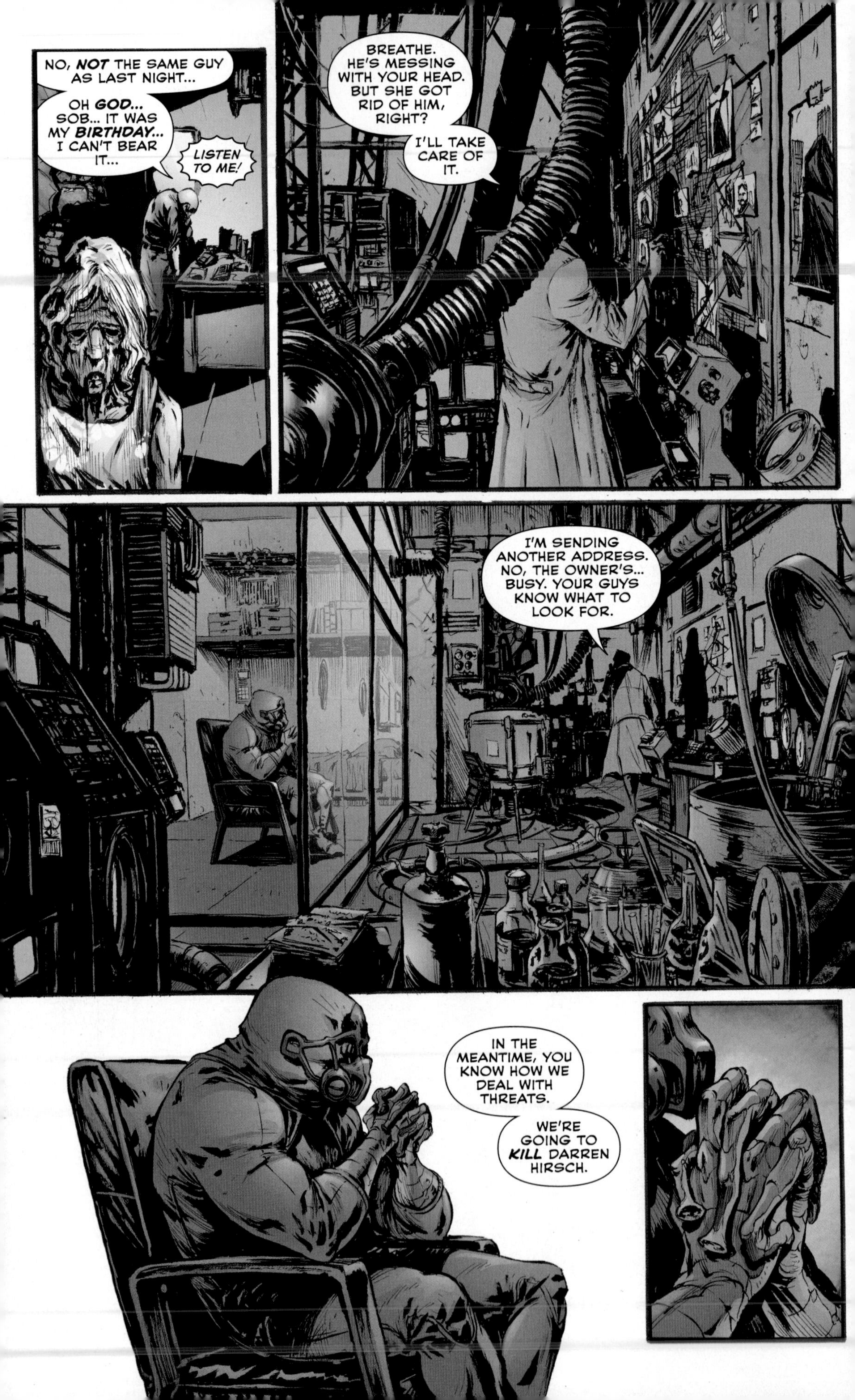
NO, NOT THE SAME GUY AS LAST NIGHT...
OH GOD... SOB... IT WAS MY BIRTHDAY... I CAN'T BEAR IT...
LISTEN TO ME!
BREATHE. HE'S MESSING WITH YOUR HEAD. BUT SHE GOT RID OF HIM, RIGHT?
I'LL TAKE CARE OF IT.
I'M SENDING ANOTHER ADDRESS. NO, THE OWNER'S... BUSY. YOUR GUYS KNOW WHAT TO LOOK FOR.
IN THE MEANTIME, YOU KNOW HOW WE DEAL WITH THREATS.
WE'RE GOING TO KILL DARREN HIRSCH.

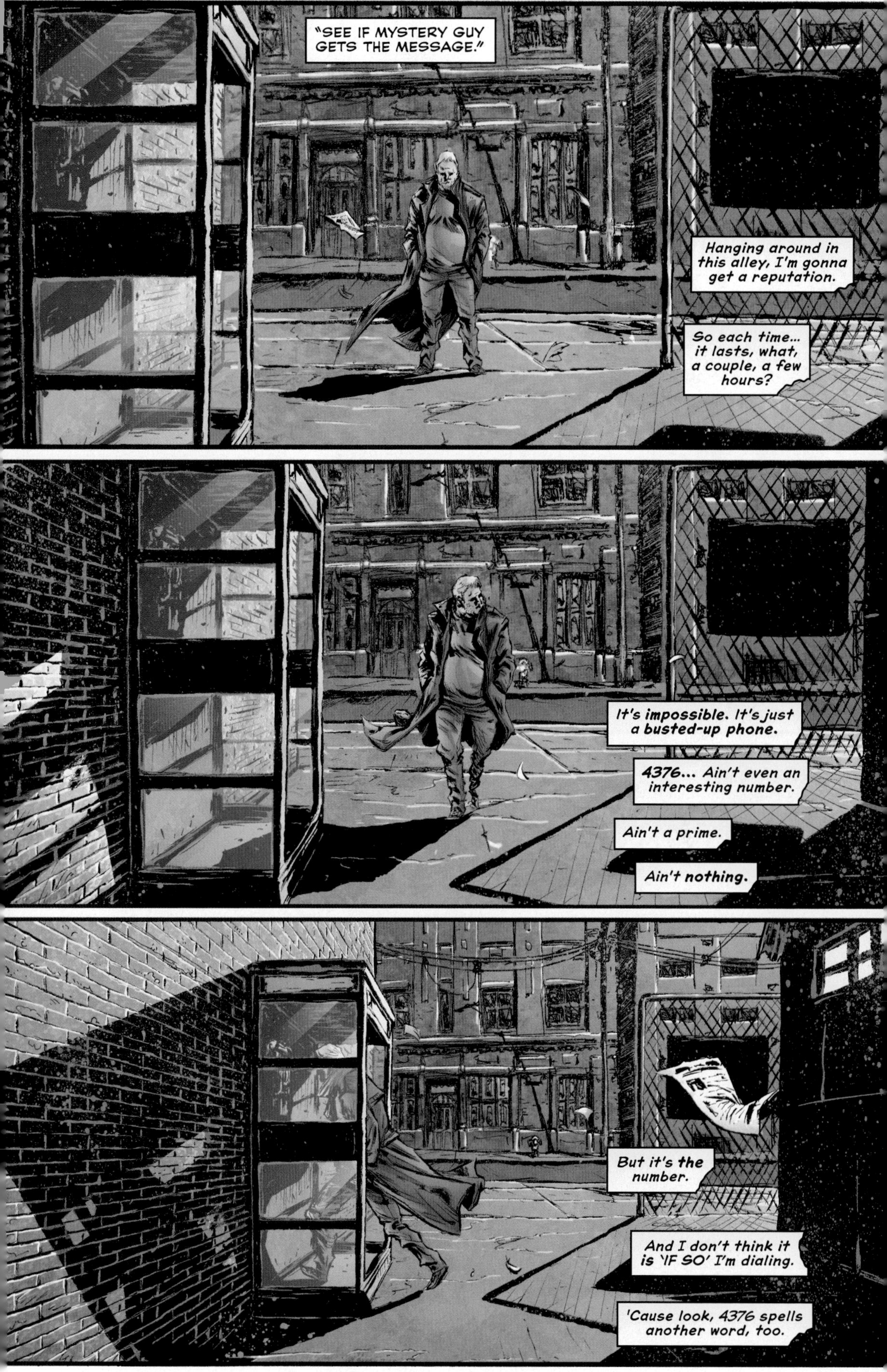
"SEE IF MYSTERY GUY GETS THE MESSAGE."
Hanging around in this alley, I'm gonna get a reputation.
So each time... it lasts, what, a couple, a few hours?
It's impossible. It's just a busted-up phone.
4376... Ain't even an interesting number.
Ain't a prime.
Ain't nothing.
But it's the number.
And I don't think it is 'IF SO' I'm dialing.
'Cause look, 4376 spells another word, too.

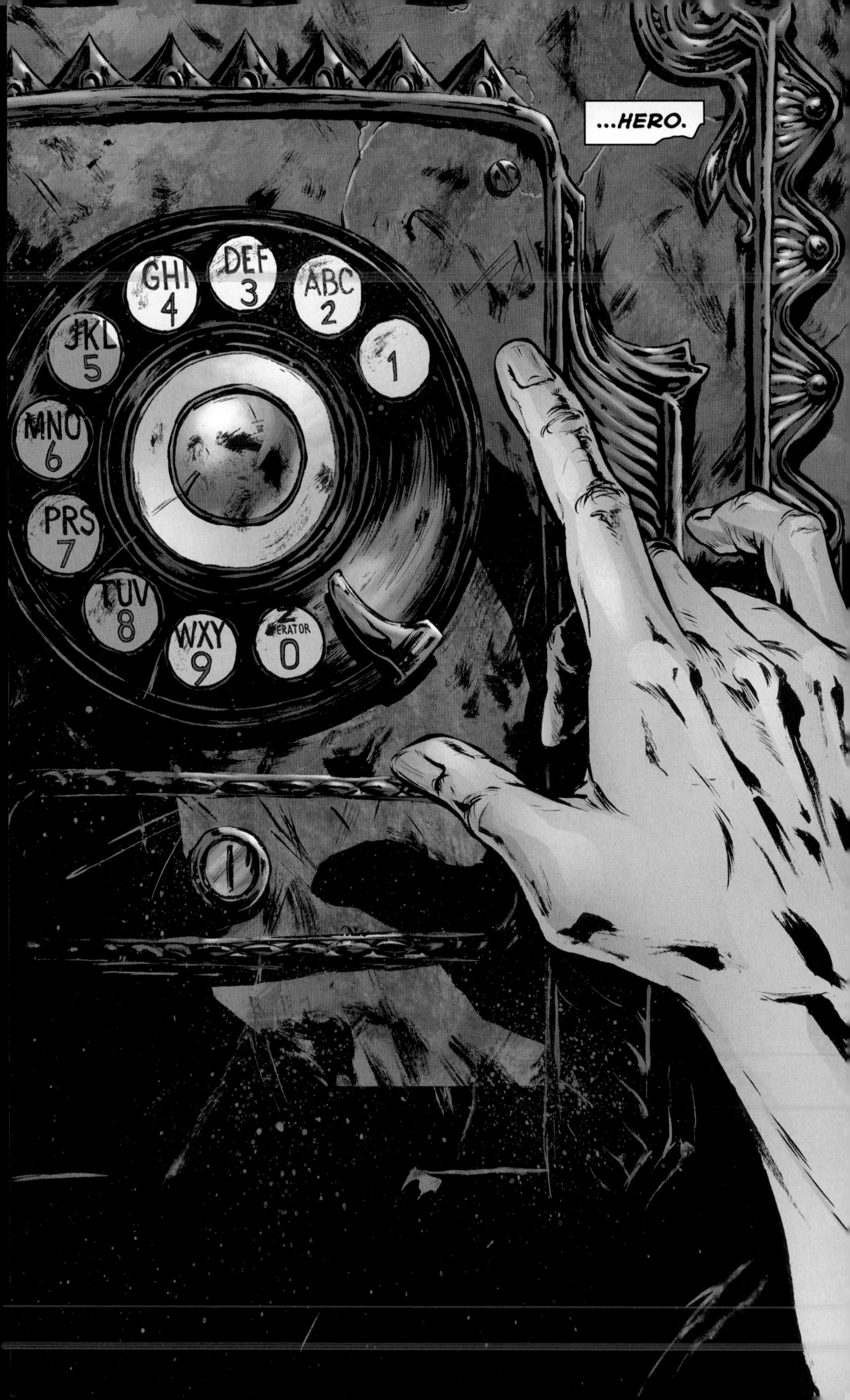
...HERO.

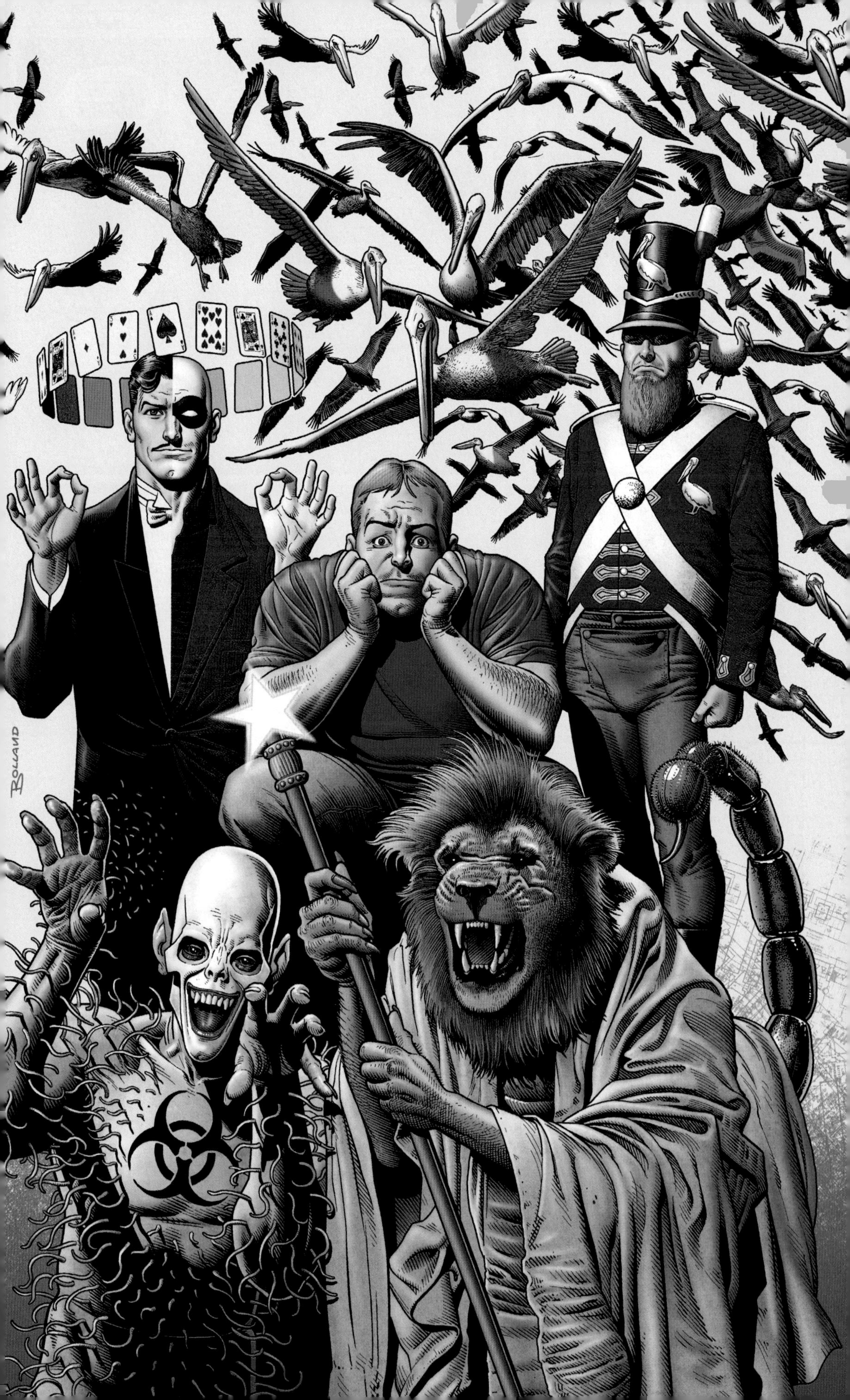
BOLLAND

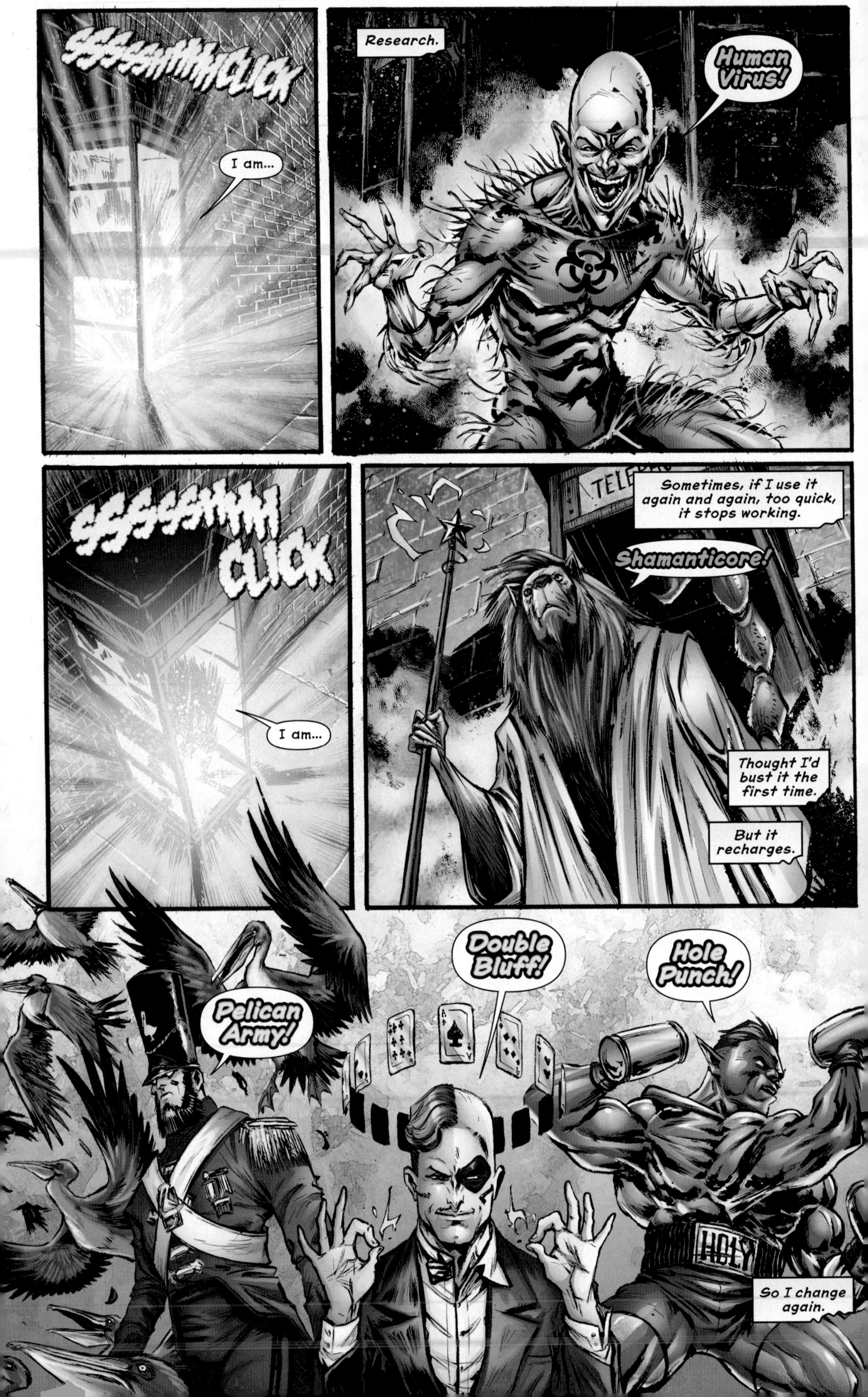
SSSSSHHHHCLICK
I am...
Research.
Human Virus!
SSSSSHHH CLICK
I am...
Sometimes, if I use it again and again, too quick, it stops working.
Shamanticore!
Thought I'd bust it the first time.
But it recharges.
Pelican Army!
Double Bluff!
Hole Punch!
So I change again.

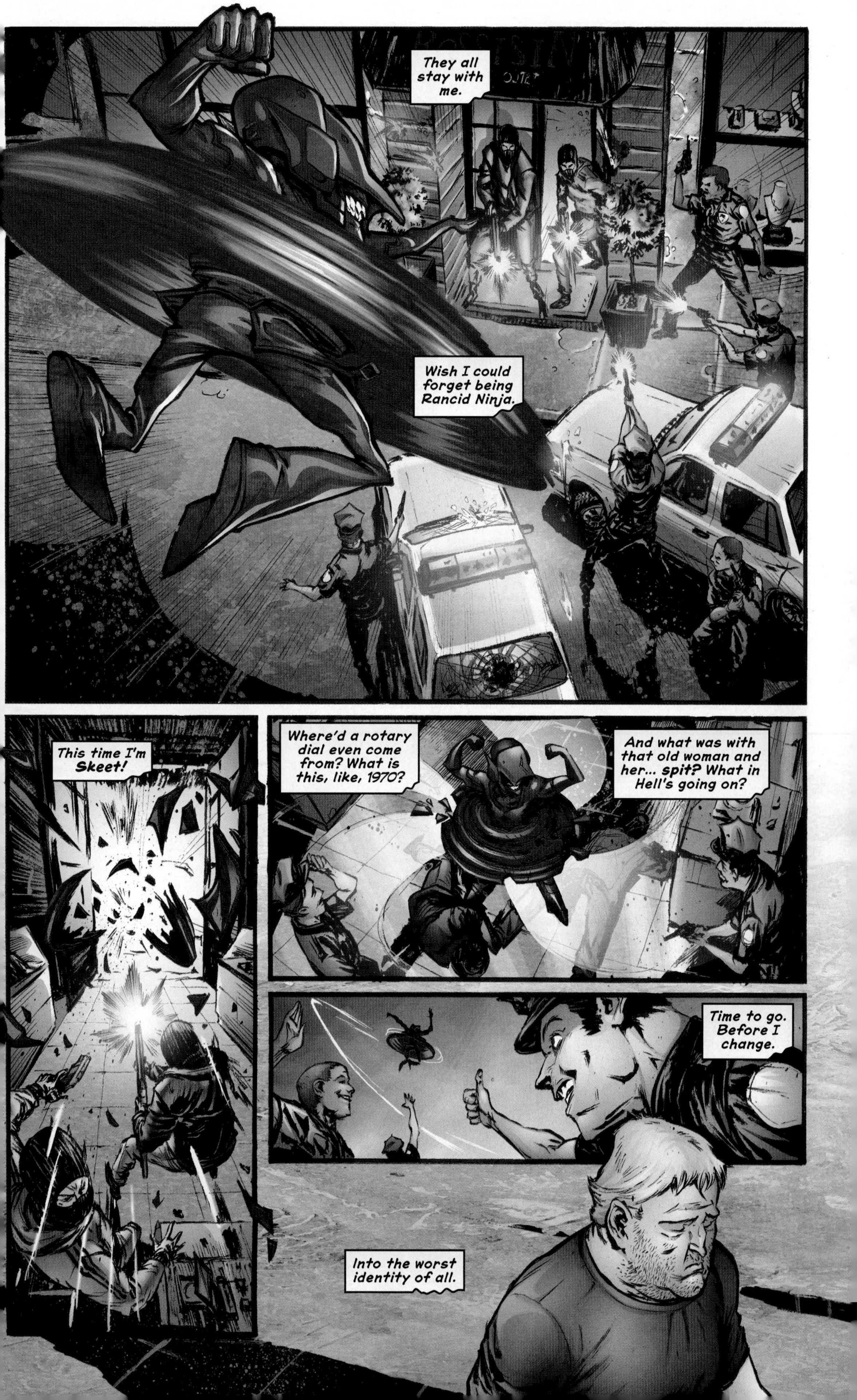
They all stay with me.
Wish I could forget being Rancid Ninja.
This time I'm Skeet!
Where'd a rotary dial even come from? What is this, like, 1970?
And what was with that old woman and her... spit? What in Hell's going on?
Time to go. Before I change.
Into the worst identity of all.

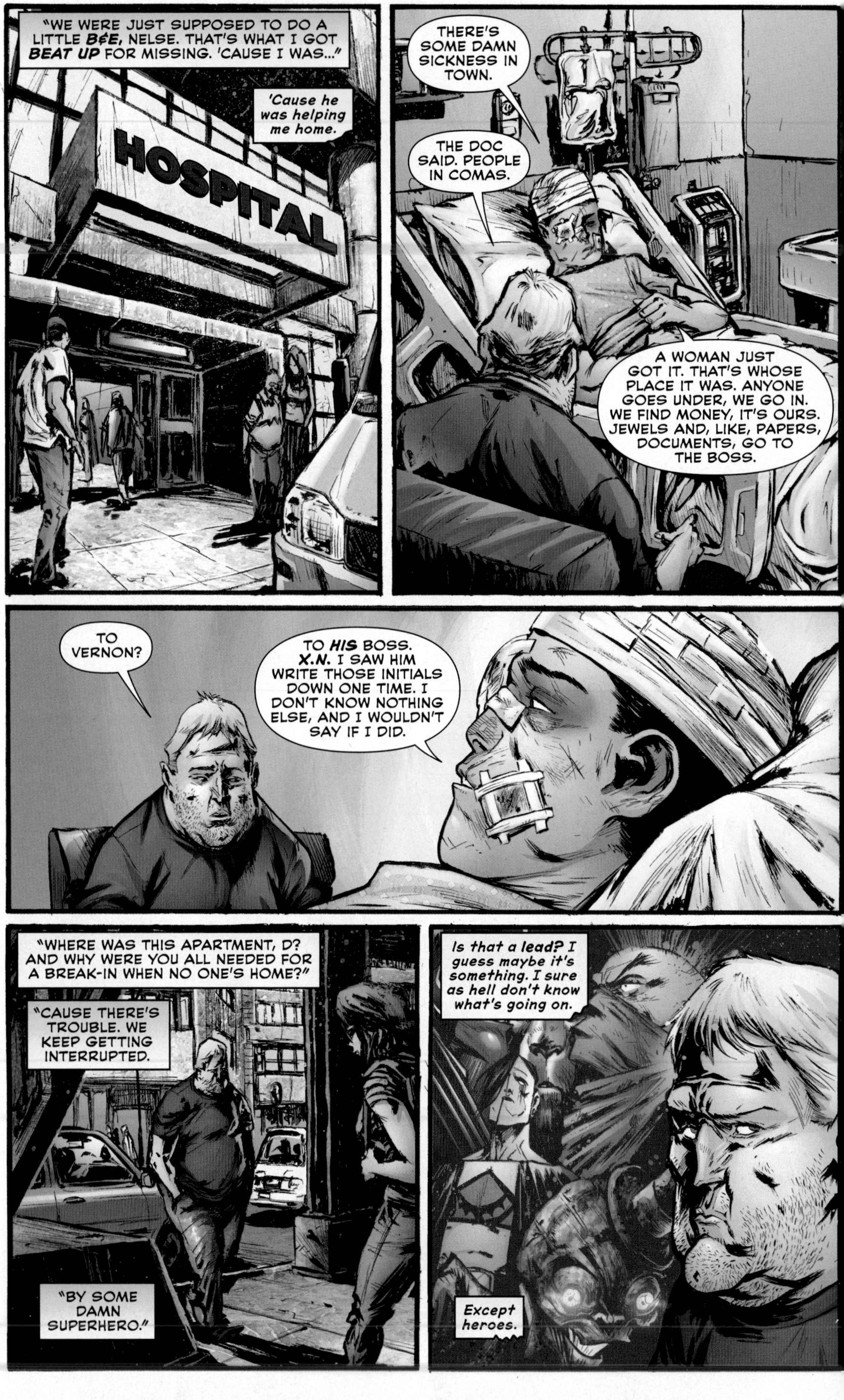
"WE WERE JUST SUPPOSED TO DO A LITTLE B&E, NELSE. THAT'S WHAT I GOT BEAT UP FOR MISSING. 'CAUSE I WAS..."
'Cause he was helping me home.
HOSPITAL
THERE'S SOME DAMN SICKNESS IN TOWN.
THE DOC SAID. PEOPLE IN COMAS.
A WOMAN JUST GOT IT. THAT'S WHOSE PLACE IT WAS. ANYONE GOES UNDER, WE GO IN. WE FIND MONEY, IT'S OURS. JEWELS AND, LIKE, PAPERS, DOCUMENTS, GO TO THE BOSS.
TO VERNON?
TO HIS BOSS. X.N. I SAW HIM WRITE THOSE INITIALS DOWN ONE TIME. I DON'T KNOW NOTHING ELSE, AND I WOULDN'T SAY IF I DID.
"WHERE WAS THIS APARTMENT, D? AND WHY WERE YOU ALL NEEDED FOR A BREAK-IN WHEN NO ONE'S HOME?"
"CAUSE THERE'S TROUBLE. WE KEEP GETTING INTERRUPTED.
"BY SOME DAMN SUPERHERO."
Is that a lead? I guess maybe it's something. I sure as hell don't know what's going on.
Except heroes.

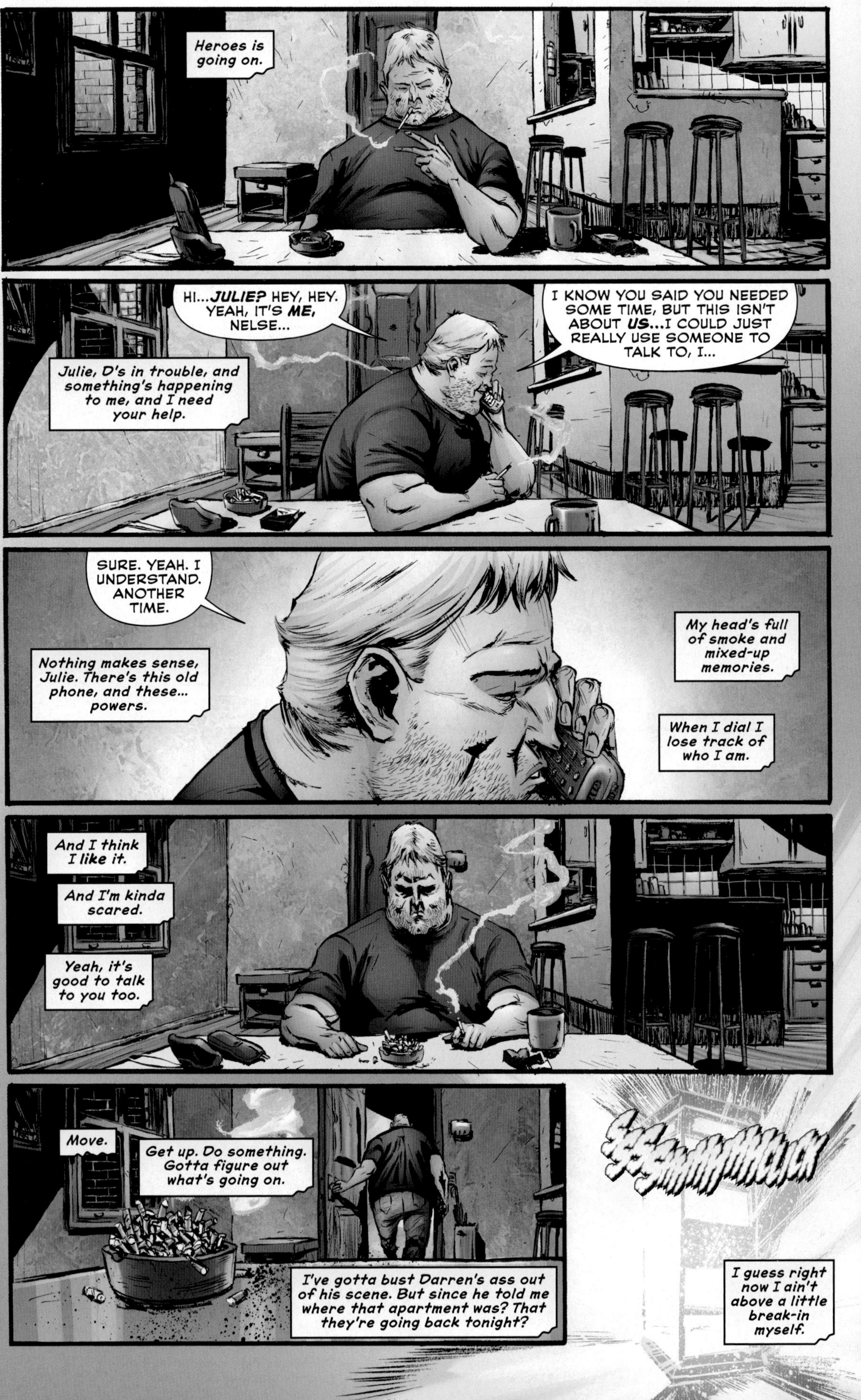
Heroes is going on.
HI...JULIE? HEY, HEY. YEAH, IT'S ME, NELSE...
Julie, D's in trouble, and something's happening to me, and I need your help.
I KNOW YOU SAID YOU NEEDED SOME TIME, BUT THIS ISN'T ABOUT US...I COULD JUST REALLY USE SOMEONE TO TALK TO, I...
SURE. YEAH. I UNDERSTAND. ANOTHER TIME.
Nothing makes sense, Julie. There's this old phone, and these... powers.
My head's full of smoke and mixed-up memories.
When I dial I lose track of who I am.
And I think I like it.
And I'm kinda scared.
Yeah, it's good to talk to you too.
Move.
Get up. Do something. Gotta figure out what's going on.
I've gotta bust Darren's ass out of his scene. But since he told me where that apartment was? That they're going back tonight?
I guess right now I ain't above a little break-in myself.

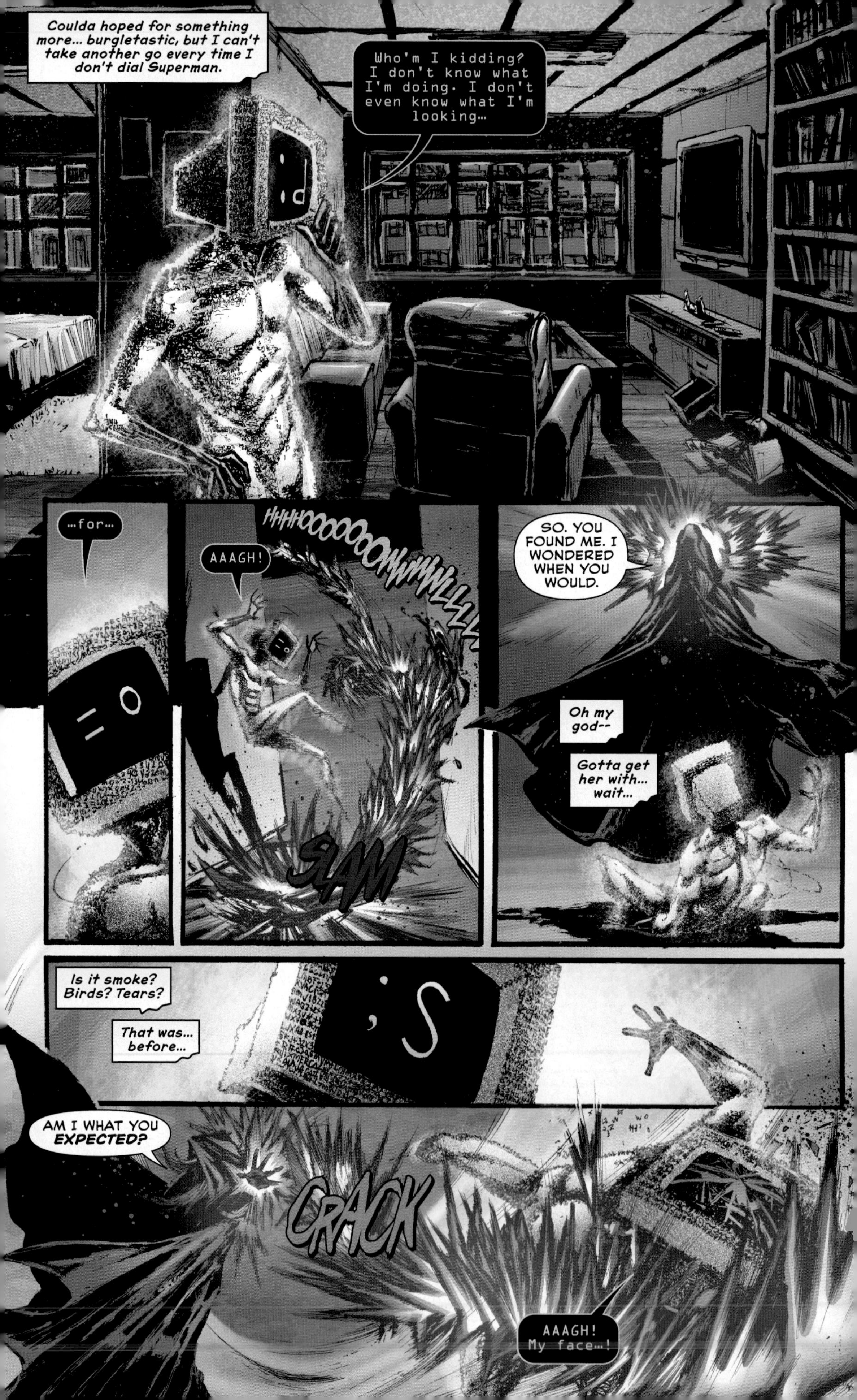

Coulda hoped for something more... burgletastic, but I can't take another go every time I don't dial Superman.
Who'm I kidding? I don't know what I'm doing. I don't even know what I'm looking…
…for…
AAAGH!
HHHHOOOOOOOWWWWLLLL
SLAM
SO. YOU FOUND ME. I WONDERED WHEN YOU WOULD.
Oh my god--
Gotta get her with... wait...
Is it smoke? Birds? Tears?
That was... before...
AM I WHAT YOU EXPECTED?
CRACK
AAAGH! My face…!

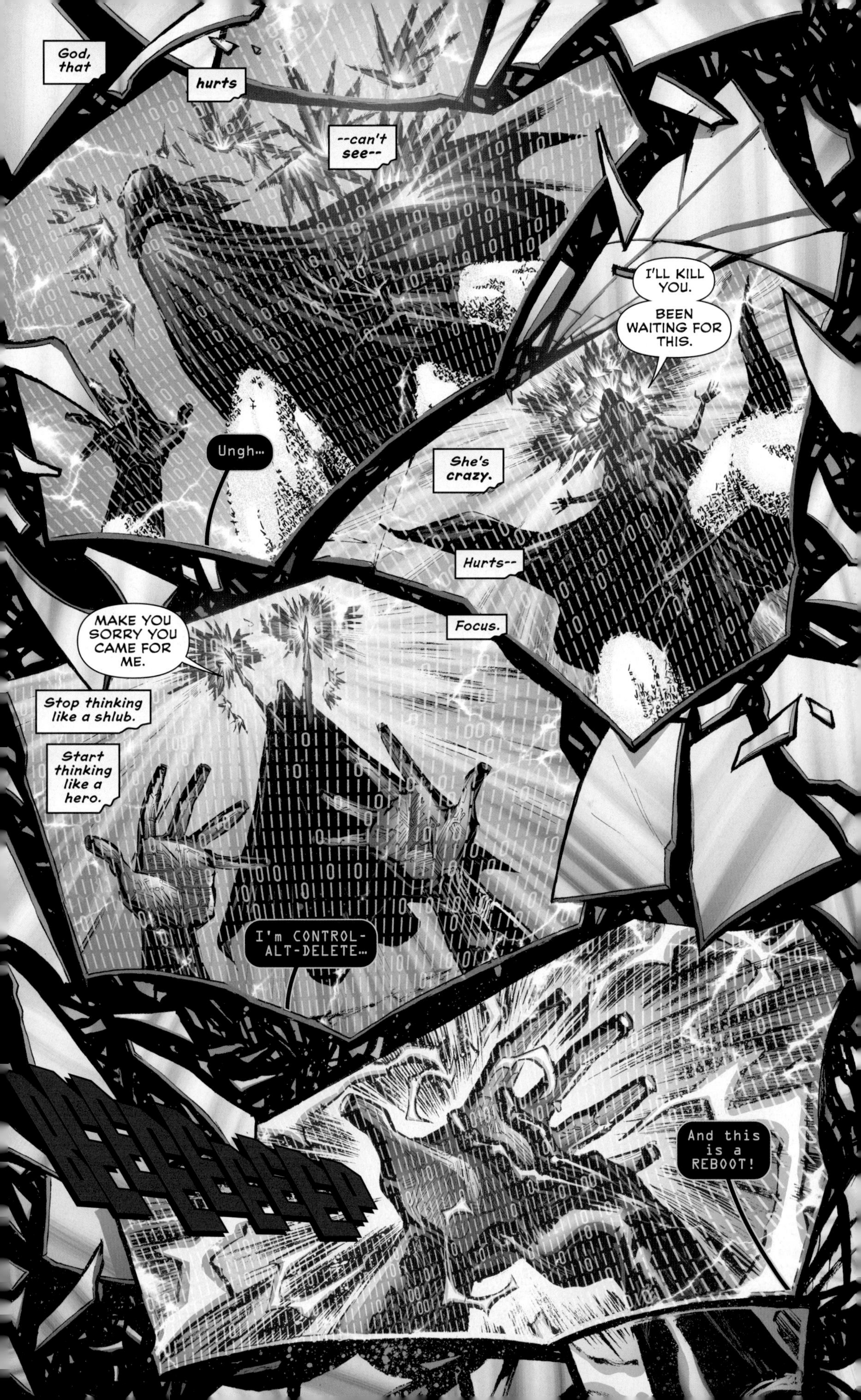
God, that
hurts
--can't see--
I'LL KILL YOU.
BEEN WAITING FOR THIS.
Ungh...
She's crazy.
Hurts--
Focus.
MAKE YOU SORRY YOU CAME FOR ME.
Stop thinking like a shlub.
Start thinking like a hero.
I'm CONTROL-ALT-DELETE...
And this is a REBOOT!

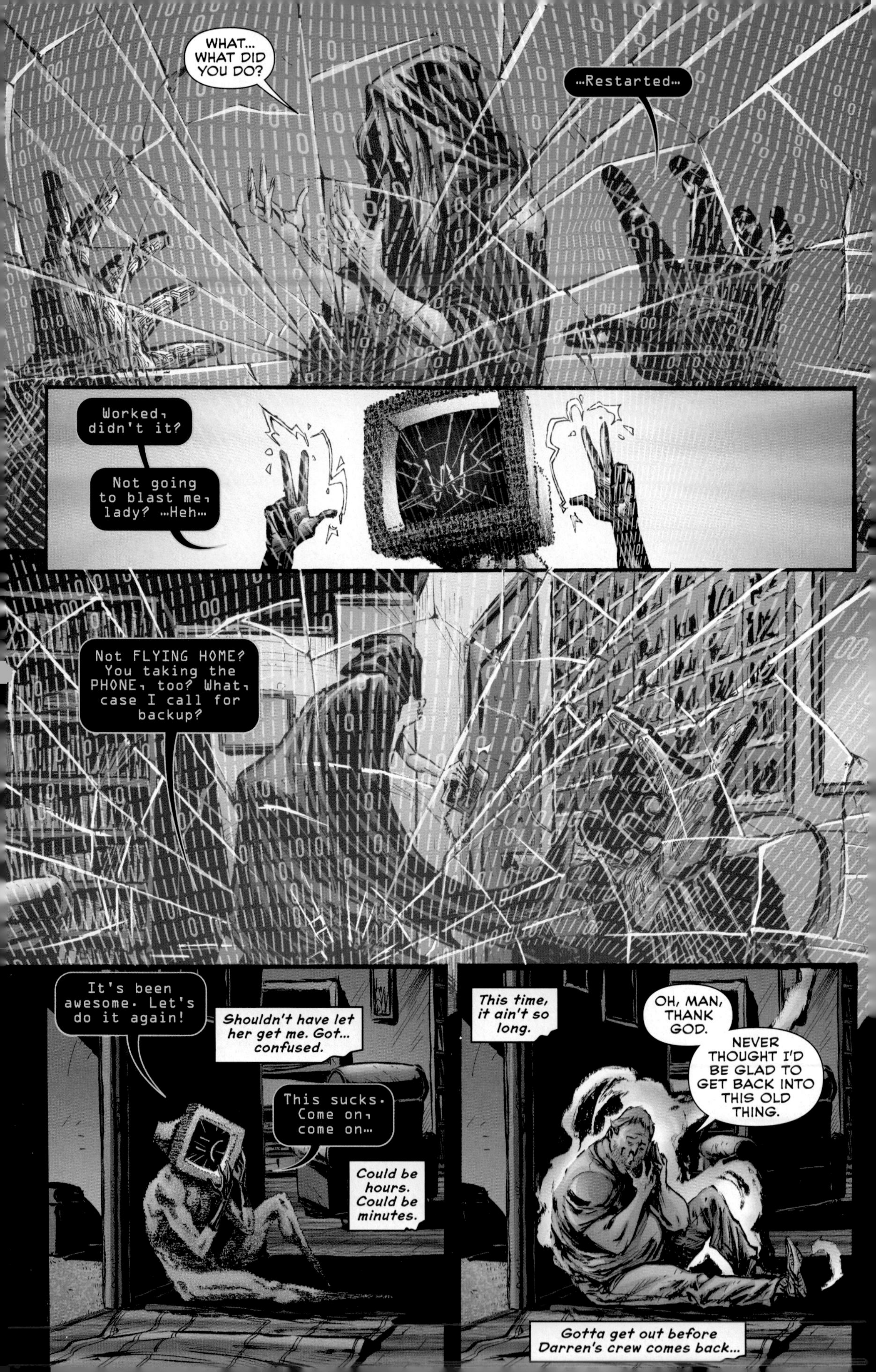
WHAT... WHAT DID YOU DO?
...Restarted...
Worked, didn't it?
Not going to blast me, lady? ...Heh...
Not FLYING HOME? You taking the PHONE, too? What, case I call for backup?
It's been awesome. Let's do it again!
Shouldn't have let her get me. Got... confused.
This sucks. Come on, come on...
Could be hours. Could be minutes.
This time, it ain't so long.
OH, MAN, THANK GOD.
NEVER THOUGHT I'D BE GLAD TO GET BACK INTO THIS OLD THING.
Gotta get out before Darren's crew comes back...

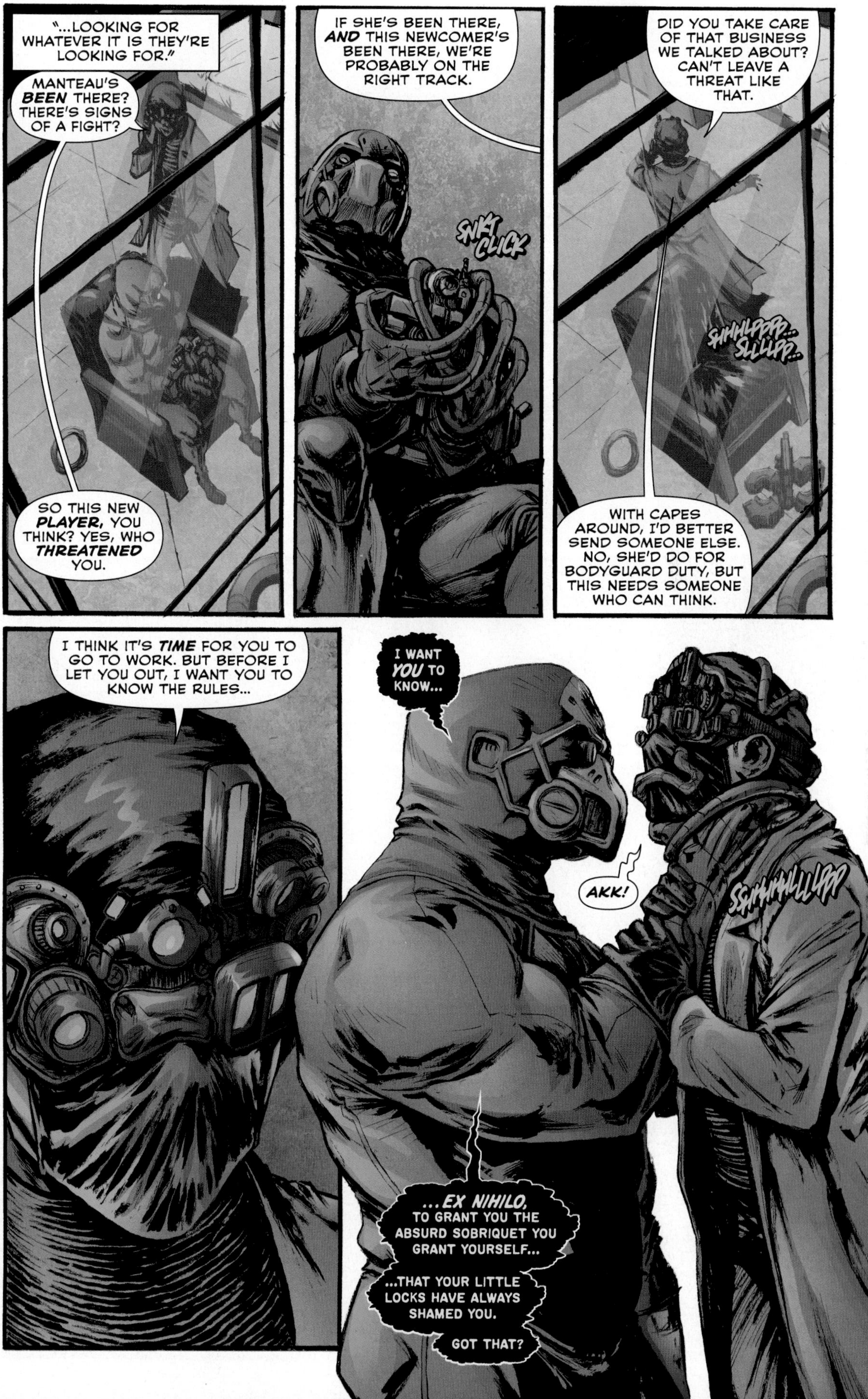
"...LOOKING FOR WHATEVER IT IS THEY'RE LOOKING FOR."
MANTEAU'S **BEEN** THERE? THERE'S SIGNS OF A FIGHT?
SO THIS NEW **PLAYER,** YOU THINK? YES, WHO **THREATENED** YOU.
IF SHE'S BEEN THERE, **AND** THIS NEWCOMER'S BEEN THERE, WE'RE PROBABLY ON THE RIGHT TRACK.
SNKT CLICK
DID YOU TAKE CARE OF THAT BUSINESS WE TALKED ABOUT? CAN'T LEAVE A THREAT LIKE THAT.
SHHHLPPP... SLLLPP...
WITH CAPES AROUND, I'D BETTER SEND SOMEONE ELSE. NO, SHE'D DO FOR BODYGUARD DUTY, BUT THIS NEEDS SOMEONE WHO CAN THINK.
I THINK IT'S **TIME** FOR YOU TO GO TO WORK. BUT BEFORE I LET YOU OUT, I WANT YOU TO KNOW THE RULES...
I WANT **YOU** TO KNOW...
AKK!
SSHHHHLLLPPP
...**EX NIHILO,** TO GRANT YOU THE ABSURD SOBRIQUET YOU GRANT YOURSELF...
...THAT YOUR LITTLE LOCKS HAVE ALWAYS SHAMED YOU.
GOT THAT?

MMMMM! MMMMM!

GLOOOP

SUCH INKS I HAVE. I COULD GIVE YOU SUCH DREAMS.

OR MAKE YOU DROWN ON YOUR OWN MELTING LUNGS.

I'LL *DO* YOUR DIRTY WORK. NOT NOW, NOT EVER, BECAUSE YOU *MAKE* ME. YOU NEVER COULD.

BUT BECAUSE YOU'RE *CLOSE.*

BECAUSE I WANT YOU TO SUCCEED.

COUGH! COUGH!

HOW *LONG* HAVE I BEEN HERE? WHEN DID YOU FIND ME?

I WAS NEVER YOUR PRISONER.

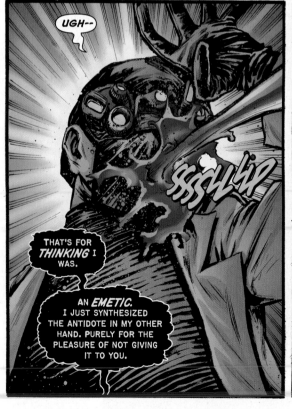

UGH--

SSSSLLIP

THAT'S FOR *THINKING* I WAS.

AN *EMETIC.* I JUST SYNTHESIZED THE ANTIDOTE IN MY OTHER HAND. PURELY FOR THE PLEASURE OF NOT GIVING IT TO YOU.

YOU NEED NEITHER SPELLS NOR THREATS. I'LL TAKE CARE OF YOUR PROBLEM. YOU GET BACK TO WORK.

THEY CAN BE *AWKWARD,* MASKS, CAN'T THEY? WHEN ONE'S PRODUCING MATTER *EX NIHILO.*

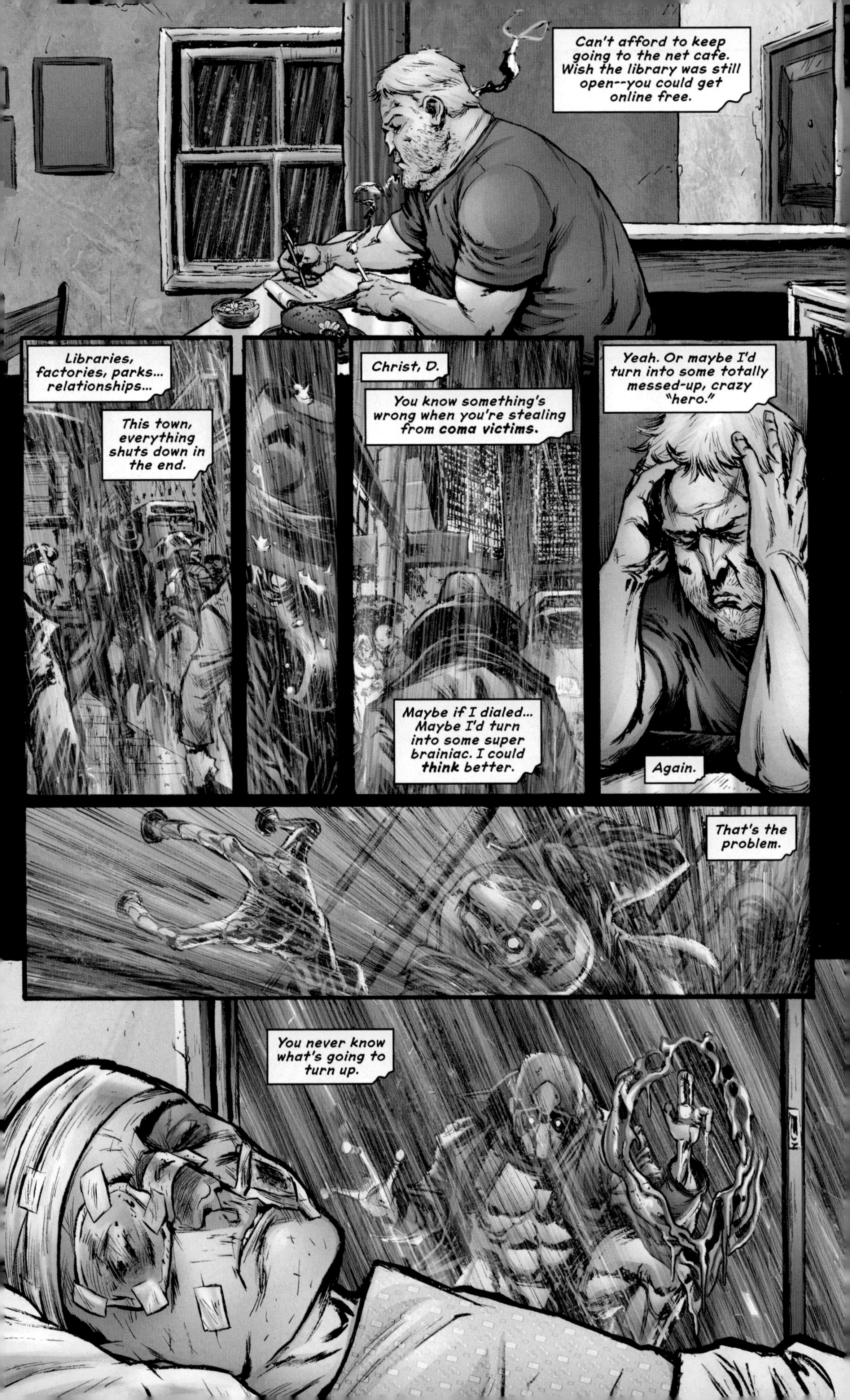
Can't afford to keep going to the net cafe. Wish the library was still open--you could get online free.
Libraries, factories, parks... relationships...
This town, everything shuts down in the end.
Christ, D.
You know something's wrong when you're stealing from **coma victims.**
Maybe if I dialed... Maybe I'd turn into some super brainiac. I could **think** better.
Yeah. Or maybe I'd turn into some totally messed-up, crazy "hero."
Again.
That's the problem.
You never know what's going to turn up.

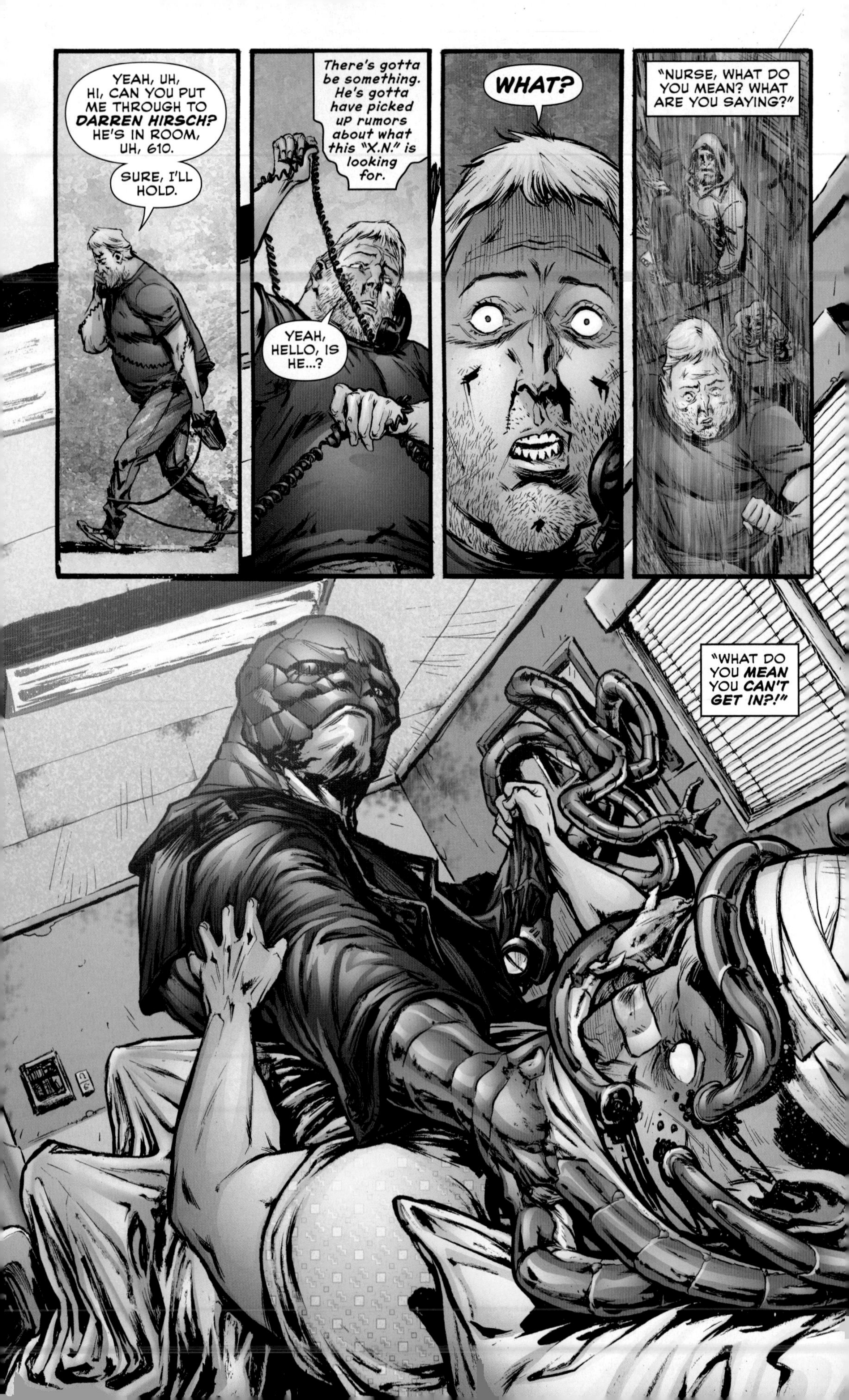

YEAH, UH, HI, CAN YOU PUT ME THROUGH TO **DARREN HIRSCH?** HE'S IN ROOM, UH, 610.
SURE, I'LL HOLD.
There's gotta be something. He's gotta have picked up rumors about what this "X.N." is looking for.
YEAH, HELLO, IS HE...?
WHAT?
"NURSE, WHAT DO YOU MEAN? WHAT ARE YOU SAYING?"
"WHAT DO YOU **MEAN** YOU **CAN'T GET IN?!**"

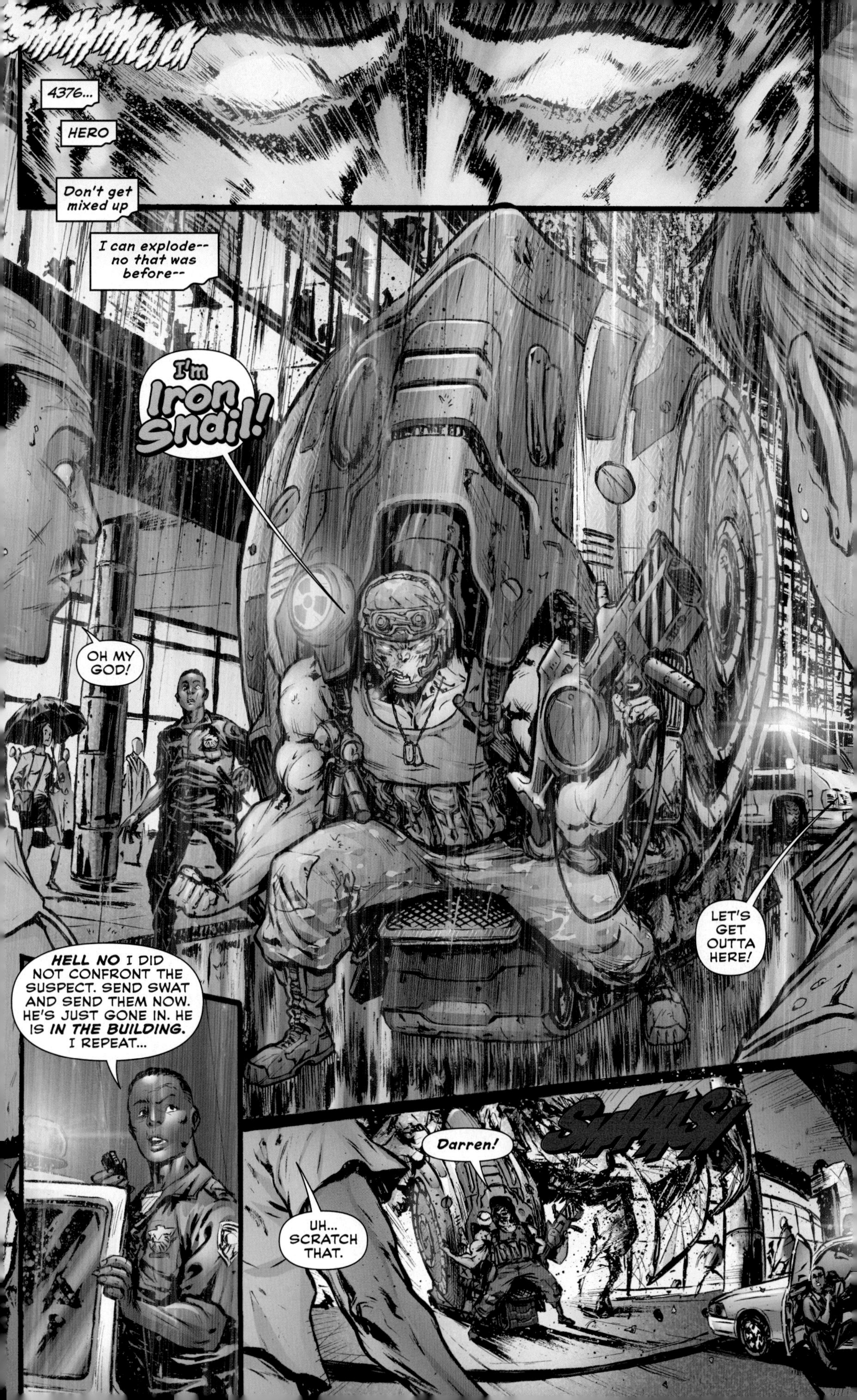
4376...
HERO
Don't get mixed up
I can explode-- no that was before--
I'm Iron Snail!
OH MY GOD!
LET'S GET OUTTA HERE!
HELL NO I DID NOT CONFRONT THE SUSPECT. SEND SWAT AND SEND THEM NOW. HE'S JUST GONE IN. HE IS IN THE BUILDING. I REPEAT...
Darren!
UH... SCRATCH THAT.

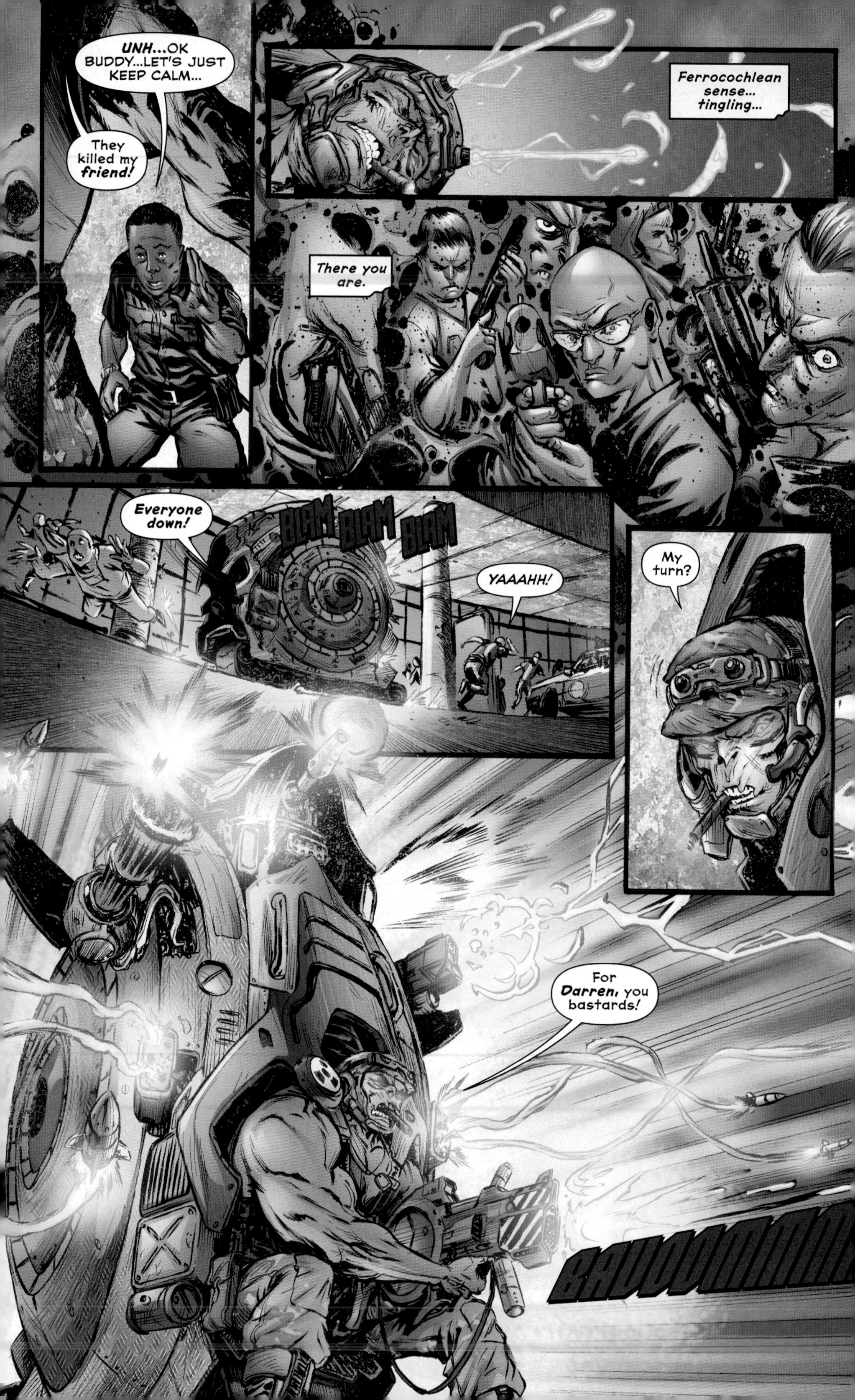

UNH...OK BUDDY...LET'S JUST KEEP CALM...
They killed my friend!
Ferrocochlean sense... tingling...
There you are.
Everyone down!
BLAM BLAM BLAM
YAAAHH!
My turn?
For Darren, you bastards!

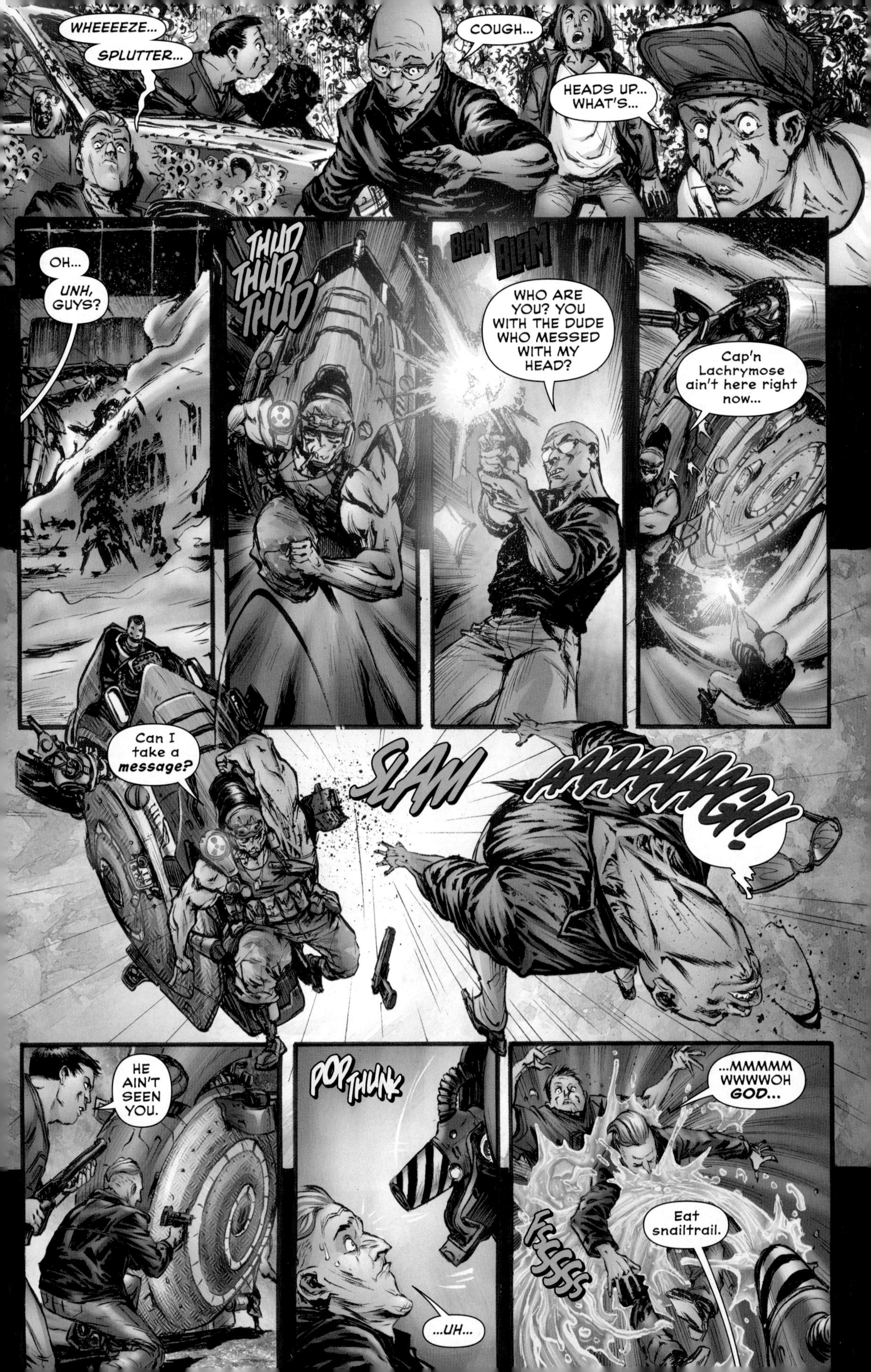
WHEEEEZE...
SPLUTTER...
COUGH...
HEADS UP... WHAT'S...
OH...
UNH, GUYS?
THUD THUD THUD
BLAM BLAM
WHO ARE YOU? YOU WITH THE DUDE WHO MESSED WITH MY HEAD?
Cap'n Lachrymose ain't here right now...
Can I take a *message?*
SLAM
AAAAAAAGH!
HE AIN'T SEEN YOU.
POP THUNK
...UH...
...MMMMM WWWWOH *GOD...*
Eat snailtrail.

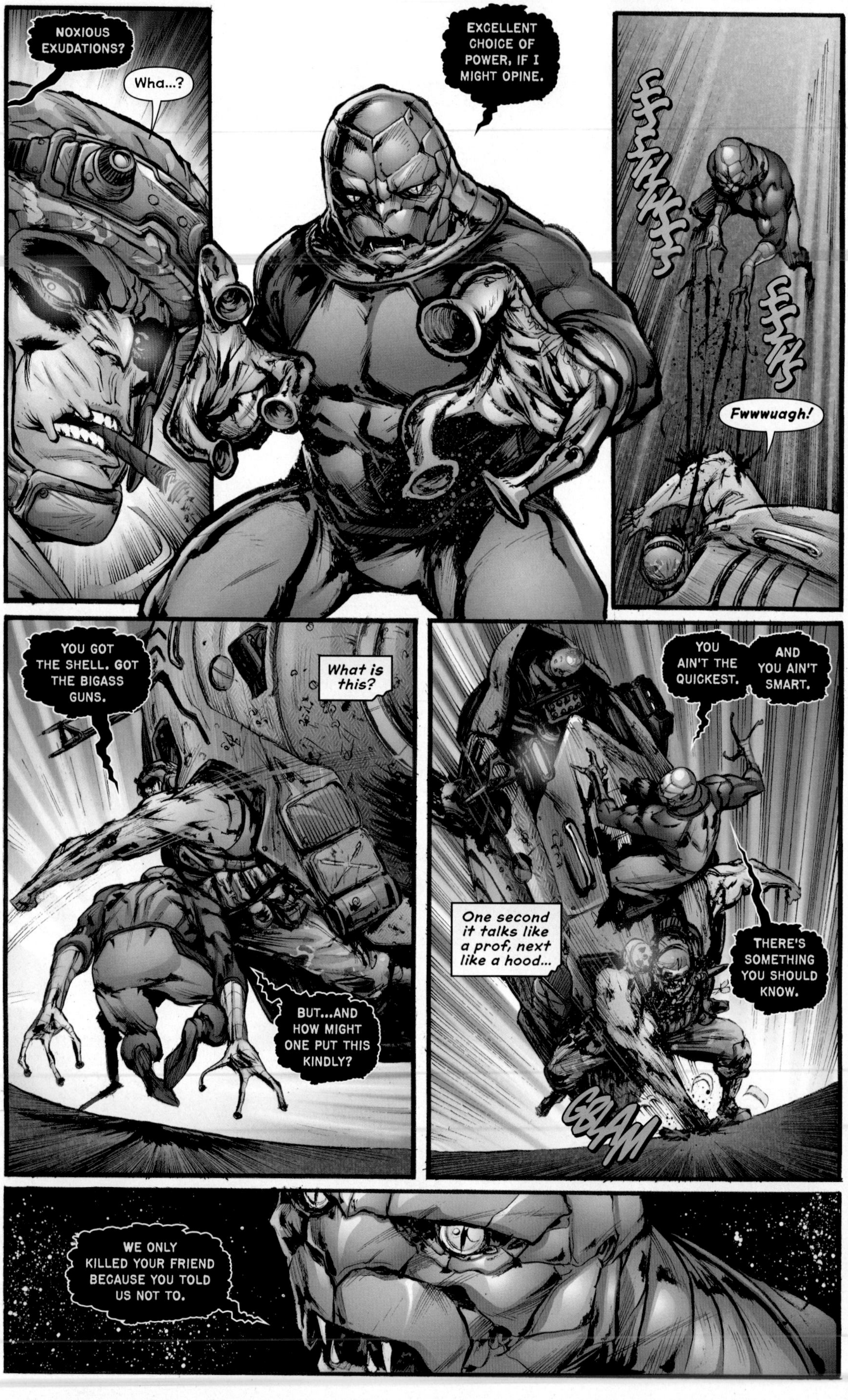

NOXIOUS EXUDATIONS?
Wha...?
EXCELLENT CHOICE OF POWER, IF I MIGHT OPINE.
FSSHHKKSSS
FSSKKS
Fwwwuagh!
YOU GOT THE SHELL. GOT THE BIGASS GUNS.
What is this?
BUT...AND HOW MIGHT ONE PUT THIS KINDLY?
YOU AIN'T THE QUICKEST.
AND YOU AIN'T SMART.
One second it talks like a prof, next like a hood...
THERE'S SOMETHING YOU SHOULD KNOW.
GBLAM
WE ONLY KILLED YOUR FRIEND BECAUSE YOU TOLD US NOT TO.

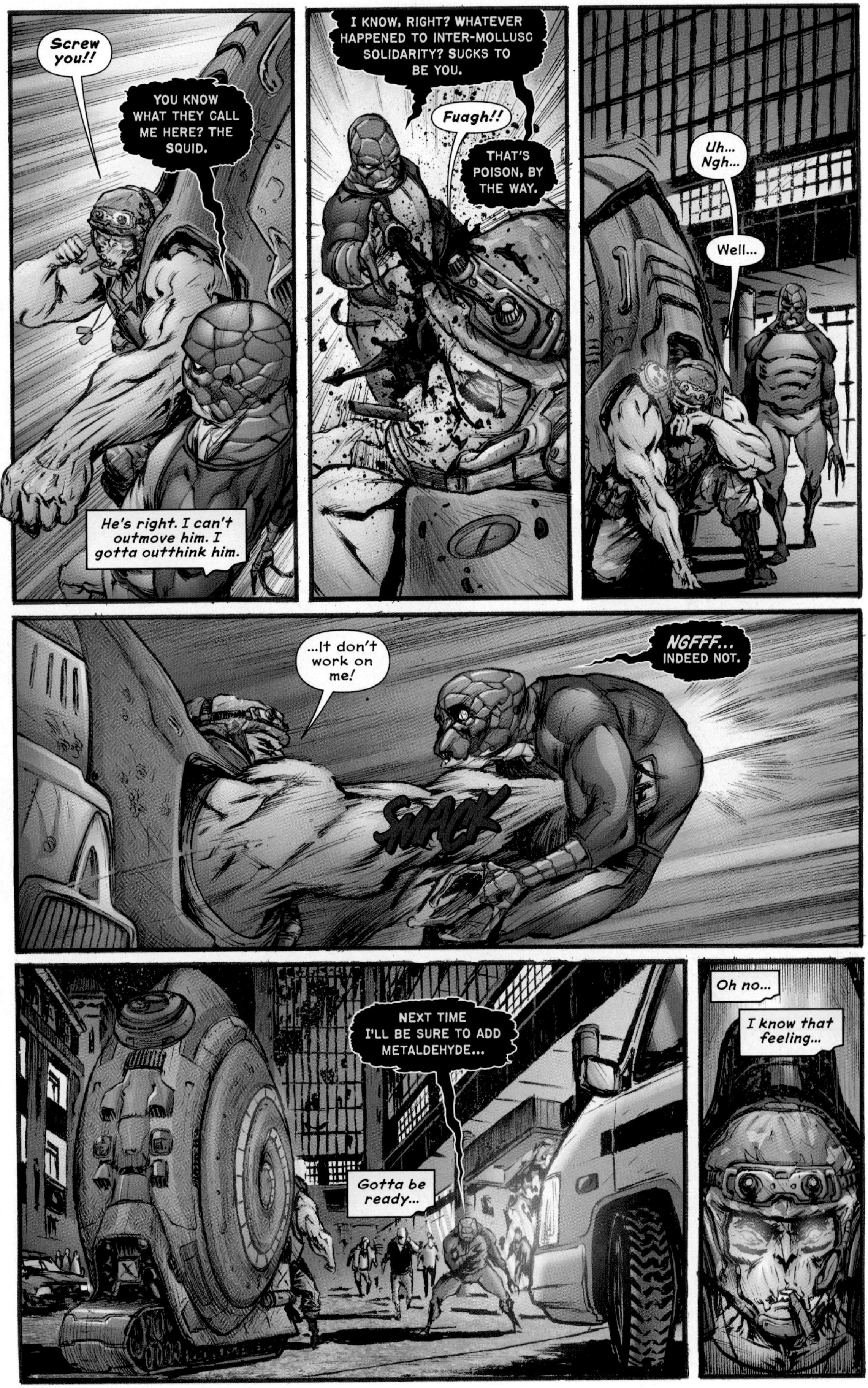
Screw you!!
YOU KNOW WHAT THEY CALL ME HERE? THE SQUID.
He's right. I can't outmove him. I gotta outthink him.
I KNOW, RIGHT? WHATEVER HAPPENED TO INTER-MOLLUSC SOLIDARITY? SUCKS TO BE YOU.
Fuagh!!
THAT'S POISON, BY THE WAY.
Uh... Ngh...
Well...
...It don't work on me!
NGFFF... INDEED NOT.
SMACK
NEXT TIME I'LL BE SURE TO ADD METALDEHYDE...
Gotta be ready...
Oh no...
I know that feeling...

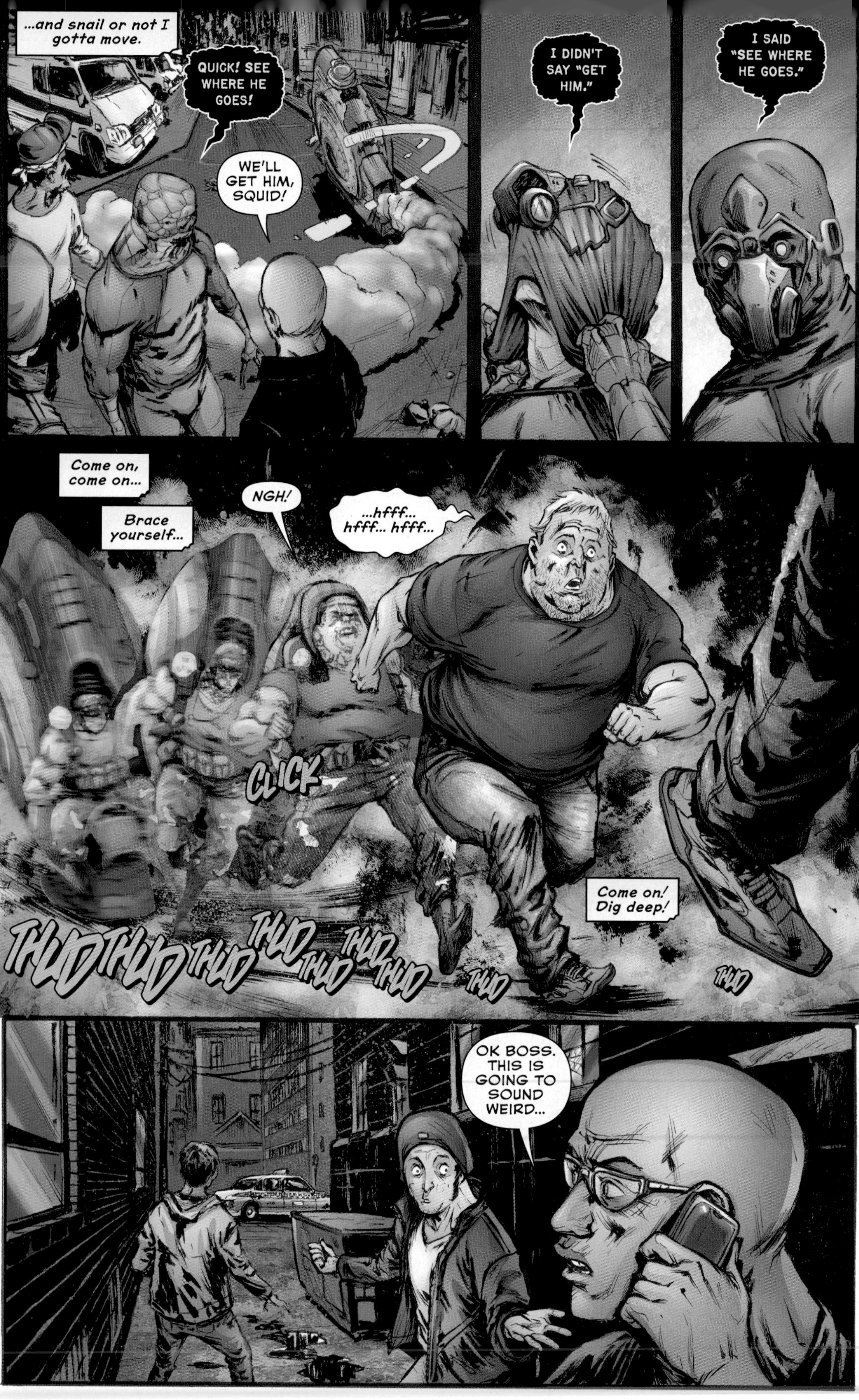

...and snail or not I gotta move.
QUICK! SEE WHERE HE GOES!
WE'LL GET HIM, SQUID!
I DIDN'T SAY "GET HIM."
I SAID "SEE WHERE HE GOES."
Come on, come on...
Brace yourself...
NGH!
...hfff... hfff... hfff...
CLICK
Come on! Dig deep!
THUD THUD THUD THUD THUD THUD THUD THUD THUD
OK BOSS. THIS IS GOING TO SOUND WEIRD...

HE *HAILED A CAB?* THE GUY WHO WAS IN HERE IN BODY ARMOR?

HOW DID HE EVEN FIT INSIDE?

BECAUSE IT AIN'T HIM, *EX NIHILO.* AT LEAST...NOT QUITE.

TELL VERN TO FOLLOW HIM. OUTTA SIGHT.

TAIL HIM. DON'T LET HIM SEE YOU. CALL ME WHEN HE'S GOT WHERE HE'S GOING.

GOOD.

YOU... I'M WARNING YOU...

WHATEVER SPECIAL WEAPON THAT IS, KEEP IT IN YOUR POCKET.

I DON'T LIKE YOU, DOCTOR. BUT I NEED YOU. YOU'VE NEARLY DONE IT.

LOOK TO YOUR PATIENT.

I'VE BEEN YOUR...GUEST... BECAUSE OF WHAT I KNOW.

AND I'LL HELP YOU.

WITH INFORMATION. TECHNIQUES. WITH THESE IDIOTS IN COSTUME. BECAUSE I DON'T WANT THEM CAUSING TROUBLE. NOT NOW.

LOOK AT HIM.

YOU KNOW WHO... YOU KNOW WHAT *TOUCHED* HIM, DOC. WHAT TOUCHED ALL OF THEM. YOU KNOW IT'S GETTING *CLOSER* AND CLOSER.

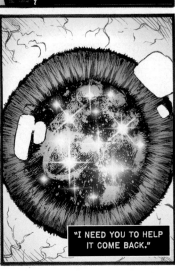

"I NEED YOU TO HELP IT COME BACK."

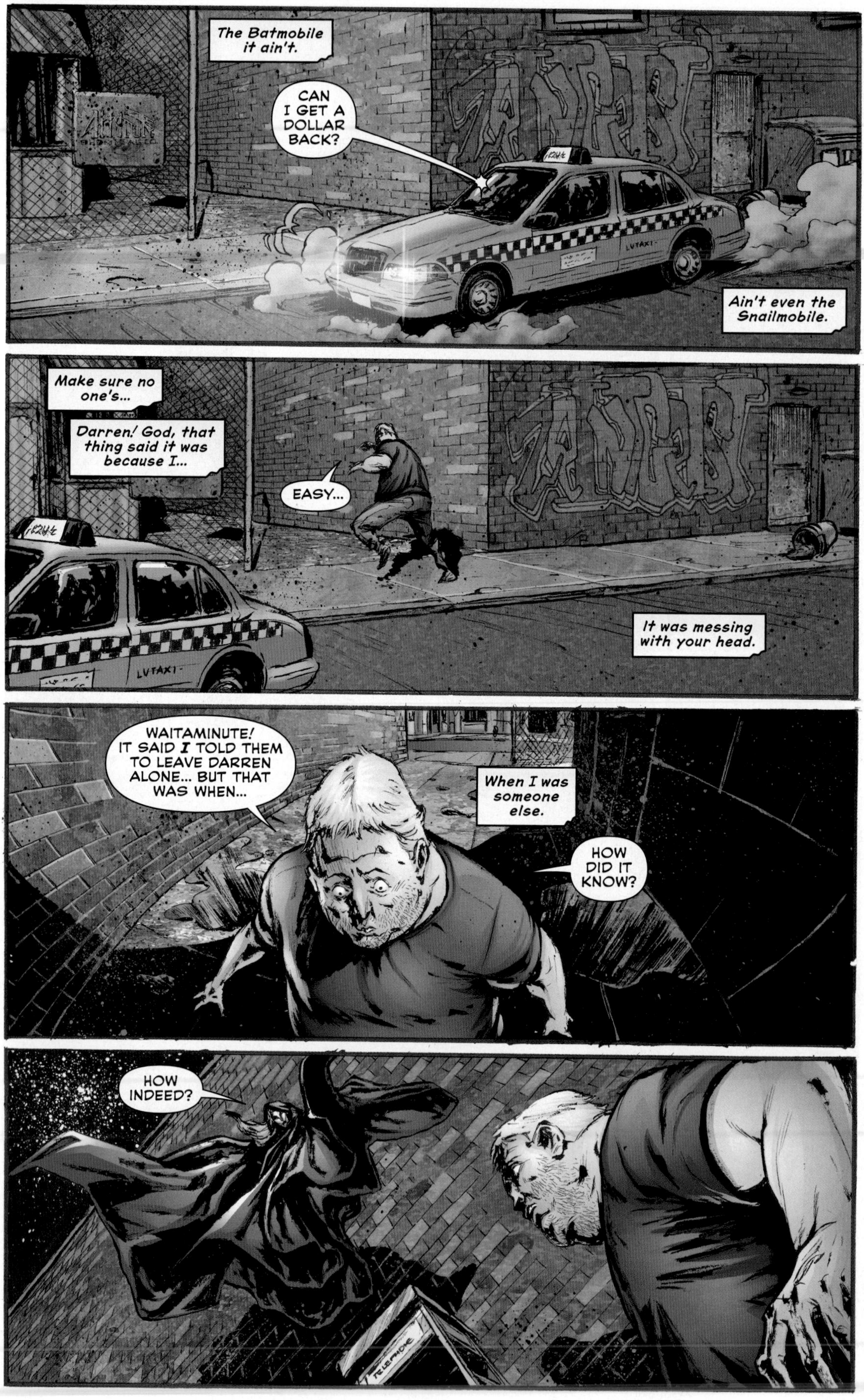
The Batmobile it ain't.
CAN I GET A DOLLAR BACK?
Ain't even the Snailmobile.
Make sure no one's...
Darren! God, that thing said it was because I...
EASY...
It was messing with your head.
WAITAMINUTE! IT SAID *I* TOLD THEM TO LEAVE DARREN ALONE... BUT THAT WAS WHEN...
When I was someone else.
HOW DID IT KNOW?
HOW INDEED?
LV TAXI
TELEPHONE

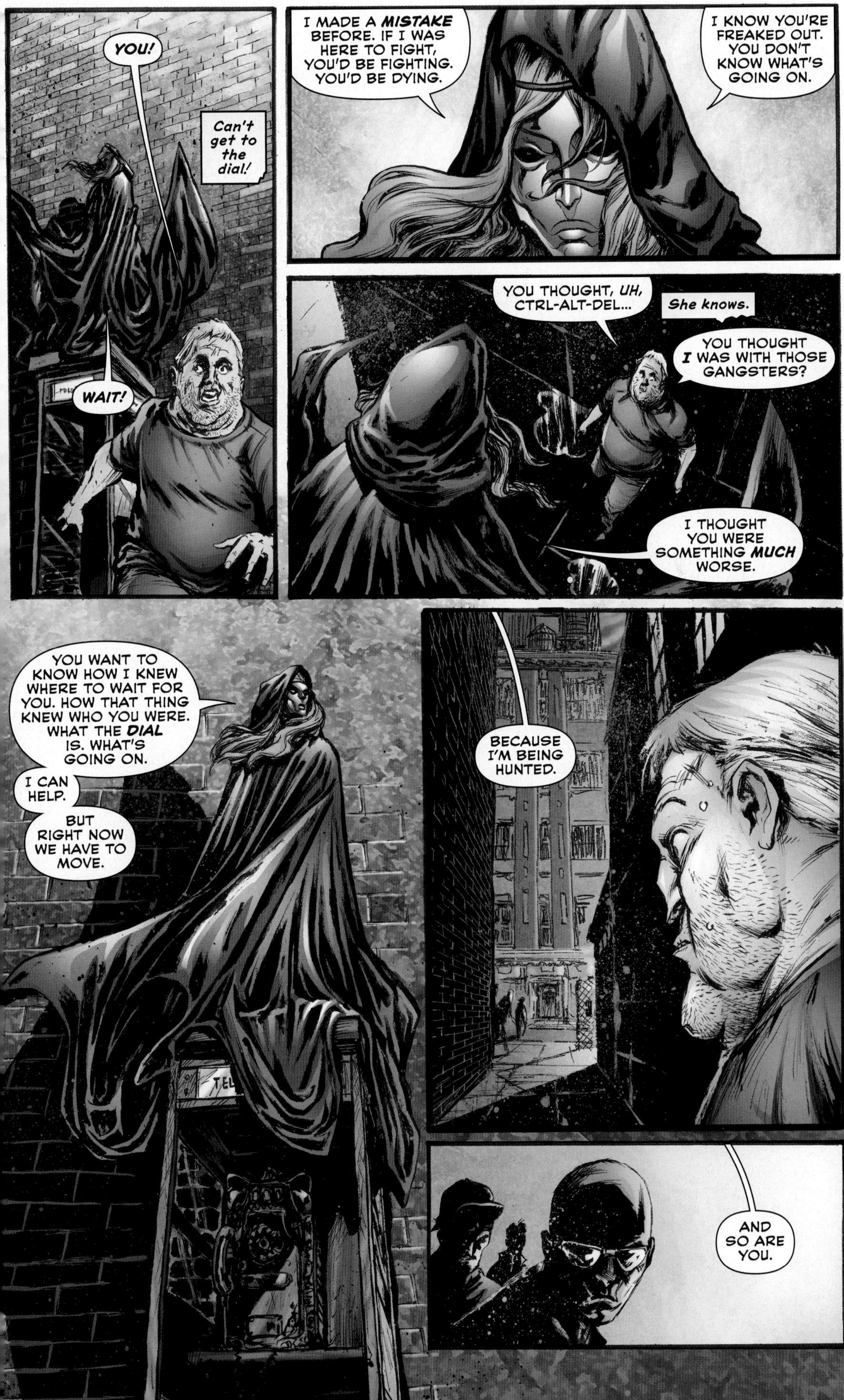
YOU!
Can't get to the dial!
WAIT!
I MADE A MISTAKE BEFORE. IF I WAS HERE TO FIGHT, YOU'D BE FIGHTING. YOU'D BE DYING.
I KNOW YOU'RE FREAKED OUT. YOU DON'T KNOW WHAT'S GOING ON.
YOU THOUGHT, UH, CTRL-ALT-DEL...
She knows.
YOU THOUGHT I WAS WITH THOSE GANGSTERS?
I THOUGHT YOU WERE SOMETHING MUCH WORSE.
YOU WANT TO KNOW HOW I KNEW WHERE TO WAIT FOR YOU. HOW THAT THING KNEW WHO YOU WERE. WHAT THE DIAL IS. WHAT'S GOING ON.
I CAN HELP.
BUT RIGHT NOW WE HAVE TO MOVE.
BECAUSE I'M BEING HUNTED.
AND SO ARE YOU.

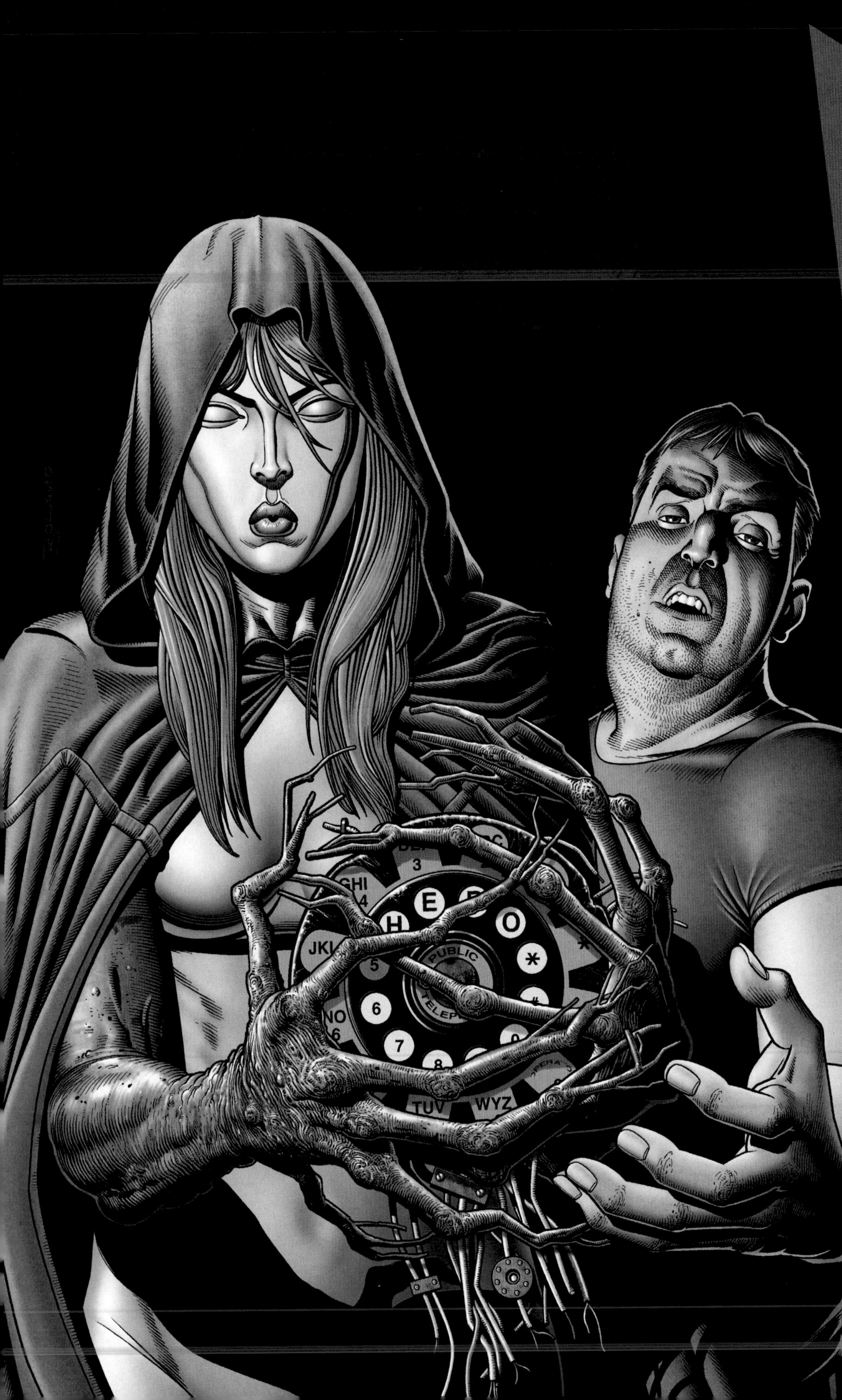

GHI
JKL
PUBLIC
TUV
WYZ

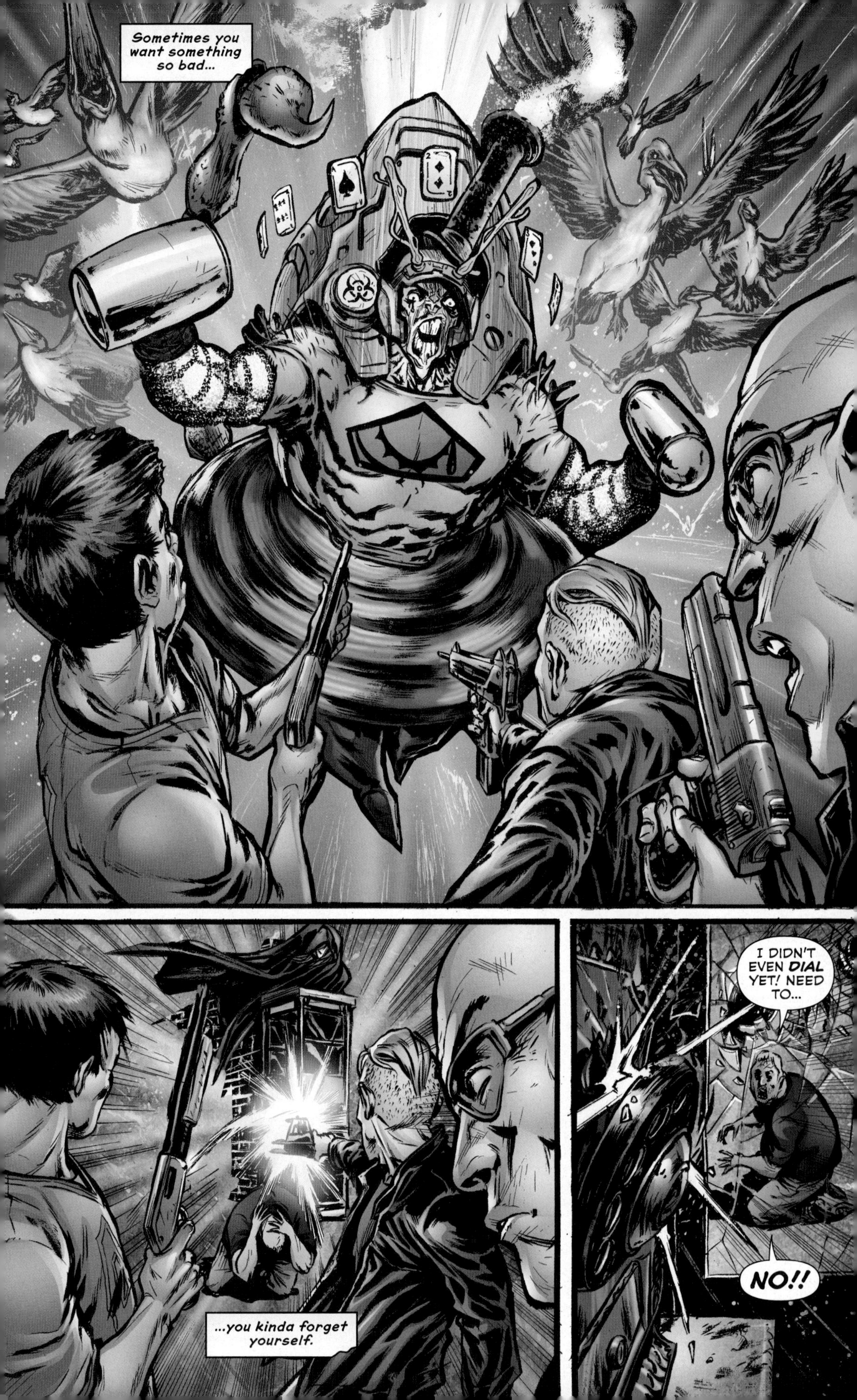
Sometimes you want something so bad...
...you kinda forget yourself.
I DIDN'T EVEN DIAL YET! NEED TO...
NO!!

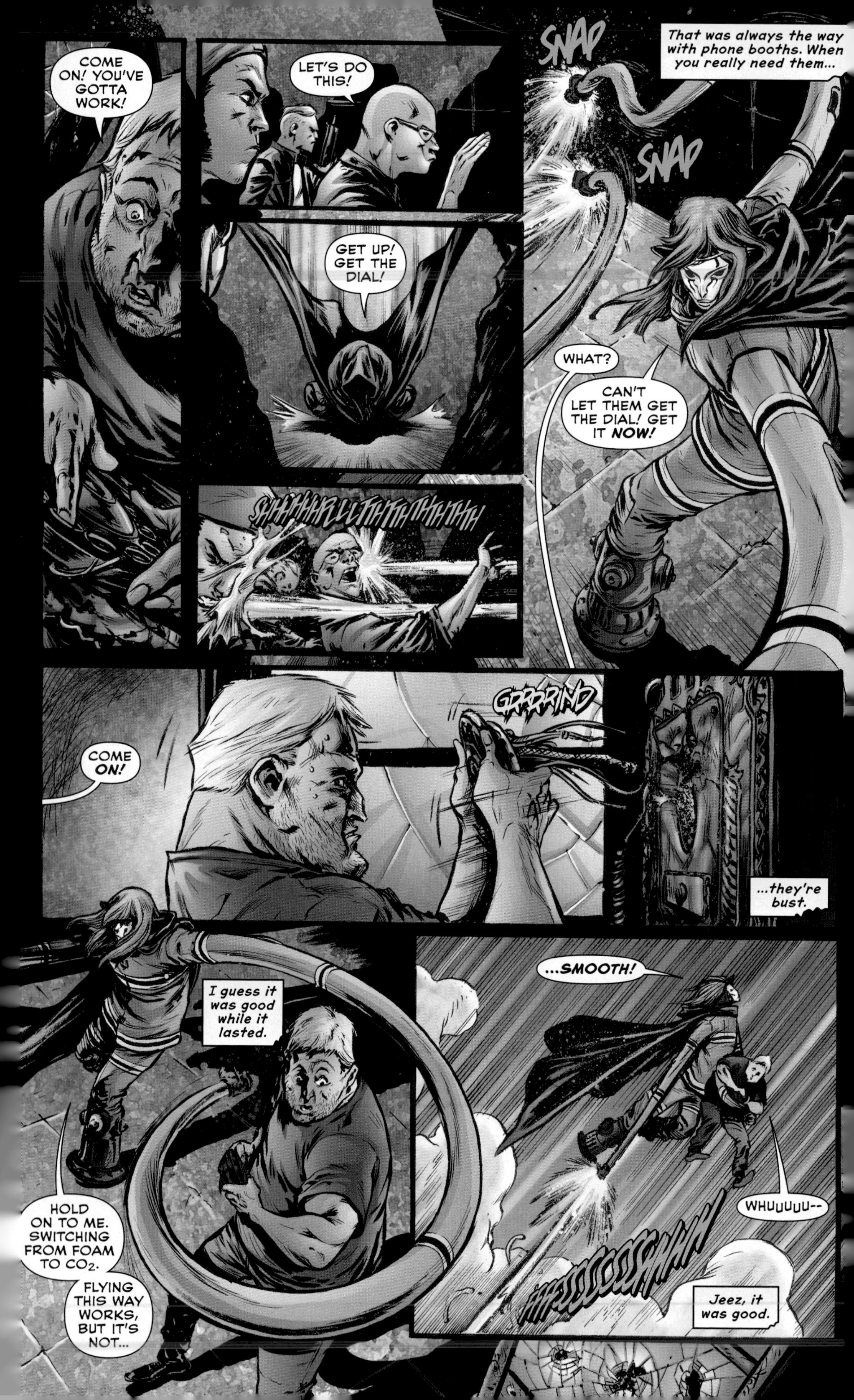
COME ON! YOU'VE GOTTA WORK!
LET'S DO THIS!
SNAP
That was always the way with phone booths. When you really need them...
SNAP
GET UP! GET THE DIAL!
WHAT?
CAN'T LET THEM GET THE DIAL! GET IT NOW!
SHHHHHHRLLLTHTHTHTHTHTH
GRRRRIND
COME ON!
...they're bust.
I guess it was good while it lasted.
...SMOOTH!
WHUUUUU--
HOLD ON TO ME. SWITCHING FROM FOAM TO CO_2.
FLYING THIS WAY WORKS, BUT IT'S NOT...
FHHSSSSSSHHHH
Jeez, it was good.

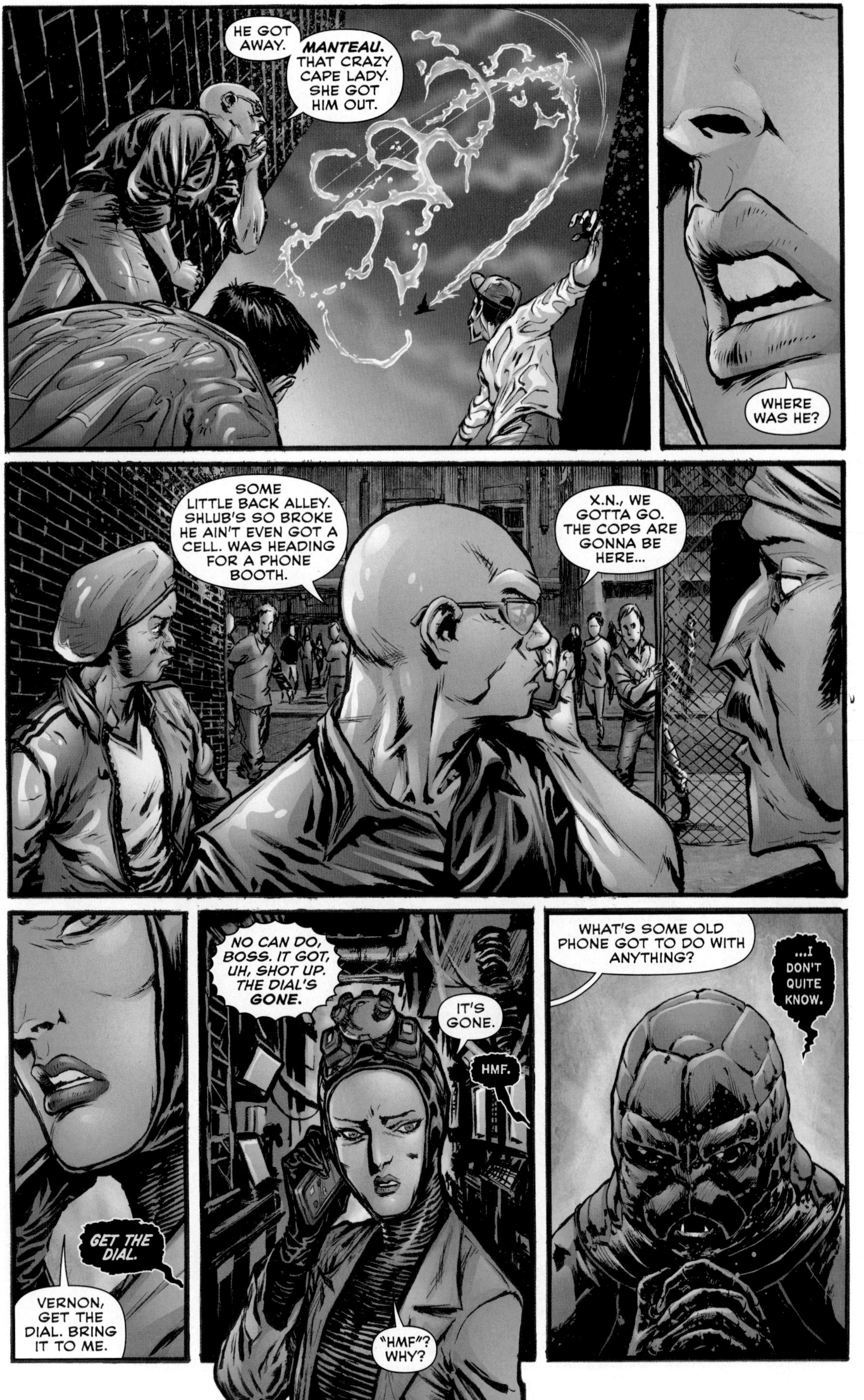
HE GOT AWAY.
MANTEAU. THAT CRAZY CAPE LADY. SHE GOT HIM OUT.
WHERE WAS HE?
SOME LITTLE BACK ALLEY. SHLUB'S SO BROKE HE AIN'T EVEN GOT A CELL. WAS HEADING FOR A PHONE BOOTH.
X.N., WE GOTTA GO. THE COPS ARE GONNA BE HERE...
GET THE DIAL.
VERNON, GET THE DIAL. BRING IT TO ME.
NO CAN DO, BOSS. IT GOT, UH, SHOT UP. THE DIAL'S GONE.
IT'S GONE.
HMF.
"HMF"? WHY?
WHAT'S SOME OLD PHONE GOT TO DO WITH ANYTHING?
...I DON'T QUITE KNOW.

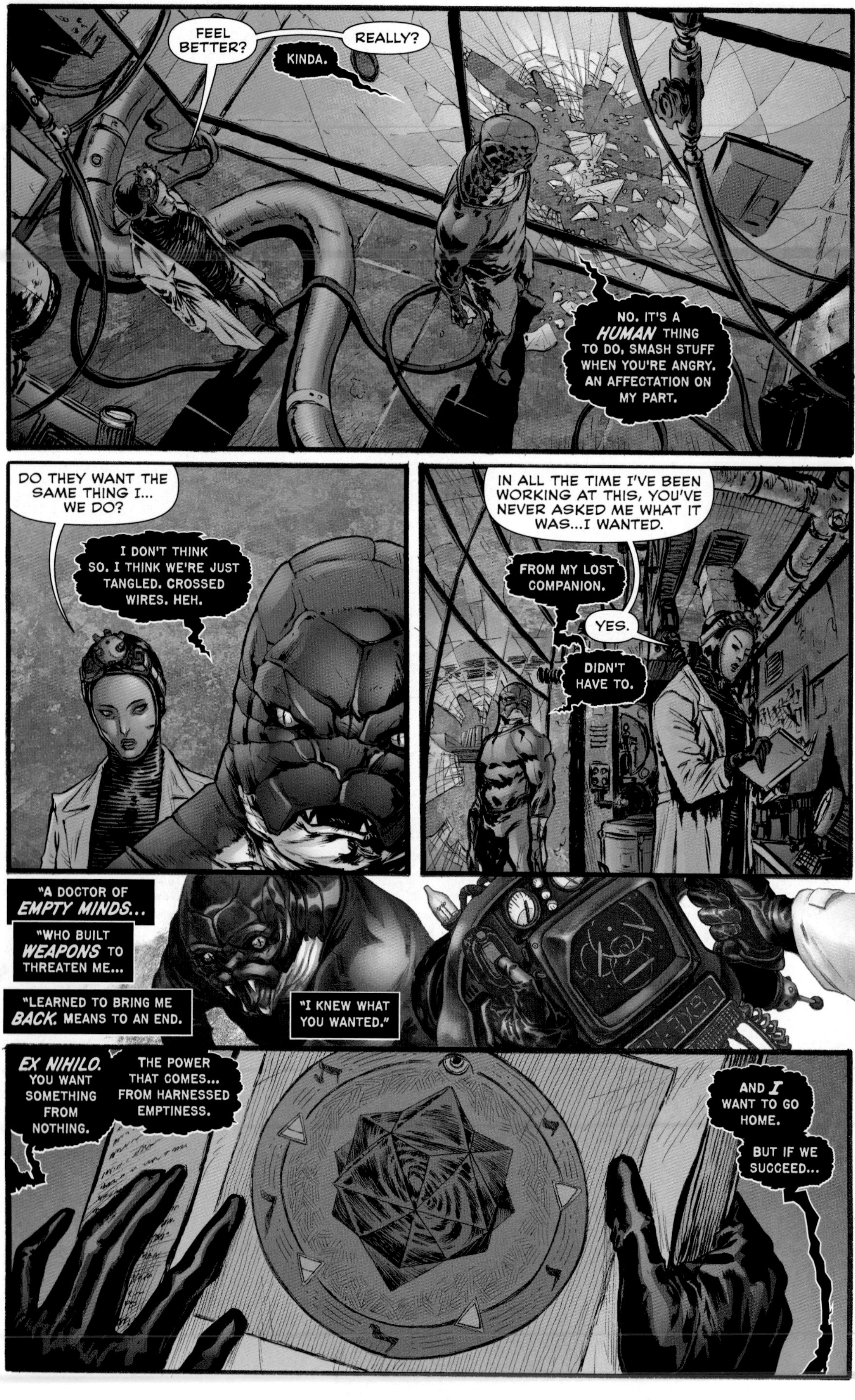
FEEL BETTER?
KINDA.
REALLY?
NO. IT'S A HUMAN THING TO DO, SMASH STUFF WHEN YOU'RE ANGRY. AN AFFECTATION ON MY PART.
DO THEY WANT THE SAME THING I... WE DO?
I DON'T THINK SO. I THINK WE'RE JUST TANGLED. CROSSED WIRES. HEH.
IN ALL THE TIME I'VE BEEN WORKING AT THIS, YOU'VE NEVER ASKED ME WHAT IT WAS...I WANTED.
FROM MY LOST COMPANION.
YES.
DIDN'T HAVE TO.
"A DOCTOR OF EMPTY MINDS...
"WHO BUILT WEAPONS TO THREATEN ME...
"LEARNED TO BRING ME BACK. MEANS TO AN END.
"I KNEW WHAT YOU WANTED."
EX NIHILO. YOU WANT SOMETHING FROM NOTHING.
THE POWER THAT COMES... FROM HARNESSED EMPTINESS.
AND I WANT TO GO HOME.
BUT IF WE SUCCEED...

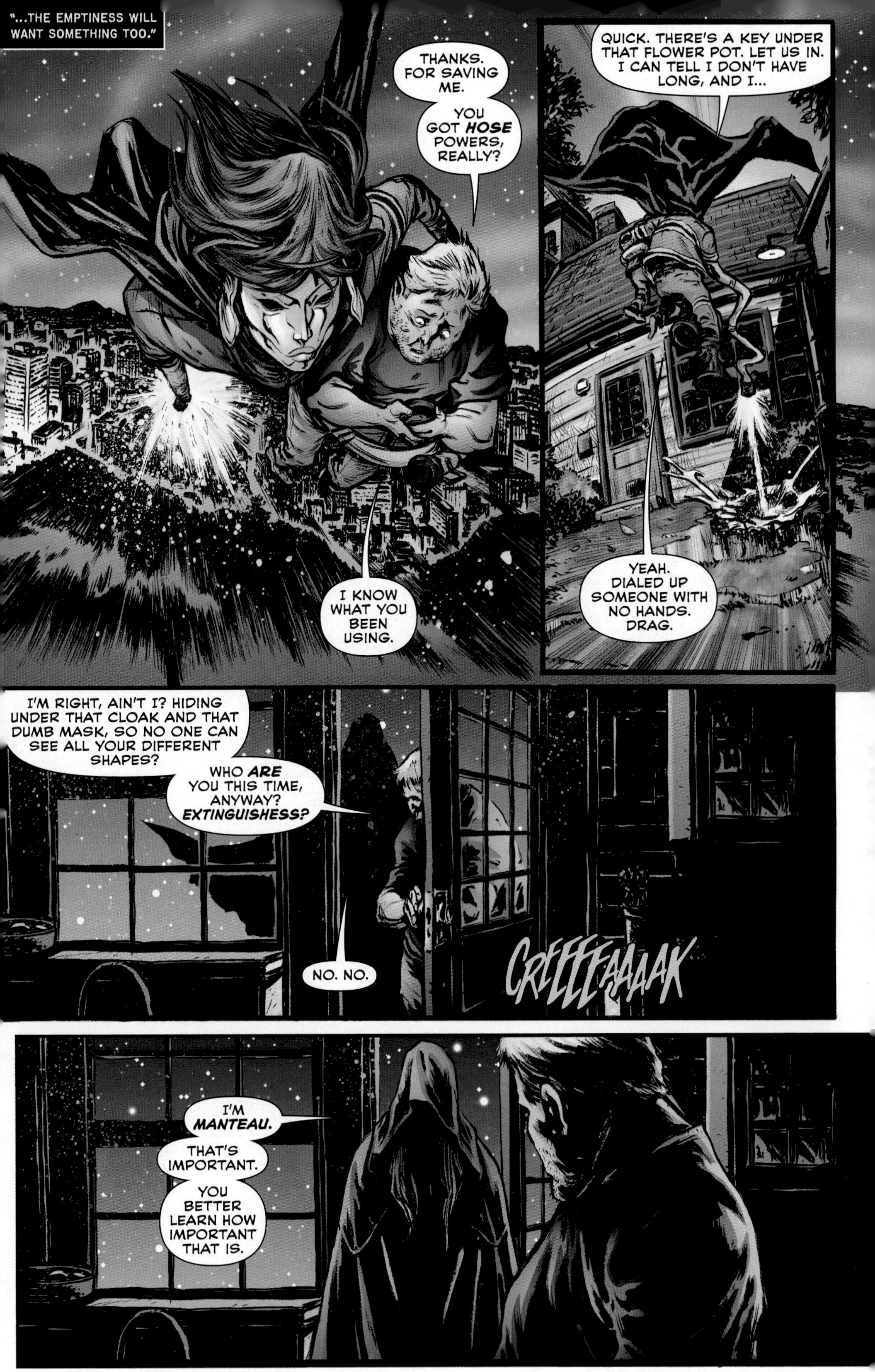
"...THE EMPTINESS WILL WANT SOMETHING TOO."
THANKS. FOR SAVING ME.
YOU GOT HOSE POWERS, REALLY?
I KNOW WHAT YOU BEEN USING.
QUICK. THERE'S A KEY UNDER THAT FLOWER POT. LET US IN. I CAN TELL I DON'T HAVE LONG, AND I...
YEAH. DIALED UP SOMEONE WITH NO HANDS. DRAG.
I'M RIGHT, AIN'T I? HIDING UNDER THAT CLOAK AND THAT DUMB MASK, SO NO ONE CAN SEE ALL YOUR DIFFERENT SHAPES?
WHO ARE YOU THIS TIME, ANYWAY? EXTINGUISHESS?
NO. NO.
CREEEEAAAAK
I'M MANTEAU.
THAT'S IMPORTANT.
YOU BETTER LEARN HOW IMPORTANT THAT IS.

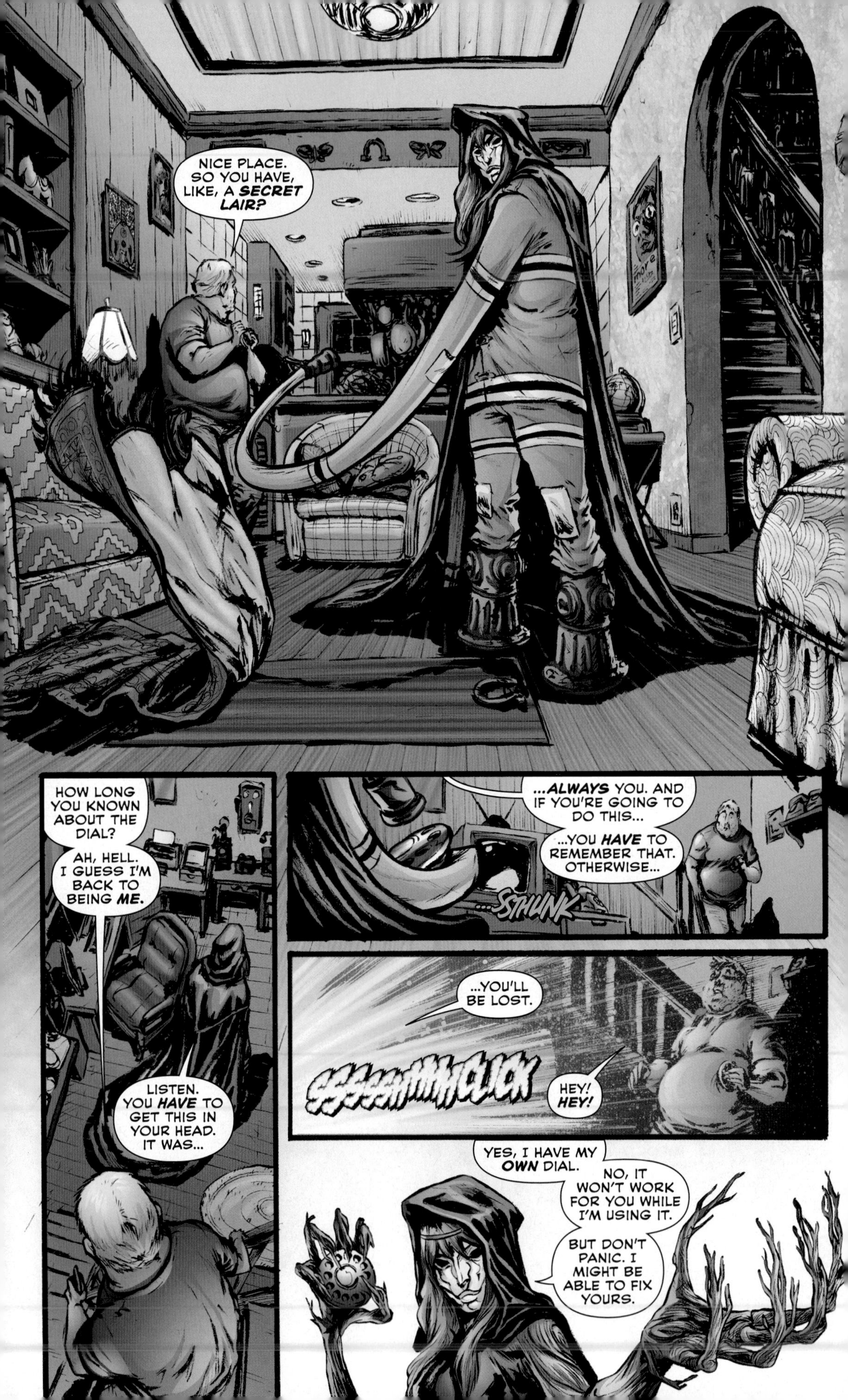
NICE PLACE. SO YOU HAVE, LIKE, A SECRET LAIR?
HOW LONG YOU KNOWN ABOUT THE DIAL?
AH, HELL. I GUESS I'M BACK TO BEING ME.
LISTEN. YOU HAVE TO GET THIS IN YOUR HEAD. IT WAS...
...ALWAYS YOU. AND IF YOU'RE GOING TO DO THIS...
...YOU HAVE TO REMEMBER THAT. OTHERWISE...
...SSTHUNK
...YOU'LL BE LOST.
SSSSSSHHHHHCLICK
HEY! HEY!
YES, I HAVE MY OWN DIAL.
NO, IT WON'T WORK FOR YOU WHILE I'M USING IT.
BUT DON'T PANIC. I MIGHT BE ABLE TO FIX YOURS.

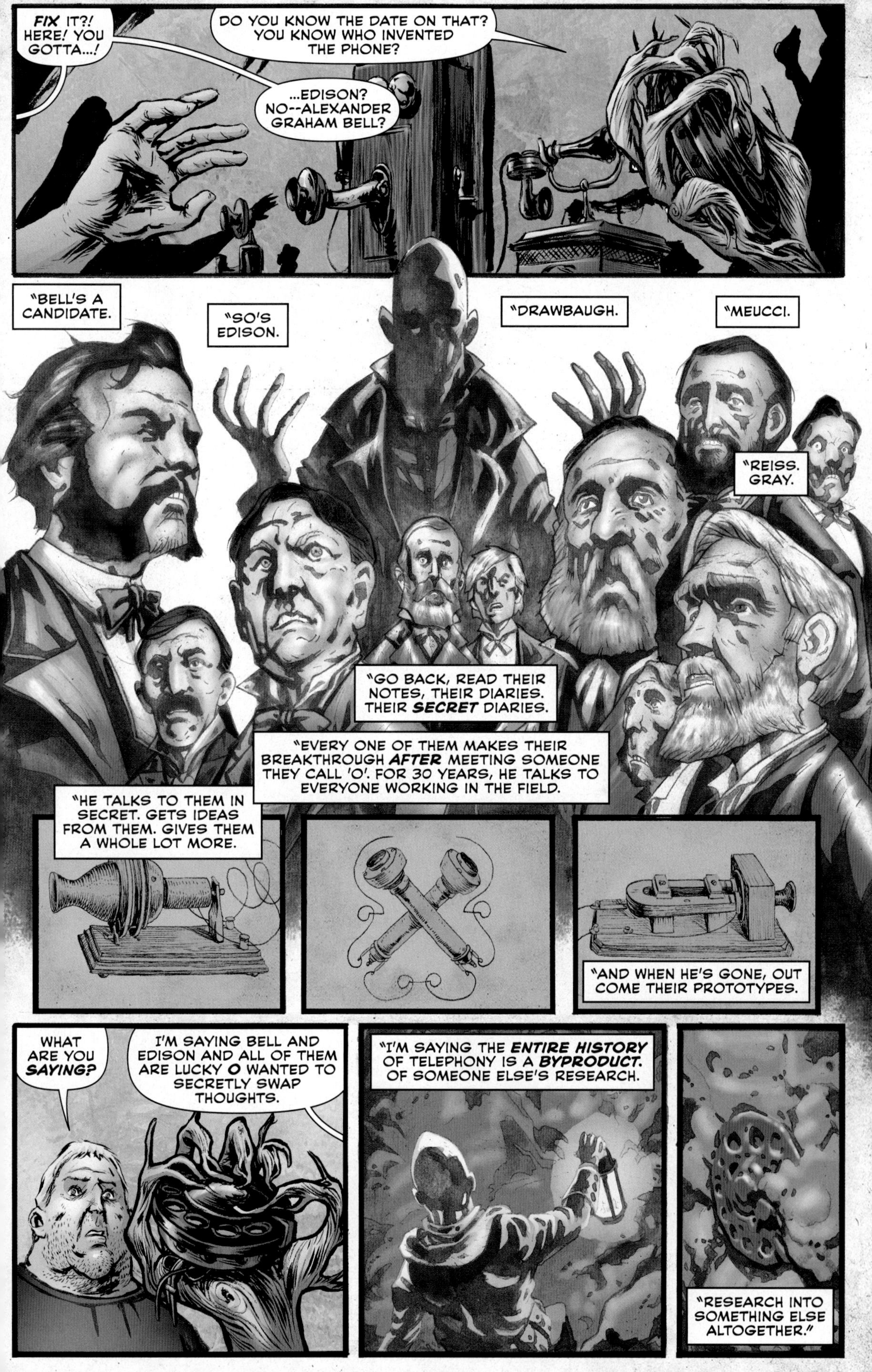
FIX IT?! HERE! YOU GOTTA...!
DO YOU KNOW THE DATE ON THAT? YOU KNOW WHO INVENTED THE PHONE?
...EDISON? NO--ALEXANDER GRAHAM BELL?
"BELL'S A CANDIDATE.
"SO'S EDISON.
"DRAWBAUGH.
"MEUCCI.
"REISS. GRAY.
"GO BACK, READ THEIR NOTES, THEIR DIARIES. THEIR SECRET DIARIES.
"EVERY ONE OF THEM MAKES THEIR BREAKTHROUGH AFTER MEETING SOMEONE THEY CALL 'O'. FOR 30 YEARS, HE TALKS TO EVERYONE WORKING IN THE FIELD.
"HE TALKS TO THEM IN SECRET. GETS IDEAS FROM THEM. GIVES THEM A WHOLE LOT MORE.
"AND WHEN HE'S GONE, OUT COME THEIR PROTOTYPES.
WHAT ARE YOU SAYING?
I'M SAYING BELL AND EDISON AND ALL OF THEM ARE LUCKY O WANTED TO SECRETLY SWAP THOUGHTS.
"I'M SAYING THE ENTIRE HISTORY OF TELEPHONY IS A BYPRODUCT. OF SOMEONE ELSE'S RESEARCH.
"RESEARCH INTO SOMETHING ELSE ALTOGETHER."

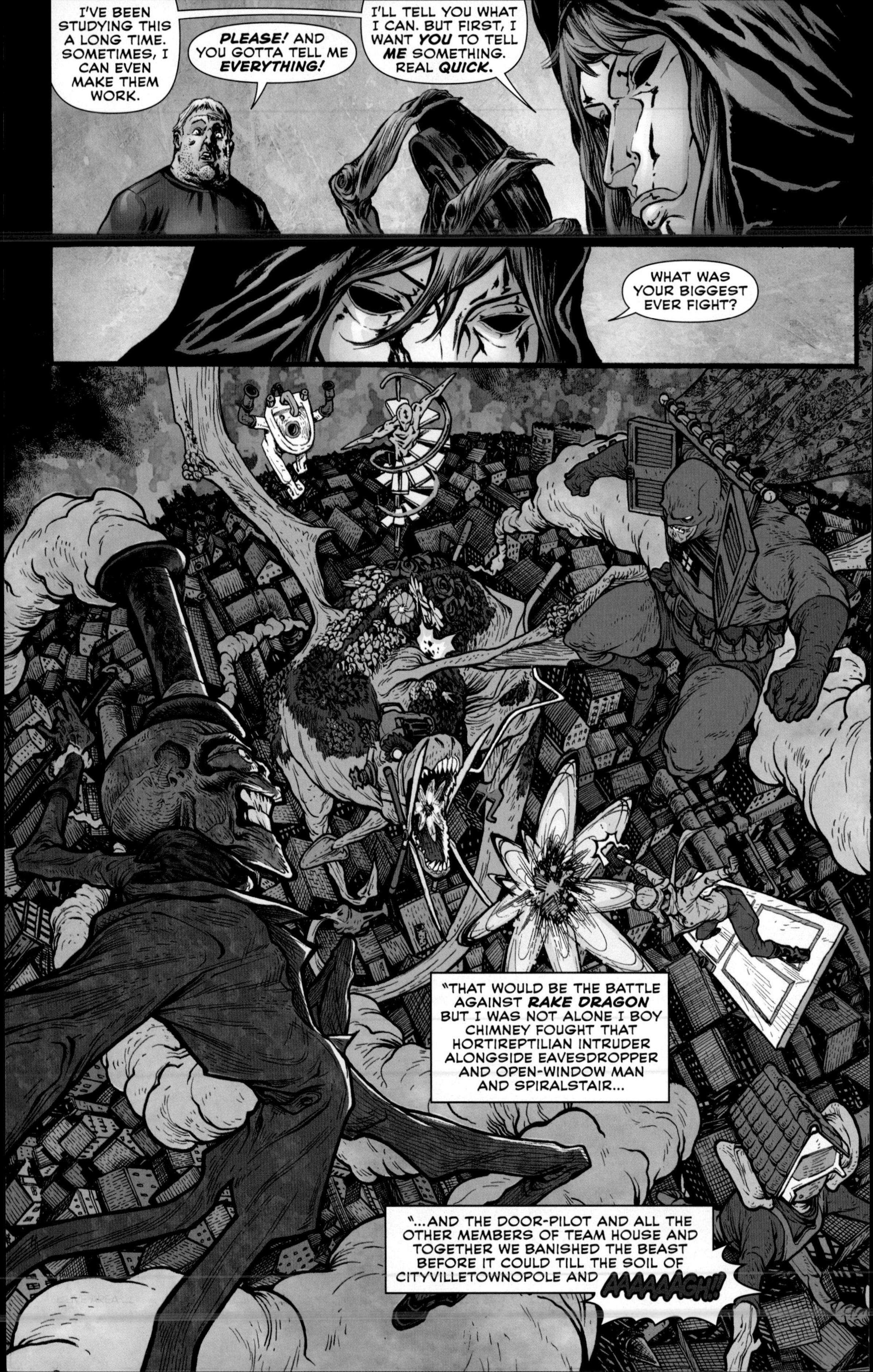

I'VE BEEN STUDYING THIS A LONG TIME. SOMETIMES, I CAN EVEN MAKE THEM WORK.
PLEASE! AND YOU GOTTA TELL ME EVERYTHING!
I'LL TELL YOU WHAT I CAN. BUT FIRST, I WANT YOU TO TELL ME SOMETHING. REAL QUICK.
WHAT WAS YOUR BIGGEST EVER FIGHT?
"THAT WOULD BE THE BATTLE AGAINST RAKE DRAGON BUT I WAS NOT ALONE I BOY CHIMNEY FOUGHT THAT HORTIREPTILIAN INTRUDER ALONGSIDE EAVESDROPPER AND OPEN-WINDOW MAN AND SPIRALSTAIR...
"...AND THE DOOR-PILOT AND ALL THE OTHER MEMBERS OF TEAM HOUSE AND TOGETHER WE BANISHED THE BEAST BEFORE IT COULD TILL THE SOIL OF CITYVILLETOWNOPOLE AND
AAAAAAGH!!

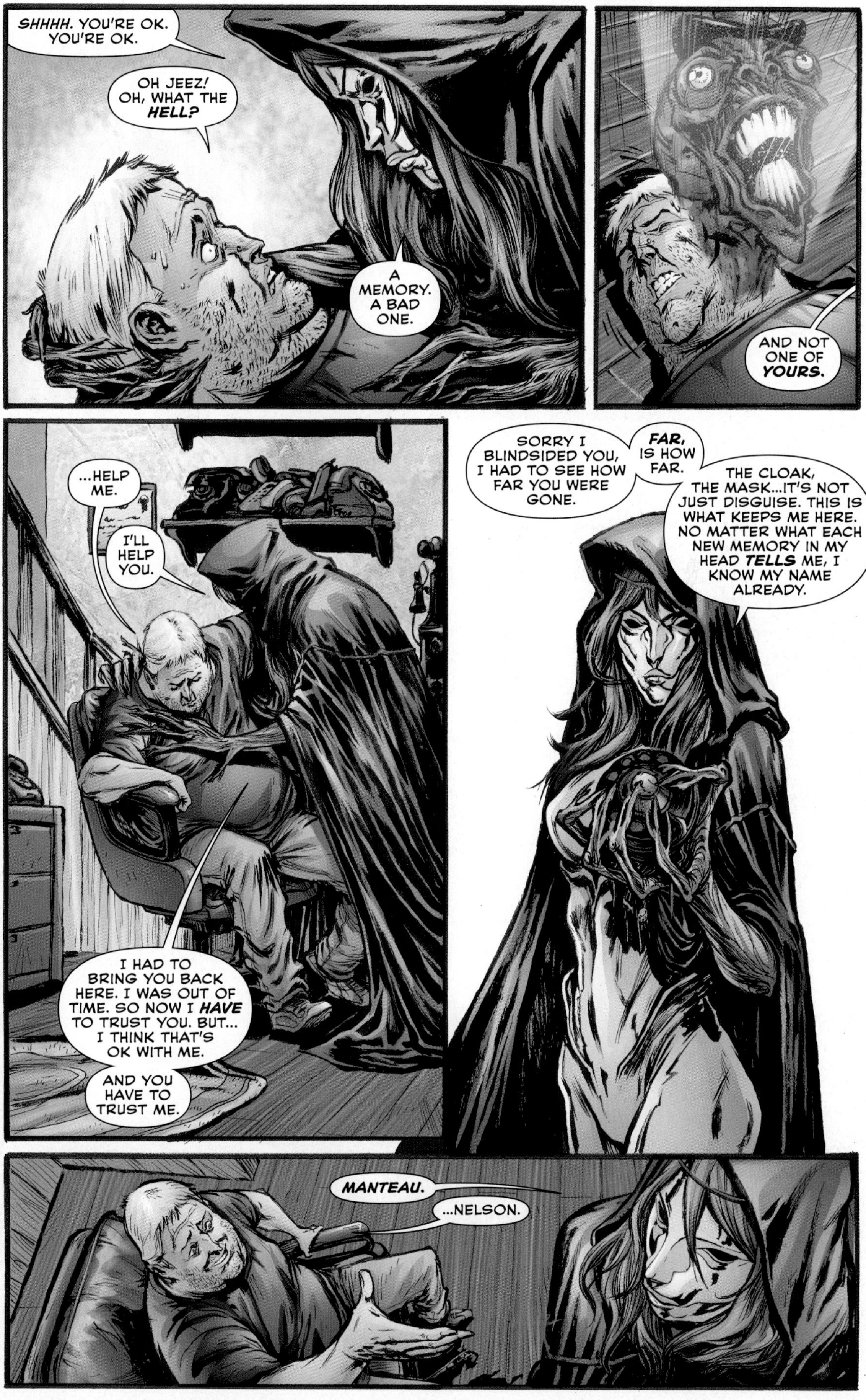
SHHHH. YOU'RE OK. YOU'RE OK.
OH JEEZ! OH, WHAT THE HELL?
A MEMORY. A BAD ONE.
AND NOT ONE OF YOURS.
...HELP ME.
I'LL HELP YOU.
I HAD TO BRING YOU BACK HERE. I WAS OUT OF TIME. SO NOW I HAVE TO TRUST YOU. BUT... I THINK THAT'S OK WITH ME.
AND YOU HAVE TO TRUST ME.
SORRY I BLINDSIDED YOU, I HAD TO SEE HOW FAR YOU WERE GONE.
FAR, IS HOW FAR.
THE CLOAK, THE MASK...IT'S NOT JUST DISGUISE. THIS IS WHAT KEEPS ME HERE. NO MATTER WHAT EACH NEW MEMORY IN MY HEAD TELLS ME, I KNOW MY NAME ALREADY.
MANTEAU.
...NELSON.

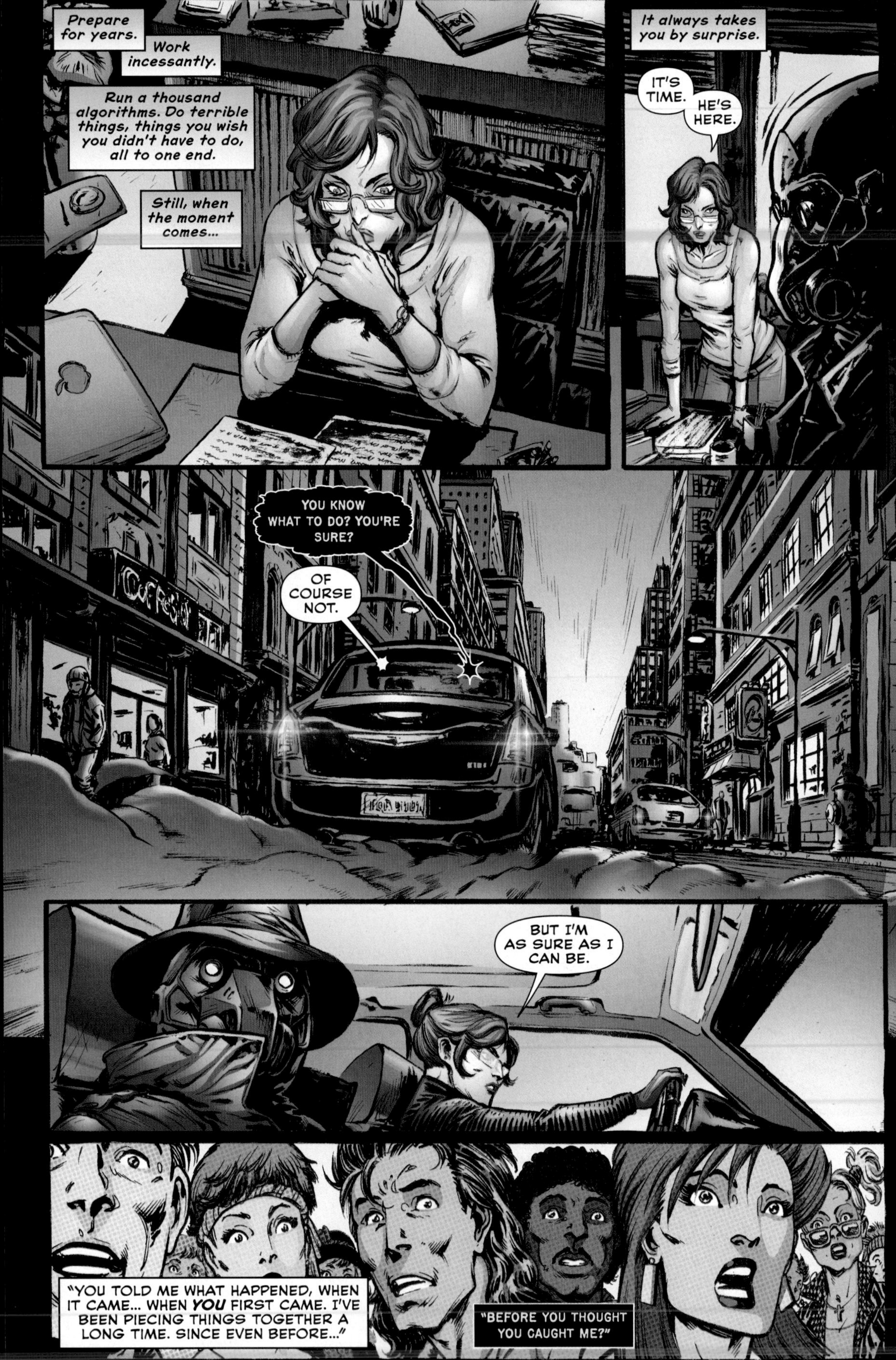

Prepare for years.
Work incessantly.
Run a thousand algorithms. Do terrible things, things you wish you didn't have to do, all to one end.
Still, when the moment comes...
It always takes you by surprise.
IT'S TIME.
HE'S HERE.
YOU KNOW WHAT TO DO? YOU'RE SURE?
OF COURSE NOT.
BUT I'M AS SURE AS I CAN BE.
"YOU TOLD ME WHAT HAPPENED, WHEN IT CAME... WHEN YOU FIRST CAME. I'VE BEEN PIECING THINGS TOGETHER A LONG TIME. SINCE EVEN BEFORE..."
"BEFORE YOU THOUGHT YOU CAUGHT ME?"

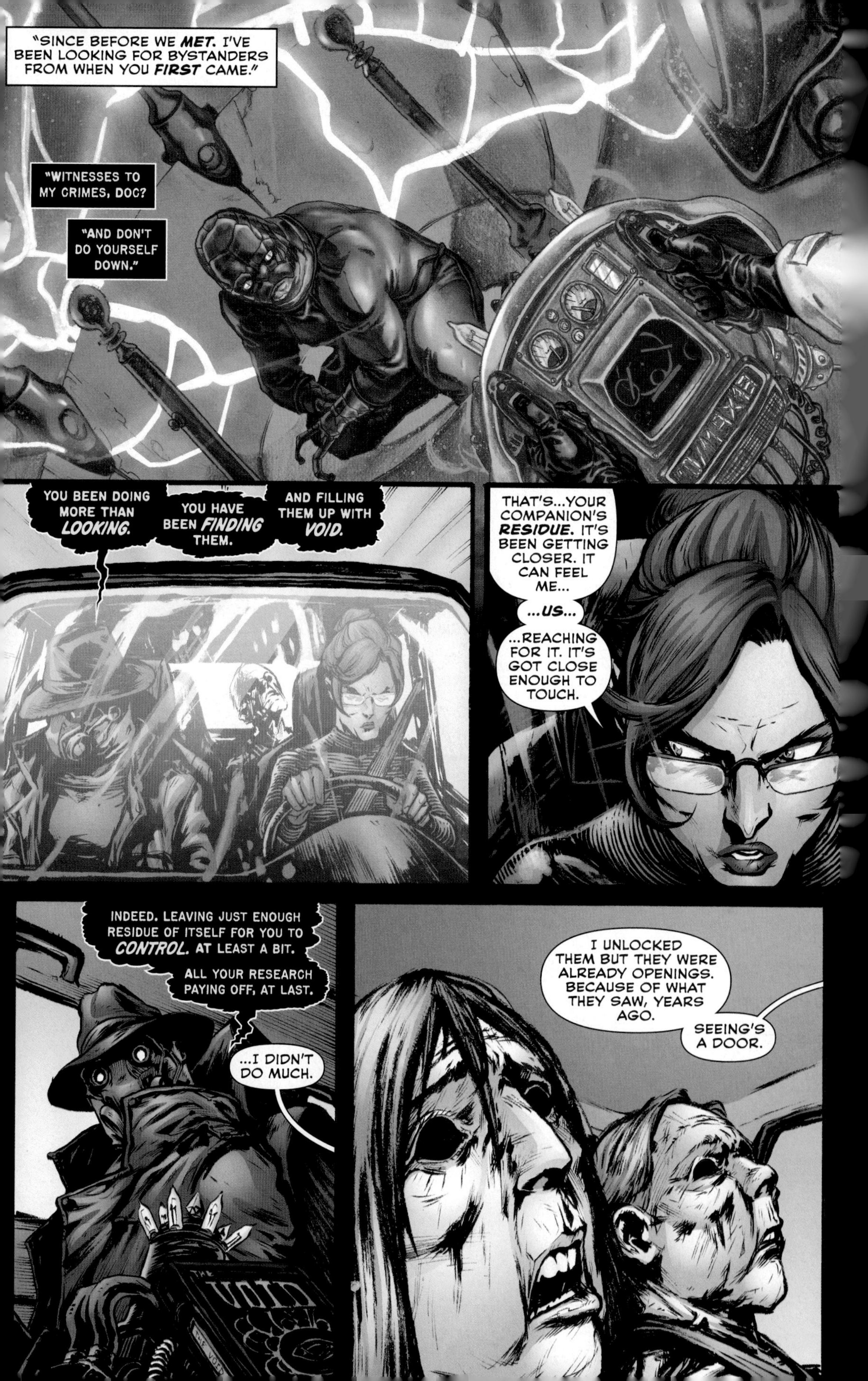
"SINCE BEFORE WE MET. I'VE BEEN LOOKING FOR BYSTANDERS FROM WHEN YOU FIRST CAME."
"WITNESSES TO MY CRIMES, DOC?
"AND DON'T DO YOURSELF DOWN."
YOU BEEN DOING MORE THAN LOOKING.
YOU HAVE BEEN FINDING THEM.
AND FILLING THEM UP WITH VOID.
THAT'S...YOUR COMPANION'S RESIDUE. IT'S BEEN GETTING CLOSER. IT CAN FEEL ME...
...US...
...REACHING FOR IT. IT'S GOT CLOSE ENOUGH TO TOUCH.
INDEED. LEAVING JUST ENOUGH RESIDUE OF ITSELF FOR YOU TO CONTROL. AT LEAST A BIT.
ALL YOUR RESEARCH PAYING OFF, AT LAST.
...I DIDN'T DO MUCH.
I UNLOCKED THEM BUT THEY WERE ALREADY OPENINGS. BECAUSE OF WHAT THEY SAW, YEARS AGO.
SEEING'S A DOOR.

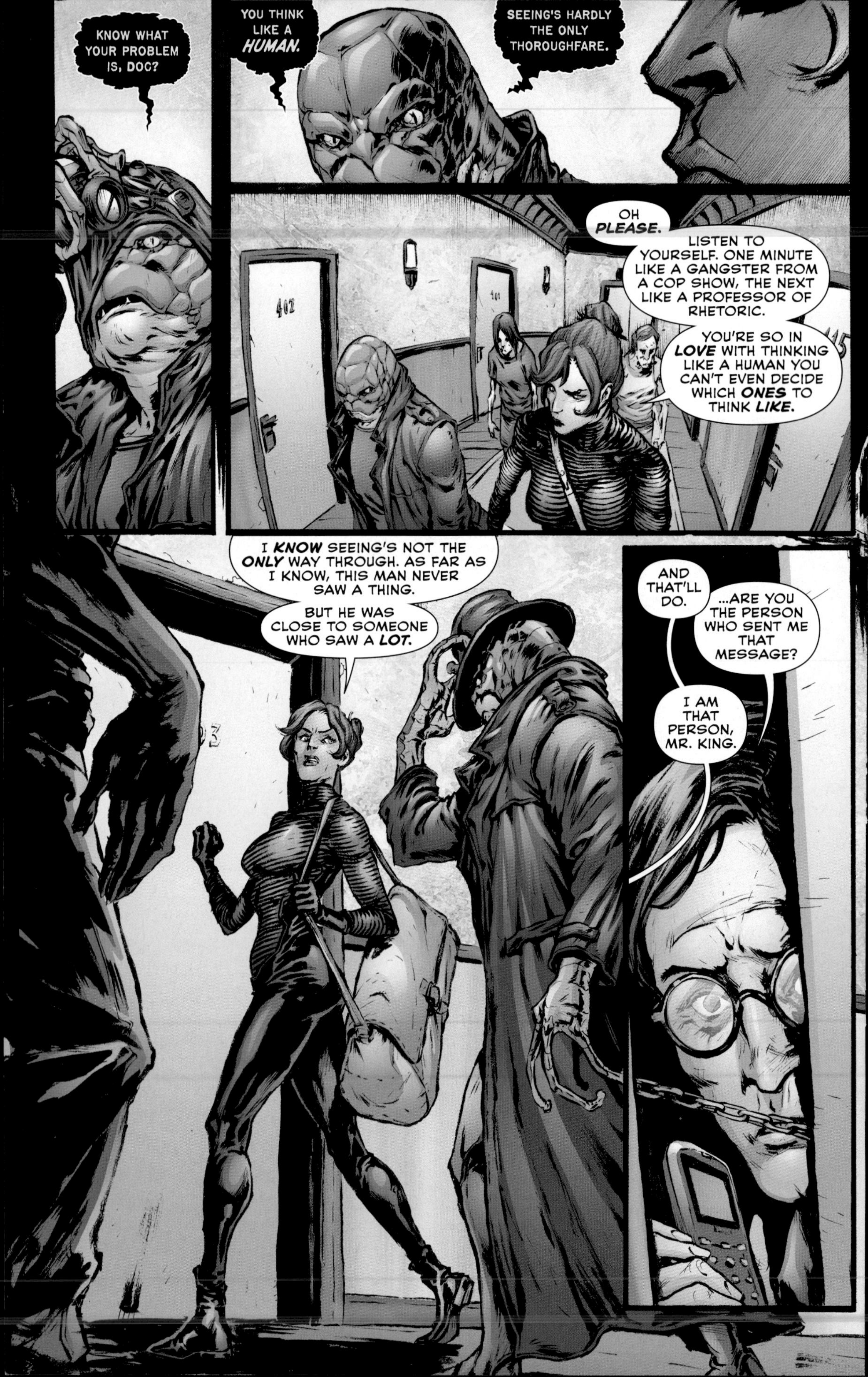

KNOW WHAT YOUR PROBLEM IS, DOC?
YOU THINK LIKE A *HUMAN.*
SEEING'S HARDLY THE ONLY THOROUGHFARE.
OH *PLEASE.*
LISTEN TO YOURSELF. ONE MINUTE LIKE A GANGSTER FROM A COP SHOW, THE NEXT LIKE A PROFESSOR OF RHETORIC.
YOU'RE SO IN *LOVE* WITH THINKING LIKE A HUMAN YOU CAN'T EVEN DECIDE WHICH *ONES* TO THINK *LIKE.*
I *KNOW* SEEING'S NOT THE *ONLY* WAY THROUGH. AS FAR AS I KNOW, THIS MAN NEVER SAW A THING.
BUT HE WAS CLOSE TO SOMEONE WHO SAW A *LOT.*
AND THAT'LL DO.
...ARE YOU THE PERSON WHO SENT ME THAT MESSAGE?
I AM THAT PERSON, MR. KING.

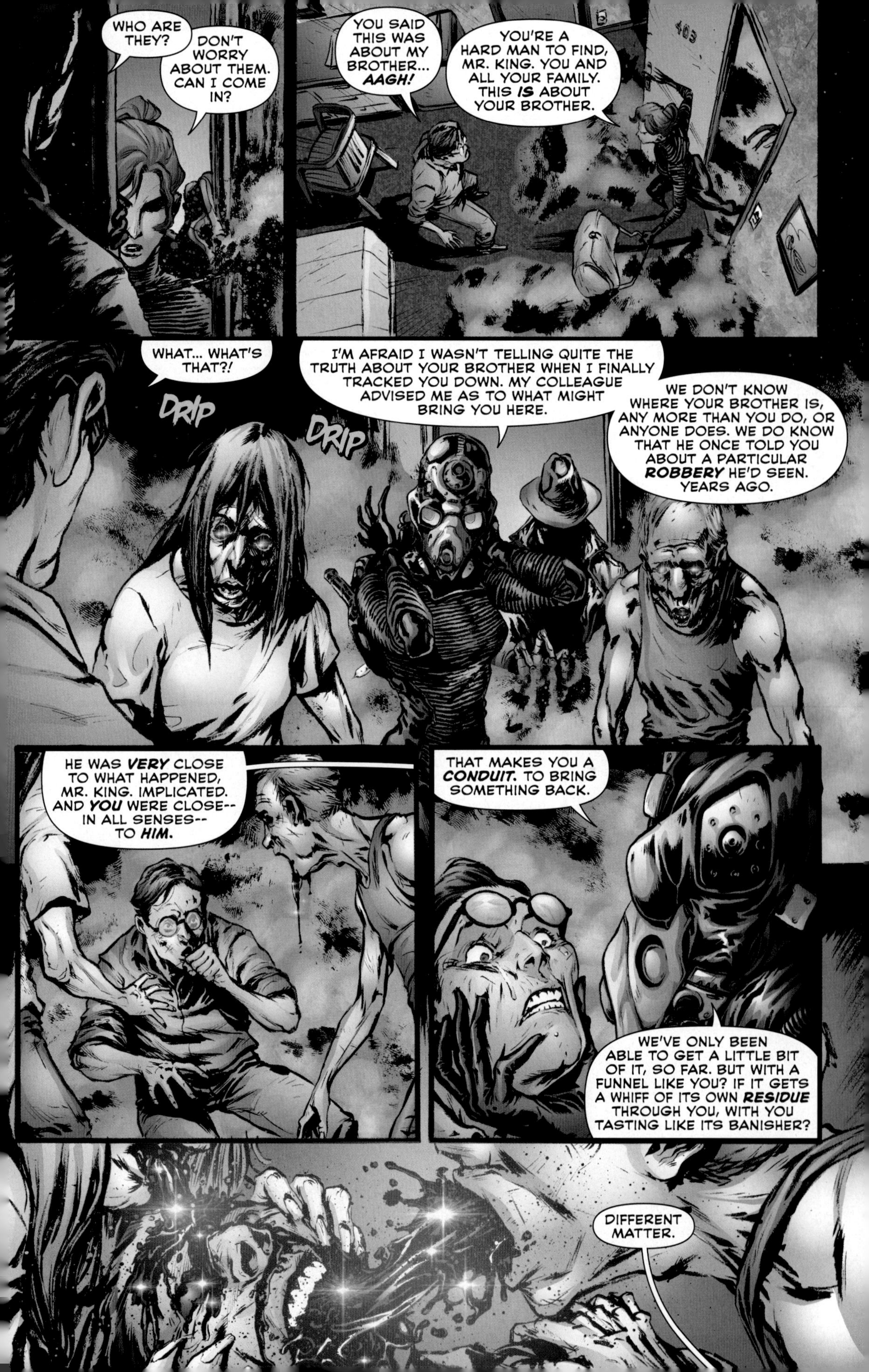
WHO ARE THEY?
DON'T WORRY ABOUT THEM. CAN I COME IN?
YOU SAID THIS WAS ABOUT MY BROTHER... AAGH!
YOU'RE A HARD MAN TO FIND, MR. KING. YOU AND ALL YOUR FAMILY. THIS IS ABOUT YOUR BROTHER.
403
WHAT... WHAT'S THAT?!
DRIP
DRIP
I'M AFRAID I WASN'T TELLING QUITE THE TRUTH ABOUT YOUR BROTHER WHEN I FINALLY TRACKED YOU DOWN. MY COLLEAGUE ADVISED ME AS TO WHAT MIGHT BRING YOU HERE.
WE DON'T KNOW WHERE YOUR BROTHER IS, ANY MORE THAN YOU DO, OR ANYONE DOES. WE DO KNOW THAT HE ONCE TOLD YOU ABOUT A PARTICULAR ROBBERY HE'D SEEN. YEARS AGO.
HE WAS VERY CLOSE TO WHAT HAPPENED, MR. KING. IMPLICATED. AND YOU WERE CLOSE-- IN ALL SENSES-- TO HIM.
THAT MAKES YOU A CONDUIT. TO BRING SOMETHING BACK.
WE'VE ONLY BEEN ABLE TO GET A LITTLE BIT OF IT, SO FAR. BUT WITH A FUNNEL LIKE YOU? IF IT GETS A WHIFF OF ITS OWN RESIDUE THROUGH YOU, WITH YOU TASTING LIKE ITS BANISHER?
DIFFERENT MATTER.

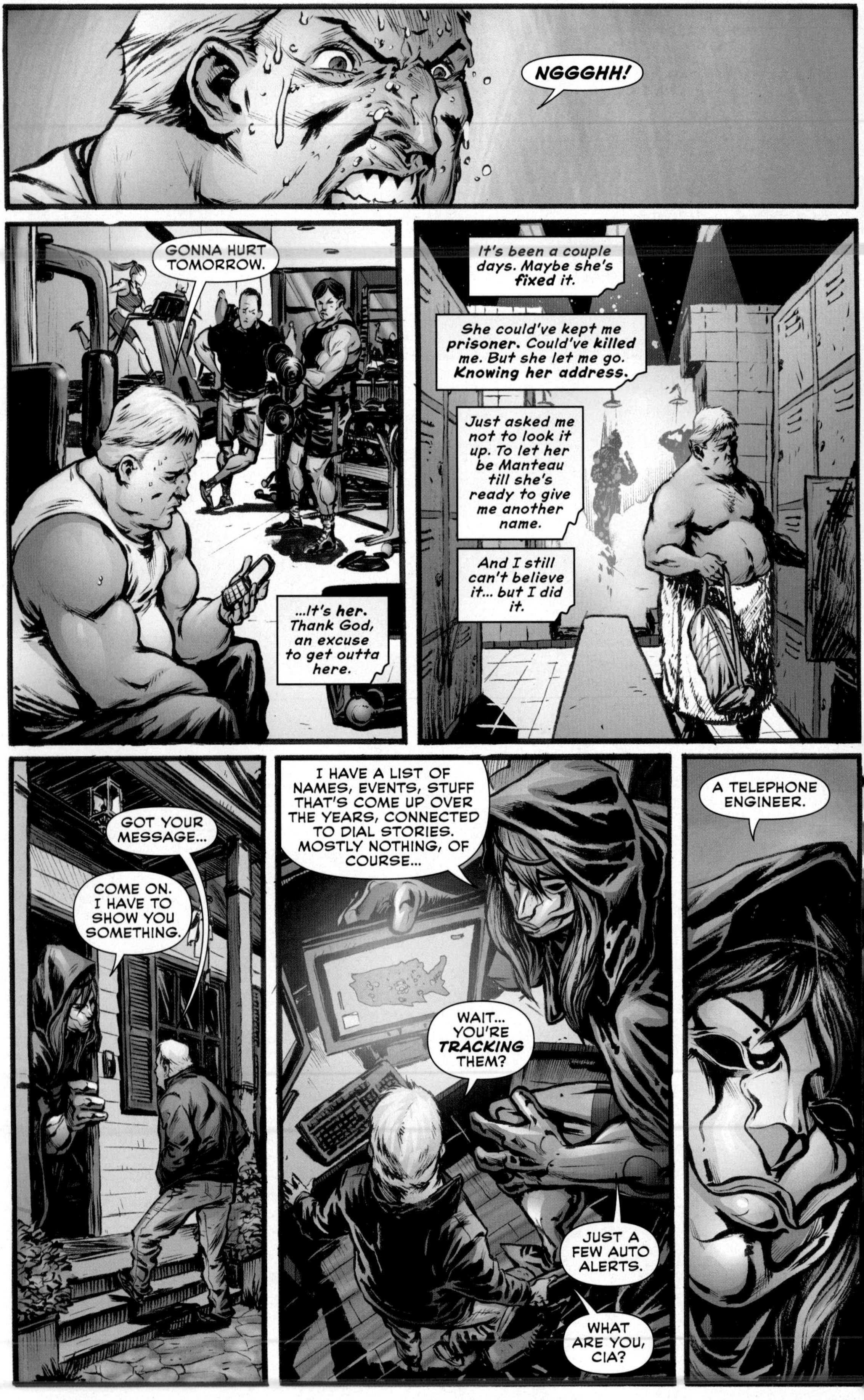
NGGGHH!
GONNA HURT TOMORROW.
...It's her. Thank God, an excuse to get outta here.
It's been a couple days. Maybe she's fixed it.
She could've kept me prisoner. Could've killed me. But she let me go. Knowing her address.
Just asked me not to look it up. To let her be Manteau till she's ready to give me another name.
And I still can't believe it... but I did it.
GOT YOUR MESSAGE...
COME ON. I HAVE TO SHOW YOU SOMETHING.
I HAVE A LIST OF NAMES, EVENTS, STUFF THAT'S COME UP OVER THE YEARS, CONNECTED TO DIAL STORIES. MOSTLY NOTHING, OF COURSE...
WAIT... YOU'RE TRACKING THEM?
JUST A FEW AUTO ALERTS.
WHAT ARE YOU, CIA?
A TELEPHONE ENGINEER.

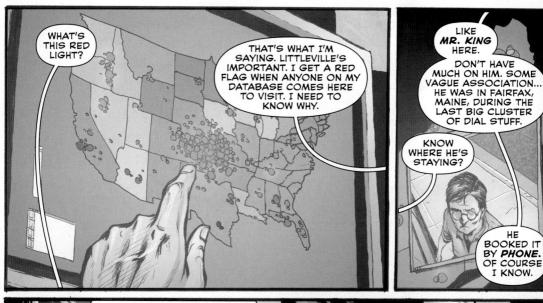

WHAT'S THIS RED LIGHT?

THAT'S WHAT I'M SAYING. LITTLEVILLE'S IMPORTANT. I GET A RED FLAG WHEN ANYONE ON MY DATABASE COMES HERE TO VISIT. I NEED TO KNOW WHY.

LIKE *MR. KING* HERE. DON'T HAVE MUCH ON HIM. SOME VAGUE ASSOCIATION... HE WAS IN FAIRFAX, MAINE, DURING THE LAST BIG CLUSTER OF DIAL STUFF.

KNOW WHERE HE'S STAYING?

HE BOOKED IT BY *PHONE*. OF COURSE I KNOW.

HOLD ON, LET ME ACCESS THE LAST CALL HE...THERE.

...YEAH, IF IT'S A REAL LEAD, IT'S HUGE... HONEY, I'LL BE HOME AS SOON AS I... HOLD ON, SOMEONE'S AT THE DOOR.

MUMBLE MUMBLE...

I AM THAT PERSON, MR. KING.

YOU SAID THIS WAS ABOUT MY BROTHER... AAGH!

CLICK!!

THAT SQUID THING! IT'S GOTTA BE. WE GOTTA GET TO THIS KING GUY, BUT MANTEAU, JEEZ, HOW CAN I HELP...?

LOOK AT ME.

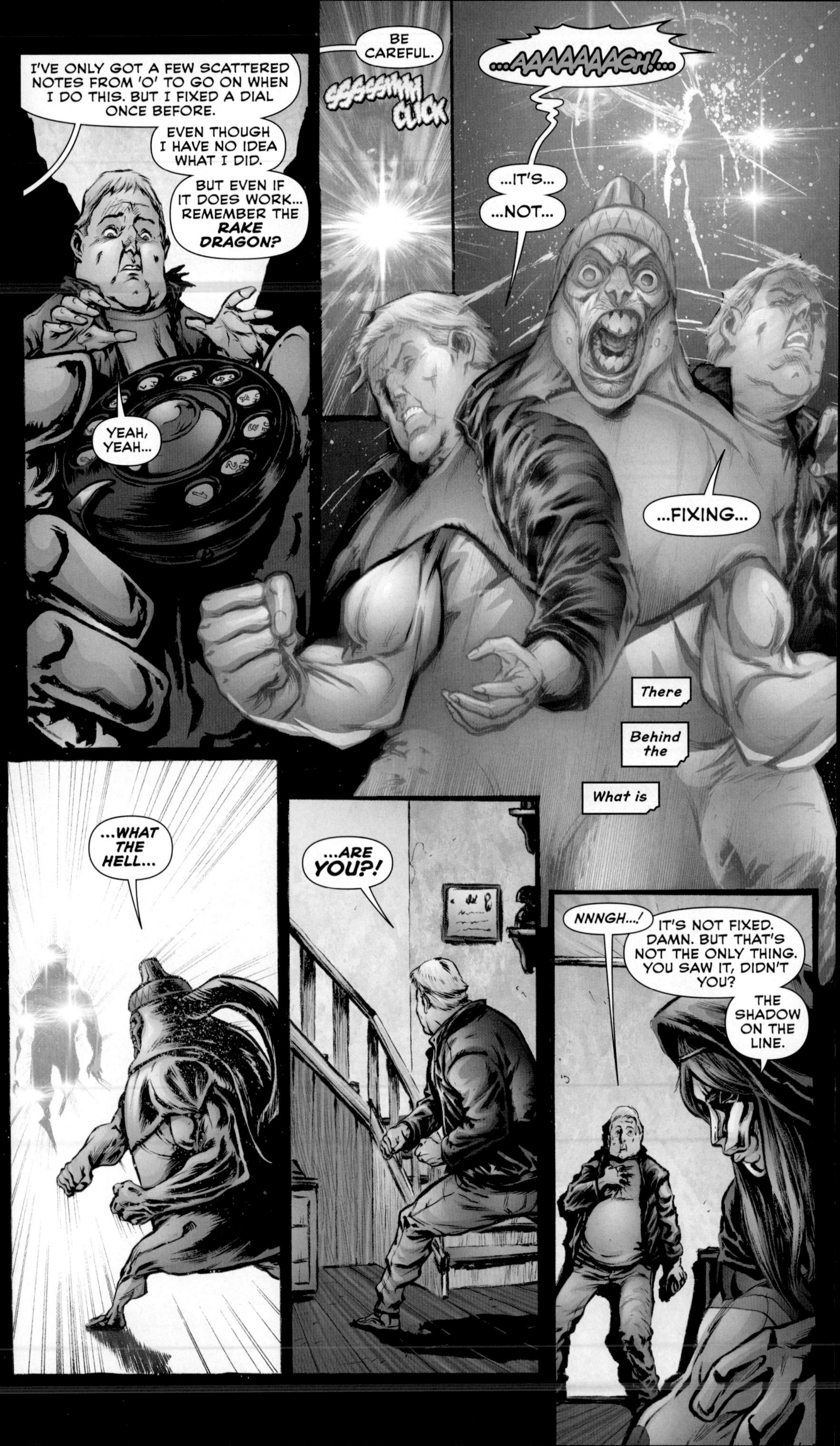
I'VE ONLY GOT A FEW SCATTERED NOTES FROM 'O' TO GO ON WHEN I DO THIS. BUT I FIXED A DIAL ONCE BEFORE.
EVEN THOUGH I HAVE NO IDEA WHAT I DID.
BUT EVEN IF IT DOES WORK... REMEMBER THE RAKE DRAGON?
YEAH, YEAH...
BE CAREFUL.
SSSSSHHH CLICK
...AAAAAAAGH!...
...IT'S...
...NOT...
...FIXING...
There
Behind the
What is
...WHAT THE HELL...
...ARE YOU?!
NNNGH...!
IT'S NOT FIXED. DAMN. BUT THAT'S NOT THE ONLY THING. YOU SAW IT, DIDN'T YOU?
THE SHADOW ON THE LINE.

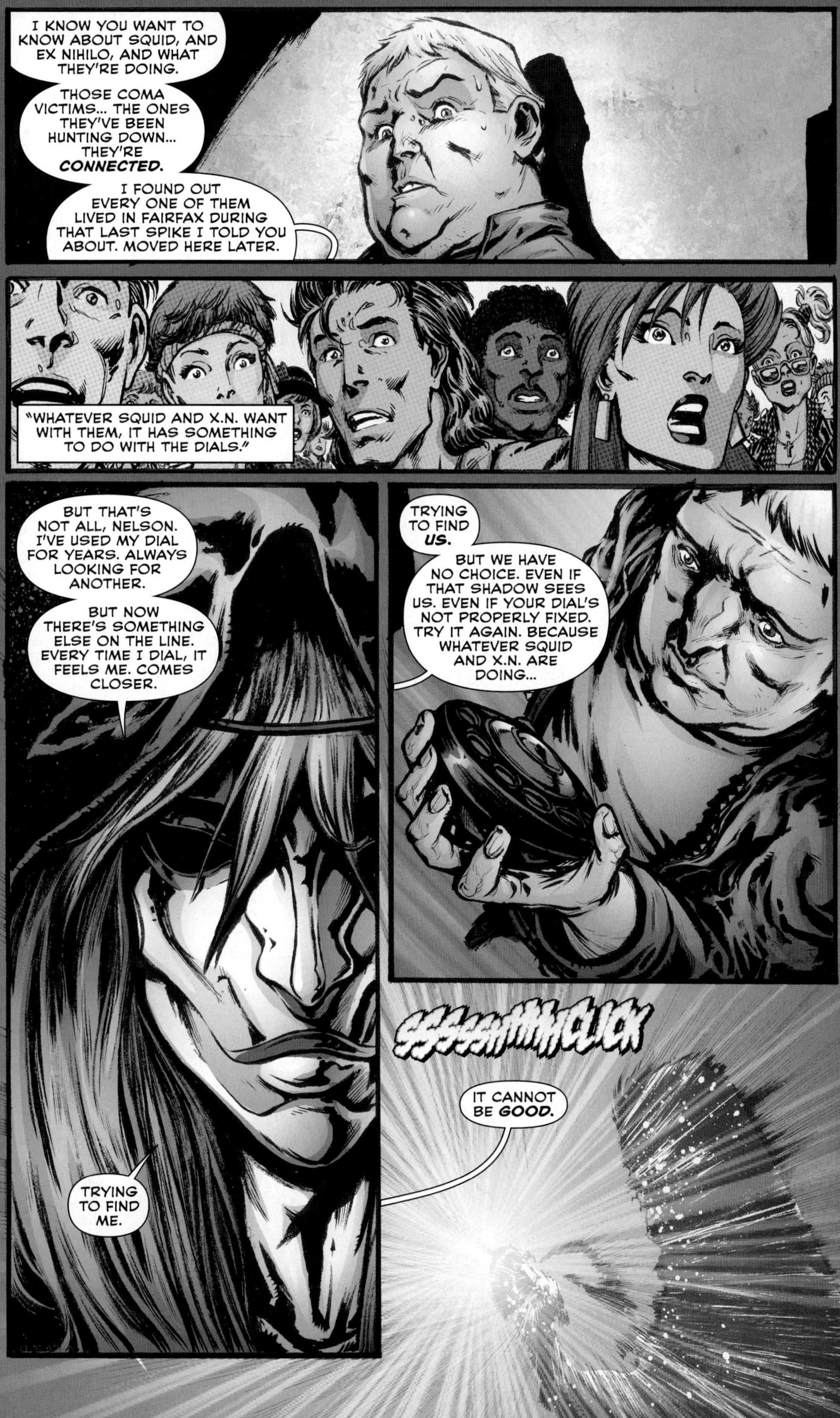
I KNOW YOU WANT TO KNOW ABOUT SQUID, AND EX NIHILO, AND WHAT THEY'RE DOING.
THOSE COMA VICTIMS... THE ONES THEY'VE BEEN HUNTING DOWN... THEY'RE CONNECTED.
I FOUND OUT EVERY ONE OF THEM LIVED IN FAIRFAX DURING THAT LAST SPIKE I TOLD YOU ABOUT. MOVED HERE LATER.
"WHATEVER SQUID AND X.N. WANT WITH THEM, IT HAS SOMETHING TO DO WITH THE DIALS."
BUT THAT'S NOT ALL, NELSON. I'VE USED MY DIAL FOR YEARS. ALWAYS LOOKING FOR ANOTHER.
BUT NOW THERE'S SOMETHING ELSE ON THE LINE. EVERY TIME I DIAL, IT FEELS ME. COMES CLOSER.
TRYING TO FIND ME.
TRYING TO FIND US.
BUT WE HAVE NO CHOICE. EVEN IF THAT SHADOW SEES US. EVEN IF YOUR DIAL'S NOT PROPERLY FIXED. TRY IT AGAIN. BECAUSE WHATEVER SQUID AND X.N. ARE DOING...
SSSSSHHHMCLICK
IT CANNOT BE GOOD.

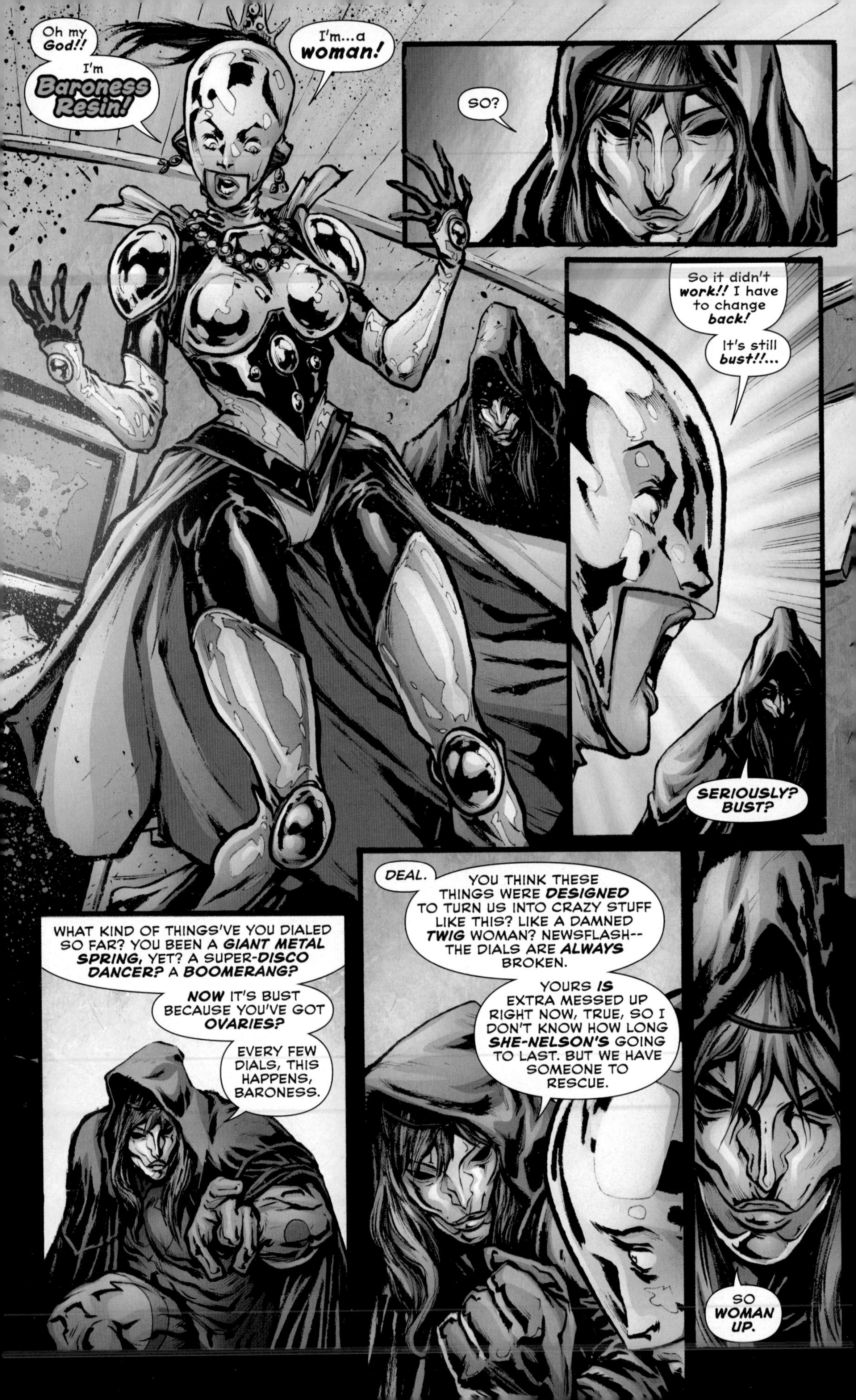

Oh my God!!
I'm Baroness Resin!
I'm...a woman!
SO?
So it didn't work!! I have to change back!
It's still bust!!...
SERIOUSLY? BUST?
WHAT KIND OF THINGS'VE YOU DIALED SO FAR? YOU BEEN A GIANT METAL SPRING, YET? A SUPER-DISCO DANCER? A BOOMERANG?
NOW IT'S BUST BECAUSE YOU'VE GOT OVARIES?
EVERY FEW DIALS, THIS HAPPENS, BARONESS.
DEAL.
YOU THINK THESE THINGS WERE DESIGNED TO TURN US INTO CRAZY STUFF LIKE THIS? LIKE A DAMNED TWIG WOMAN? NEWSFLASH-- THE DIALS ARE ALWAYS BROKEN.
YOURS IS EXTRA MESSED UP RIGHT NOW, TRUE, SO I DON'T KNOW HOW LONG SHE-NELSON'S GOING TO LAST. BUT WE HAVE SOMEONE TO RESCUE.
SO WOMAN UP.

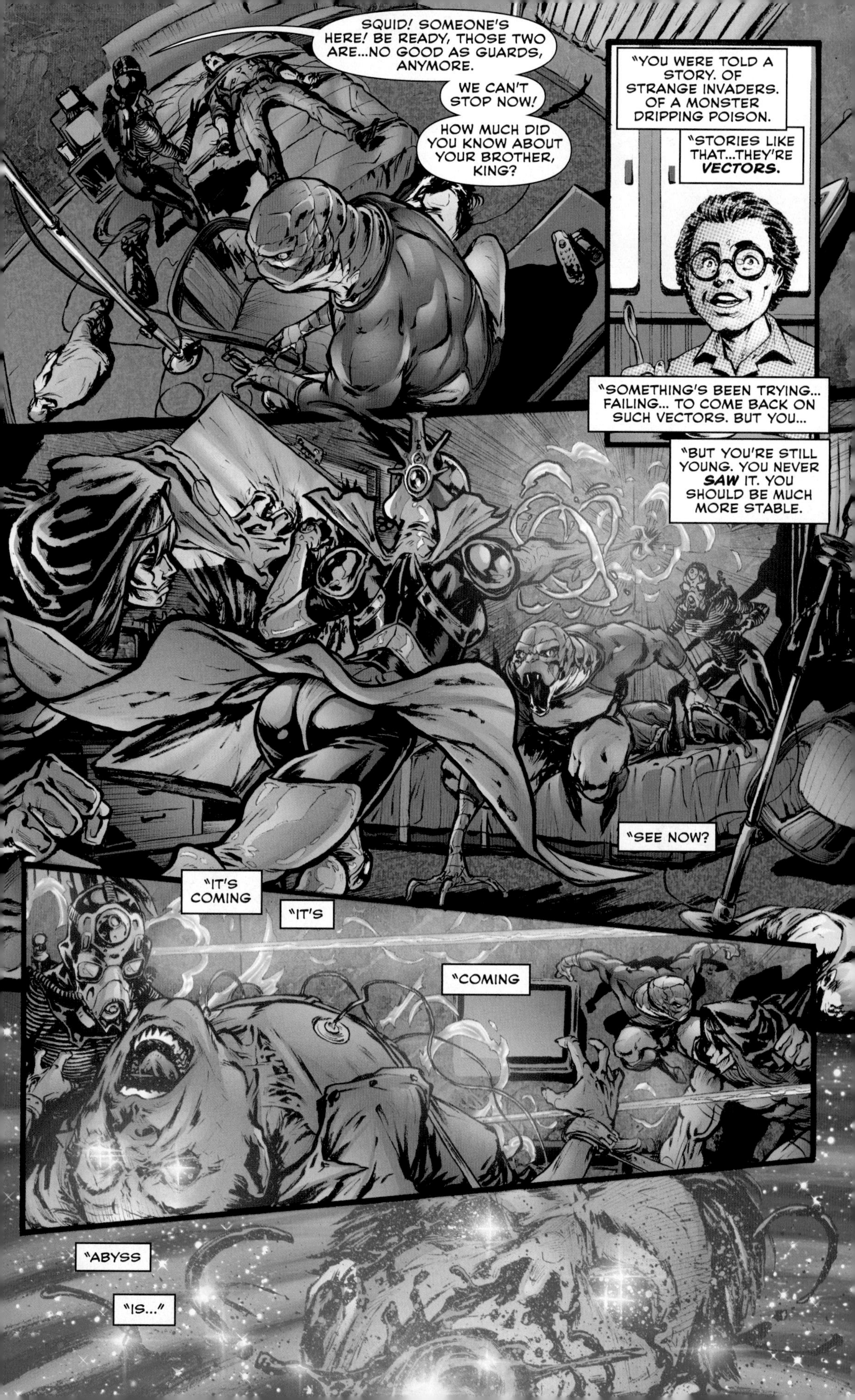
SQUID! SOMEONE'S HERE! BE READY, THOSE TWO ARE...NO GOOD AS GUARDS, ANYMORE.
WE CAN'T STOP NOW!
HOW MUCH DID YOU KNOW ABOUT YOUR BROTHER, KING?
"YOU WERE TOLD A STORY. OF STRANGE INVADERS. OF A MONSTER DRIPPING POISON.
"STORIES LIKE THAT...THEY'RE VECTORS.
"SOMETHING'S BEEN TRYING... FAILING... TO COME BACK ON SUCH VECTORS. BUT YOU...
"BUT YOU'RE STILL YOUNG. YOU NEVER SAW IT. YOU SHOULD BE MUCH MORE STABLE.
"SEE NOW?
"IT'S COMING
"IT'S
"COMING
"ABYSS
"IS..."

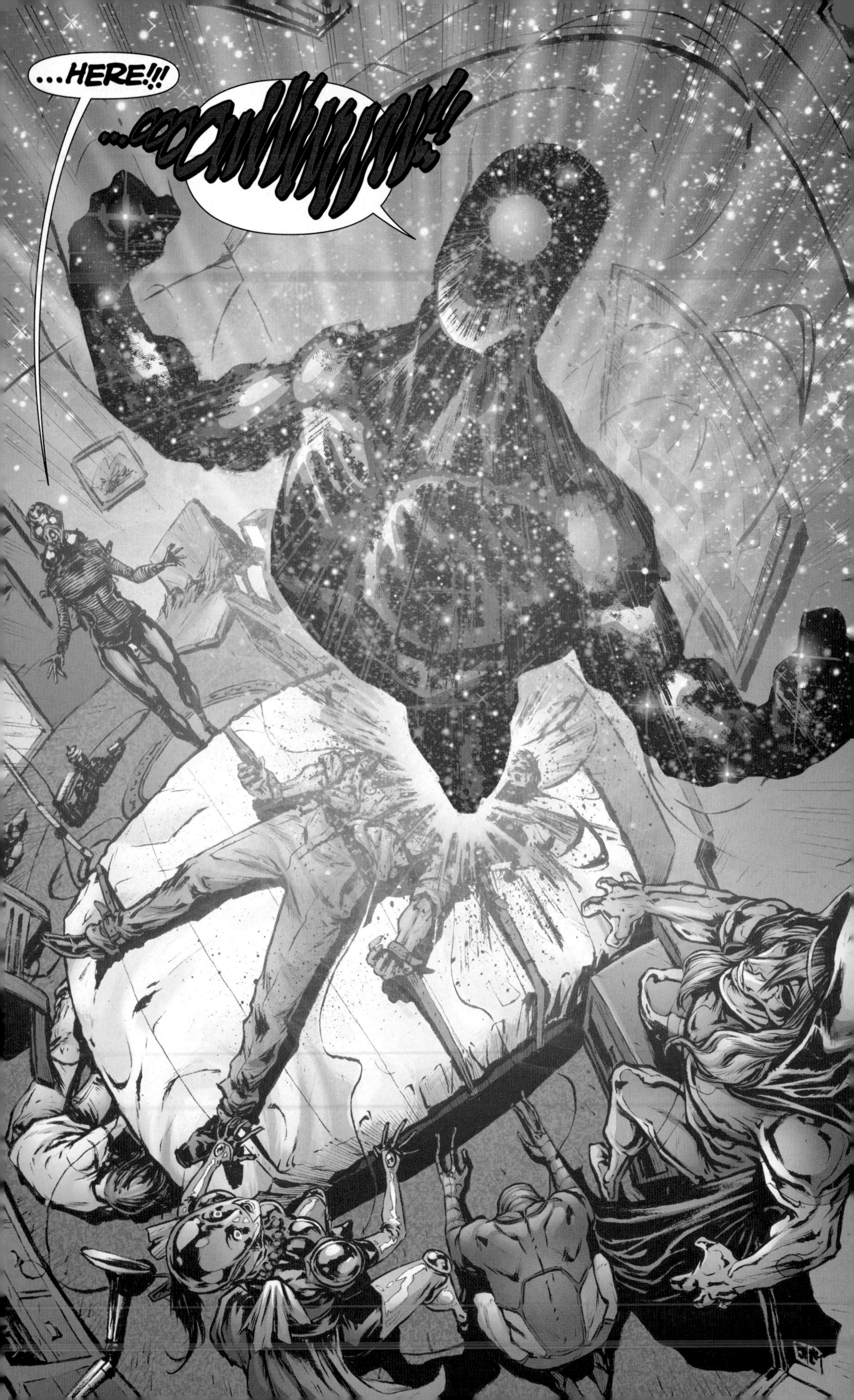
...HERE!!!

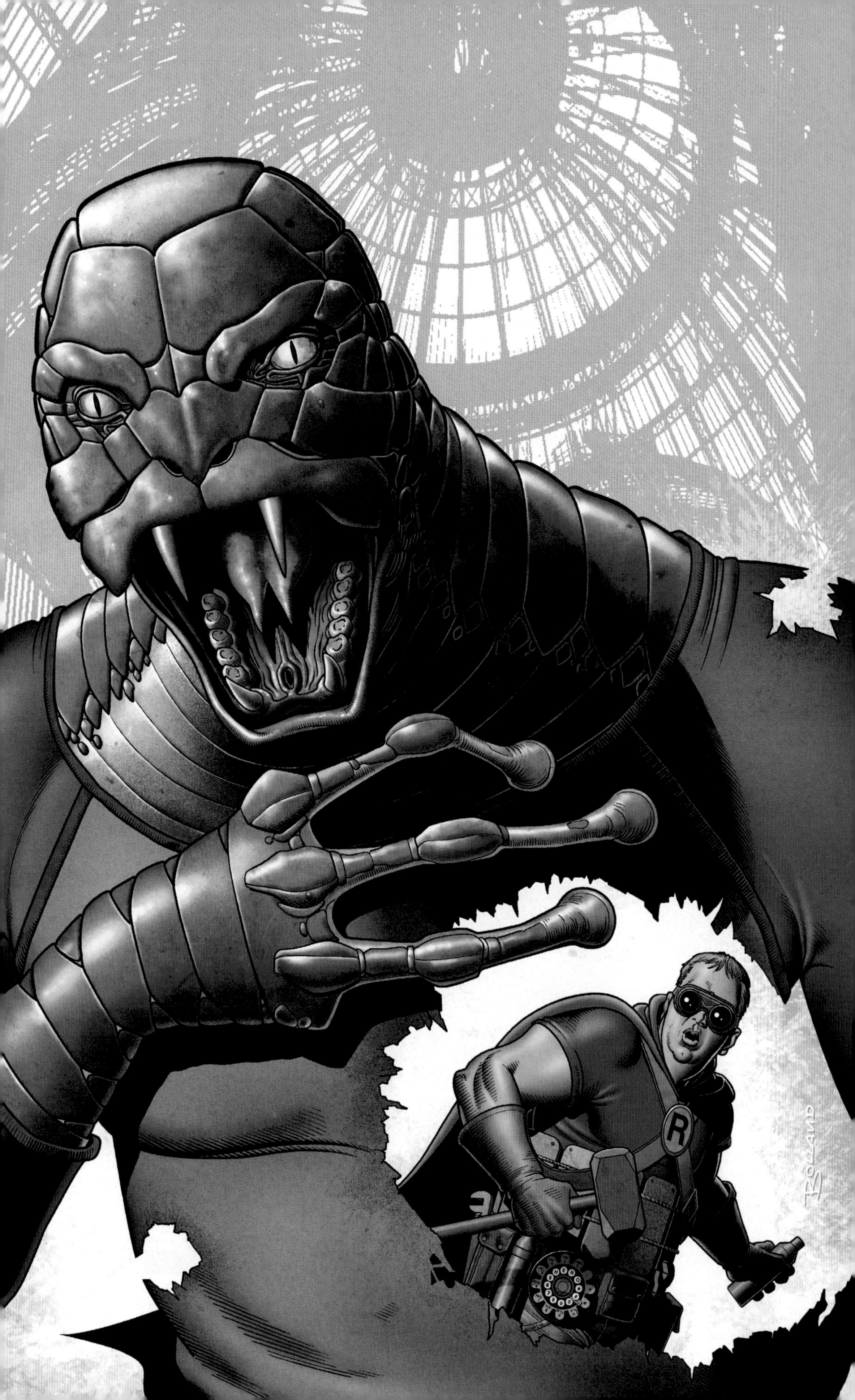

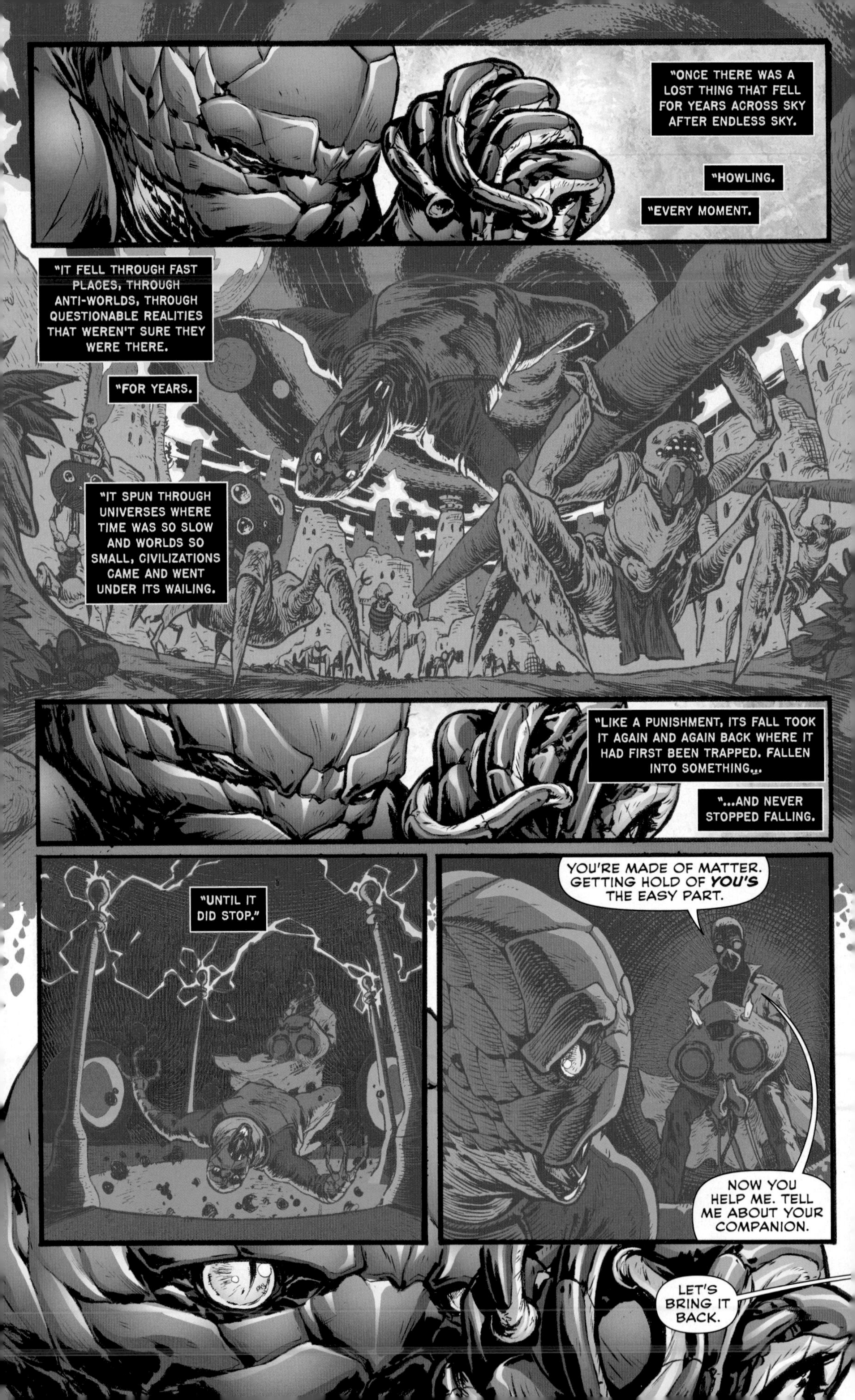
"ONCE THERE WAS A LOST THING THAT FELL FOR YEARS ACROSS SKY AFTER ENDLESS SKY.
"HOWLING.
"EVERY MOMENT.
"IT FELL THROUGH FAST PLACES, THROUGH ANTI-WORLDS, THROUGH QUESTIONABLE REALITIES THAT WEREN'T SURE THEY WERE THERE.
"FOR YEARS.
"IT SPUN THROUGH UNIVERSES WHERE TIME WAS SO SLOW AND WORLDS SO SMALL, CIVILIZATIONS CAME AND WENT UNDER ITS WAILING.
"LIKE A PUNISHMENT, ITS FALL TOOK IT AGAIN AND AGAIN BACK WHERE IT HAD FIRST BEEN TRAPPED. FALLEN INTO SOMETHING...
"...AND NEVER STOPPED FALLING.
"UNTIL IT DID STOP."
YOU'RE MADE OF MATTER. GETTING HOLD OF *YOU'S* THE EASY PART.
NOW YOU HELP ME. TELL ME ABOUT YOUR COMPANION.
LET'S BRING IT BACK.

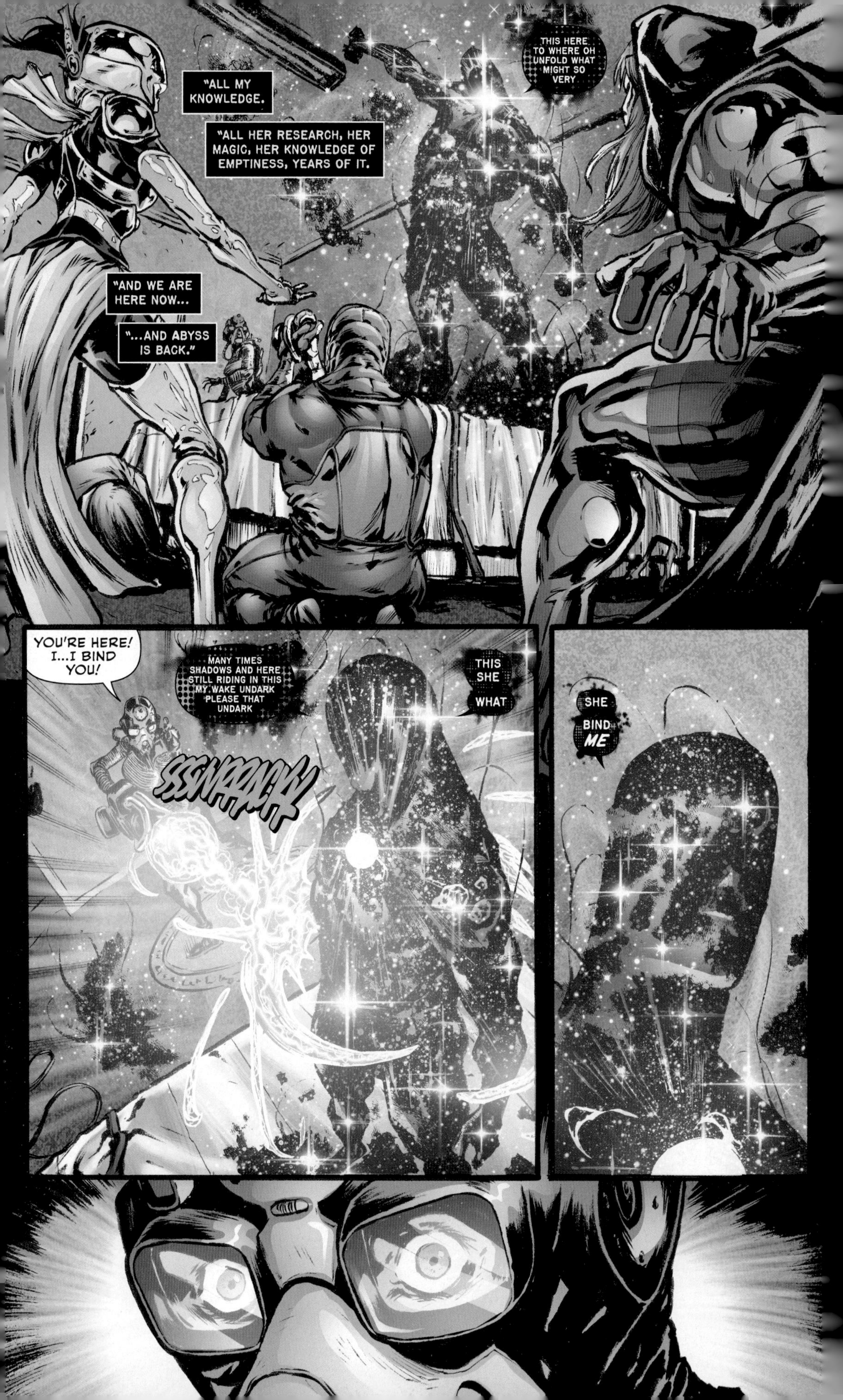
"ALL MY KNOWLEDGE.
"ALL HER RESEARCH, HER MAGIC, HER KNOWLEDGE OF EMPTINESS, YEARS OF IT.
THIS HERE TO WHERE OH UNFOLD WHAT MIGHT SO VERY
"AND WE ARE HERE NOW...
"...AND ABYSS IS BACK."
YOU'RE HERE! I...I BIND YOU!
MANY TIMES SHADOWS AND HERE STILL RIDING IN THIS MY WAKE UNDARK PLEASE THAT UNDARK
THIS
SHE
WHAT
SSSNRRRACK!
SHE
BIND
ME

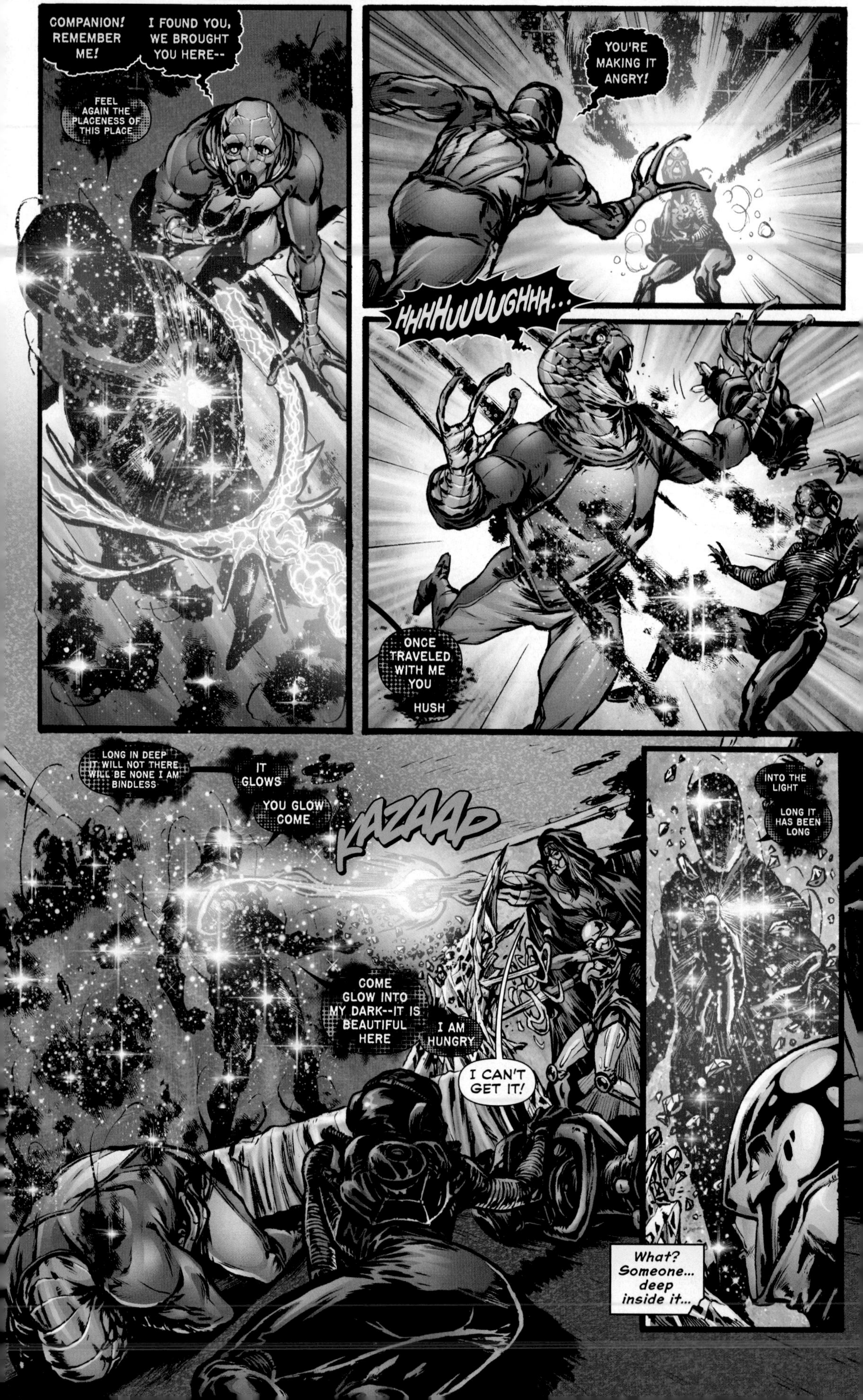
COMPANION! REMEMBER ME!
I FOUND YOU, WE BROUGHT YOU HERE--
FEEL AGAIN THE PLACENESS OF THIS PLACE
YOU'RE MAKING IT ANGRY!
HHHHUUUUGHHH...
ONCE TRAVELED WITH ME YOU
HUSH
LONG IN DEEP IT WILL NOT THERE WILL BE NONE I AM BINDLESS
IT GLOWS
YOU GLOW COME
KAZAAP
COME GLOW INTO MY DARK--IT IS BEAUTIFUL HERE
I AM HUNGRY
I CAN'T GET IT!
INTO THE LIGHT
LONG IT HAS BEEN LONG
What? Someone... deep inside it...

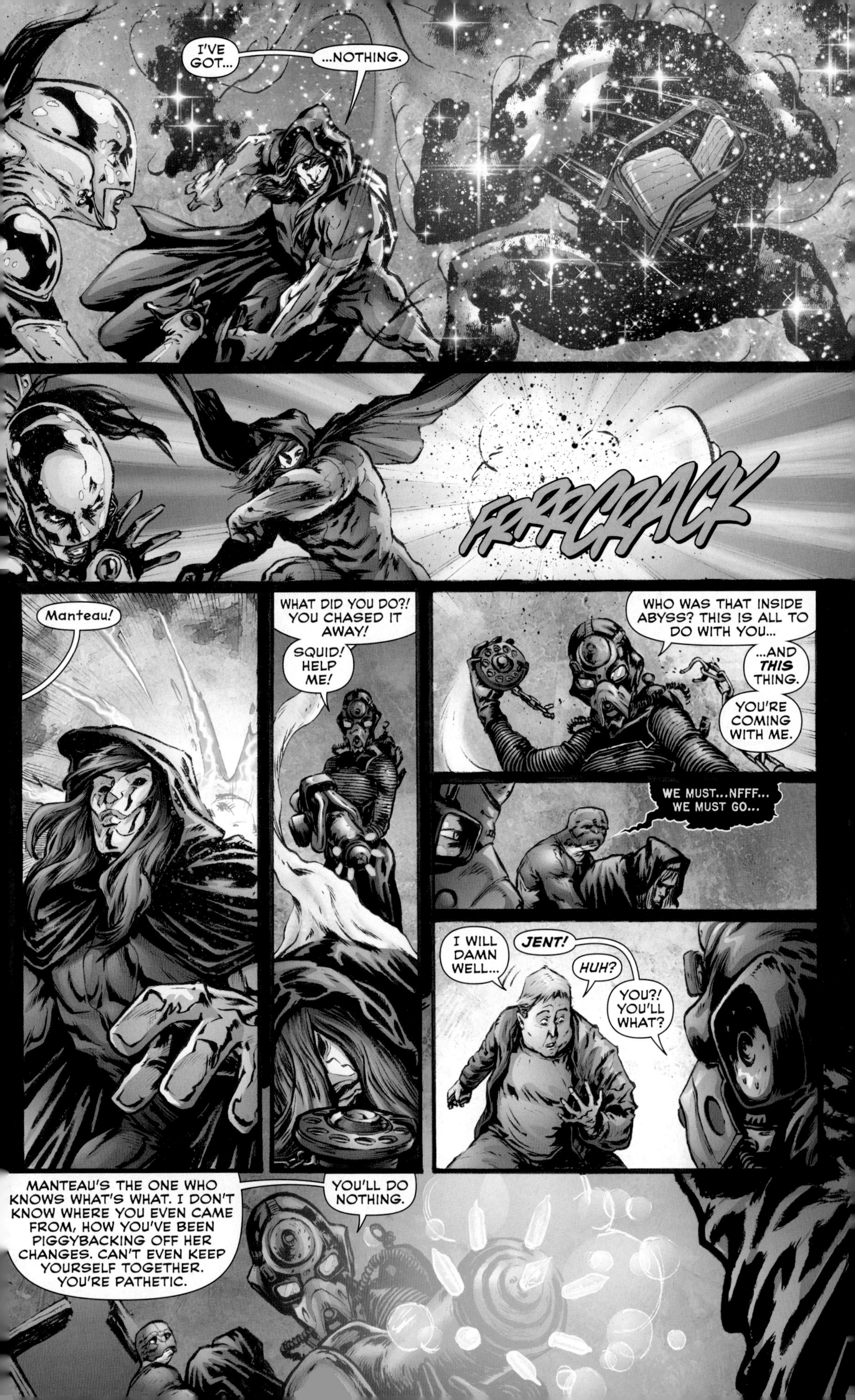

I'VE GOT...
...NOTHING.
FRRRCRACK
Manteau!
WHAT DID YOU DO?! YOU CHASED IT AWAY!
SQUID! HELP ME!
WHO WAS THAT INSIDE ABYSS? THIS IS ALL TO DO WITH YOU...
...AND THIS THING.
YOU'RE COMING WITH ME.
WE MUST...NFFF... WE MUST GO...
I WILL DAMN WELL...
JENT!
HUH?
YOU?! YOU'LL WHAT?
YOU'LL DO NOTHING.
MANTEAU'S THE ONE WHO KNOWS WHAT'S WHAT. I DON'T KNOW WHERE YOU EVEN CAME FROM, HOW YOU'VE BEEN PIGGYBACKING OFF HER CHANGES. CAN'T EVEN KEEP YOURSELF TOGETHER. YOU'RE PATHETIC.

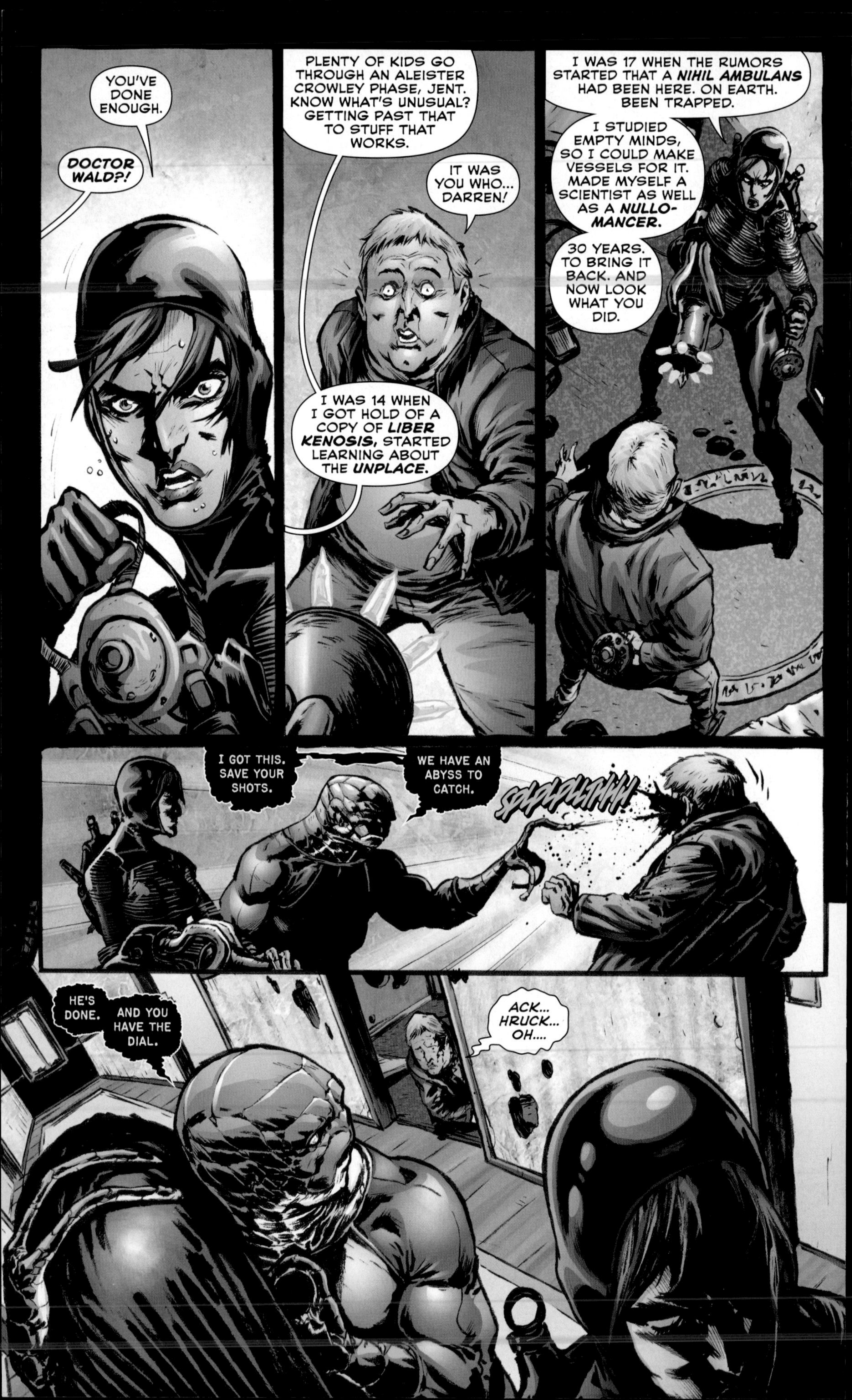
YOU'VE DONE ENOUGH.
DOCTOR WALD?!
PLENTY OF KIDS GO THROUGH AN ALEISTER CROWLEY PHASE, JENT. KNOW WHAT'S UNUSUAL? GETTING PAST THAT TO STUFF THAT WORKS.
IT WAS YOU WHO... DARREN!
I WAS 14 WHEN I GOT HOLD OF A COPY OF LIBER KENOSIS, STARTED LEARNING ABOUT THE UNPLACE.
I WAS 17 WHEN THE RUMORS STARTED THAT A NIHIL AMBULANS HAD BEEN HERE. ON EARTH. BEEN TRAPPED.
I STUDIED EMPTY MINDS, SO I COULD MAKE VESSELS FOR IT. MADE MYSELF A SCIENTIST AS WELL AS A NULLO-MANCER.
30 YEARS. TO BRING IT BACK. AND NOW LOOK WHAT YOU DID.
I GOT THIS. SAVE YOUR SHOTS.
WE HAVE AN ABYSS TO CATCH.
SPLPLPLLTHHH!
HE'S DONE.
AND YOU HAVE THE DIAL.
ACK... HRUCK... OH....

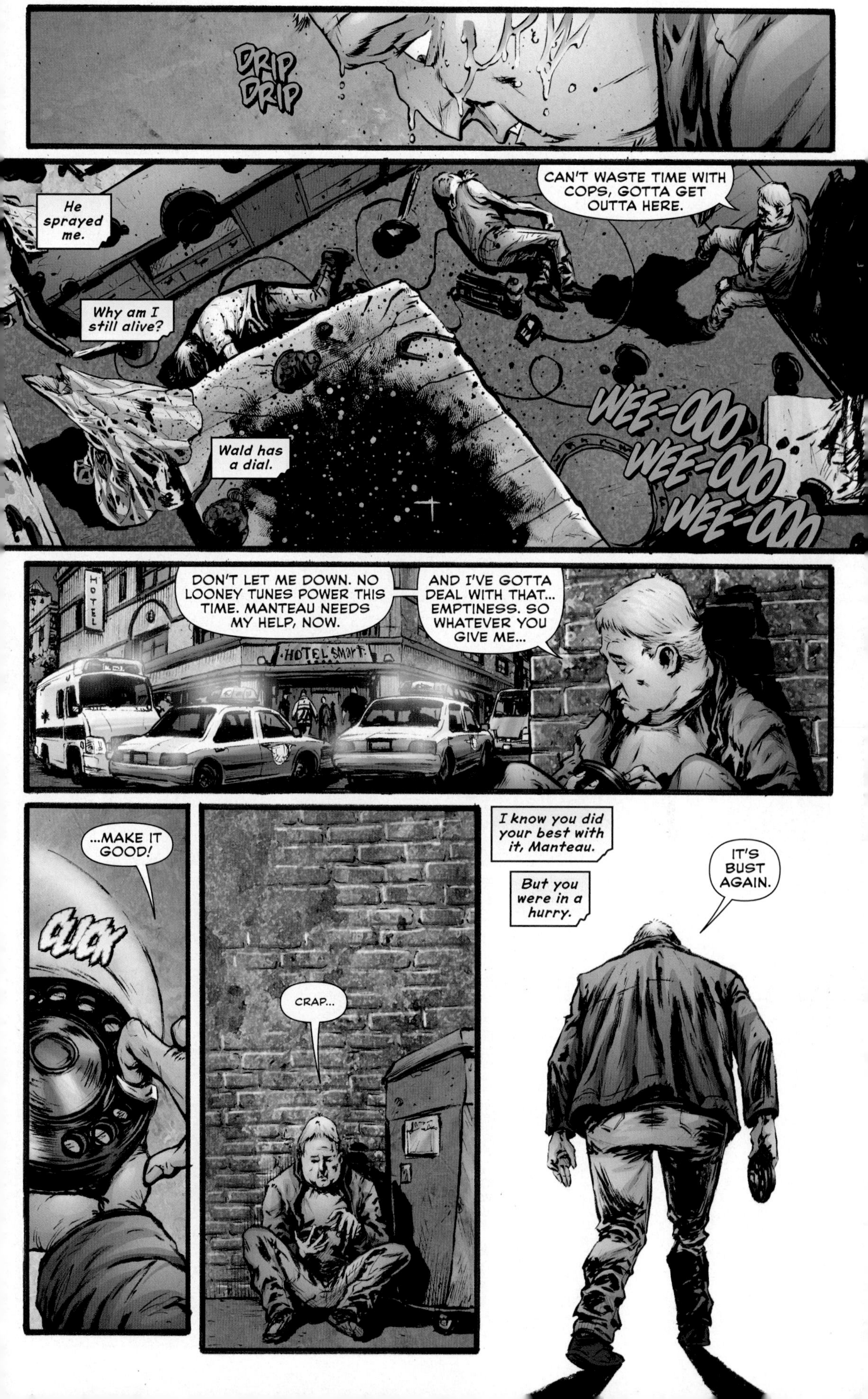
DRIP
DRIP
He sprayed me.
Why am I still alive?
Wald has a dial.
CAN'T WASTE TIME WITH COPS, GOTTA GET OUTTA HERE.
WEE-OOO
WEE-OOO
WEE-OOO
HOTEL
HOTEL SMART
DON'T LET ME DOWN. NO LOONEY TUNES POWER THIS TIME. MANTEAU NEEDS MY HELP, NOW.
AND I'VE GOTTA DEAL WITH THAT... EMPTINESS. SO WHATEVER YOU GIVE ME...
...MAKE IT GOOD!
CLICK
CRAP...
I know you did your best with it, Manteau.
But you were in a hurry.
IT'S BUST AGAIN.

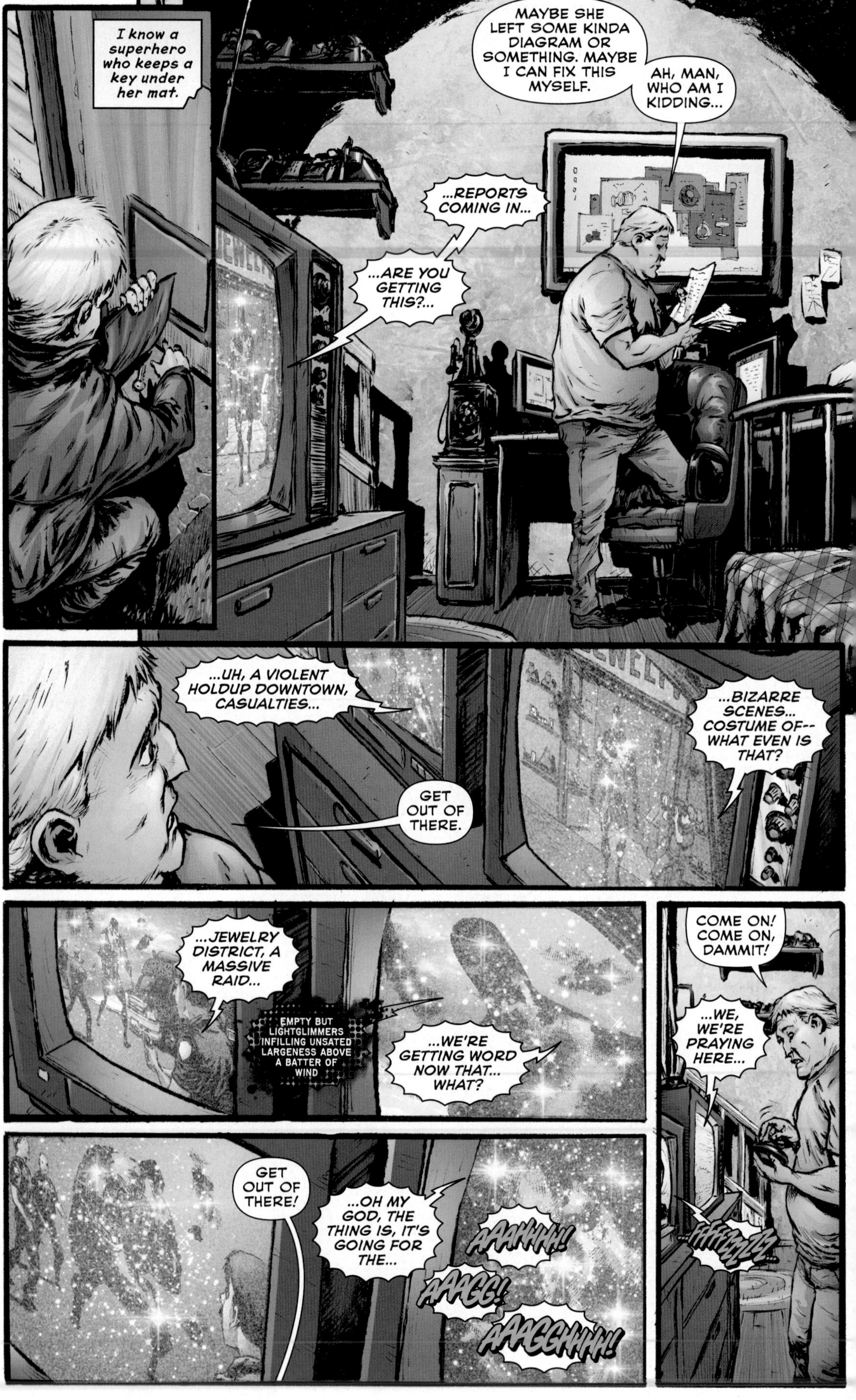
I know a superhero who keeps a key under her mat.
MAYBE SHE LEFT SOME KINDA DIAGRAM OR SOMETHING. MAYBE I CAN FIX THIS MYSELF.
AH, MAN, WHO AM I KIDDING...
...REPORTS COMING IN...
...ARE YOU GETTING THIS?...
...UH, A VIOLENT HOLDUP DOWNTOWN, CASUALTIES...
GET OUT OF THERE.
...BIZARRE SCENES... COSTUME OF-- WHAT EVEN IS THAT?
...JEWELRY DISTRICT, A MASSIVE RAID...
EMPTY BUT LIGHTGLIMMERS INFILLING UNSATED LARGENESS ABOVE A BATTER OF WIND
...WE'RE GETTING WORD NOW THAT... WHAT?
COME ON! COME ON, DAMMIT!
...WE, WE'RE PRAYING HERE...
GET OUT OF THERE!
...OH MY GOD, THE THING IS, IT'S GOING FOR THE...
AAAHHHH!
AAAGG!
AAAGGHHHH!

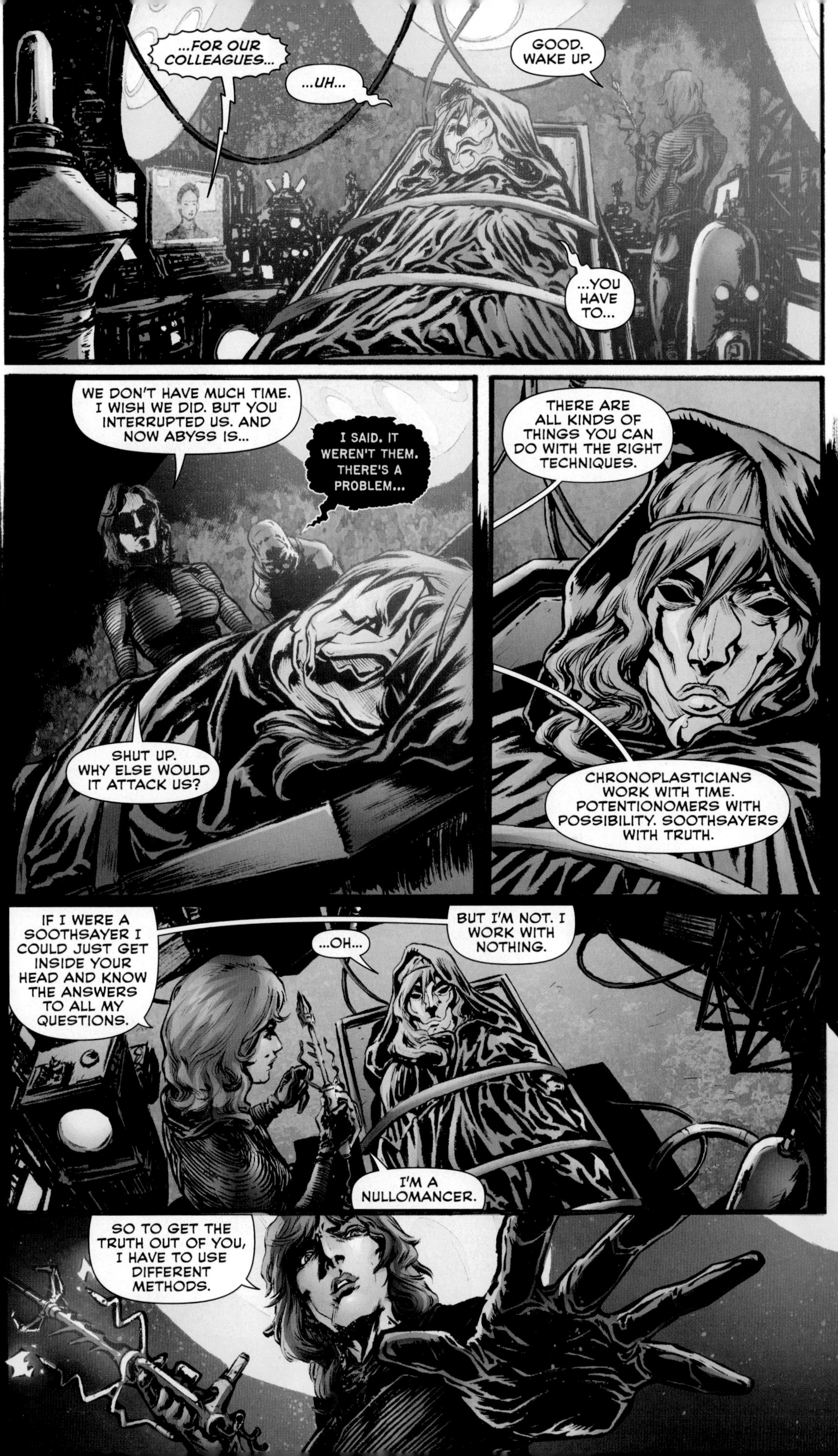
...FOR OUR COLLEAGUES...
...UH...
GOOD. WAKE UP.
...YOU HAVE TO...
WE DON'T HAVE MUCH TIME. I WISH WE DID. BUT YOU INTERRUPTED US. AND NOW ABYSS IS...
I SAID. IT WEREN'T THEM. THERE'S A PROBLEM...
SHUT UP. WHY ELSE WOULD IT ATTACK US?
THERE ARE ALL KINDS OF THINGS YOU CAN DO WITH THE RIGHT TECHNIQUES.
CHRONOPLASTICIANS WORK WITH TIME. POTENTIONOMERS WITH POSSIBILITY. SOOTHSAYERS WITH TRUTH.
IF I WERE A SOOTHSAYER I COULD JUST GET INSIDE YOUR HEAD AND KNOW THE ANSWERS TO ALL MY QUESTIONS.
...OH...
BUT I'M NOT. I WORK WITH NOTHING.
I'M A NULLOMANCER.
SO TO GET THE TRUTH OUT OF YOU, I HAVE TO USE DIFFERENT METHODS.

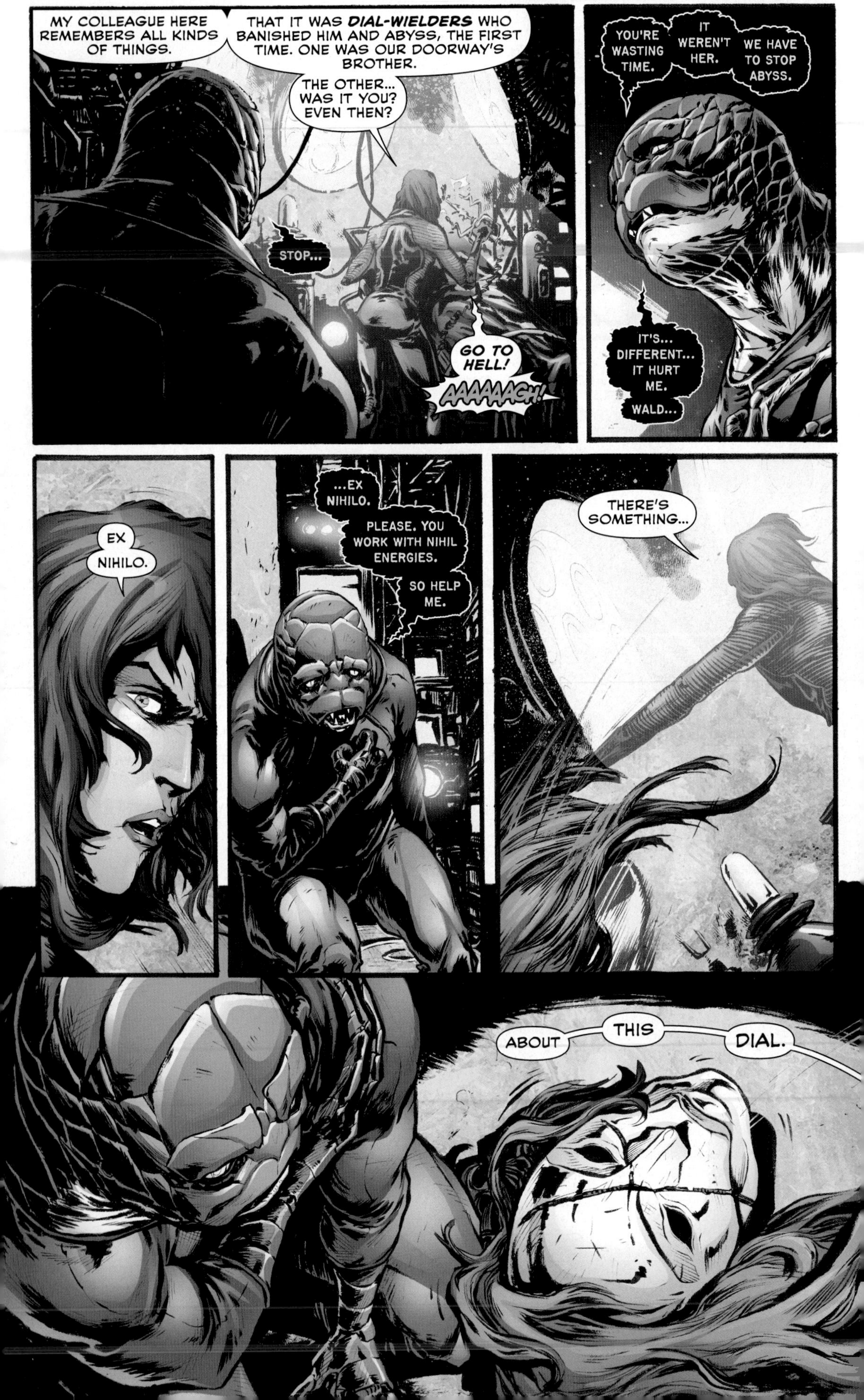
MY COLLEAGUE HERE REMEMBERS ALL KINDS OF THINGS.
THAT IT WAS DIAL-WIELDERS WHO BANISHED HIM AND ABYSS, THE FIRST TIME. ONE WAS OUR DOORWAY'S BROTHER.
THE OTHER... WAS IT YOU? EVEN THEN?
STOP...
GO TO HELL!
AAAAAAGH!
YOU'RE WASTING TIME.
IT WEREN'T HER.
WE HAVE TO STOP ABYSS.
IT'S... DIFFERENT... IT HURT ME.
WALD...
EX NIHILO.
...EX NIHILO.
PLEASE. YOU WORK WITH NIHIL ENERGIES.
SO HELP ME.
THERE'S SOMETHING...
ABOUT
THIS
DIAL.

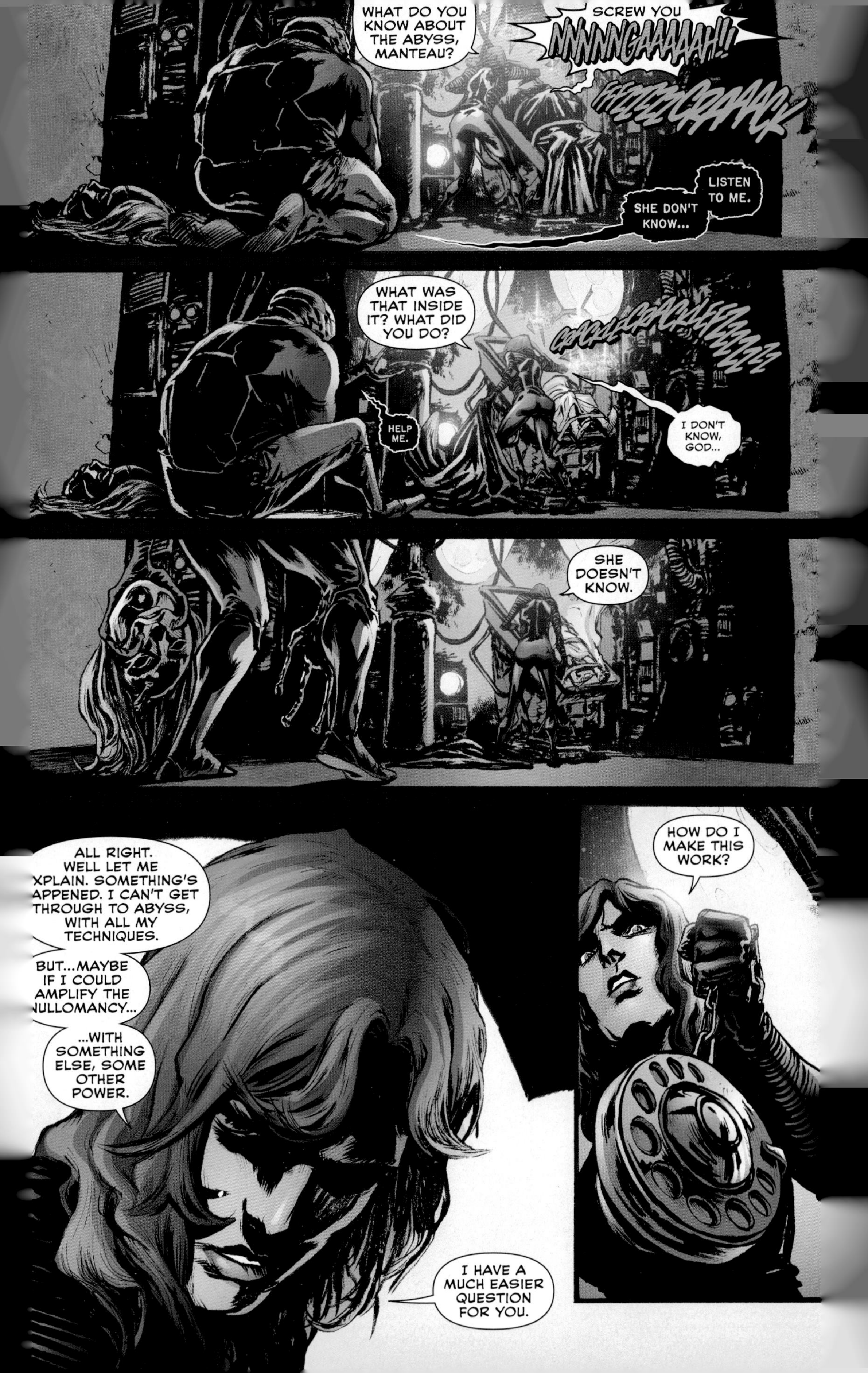
WHAT DO YOU KNOW ABOUT THE ABYSS, MANTEAU?
SCREW YOU
NNNNNGAAAAAAH!!
LISTEN TO ME.
SHE DON'T KNOW...
WHAT WAS THAT INSIDE IT? WHAT DID YOU DO?
HELP ME.
I DON'T KNOW, GOD...
SHE DOESN'T KNOW.
ALL RIGHT. WELL LET ME XPLAIN. SOMETHING'S APPENED. I CAN'T GET THROUGH TO ABYSS, WITH ALL MY TECHNIQUES.
BUT...MAYBE IF I COULD AMPLIFY THE NULLOMANCY...
...WITH SOMETHING ELSE, SOME OTHER POWER.
HOW DO I MAKE THIS WORK?
I HAVE A MUCH EASIER QUESTION FOR YOU.

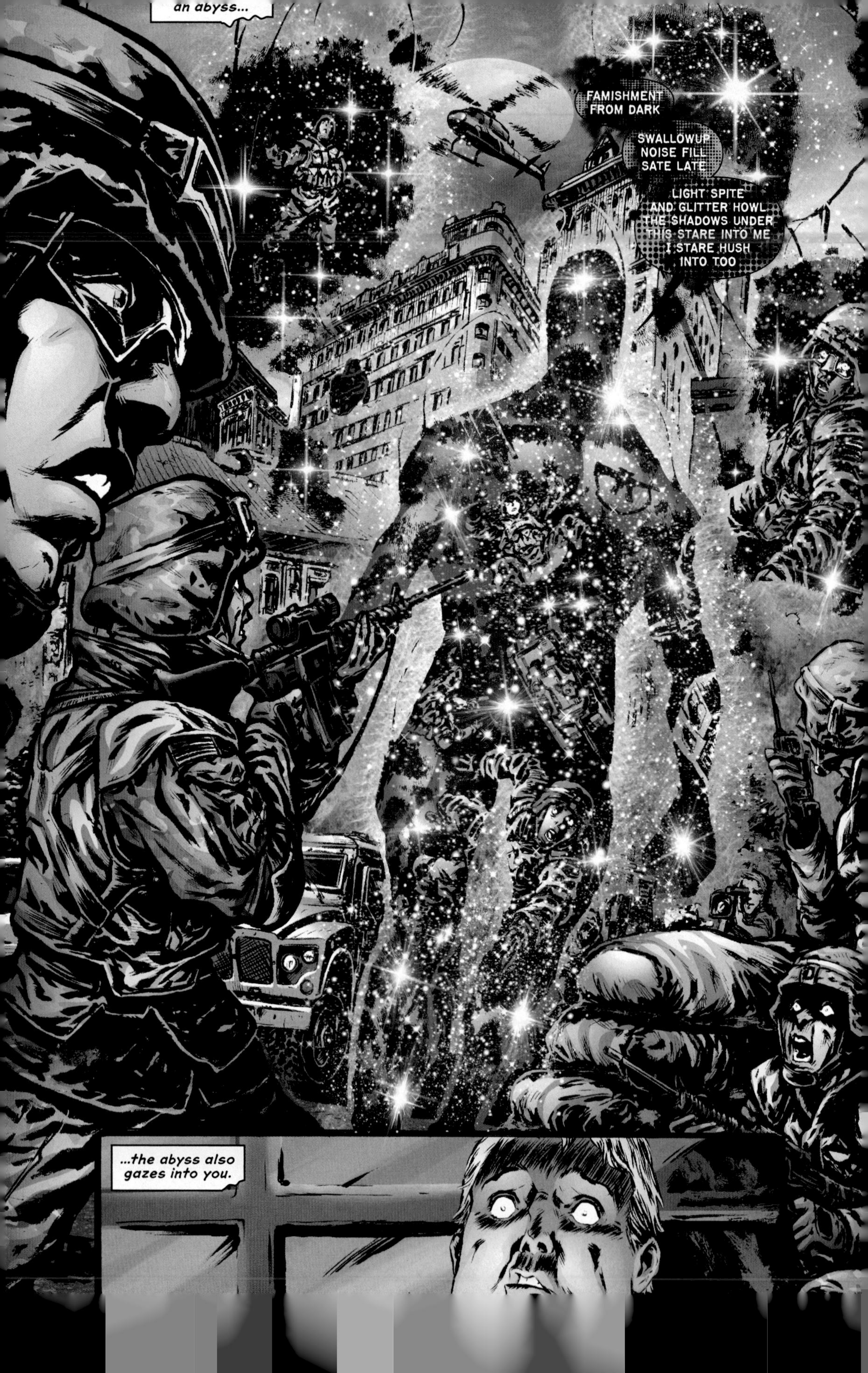
an abyss...
FAMISHMENT FROM DARK
SWALLOWUP NOISE FILL SATE LATE
LIGHT SPITE AND GLITTER HOWL THE SHADOWS UNDER THIS STARE INTO ME I STARE HUSH INTO TOO
...the abyss also gazes into you.

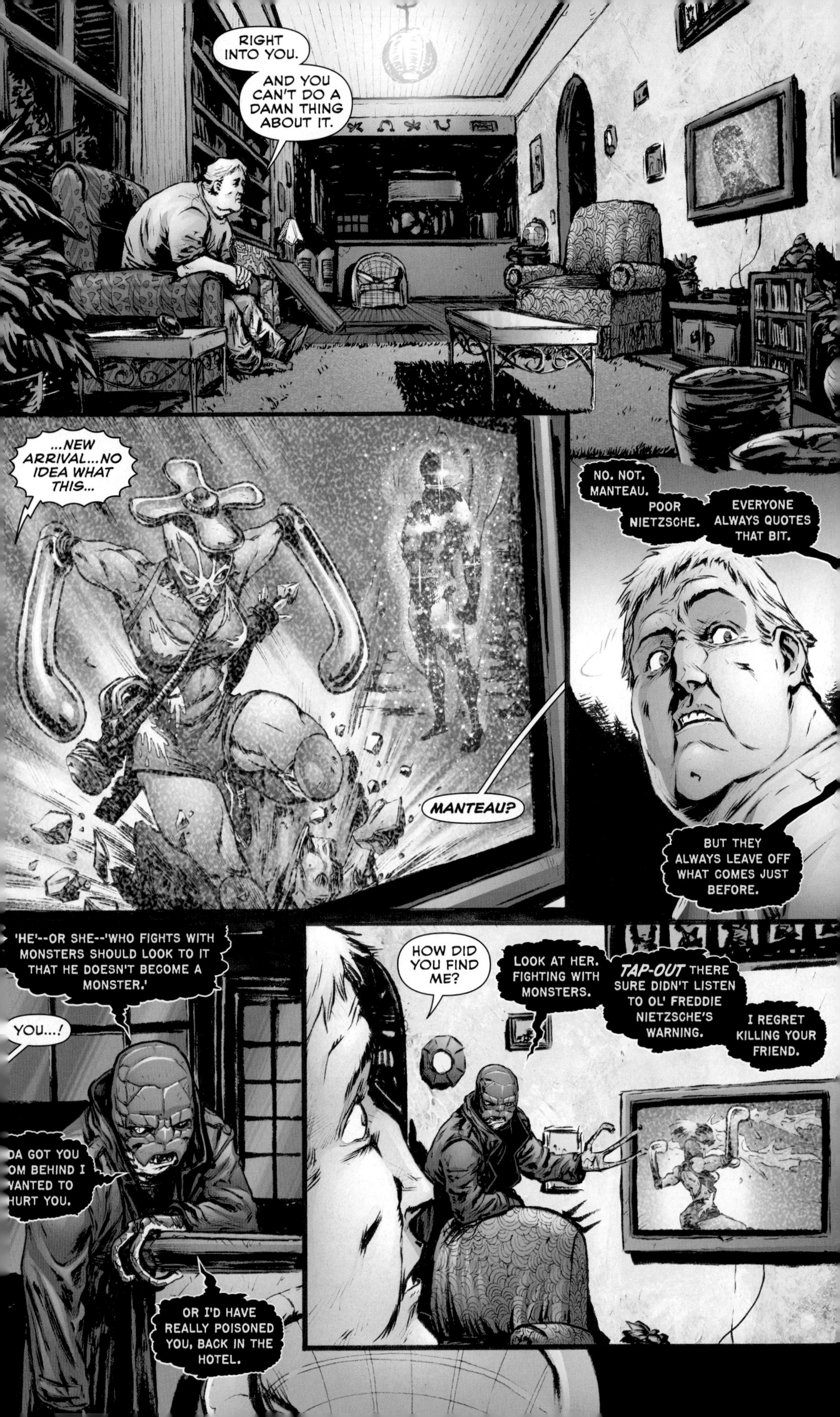
RIGHT INTO YOU.
AND YOU CAN'T DO A DAMN THING ABOUT IT.
...NEW ARRIVAL...NO IDEA WHAT THIS...
MANTEAU?
NO. NOT. MANTEAU.
POOR NIETZSCHE.
EVERYONE ALWAYS QUOTES THAT BIT.
BUT THEY ALWAYS LEAVE OFF WHAT COMES JUST BEFORE.
'HE'--OR SHE--'WHO FIGHTS WITH MONSTERS SHOULD LOOK TO IT THAT HE DOESN'T BECOME A MONSTER.'
YOU...!
OR I'D HAVE REALLY POISONED YOU, BACK IN THE HOTEL.
HOW DID YOU FIND ME?
LOOK AT HER. FIGHTING WITH MONSTERS.
TAP-OUT THERE SURE DIDN'T LISTEN TO OL' FREDDIE NIETZSCHE'S WARNING.
I REGRET KILLING YOUR FRIEND.

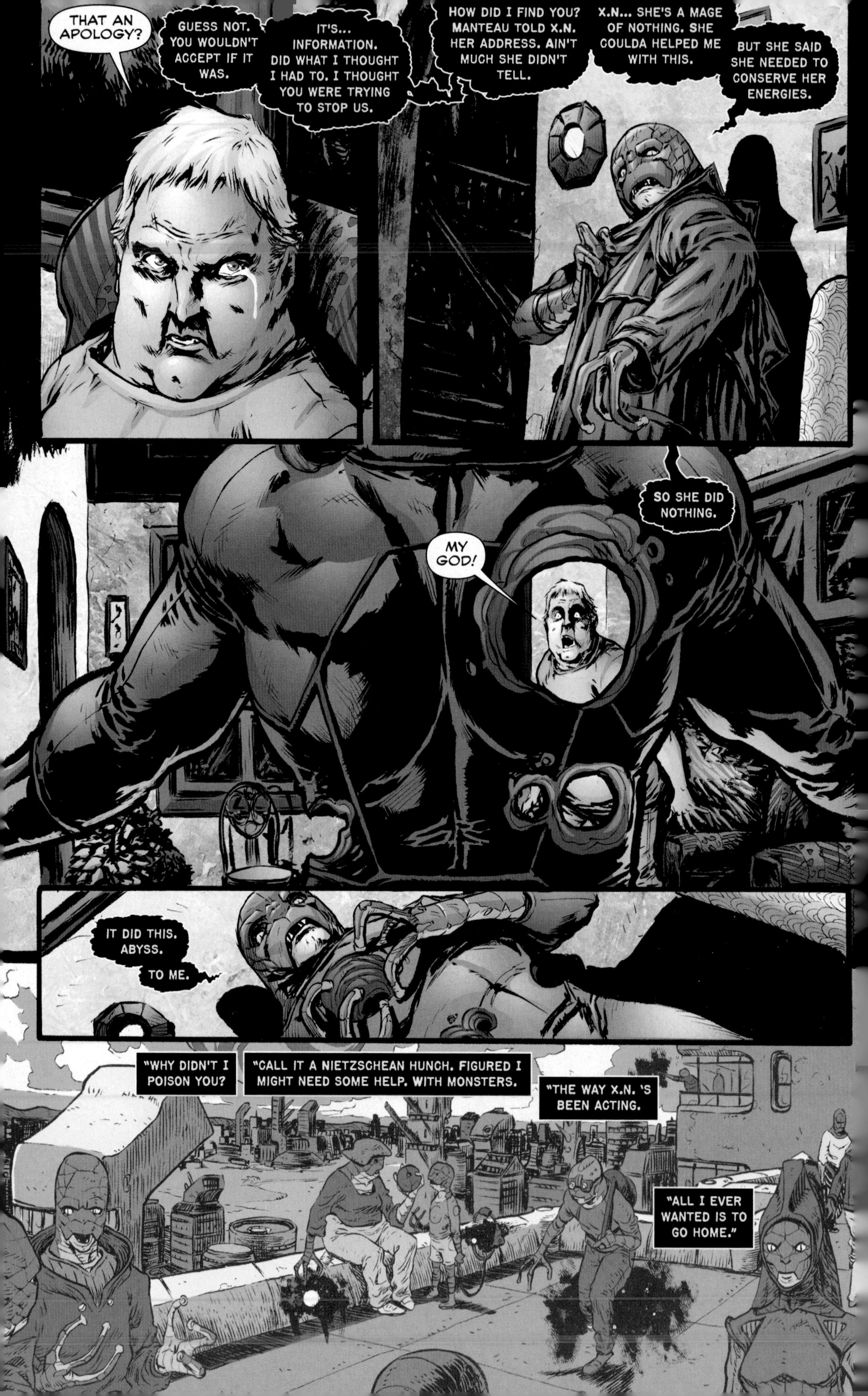
THAT AN APOLOGY?
GUESS NOT. YOU WOULDN'T ACCEPT IF IT WAS.
IT'S... INFORMATION. DID WHAT I THOUGHT I HAD TO. I THOUGHT YOU WERE TRYING TO STOP US.
HOW DID I FIND YOU? MANTEAU TOLD X.N. HER ADDRESS. AIN'T MUCH SHE DIDN'T TELL.
X.N... SHE'S A MAGE OF NOTHING. SHE COULDA HELPED ME WITH THIS.
BUT SHE SAID SHE NEEDED TO CONSERVE HER ENERGIES.
SO SHE DID NOTHING.
MY GOD!
IT DID THIS. ABYSS.
TO ME.
"WHY DIDN'T I POISON YOU?
"CALL IT A NIETZSCHEAN HUNCH. FIGURED I MIGHT NEED SOME HELP. WITH MONSTERS.
"THE WAY X.N. 'S BEEN ACTING.
"ALL I EVER WANTED IS TO GO HOME."

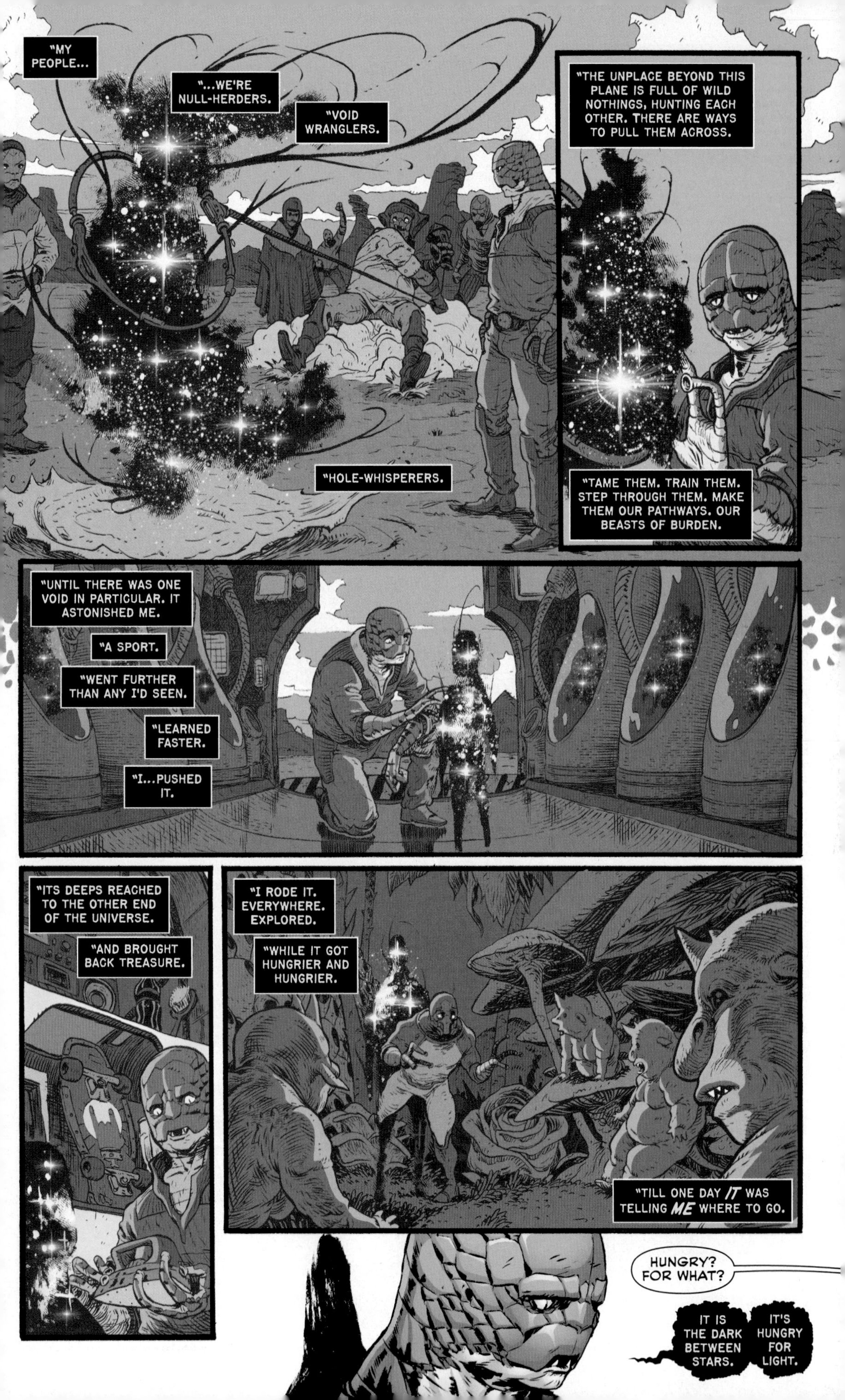
"MY PEOPLE...
"...WE'RE NULL-HERDERS.
"VOID WRANGLERS.
"HOLE-WHISPERERS.
"THE UNPLACE BEYOND THIS PLANE IS FULL OF WILD NOTHINGS, HUNTING EACH OTHER. THERE ARE WAYS TO PULL THEM ACROSS.
"TAME THEM. TRAIN THEM. STEP THROUGH THEM. MAKE THEM OUR PATHWAYS. OUR BEASTS OF BURDEN.
"UNTIL THERE WAS ONE VOID IN PARTICULAR. IT ASTONISHED ME.
"A SPORT.
"WENT FURTHER THAN ANY I'D SEEN.
"LEARNED FASTER.
"I...PUSHED IT.
"ITS DEEPS REACHED TO THE OTHER END OF THE UNIVERSE.
"AND BROUGHT BACK TREASURE.
"I RODE IT. EVERYWHERE. EXPLORED.
"WHILE IT GOT HUNGRIER AND HUNGRIER.
"TILL ONE DAY *IT* WAS TELLING *ME* WHERE TO GO.
HUNGRY? FOR WHAT?
IT IS THE DARK BETWEEN STARS.
IT'S HUNGRY FOR LIGHT.

"KNOW WHY YOUR DIALER PREDECESSORS BANISHED AN ABYSS MADE MAD, SENT ME TUMBLING INTO IT FOR AN ETERNITY OF NOTHING? NOT FOR MURDER, NOT GENOCIDE, NOT FOR WAR CRIMES.

"FOR STEALING JEWELRY.

"FOR THAT, I SPENT DECADES FALLING.

ABYSS FEEDS ON THE GLARE OF STARS. BUT THE WAY LIGHT GLINTS FROM FACETS? IT LOVES THAT.

WE WERE ONLY HERE IN THE FIRST PLACE 'CAUSE WE'D STOPPED OFF FOR A SNACK.

HER NIHIL-MAGIC AIN'T ENOUGH, BUT X.N. THINKS IF SHE USES IT ALONG WITH WHATEVER DUMBASS POWER SHE DIALS, SHE MIGHT CONTROL IT.

SHE DON'T GET IT.

IT'S BEEN LOST TOO LONG. CAME BACK MAD, WITH MAD KIDS. AND SOMETHING ELSE RIDING IT.

ALL THAT TIME NOWHERE.

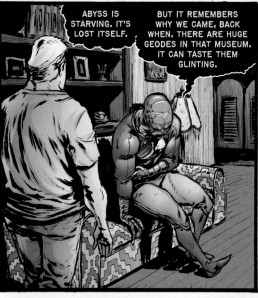

ABYSS IS STARVING. IT'S LOST ITSELF.

BUT IT REMEMBERS WHY WE CAME, BACK WHEN. THERE ARE HUGE GEODES IN THAT MUSEUM. IT CAN TASTE THEM GLINTING.

WHY YOU HERE?

BECAUSE X.N. CAN'T FIX THINGS, AND SHE'S MAKING ABYSS ANGRY.

IT MIGHT EVEN REMEMBER IT EATS SUNS.

WE HAVE TO STOP X.N. AND I'M HURT, AND I CAN'T FACE HER ALONE.

AND SHE THINKS YOU'RE DEAD. AND UNLIKE ME, SHE DIDN'T SEE WHAT YOU WERE CARRYING. SHE DON'T EVEN KNOW THERE'S ANOTHER DIAL.

THAT'S ONE THING MANTEAU DID NOT TELL HER.

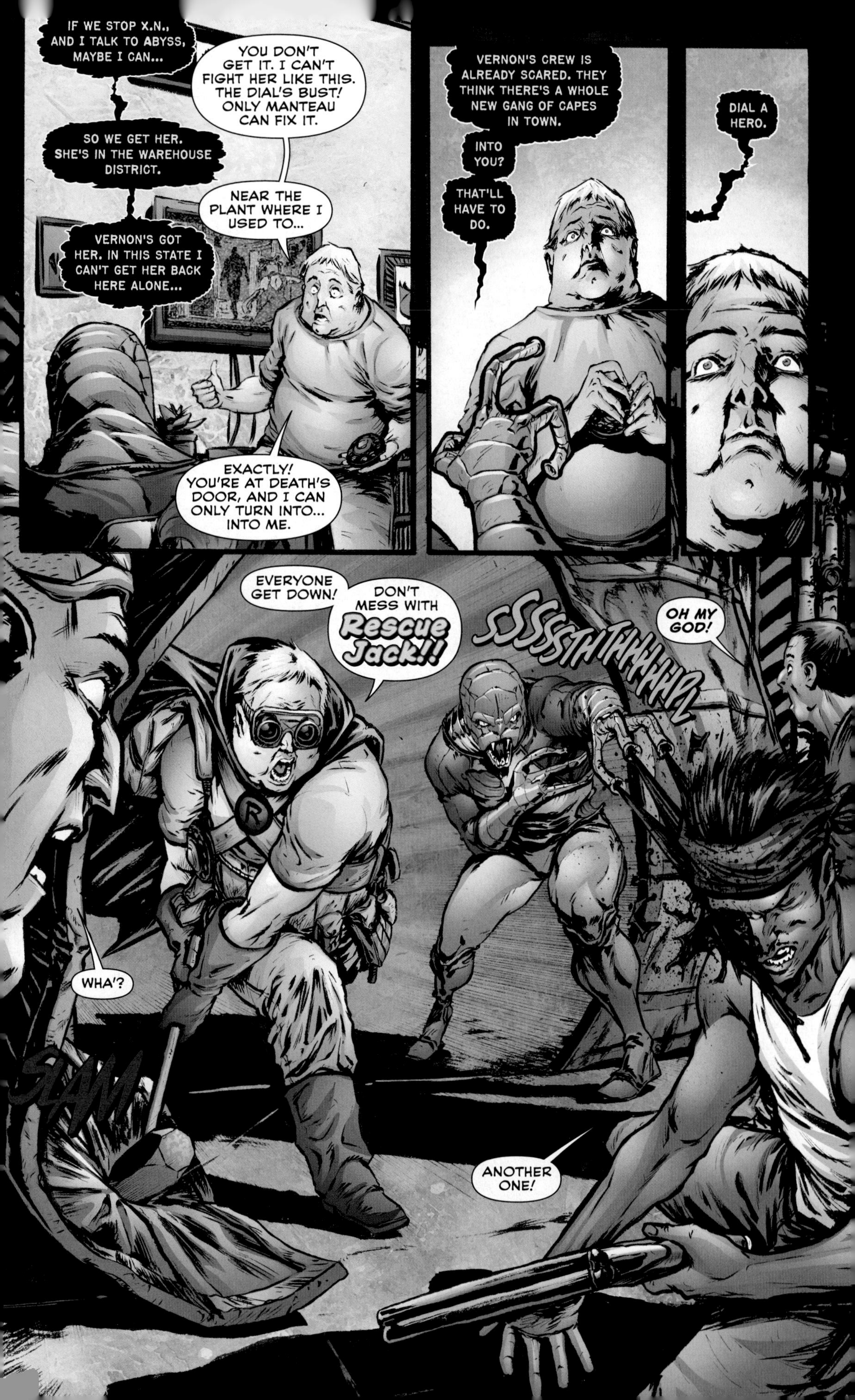
IF WE STOP X.N., AND I TALK TO ABYSS, MAYBE I CAN...
YOU DON'T GET IT. I CAN'T FIGHT HER LIKE THIS. THE DIAL'S BUST! ONLY MANTEAU CAN FIX IT.
SO WE GET HER. SHE'S IN THE WAREHOUSE DISTRICT.
NEAR THE PLANT WHERE I USED TO...
VERNON'S GOT HER. IN THIS STATE I CAN'T GET HER BACK HERE ALONE...
EXACTLY! YOU'RE AT DEATH'S DOOR, AND I CAN ONLY TURN INTO... INTO ME.
VERNON'S CREW IS ALREADY SCARED. THEY THINK THERE'S A WHOLE NEW GANG OF CAPES IN TOWN.
INTO YOU?
THAT'LL HAVE TO DO.
DIAL A HERO.
EVERYONE GET DOWN!
DON'T MESS WITH Rescue Jack!!
SSSSSTHTHWWWN
OH MY GOD!
WHA'?
SLAM
ANOTHER ONE!

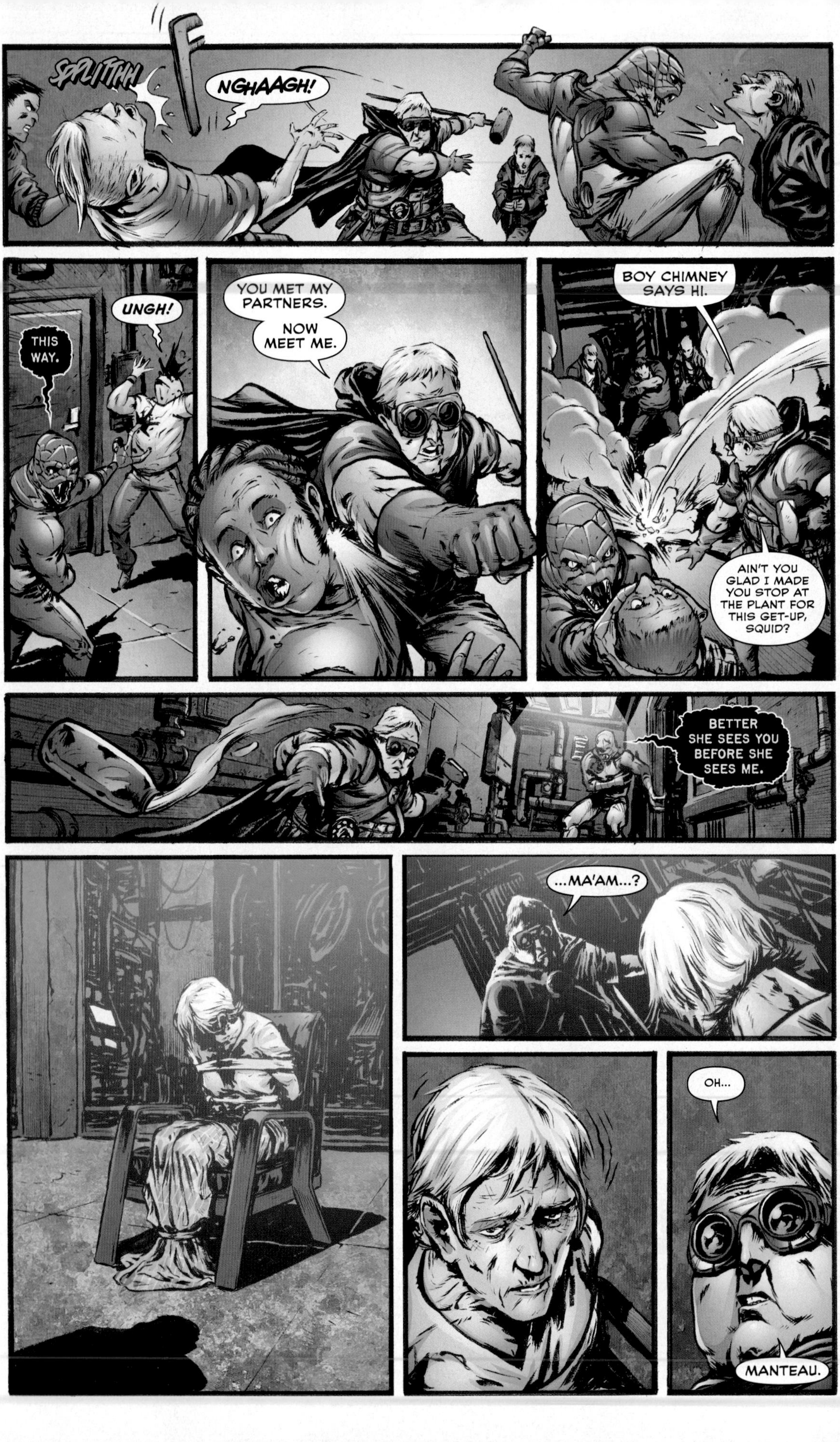
SPLITTH
NGHAAGH!
UNGH!
THIS WAY.
YOU MET MY PARTNERS.
NOW MEET ME.
BOY CHIMNEY SAYS HI.
AIN'T YOU GLAD I MADE YOU STOP AT THE PLANT FOR THIS GET-UP, SQUID?
BETTER SHE SEES YOU BEFORE SHE SEES ME.
...MA'AM...?
OH...
MANTEAU.

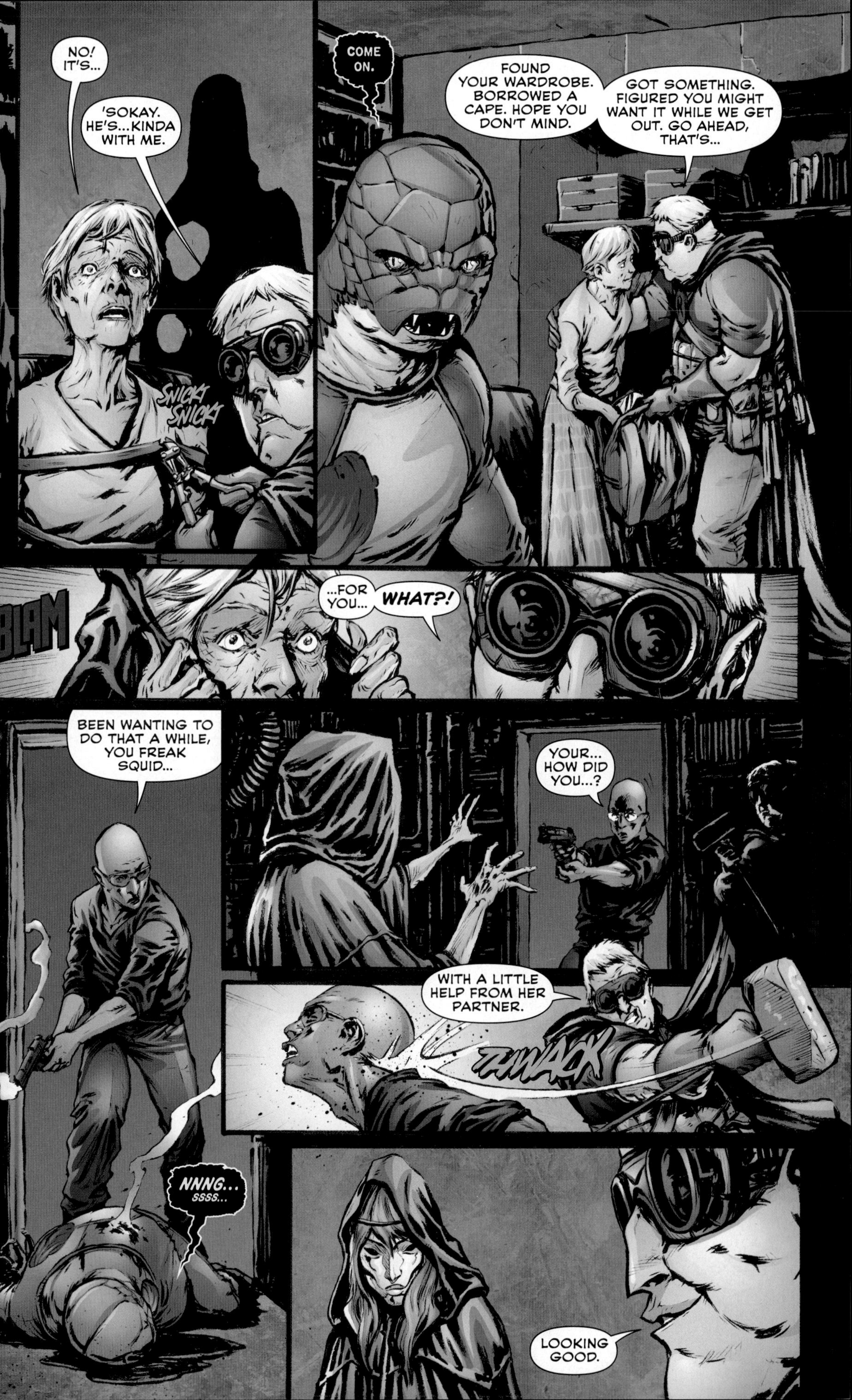
NO! IT'S...
'SOKAY. HE'S...KINDA WITH ME.
SNICK! SNICK!
COME ON.
FOUND YOUR WARDROBE. BORROWED A CAPE. HOPE YOU DON'T MIND.
GOT SOMETHING. FIGURED YOU MIGHT WANT IT WHILE WE GET OUT. GO AHEAD, THAT'S...
BLAM
...FOR YOU...
WHAT?!
BEEN WANTING TO DO THAT A WHILE, YOU FREAK SQUID...
NNNG... SSSS...
YOUR... HOW DID YOU...?
WITH A LITTLE HELP FROM HER PARTNER.
THWACK
LOOKING GOOD.

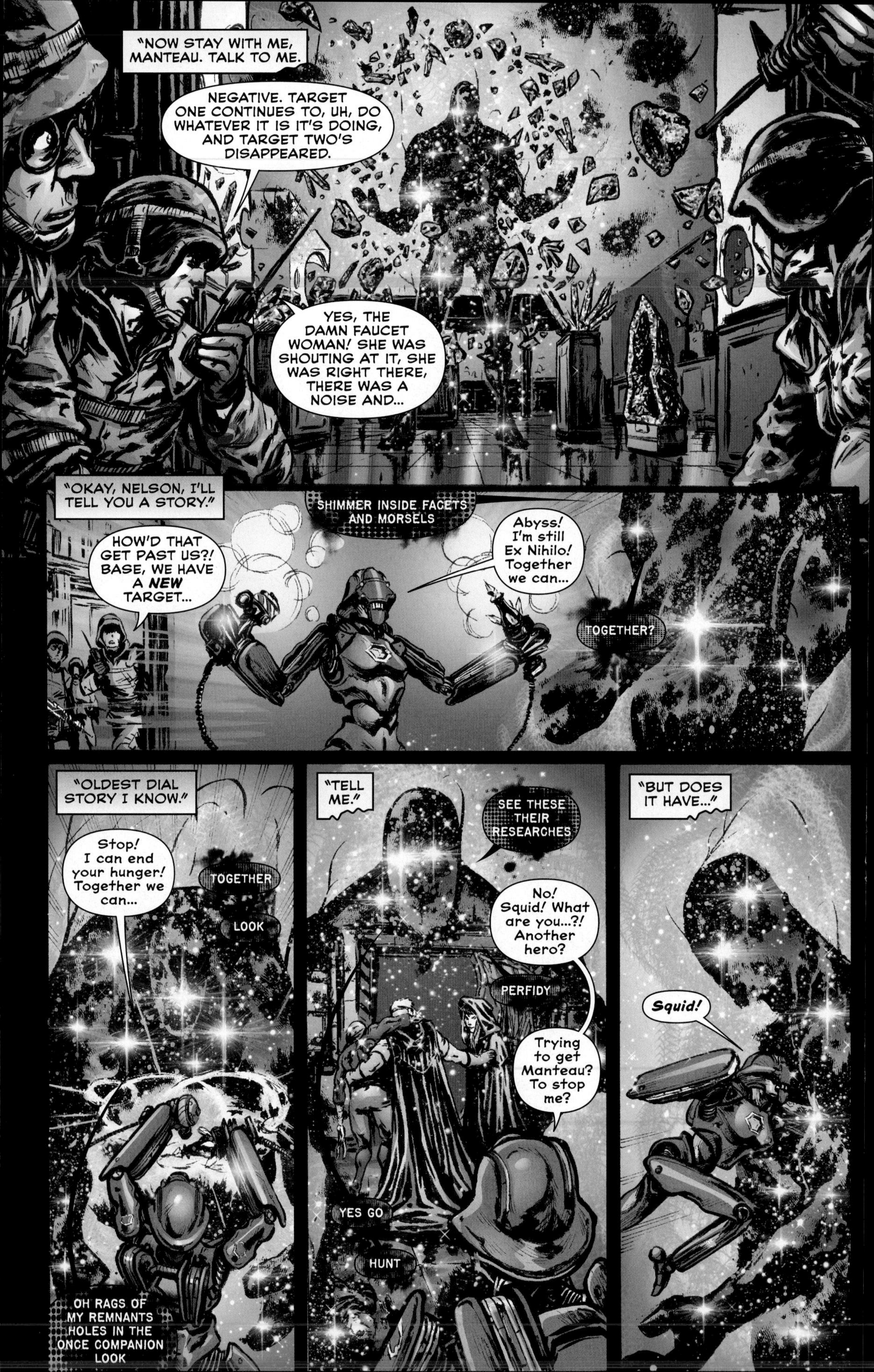
"NOW STAY WITH ME, MANTEAU. TALK TO ME.
NEGATIVE. TARGET ONE CONTINUES TO, UH, DO WHATEVER IT IS IT'S DOING, AND TARGET TWO'S DISAPPEARED.
YES, THE DAMN FAUCET WOMAN! SHE WAS SHOUTING AT IT, SHE WAS RIGHT THERE, THERE WAS A NOISE AND...
"OKAY, NELSON, I'LL TELL YOU A STORY."
HOW'D THAT GET PAST US?! BASE, WE HAVE A ***NEW*** TARGET...
SHIMMER INSIDE FACETS AND MORSELS
Abyss! I'm still Ex Nihilo! Together we can...
TOGETHER?
"OLDEST DIAL STORY I KNOW."
Stop! I can end your hunger! Together we can...
TOGETHER
LOOK
OH RAGS OF MY REMNANTS HOLES IN THE ONCE COMPANION LOOK
"TELL ME."
SEE THESE THEIR RESEARCHES
No! Squid! What are you...?! Another hero?
PERFIDY
Trying to get Manteau? To stop me?
YES GO
HUNT
"BUT DOES IT HAVE..."
Squid!

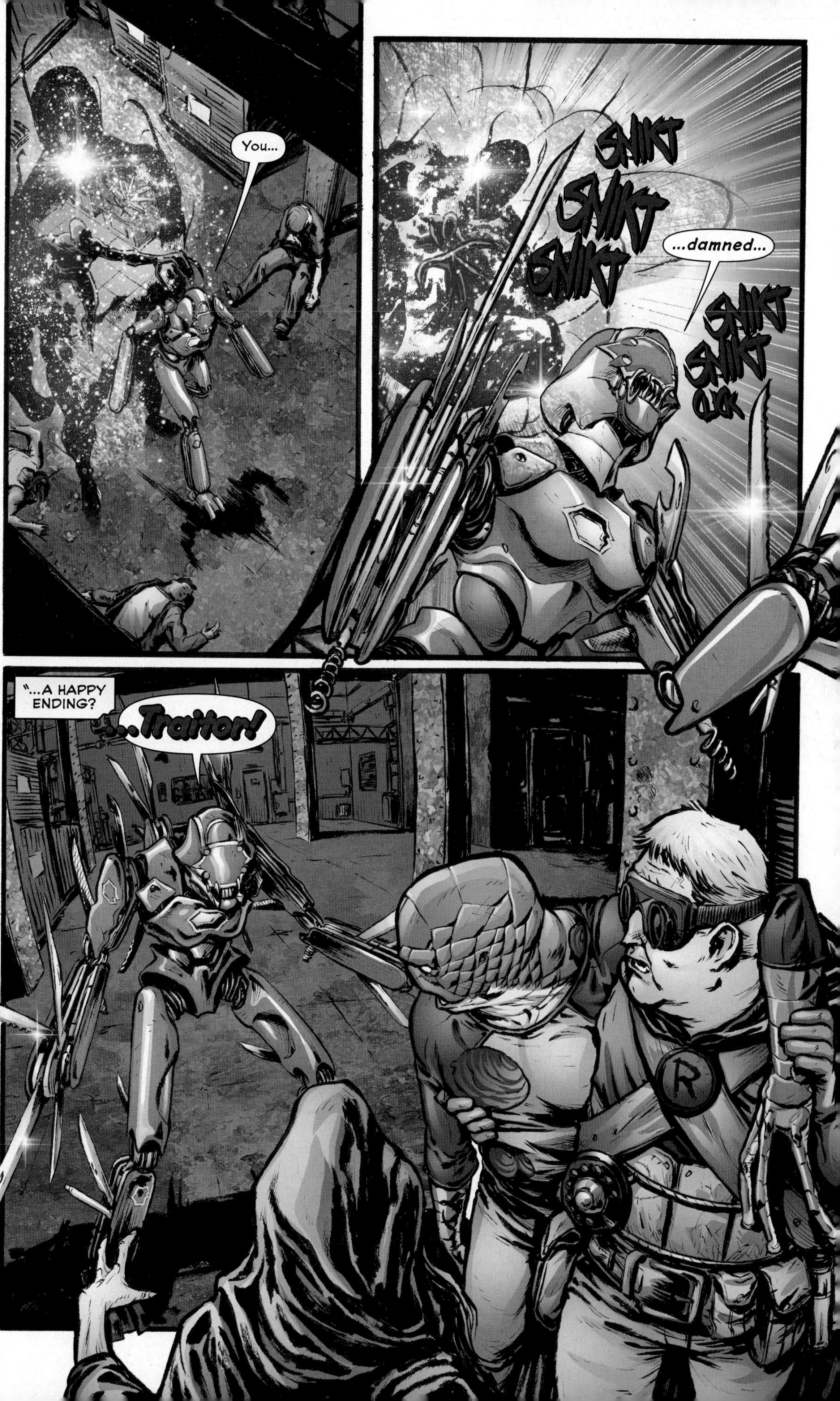
You...
SNIKT
SNIKT
SNIKT
...damned...
SNIKT
SNIKT
CLICK
"...A HAPPY ENDING?
...Traitor!

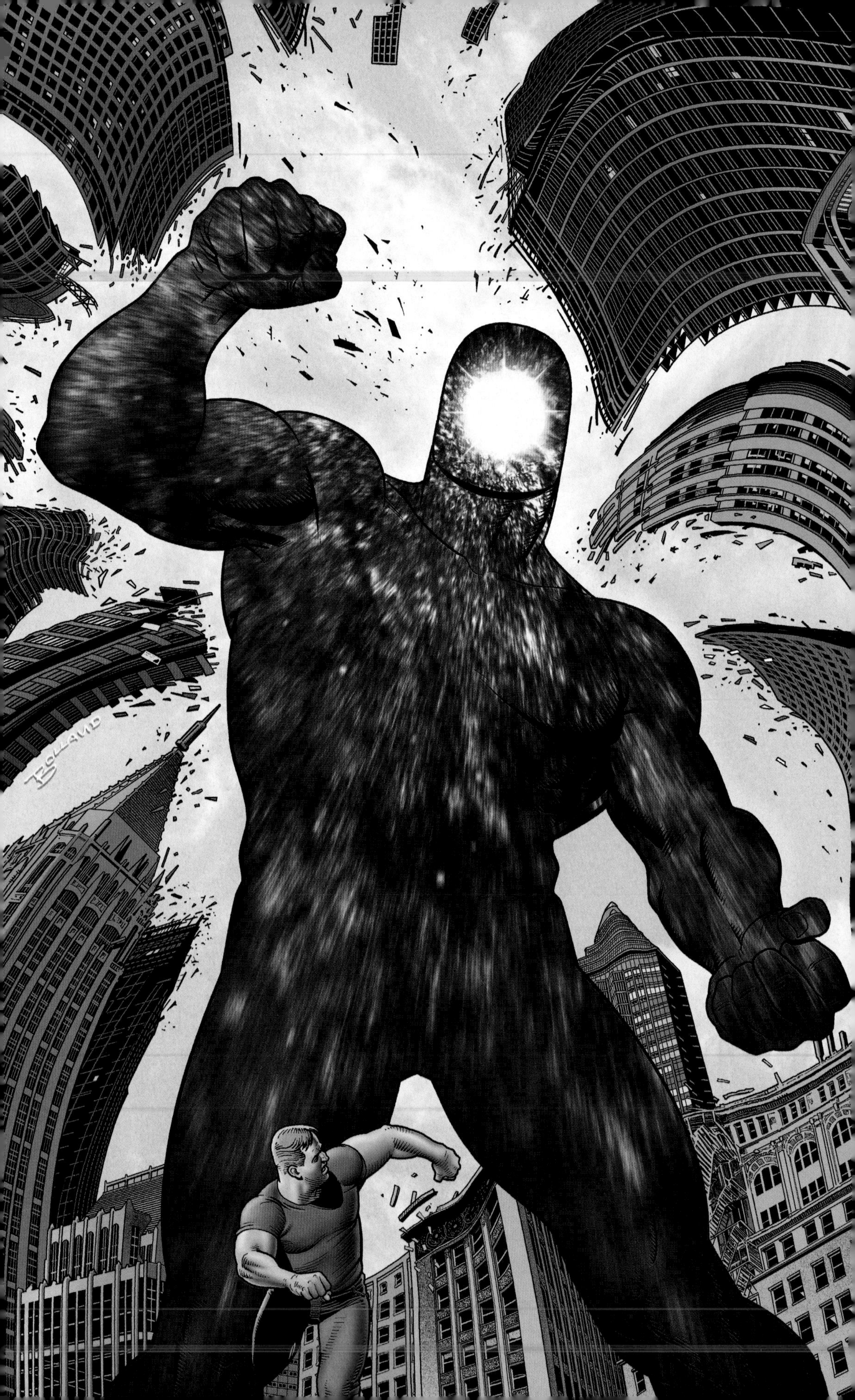

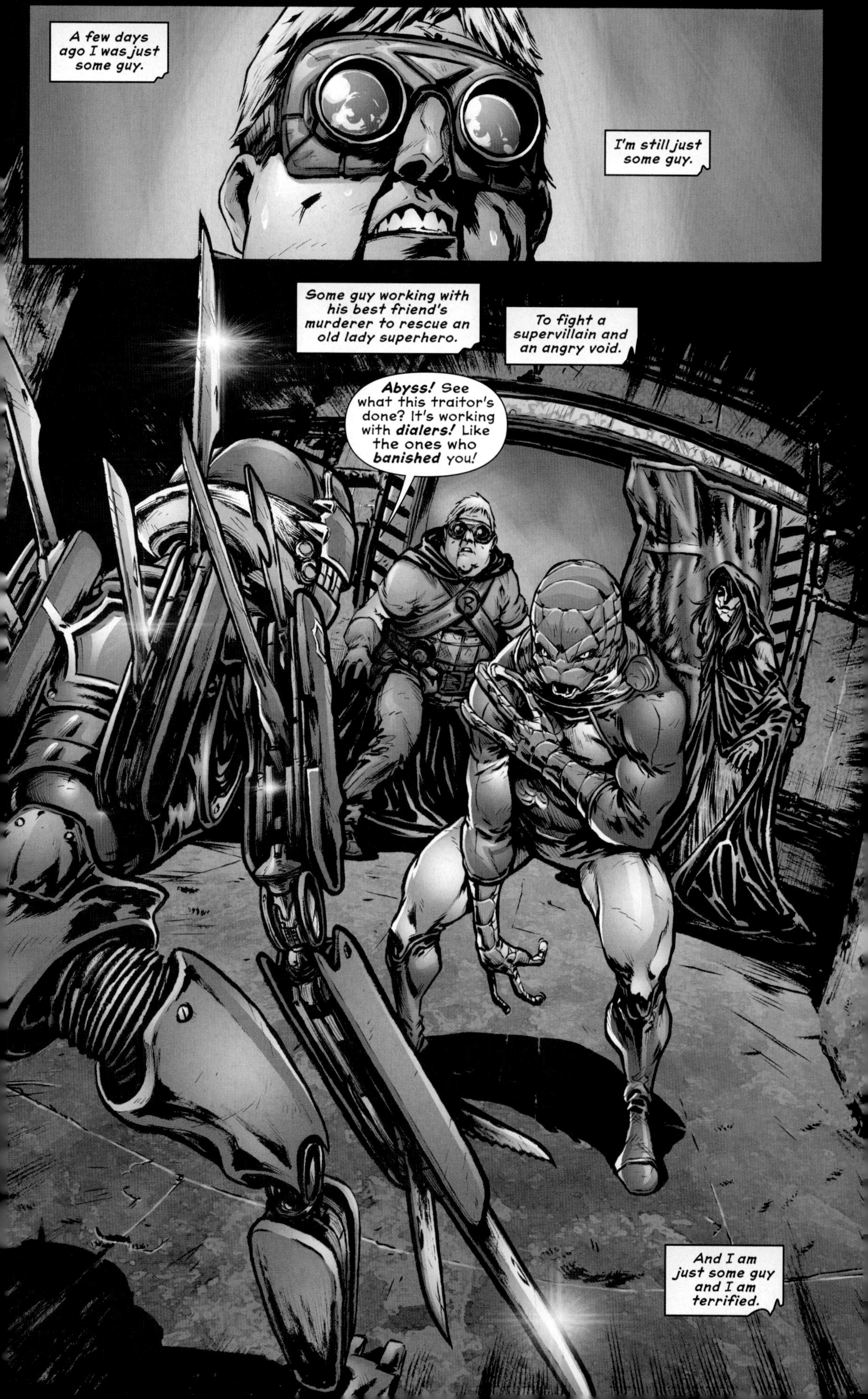

A few days ago I was just some guy.
I'm still just some guy.
Some guy working with his best friend's murderer to rescue an old lady superhero.
To fight a supervillain and an angry void.
Abyss! See what this traitor's done? It's working with dialers! Like the ones who banished you!
And I am just some guy and I am terrified.

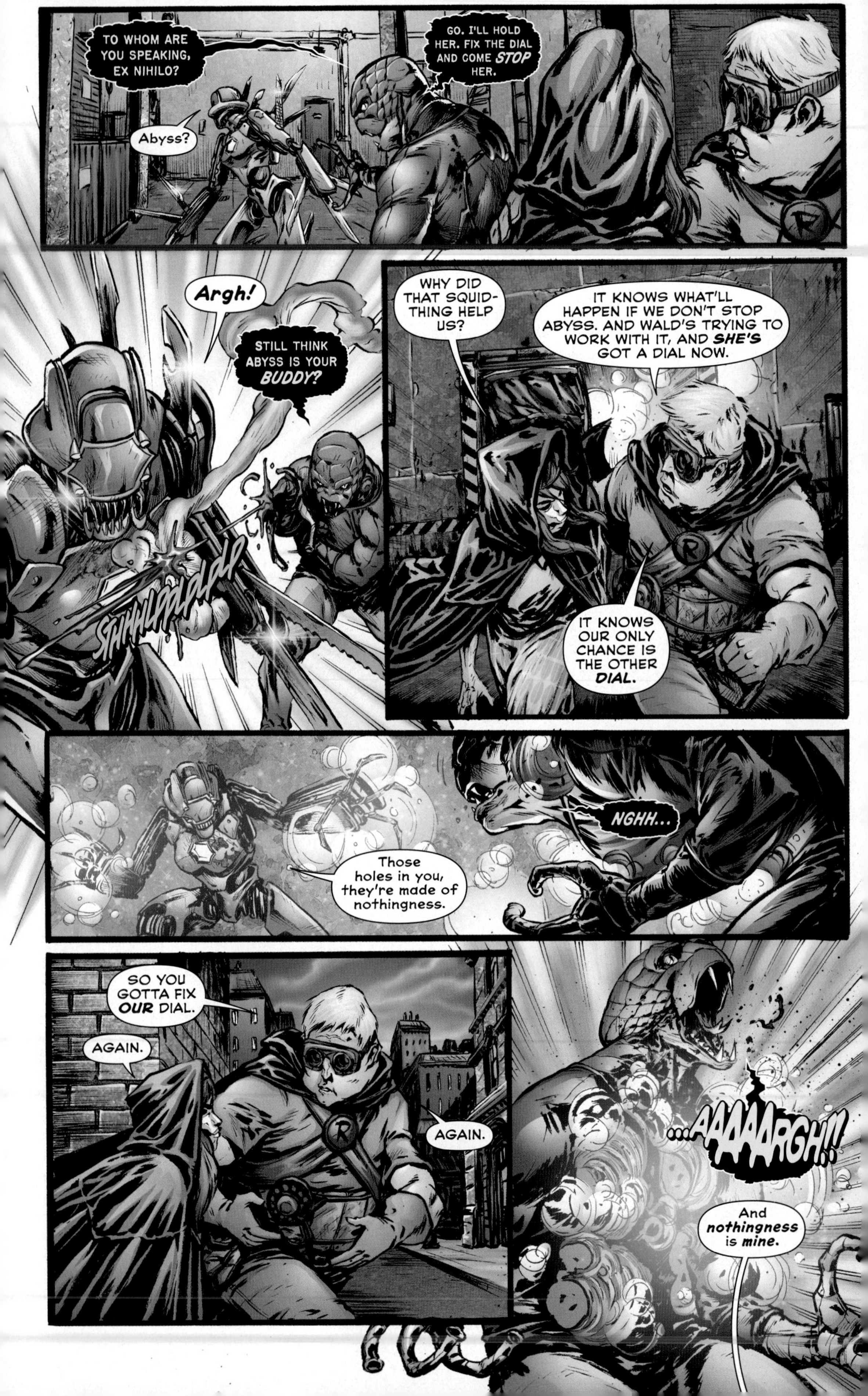
TO WHOM ARE YOU SPEAKING, EX NIHILO?
GO. I'LL HOLD HER. FIX THE DIAL AND COME STOP HER.
Abyss?
Argh!
STILL THINK ABYSS IS YOUR BUDDY?
SHHHLPPLPLPLP
WHY DID THAT SQUID-THING HELP US?
IT KNOWS WHAT'LL HAPPEN IF WE DON'T STOP ABYSS. AND WALD'S TRYING TO WORK WITH IT, AND SHE'S GOT A DIAL NOW.
IT KNOWS OUR ONLY CHANCE IS THE OTHER DIAL.
NGHH...
Those holes in you, they're made of nothingness.
SO YOU GOTTA FIX OUR DIAL.
AGAIN.
AGAIN.
...AAAAARGH!!
And nothingness is mine.

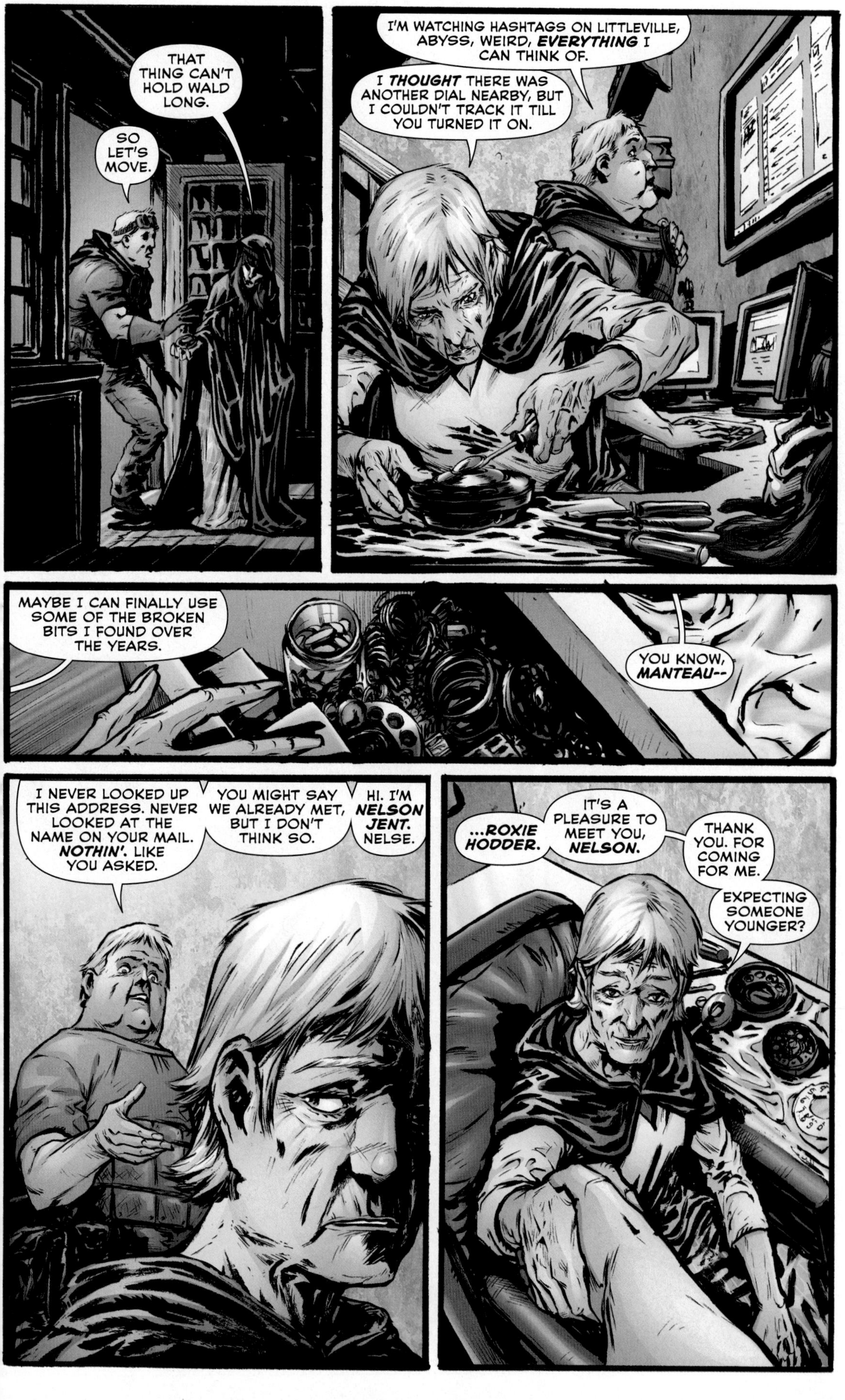

THAT THING CAN'T HOLD WALD LONG.
SO LET'S MOVE.
I'M WATCHING HASHTAGS ON LITTLEVILLE, ABYSS, WEIRD, EVERYTHING I CAN THINK OF.
I THOUGHT THERE WAS ANOTHER DIAL NEARBY, BUT I COULDN'T TRACK IT TILL YOU TURNED IT ON.
MAYBE I CAN FINALLY USE SOME OF THE BROKEN BITS I FOUND OVER THE YEARS.
YOU KNOW, MANTEAU--
I NEVER LOOKED UP THIS ADDRESS. NEVER LOOKED AT THE NAME ON YOUR MAIL. NOTHIN'. LIKE YOU ASKED.
YOU MIGHT SAY WE ALREADY MET, BUT I DON'T THINK SO.
HI. I'M NELSON JENT. NELSE.
...ROXIE HODDER.
IT'S A PLEASURE TO MEET YOU, NELSON.
THANK YOU. FOR COMING FOR ME.
EXPECTING SOMEONE YOUNGER?

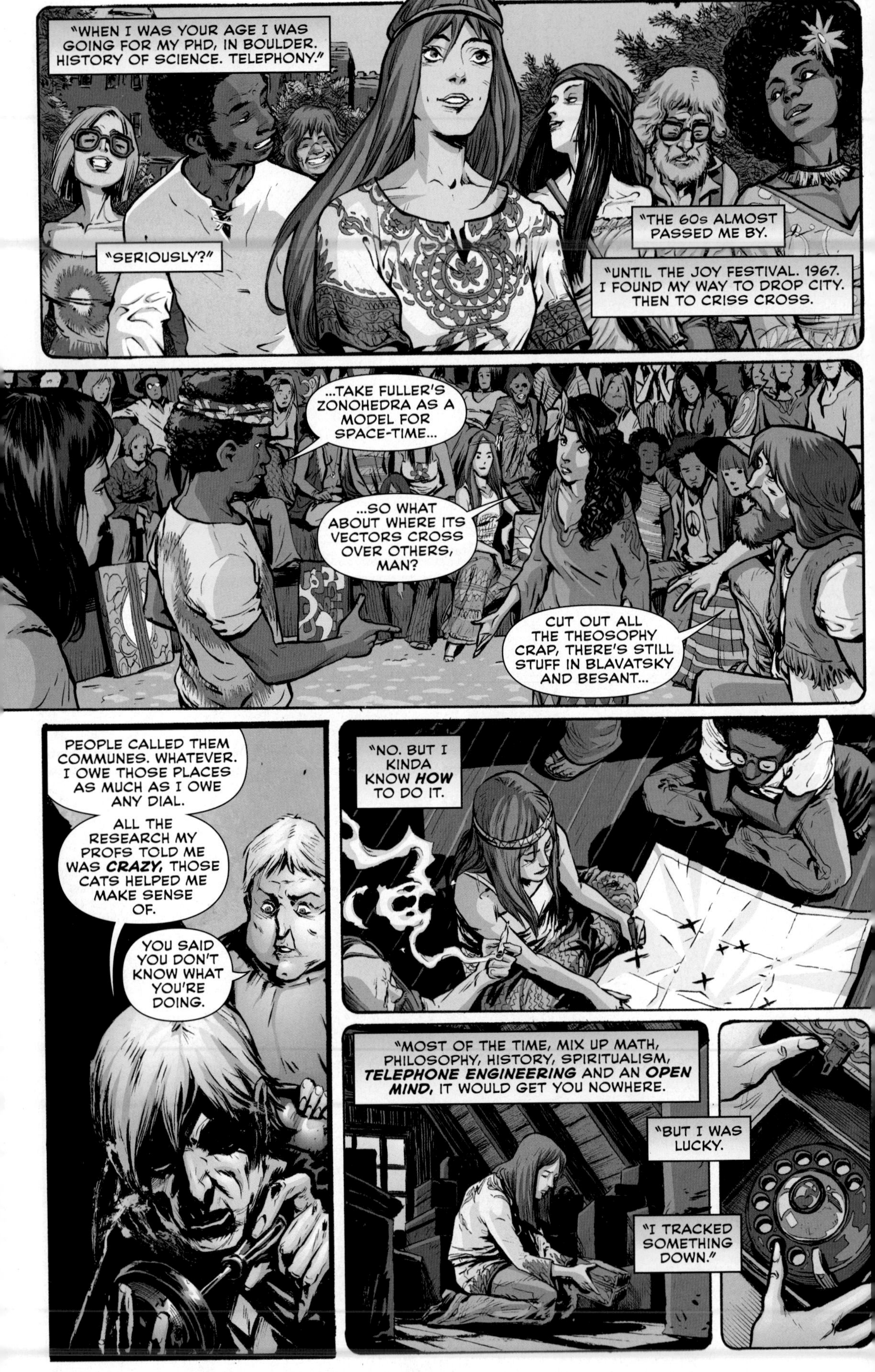

"WHEN I WAS YOUR AGE I WAS GOING FOR MY PHD, IN BOULDER. HISTORY OF SCIENCE. TELEPHONY."
"SERIOUSLY?"
"THE 60s ALMOST PASSED ME BY.
"UNTIL THE JOY FESTIVAL. 1967. I FOUND MY WAY TO DROP CITY. THEN TO CRISS CROSS.
...TAKE FULLER'S ZONOHEDRA AS A MODEL FOR SPACE-TIME...
...SO WHAT ABOUT WHERE ITS VECTORS CROSS OVER OTHERS, MAN?
CUT OUT ALL THE THEOSOPHY CRAP, THERE'S STILL STUFF IN BLAVATSKY AND BESANT...
PEOPLE CALLED THEM COMMUNES. WHATEVER. I OWE THOSE PLACES AS MUCH AS I OWE ANY DIAL.
ALL THE RESEARCH MY PROFS TOLD ME WAS *CRAZY,* THOSE CATS HELPED ME MAKE SENSE OF.
YOU SAID YOU DON'T KNOW WHAT YOU'RE DOING.
"NO. BUT I KINDA KNOW ***HOW*** TO DO IT.
"MOST OF THE TIME, MIX UP MATH, PHILOSOPHY, HISTORY, SPIRITUALISM, ***TELEPHONE ENGINEERING*** AND AN ***OPEN MIND,*** IT WOULD GET YOU NOWHERE.
"BUT I WAS LUCKY.
"I TRACKED SOMETHING DOWN."

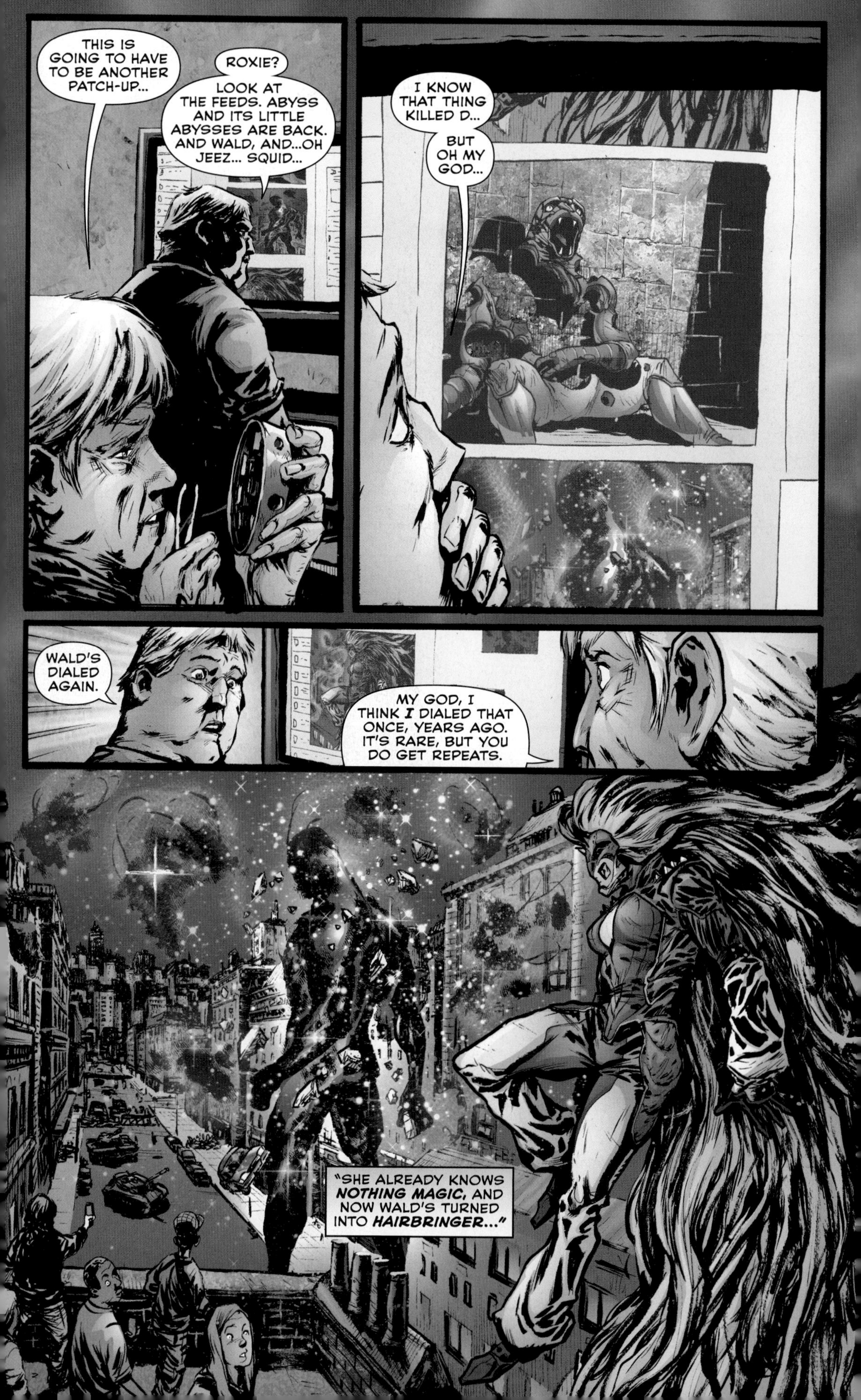
THIS IS GOING TO HAVE TO BE ANOTHER PATCH-UP...
ROXIE?
LOOK AT THE FEEDS. ABYSS AND ITS LITTLE ABYSSES ARE BACK. AND WALD, AND...OH JEEZ... SQUID...
I KNOW THAT THING KILLED D...
BUT OH MY GOD...
WALD'S DIALED AGAIN.
MY GOD, I THINK *I* DIALED THAT ONCE, YEARS AGO. IT'S RARE, BUT YOU DO GET REPEATS.
"SHE ALREADY KNOWS ***NOTHING MAGIC***, AND NOW WALD'S TURNED INTO ***HAIRBRINGER***..."

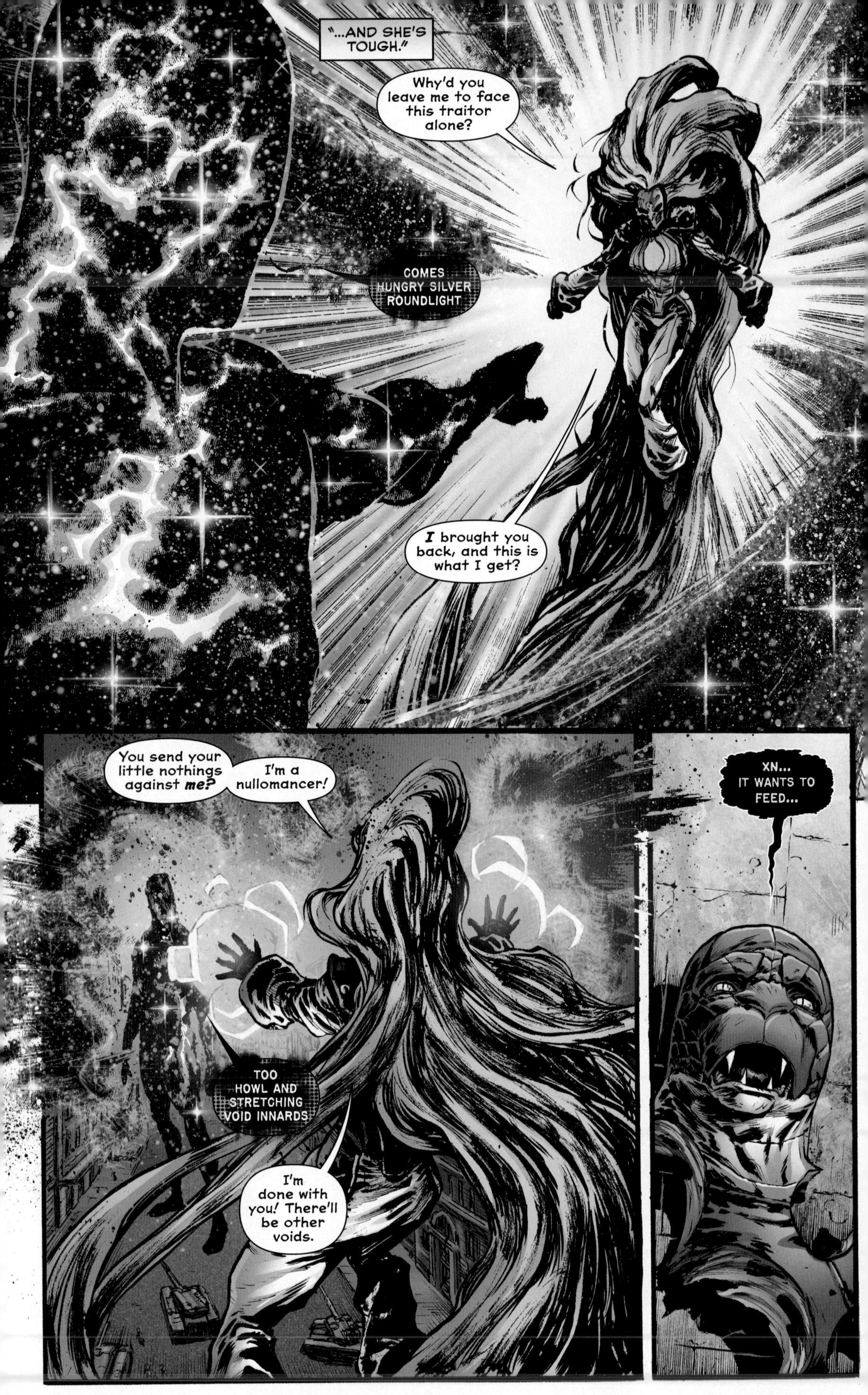
"...AND SHE'S TOUGH."
Why'd you leave me to face this traitor alone?
COMES HUNGRY SILVER ROUNDLIGHT
I brought you back, and this is what I get?
You send your little nothings against me?
I'm a nullomancer!
TOO HOWL AND STRETCHING VOID INNARDS
I'm done with you! There'll be other voids.
XN... IT WANTS TO FEED...

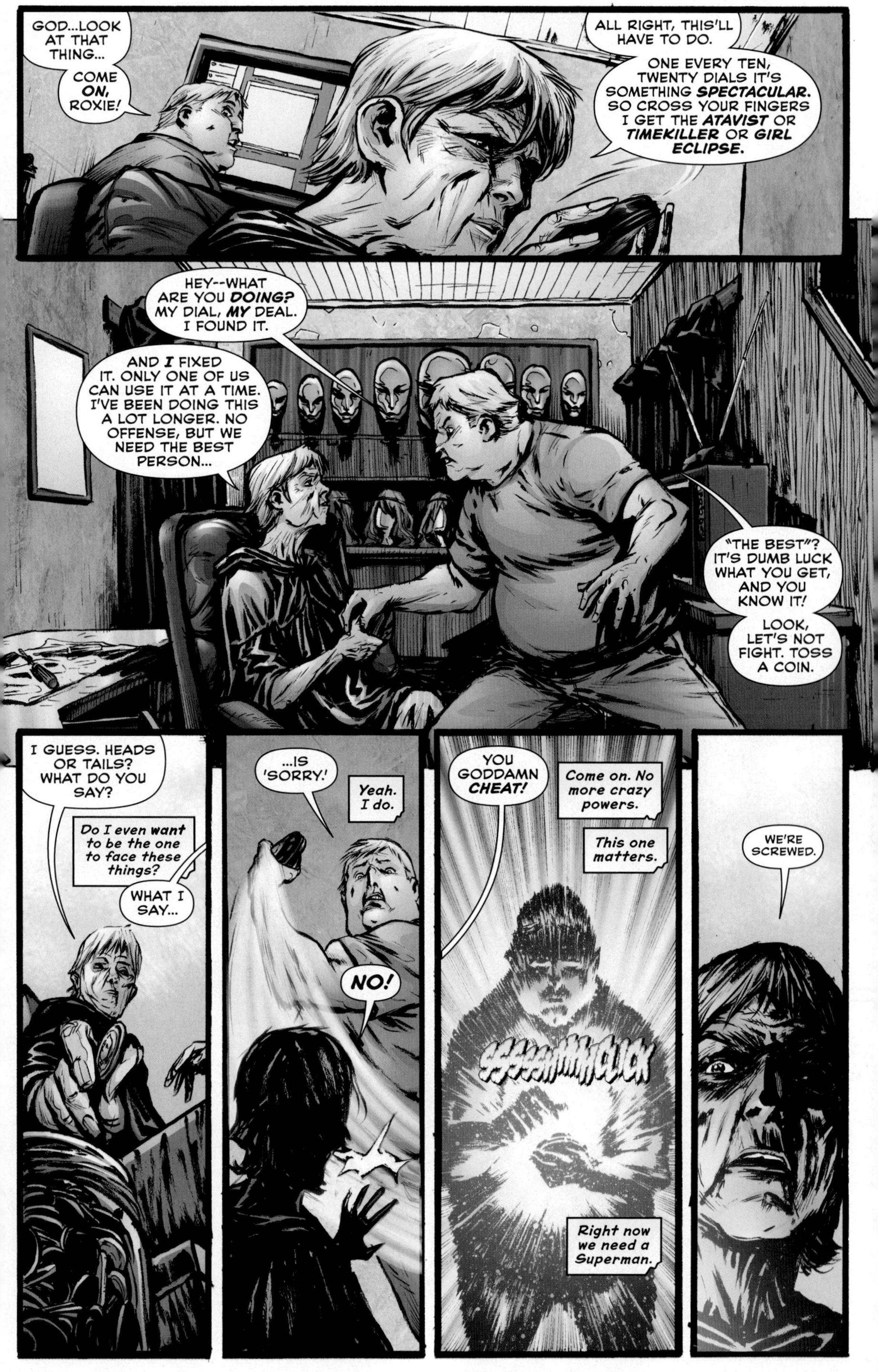
GOD...LOOK AT THAT THING...
COME ON, ROXIE!
ALL RIGHT, THIS'LL HAVE TO DO.
ONE EVERY TEN, TWENTY DIALS IT'S SOMETHING SPECTACULAR. SO CROSS YOUR FINGERS I GET THE ATAVIST OR TIMEKILLER OR GIRL ECLIPSE.
HEY--WHAT ARE YOU DOING? MY DIAL, MY DEAL. I FOUND IT.
AND I FIXED IT. ONLY ONE OF US CAN USE IT AT A TIME. I'VE BEEN DOING THIS A LOT LONGER. NO OFFENSE, BUT WE NEED THE BEST PERSON...
"THE BEST"? IT'S DUMB LUCK WHAT YOU GET, AND YOU KNOW IT!
LOOK, LET'S NOT FIGHT. TOSS A COIN.
I GUESS. HEADS OR TAILS? WHAT DO YOU SAY?
Do I even want to be the one to face these things?
WHAT I SAY...
...IS 'SORRY.'
Yeah. I do.
NO!
YOU GODDAMN CHEAT!
Come on. No more crazy powers.
This one matters.
SSSSSHHHHCLICK
Right now we need a Superman.
WE'RE SCREWED.

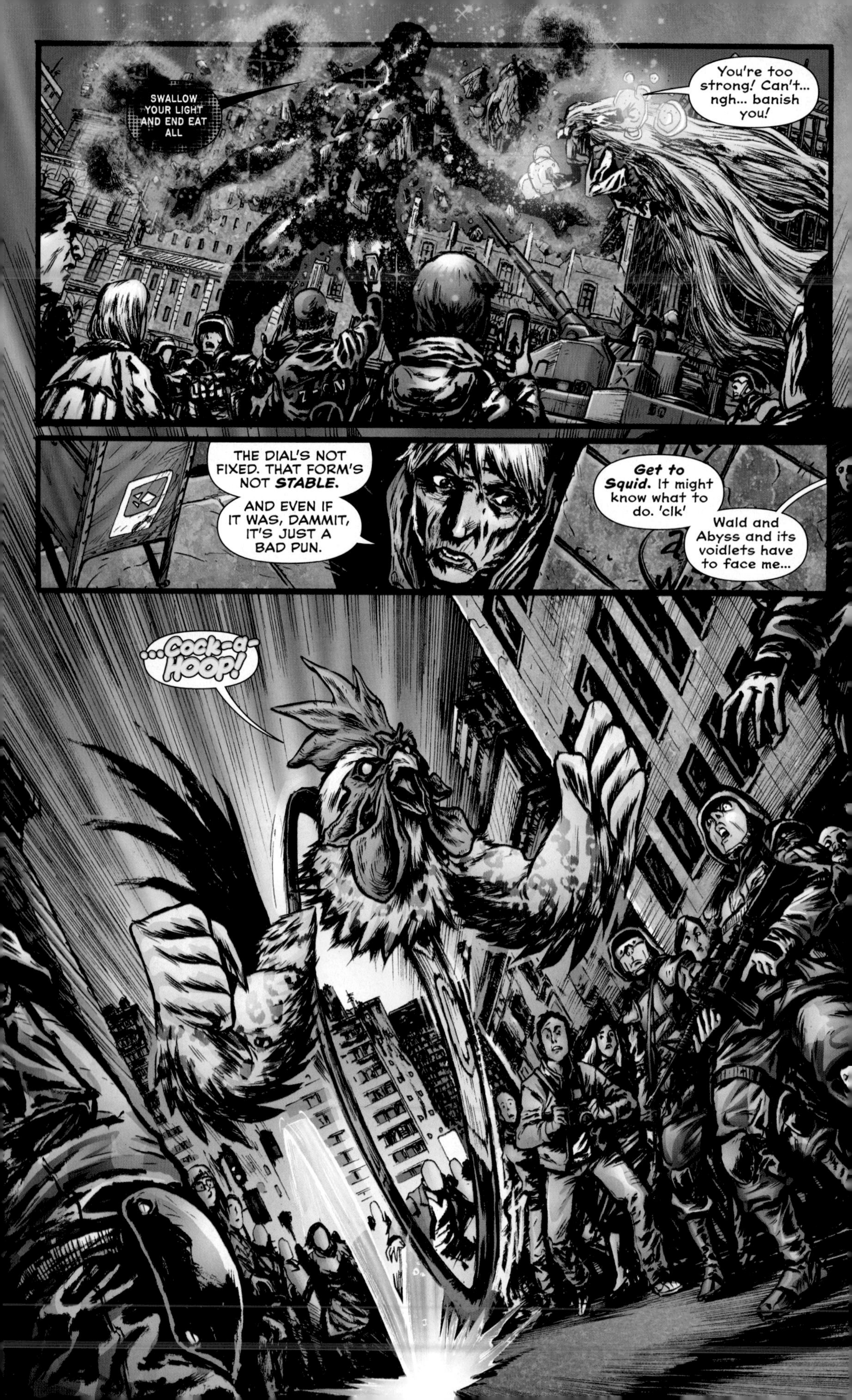
SWALLOW YOUR LIGHT AND END EAT ALL
You're too strong! Can't... ngh... banish you!
THE DIAL'S NOT FIXED. THAT FORM'S NOT *STABLE.*
AND EVEN IF IT WAS, DAMMIT, IT'S JUST A BAD PUN.
Get to Squid. It might know what to do. 'clk'
Wald and Abyss and its voidlets have to face me...
...Cock-a-HOOP!

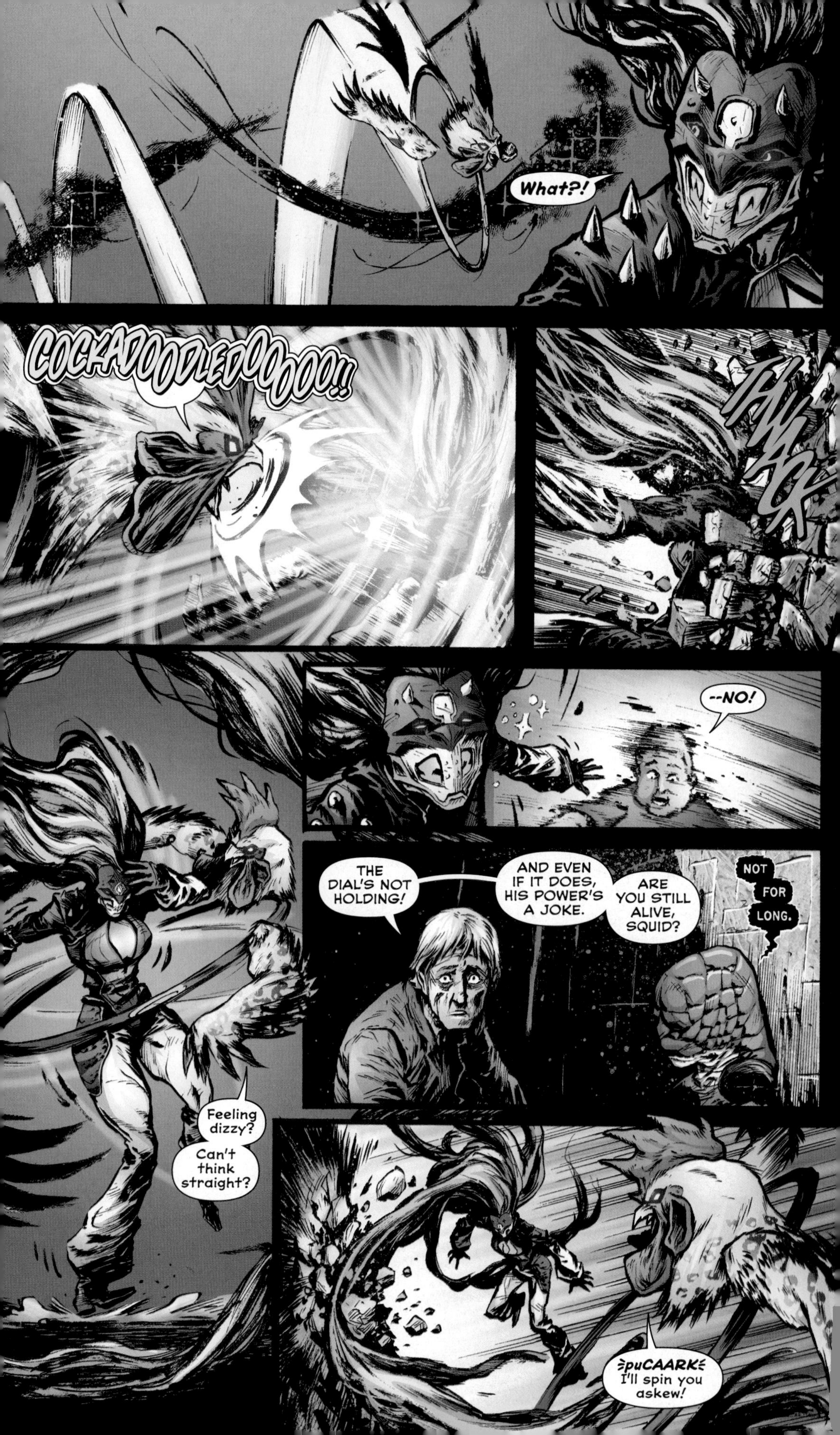
What?!
COCKADOOODLEDOOOOOOO!!
THWACK
--NO!
Feeling dizzy?
Can't think straight?
THE DIAL'S NOT HOLDING!
AND EVEN IF IT DOES, HIS POWER'S A JOKE.
ARE YOU STILL ALIVE, SQUID?
NOT FOR LONG.
puCAARK
I'll spin you askew!

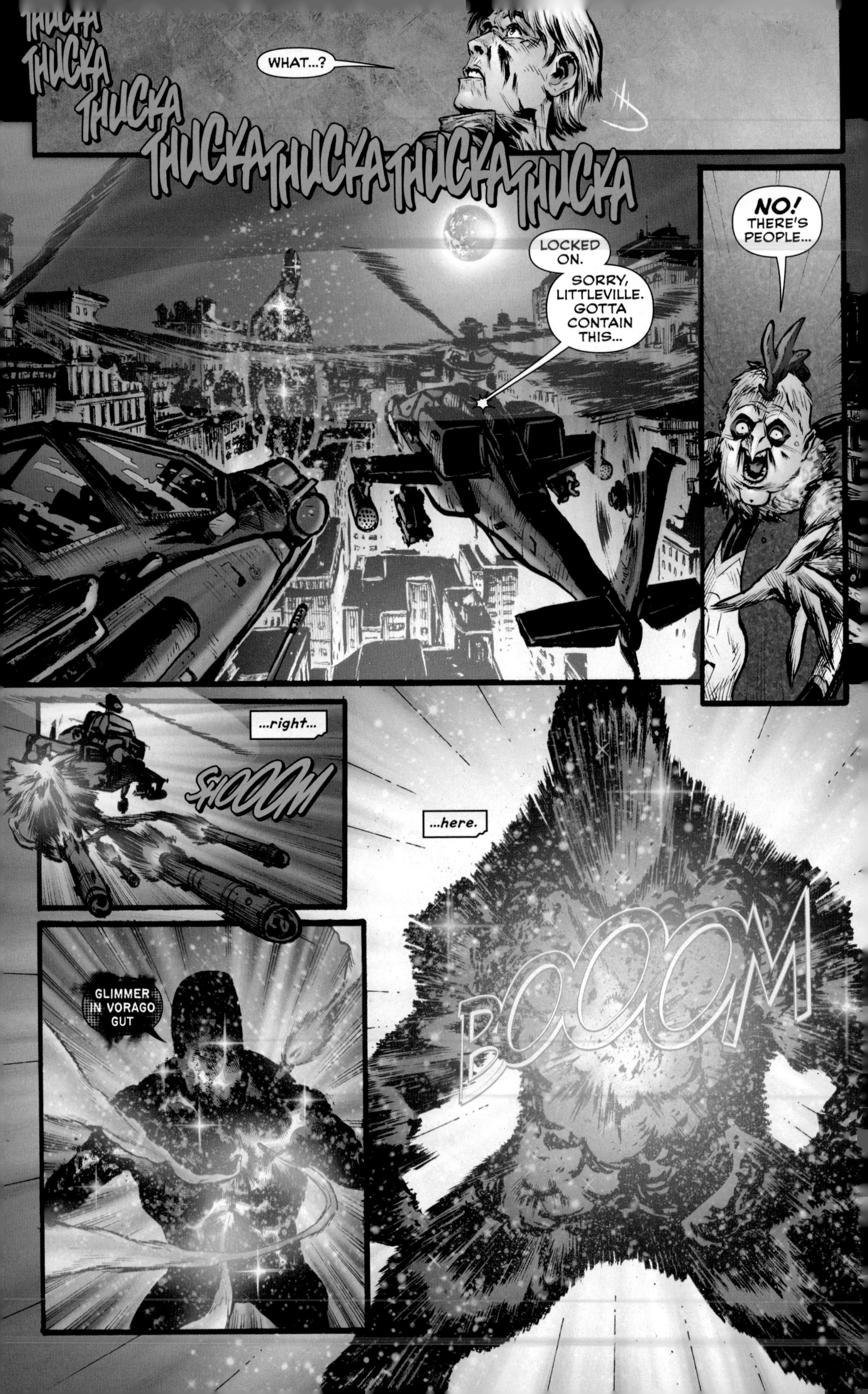
THUCKA
THUCKA
THUCKA
WHAT...?
THUCKA THUCKA THUCKA THUCKA
LOCKED ON.
SORRY, LITTLEVILLE. GOTTA CONTAIN THIS...
NO! THERE'S PEOPLE...
...right...?
SHOOOM
...here.
GLIMMER IN VORAGO GUT
BOOOOM

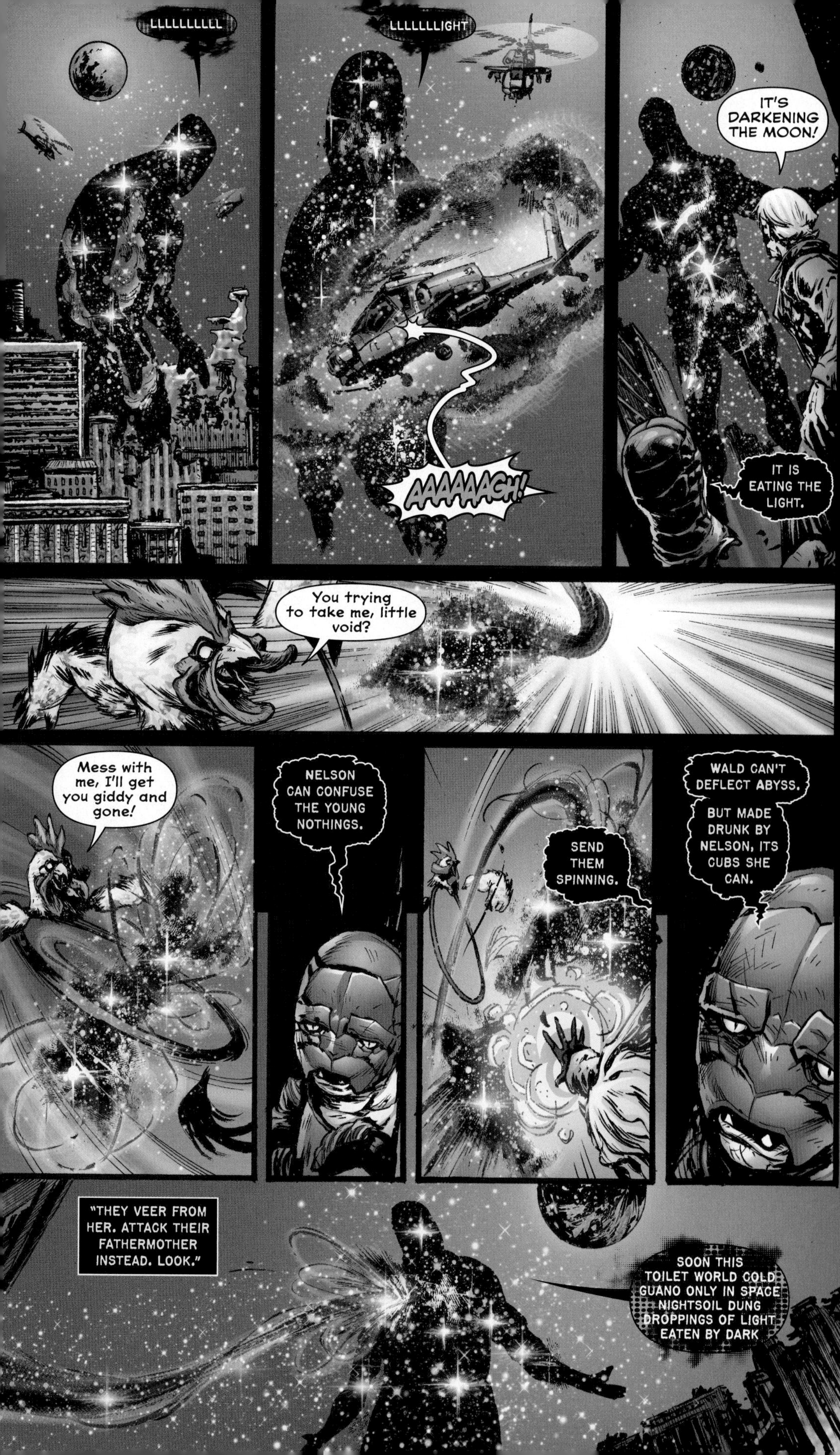
LLLLLLLLLL
LLLLLLLIGHT
AAAAAAGH!
IT'S DARKENING THE MOON!
IT IS EATING THE LIGHT.
You trying to take me, little void?
Mess with me, I'll get you giddy and gone!
NELSON CAN CONFUSE THE YOUNG NOTHINGS.
SEND THEM SPINNING.
WALD CAN'T DEFLECT ABYSS.
BUT MADE DRUNK BY NELSON, ITS CUBS SHE CAN.
"THEY VEER FROM HER. ATTACK THEIR FATHERMOTHER INSTEAD. LOOK."
SOON THIS TOILET WORLD COLD GUANO ONLY IN SPACE NIGHTSOIL DUNG DROPPINGS OF LIGHT EATEN BY DARK

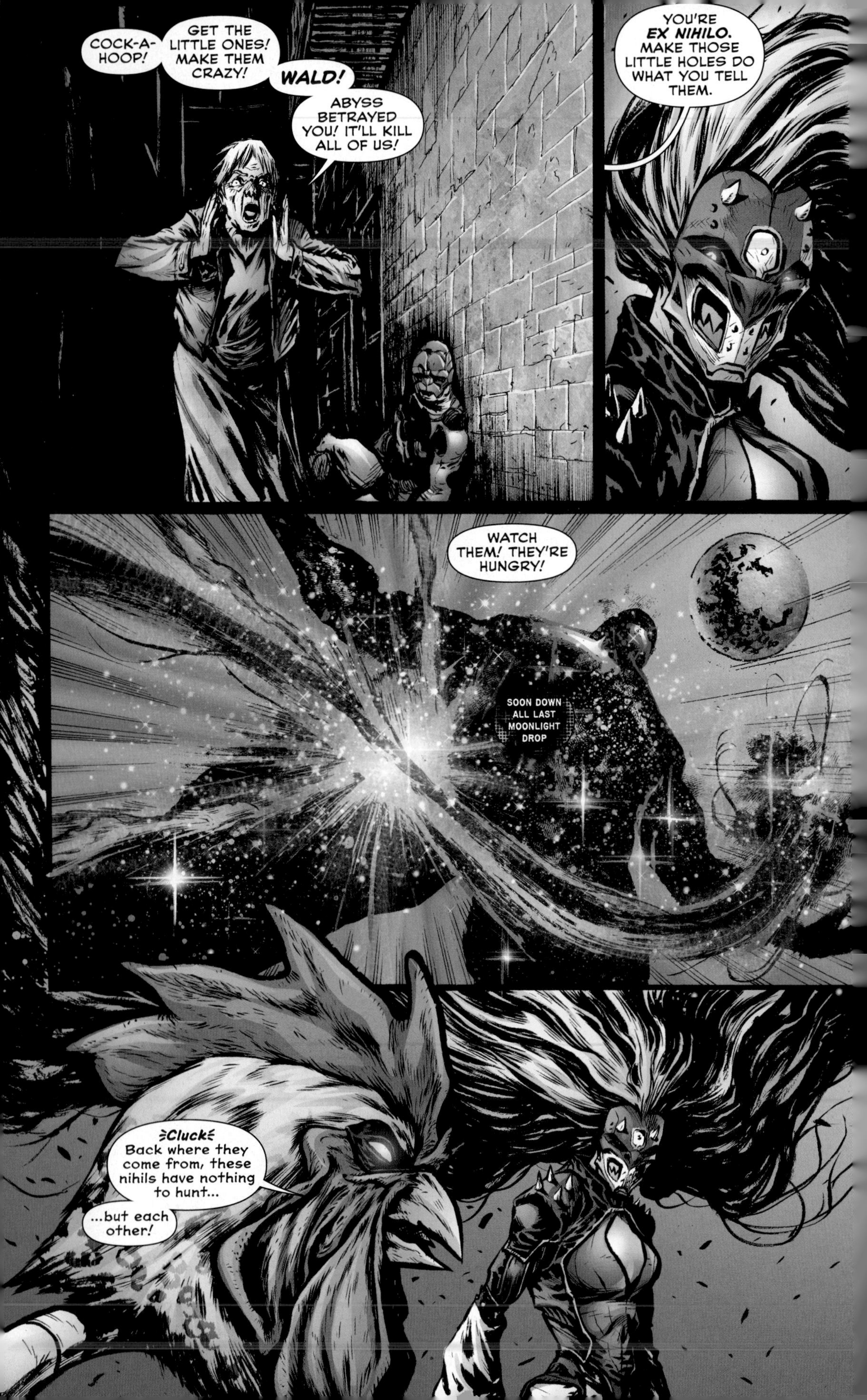
COCK-A-HOOP!
GET THE LITTLE ONES! MAKE THEM CRAZY!
WALD!
ABYSS BETRAYED YOU! IT'LL KILL ALL OF US!
YOU'RE EX NIHILO. MAKE THOSE LITTLE HOLES DO WHAT YOU TELL THEM.
WATCH THEM! THEY'RE HUNGRY!
SOON DOWN ALL LAST MOONLIGHT DROP
Cluck
Back where they come from, these nihils have nothing to hunt...
...but each other!

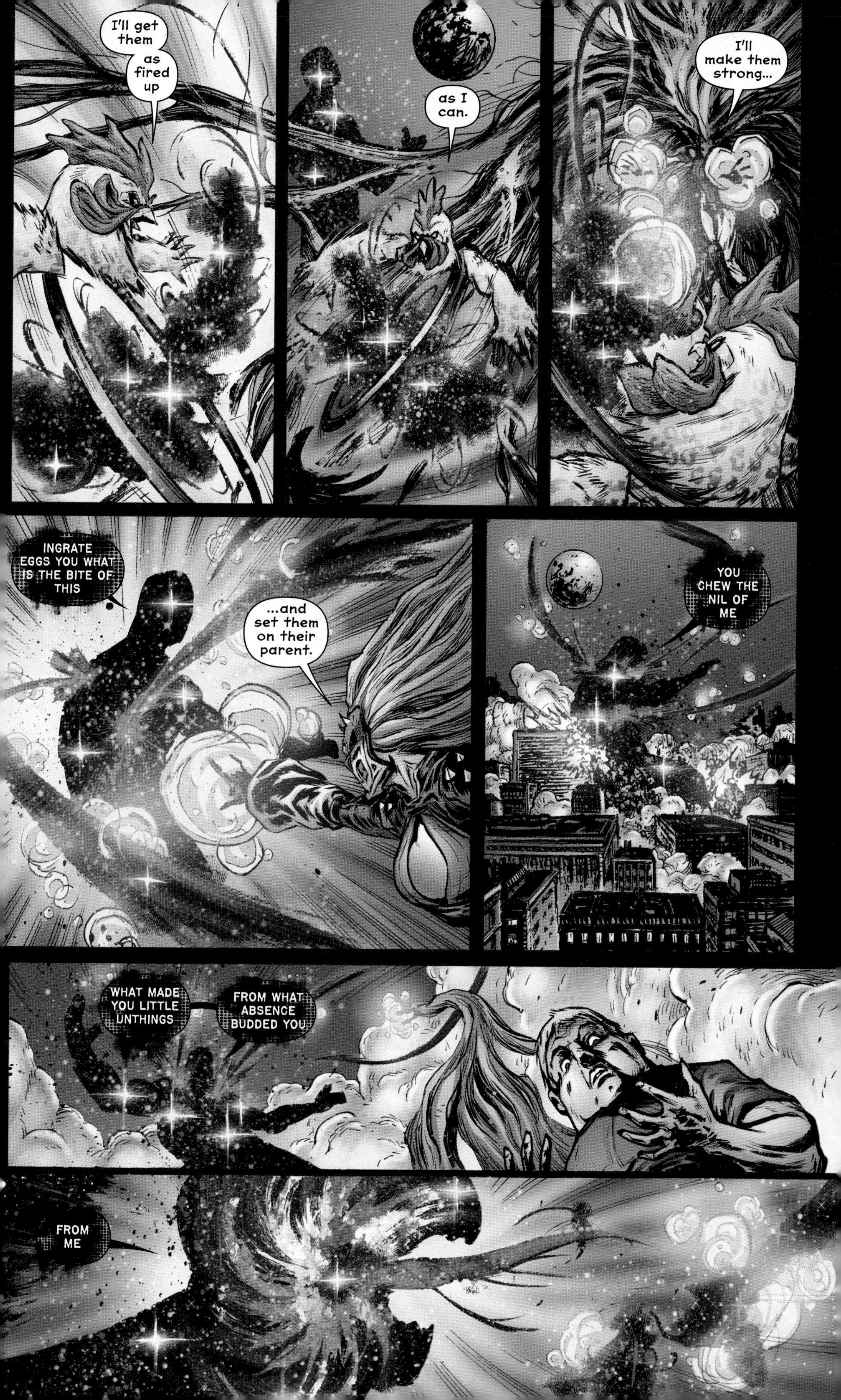
I'll get them
as fired up
as I can.
I'll make them strong...
INGRATE EGGS YOU WHAT IS THE BITE OF THIS
...and set them on their parent.
YOU CHEW THE NIL OF ME
WHAT MADE YOU LITTLE UNTHINGS
FROM WHAT ABSENCE BUDDED YOU
FROM ME

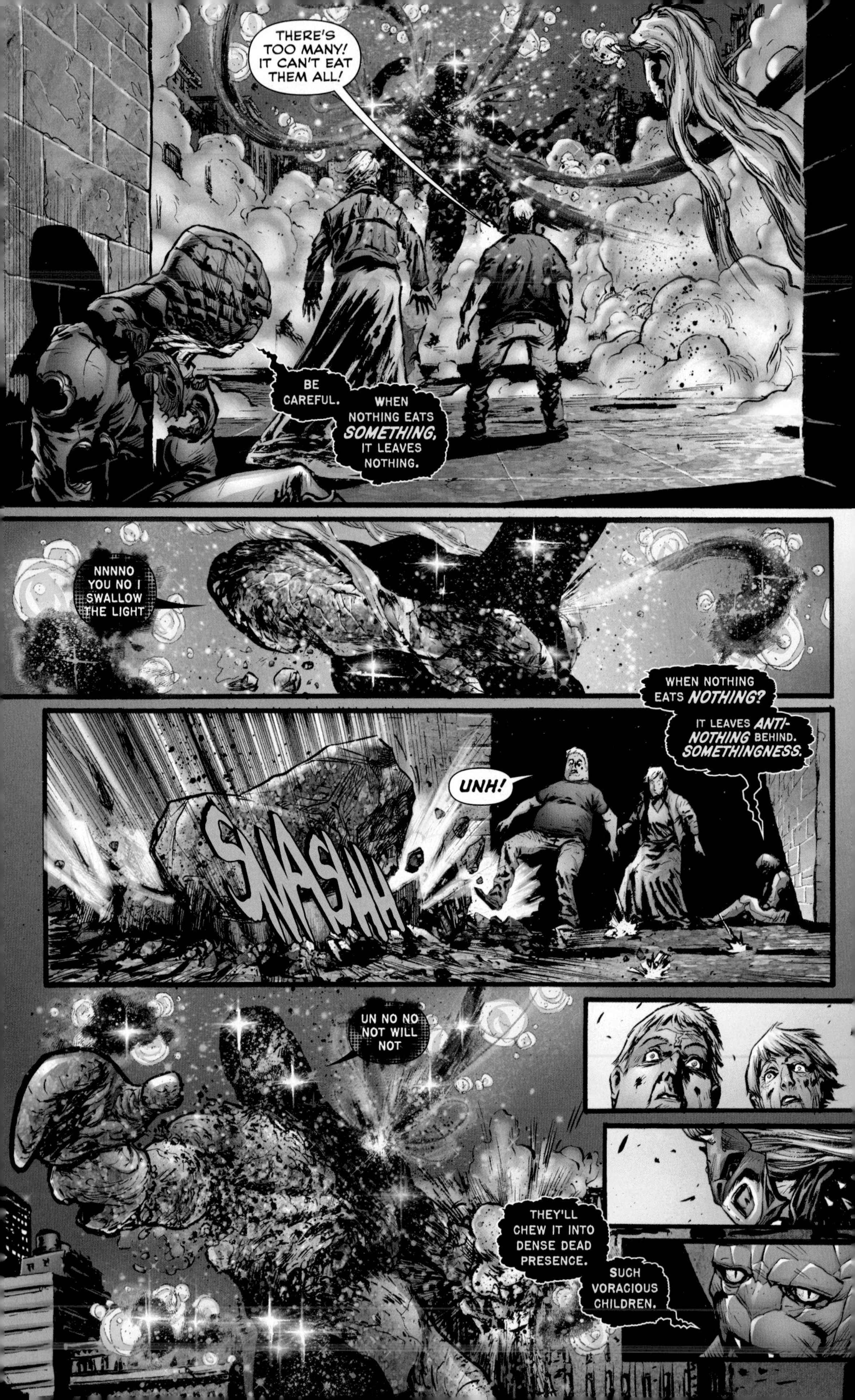

THERE'S TOO MANY! IT CAN'T EAT THEM ALL!
BE CAREFUL.
WHEN NOTHING EATS SOMETHING, IT LEAVES NOTHING.
NNNNO YOU NO I SWALLOW THE LIGHT
WHEN NOTHING EATS NOTHING?
IT LEAVES ANTI-NOTHING BEHIND. SOMETHINGNESS.
UNH!
SMASHHH
UN NO NO NOT WILL NOT
THEY'LL CHEW IT INTO DENSE DEAD PRESENCE.
SUCH VORACIOUS CHILDREN.

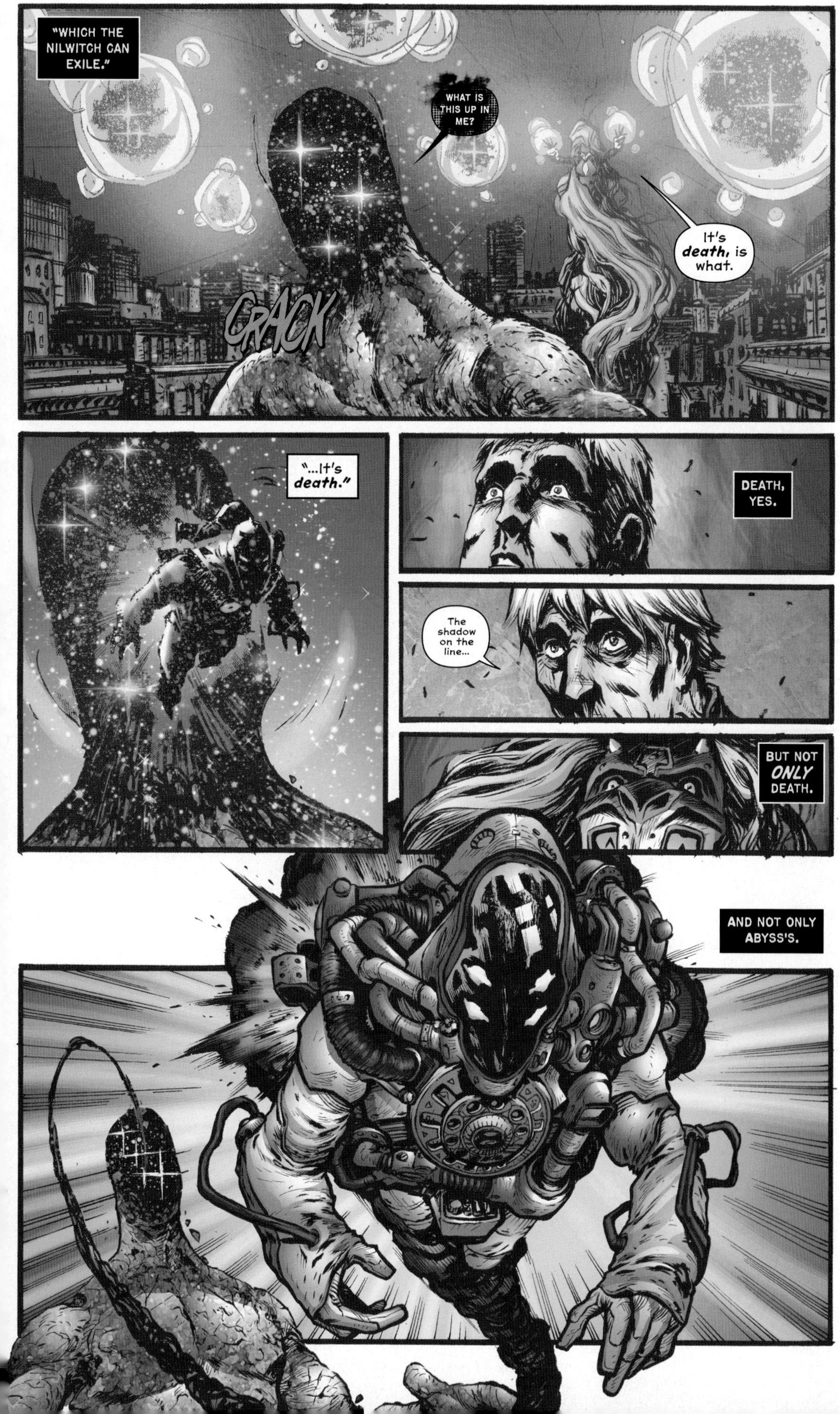
"WHICH THE NILWITCH CAN EXILE."
WHAT IS THIS UP IN ME?
It's death, is what.
CRACK
"...It's death."
DEATH, YES.
The shadow on the line...
BUT NOT ONLY DEATH.
AND NOT ONLY ABYSS'S.

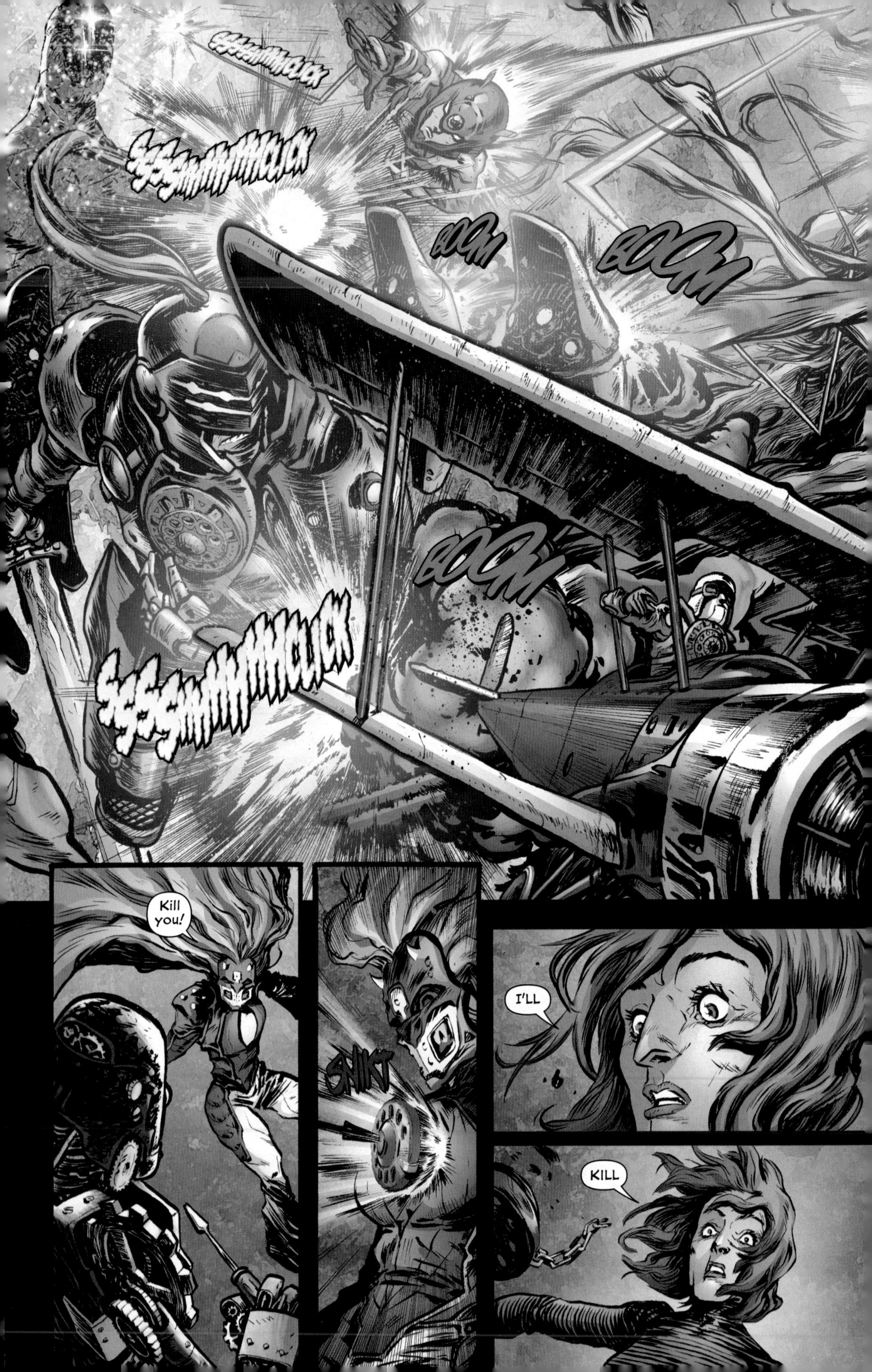
SSSSHHHHHCLICK
SSSSHHHHHCLICK
BOOM
BOOM
BOOM
SSSSHHHHHCLICK
Kill you!
SNIKT
I'LL
KILL

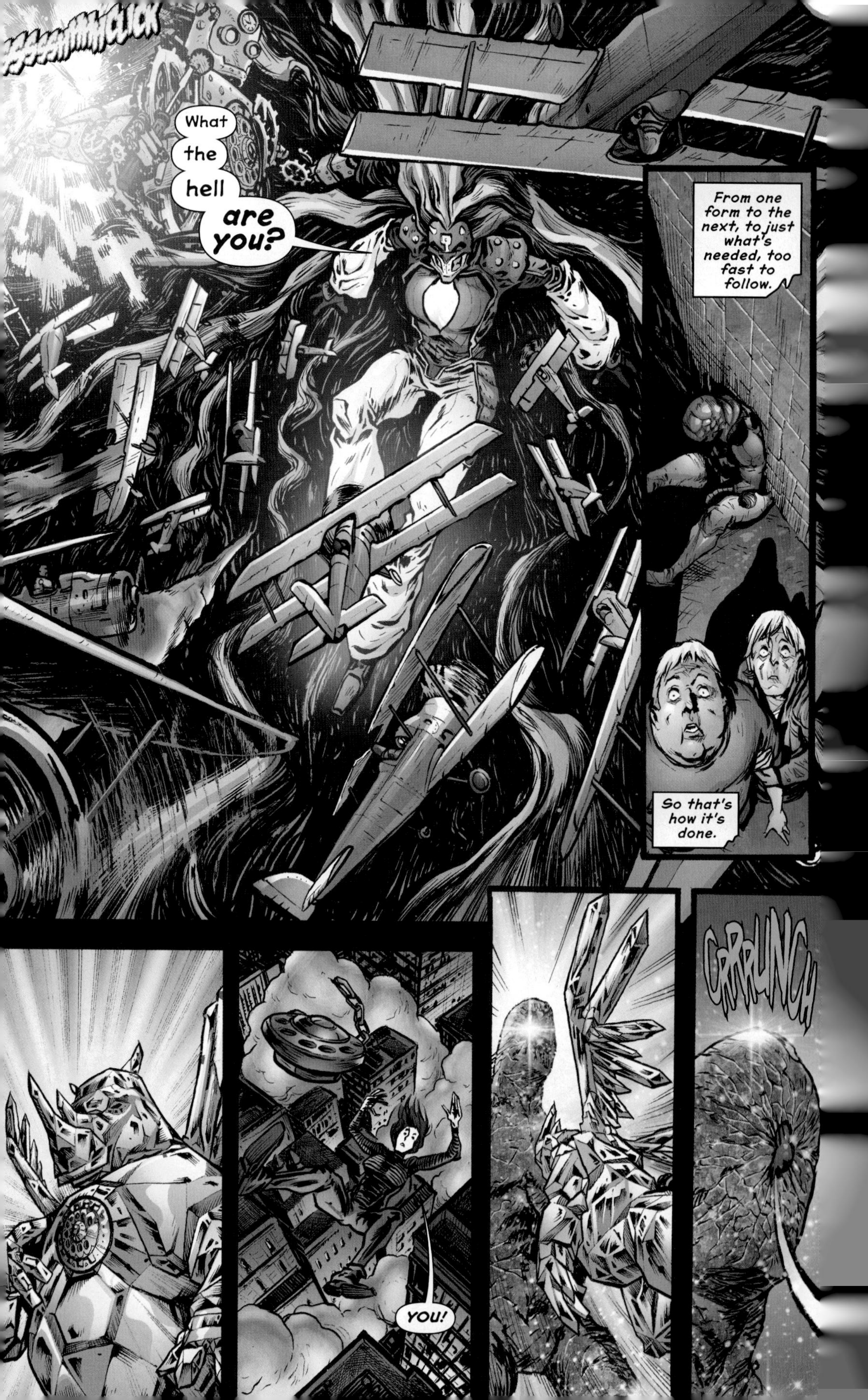
What the hell are you?
From one form to the next, to just what's needed, too fast to follow.
So that's how it's done.
YOU!
CRRRUNCH

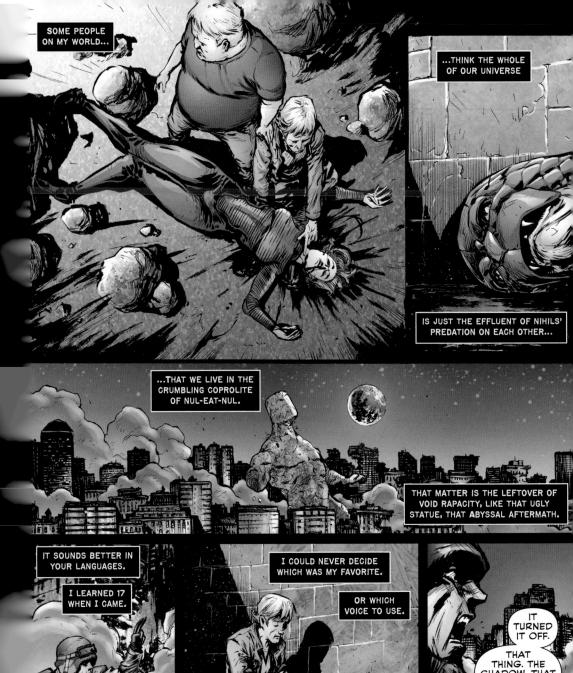

SOME PEOPLE ON MY WORLD...

...THINK THE WHOLE OF OUR UNIVERSE

IS JUST THE EFFLUENT OF NIHILS' PREDATION ON EACH OTHER...

...THAT WE LIVE IN THE CRUMBLING COPROLITE OF NUL-EAT-NUL.

THAT MATTER IS THE LEFTOVER OF VOID RAPACITY, LIKE THAT UGLY STATUE, THAT ABYSSAL AFTERMATH.

IT SOUNDS BETTER IN YOUR LANGUAGES.

I LEARNED 17 WHEN I CAME.

I COULD NEVER DECIDE WHICH WAS MY FAVORITE.

OR WHICH VOICE TO USE.

IT TURNED IT OFF.

THAT THING. THE SHADOW. THAT CAME OUT OF ABYSS.

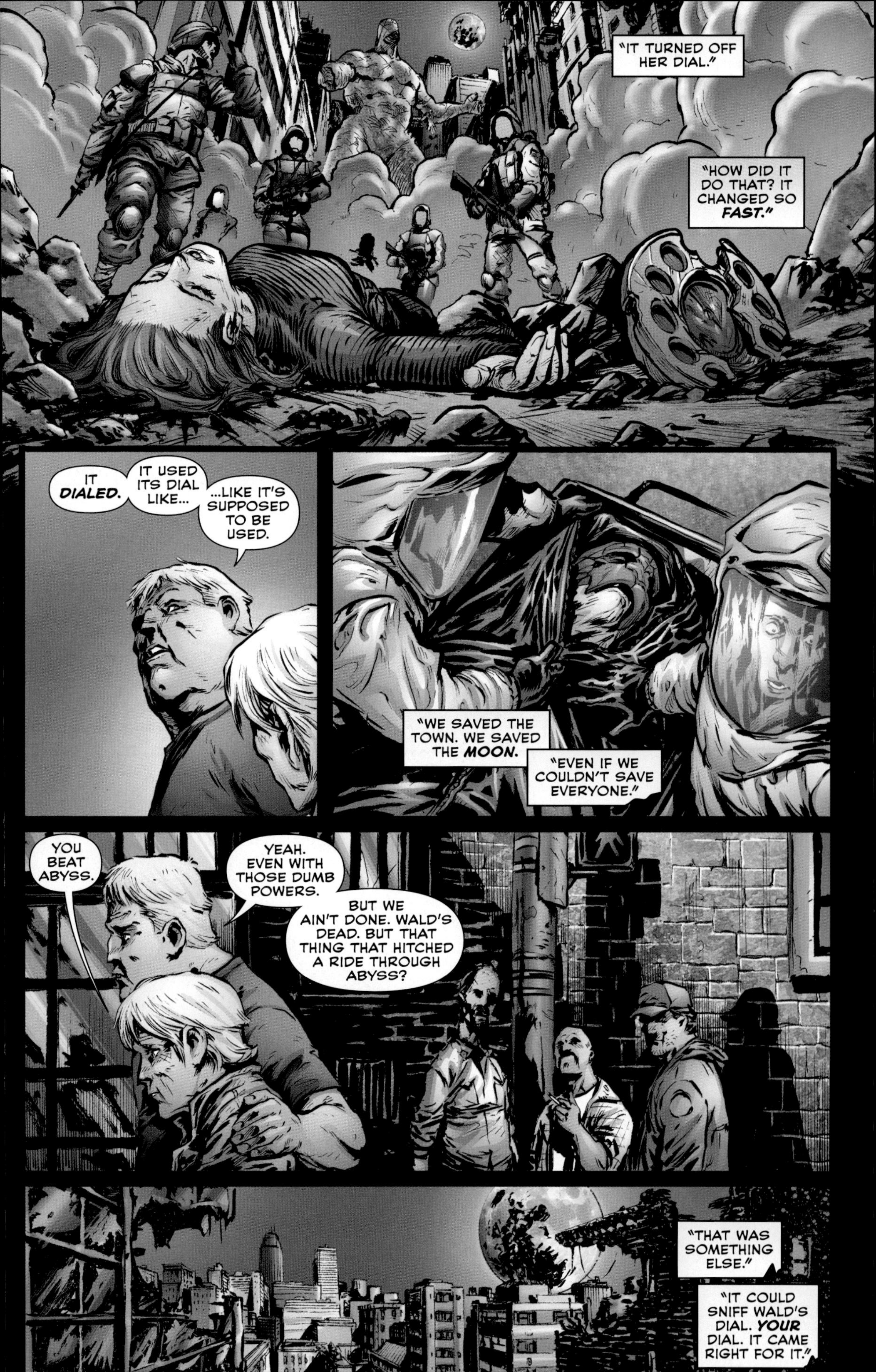
"IT TURNED OFF HER DIAL."
"HOW DID IT DO THAT? IT CHANGED SO **FAST.**"
IT ***DIALED.***
IT USED ITS DIAL LIKE...
...LIKE IT'S SUPPOSED TO BE USED.
"WE SAVED THE TOWN. WE SAVED THE ***MOON.***
"EVEN IF WE COULDN'T SAVE EVERYONE."
YOU BEAT ABYSS.
YEAH. EVEN WITH THOSE DUMB POWERS.
BUT WE AIN'T DONE. WALD'S DEAD. BUT THAT THING THAT HITCHED A RIDE THROUGH ABYSS?
"THAT WAS SOMETHING ELSE."
"IT COULD SNIFF WALD'S DIAL. ***YOUR*** DIAL. IT CAME RIGHT FOR IT."

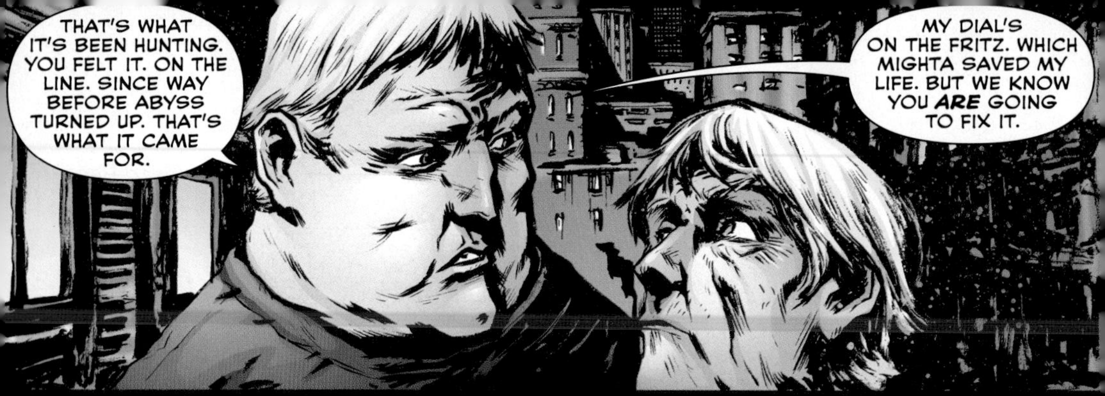
THAT'S WHAT IT'S BEEN HUNTING. YOU FELT IT. ON THE LINE. SINCE WAY BEFORE ABYSS TURNED UP. THAT'S WHAT IT CAME FOR.
MY DIAL'S ON THE FRITZ. WHICH MIGHTA SAVED MY LIFE. BUT WE KNOW YOU **ARE** GOING TO FIX IT.

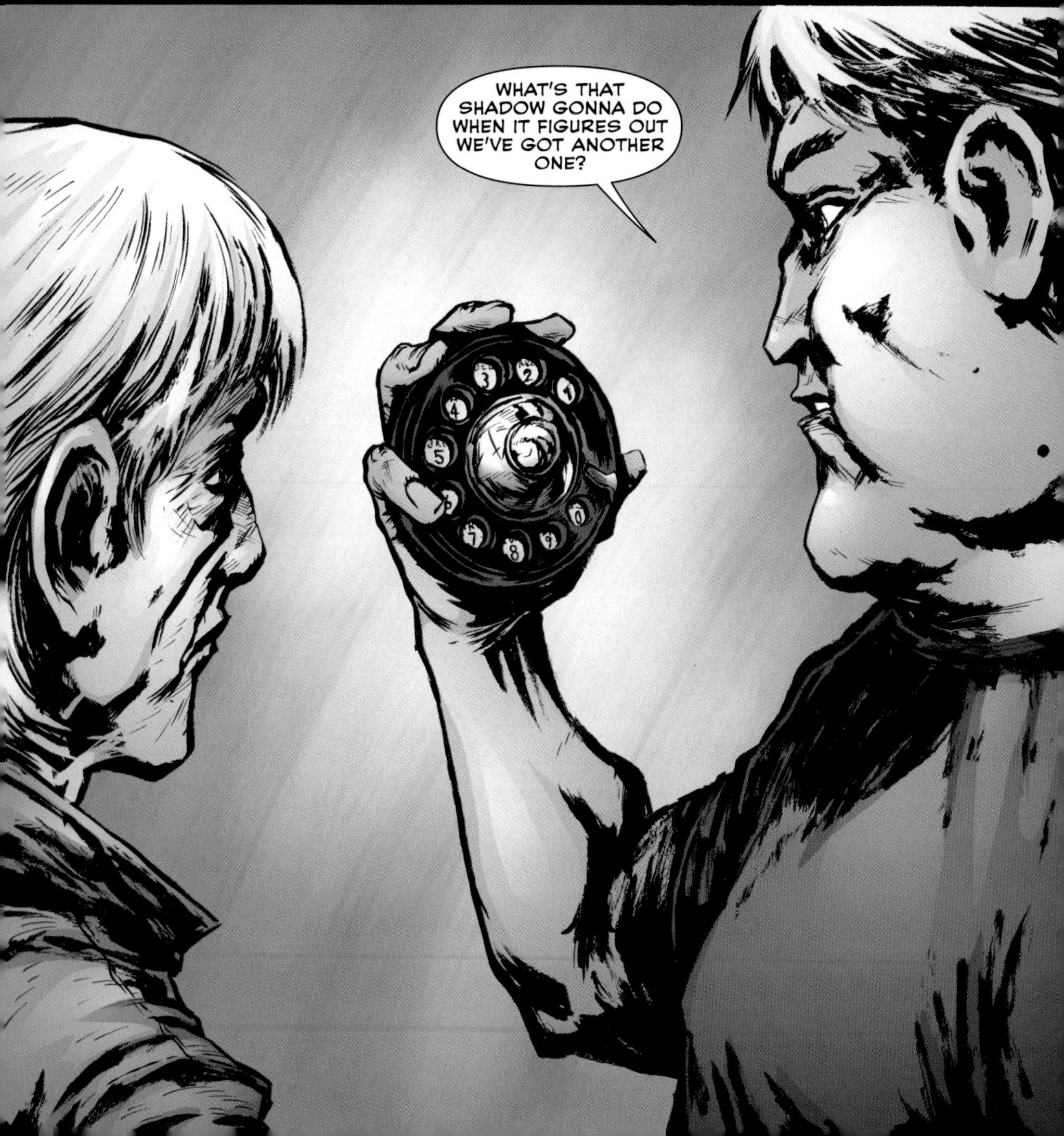
WHAT'S THAT SHADOW GONNA DO WHEN IT FIGURES OUT WE'VE GOT ANOTHER ONE?

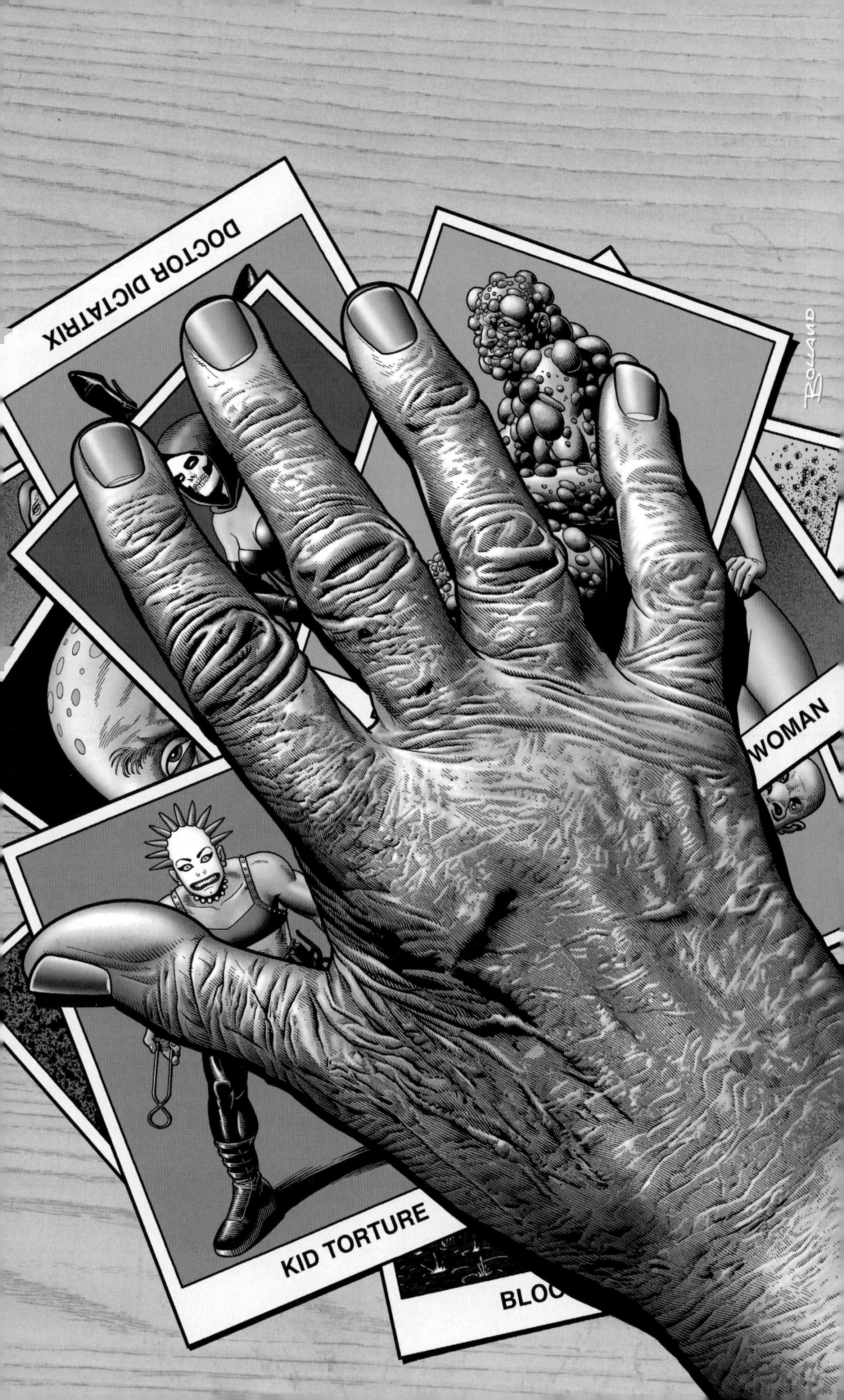
DOCTOR DICTATRIX
BOLLAND
WOMAN
KID TORTURE
BLOO

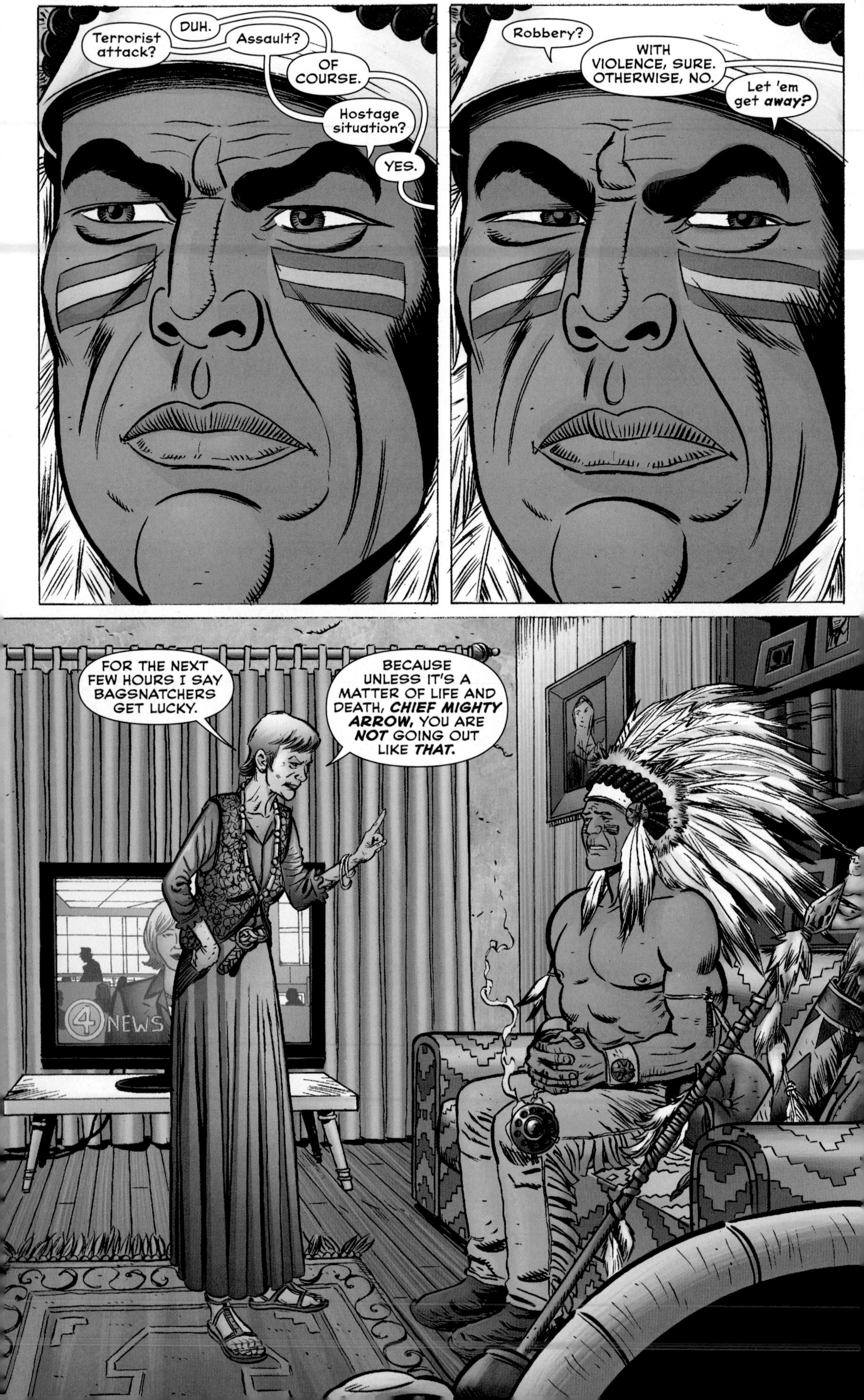

Terrorist attack?
DUH.
Assault?
OF COURSE.
Hostage situation?
YES.
Robbery?
WITH VIOLENCE, SURE. OTHERWISE, NO.
Let 'em get *away?*
FOR THE NEXT FEW HOURS I SAY BAGSNATCHERS GET LUCKY.
BECAUSE UNLESS IT'S A MATTER OF LIFE AND DEATH, ***CHIEF MIGHTY ARROW,*** YOU ARE ***NOT*** GOING OUT LIKE ***THAT.***
4 NEWS

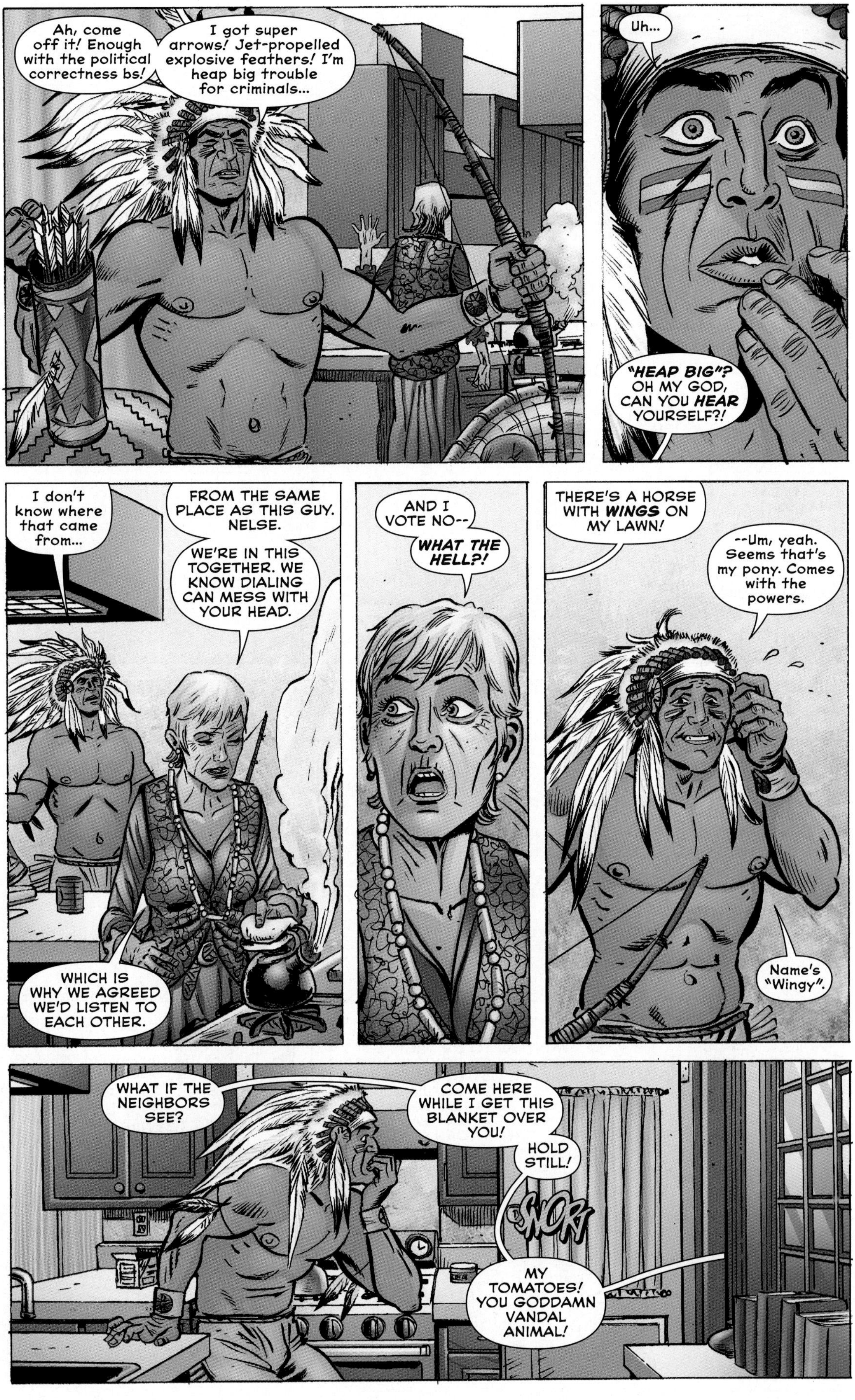
Ah, come off it! Enough with the political correctness bs!
I got super arrows! Jet-propelled explosive feathers! I'm heap big trouble for criminals...
Uh...
"HEAP BIG"? OH MY GOD, CAN YOU HEAR YOURSELF?!
I don't know where that came from...
FROM THE SAME PLACE AS THIS GUY. NELSE.
WE'RE IN THIS TOGETHER. WE KNOW DIALING CAN MESS WITH YOUR HEAD.
WHICH IS WHY WE AGREED WE'D LISTEN TO EACH OTHER.
AND I VOTE NO--
WHAT THE HELL?!
THERE'S A HORSE WITH WINGS ON MY LAWN!
--Um, yeah. Seems that's my pony. Comes with the powers.
Name's "Wingy".
WHAT IF THE NEIGHBORS SEE?
COME HERE WHILE I GET THIS BLANKET OVER YOU!
HOLD STILL!
SNORT
MY TOMATOES! YOU GODDAMN VANDAL ANIMAL!

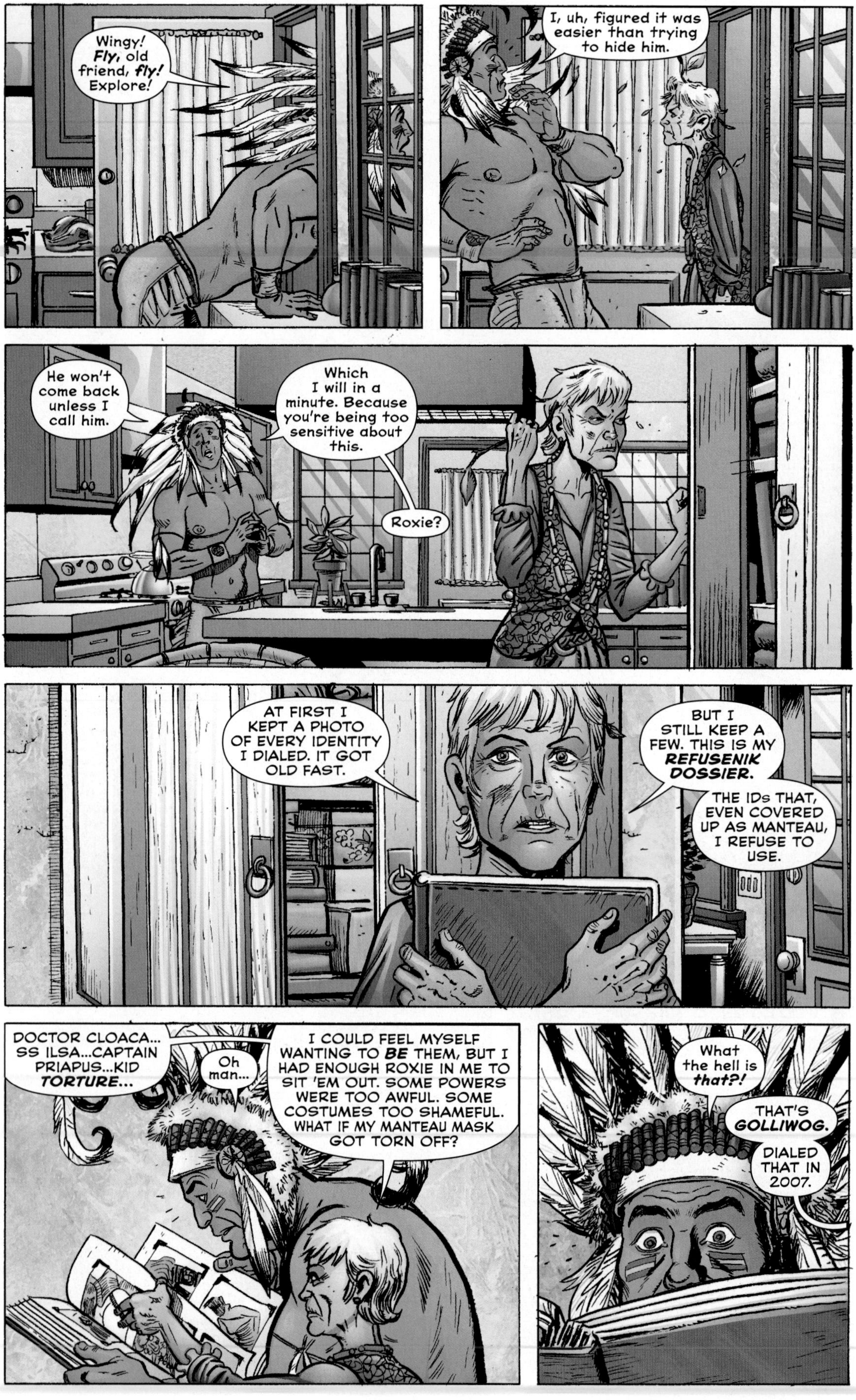
Wingy! *Fly*, old friend, *fly!* Explore!
I, uh, figured it was easier than trying to hide him.
He won't come back unless I call him.
Which I will in a minute. Because you're being too sensitive about this.
Roxie?
AT FIRST I KEPT A PHOTO OF EVERY IDENTITY I DIALED. IT GOT OLD FAST.
BUT I STILL KEEP A FEW. THIS IS MY ***REFUSENIK DOSSIER.***
THE IDs THAT, EVEN COVERED UP AS MANTEAU, I REFUSE TO USE.
DOCTOR CLOACA... SS ILSA...CAPTAIN PRIAPUS...KID ***TORTURE...***
Oh man...
I COULD FEEL MYSELF WANTING TO ***BE*** THEM, BUT I HAD ENOUGH ROXIE IN ME TO SIT 'EM OUT. SOME POWERS WERE TOO AWFUL. SOME COSTUMES TOO SHAMEFUL. WHAT IF MY MANTEAU MASK GOT TORN OFF?
What the hell is *that?!*
THAT'S ***GOLLIWOG.***
DIALED THAT IN 2007.

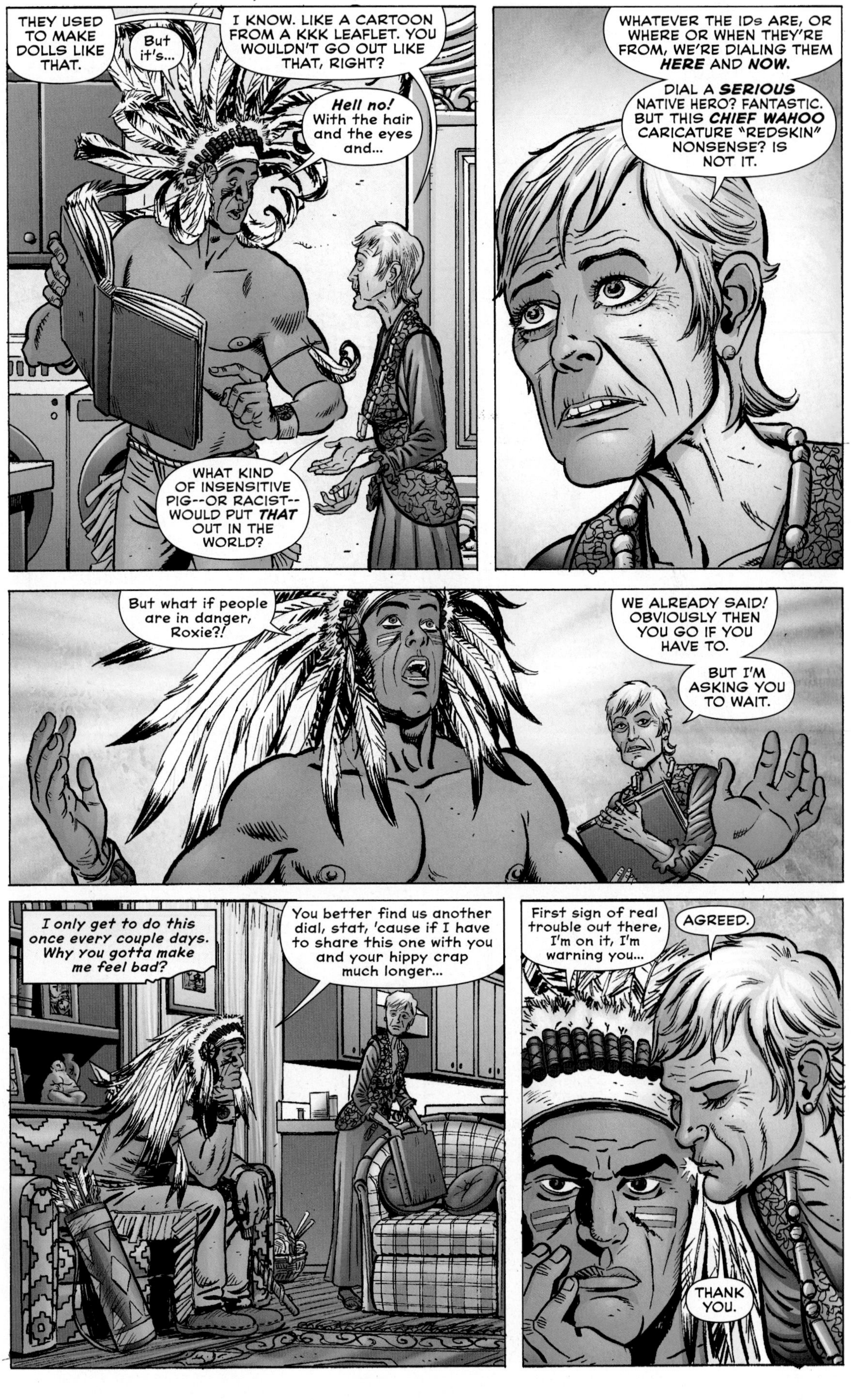
THEY USED TO MAKE DOLLS LIKE THAT.
But it's...
I KNOW. LIKE A CARTOON FROM A KKK LEAFLET. YOU WOULDN'T GO OUT LIKE THAT, RIGHT?
Hell no! With the hair and the eyes and...
WHAT KIND OF INSENSITIVE PIG--OR RACIST--WOULD PUT *THAT* OUT IN THE WORLD?
WHATEVER THE IDs ARE, OR WHERE OR WHEN THEY'RE FROM, WE'RE DIALING THEM *HERE* AND *NOW*.
DIAL A *SERIOUS* NATIVE HERO? FANTASTIC. BUT THIS *CHIEF WAHOO* CARICATURE "REDSKIN" NONSENSE? IS NOT IT.
But what if people are in danger, Roxie?!
WE ALREADY SAID! OBVIOUSLY THEN YOU GO IF YOU HAVE TO.
BUT I'M ASKING YOU TO WAIT.
I only get to do this once every couple days. Why you gotta make me feel bad?
You better find us another dial, stat, 'cause if I have to share this one with you and your hippy crap much longer...
First sign of real trouble out there, I'm on it, I'm warning you...
AGREED.
THANK YOU.

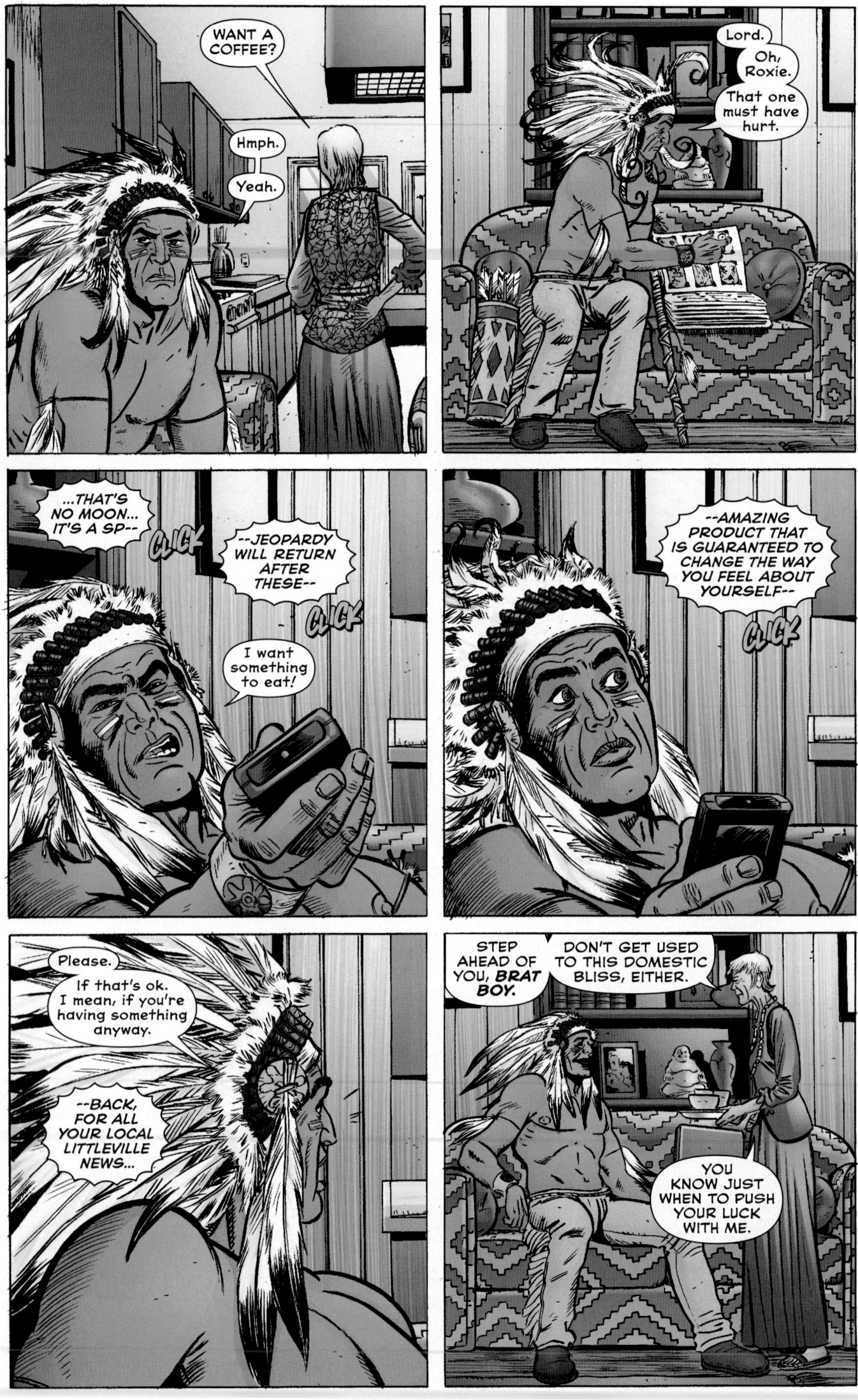
WANT A COFFEE?
Hmph.
Yeah.
Lord.
Oh, Roxie.
That one must have hurt.
...THAT'S NO MOON... IT'S A SP--
CLICK
--JEOPARDY WILL RETURN AFTER THESE--
CLICK
I want something to eat!
--AMAZING PRODUCT THAT IS GUARANTEED TO CHANGE THE WAY YOU FEEL ABOUT YOURSELF--
CLICK
Please.
If that's ok. I mean, if you're having something anyway.
--BACK, FOR ALL YOUR LOCAL LITTLEVILLE NEWS...
STEP AHEAD OF YOU, **BRAT BOY.**
DON'T GET USED TO THIS DOMESTIC BLISS, EITHER.
YOU KNOW JUST WHEN TO PUSH YOUR LUCK WITH ME.

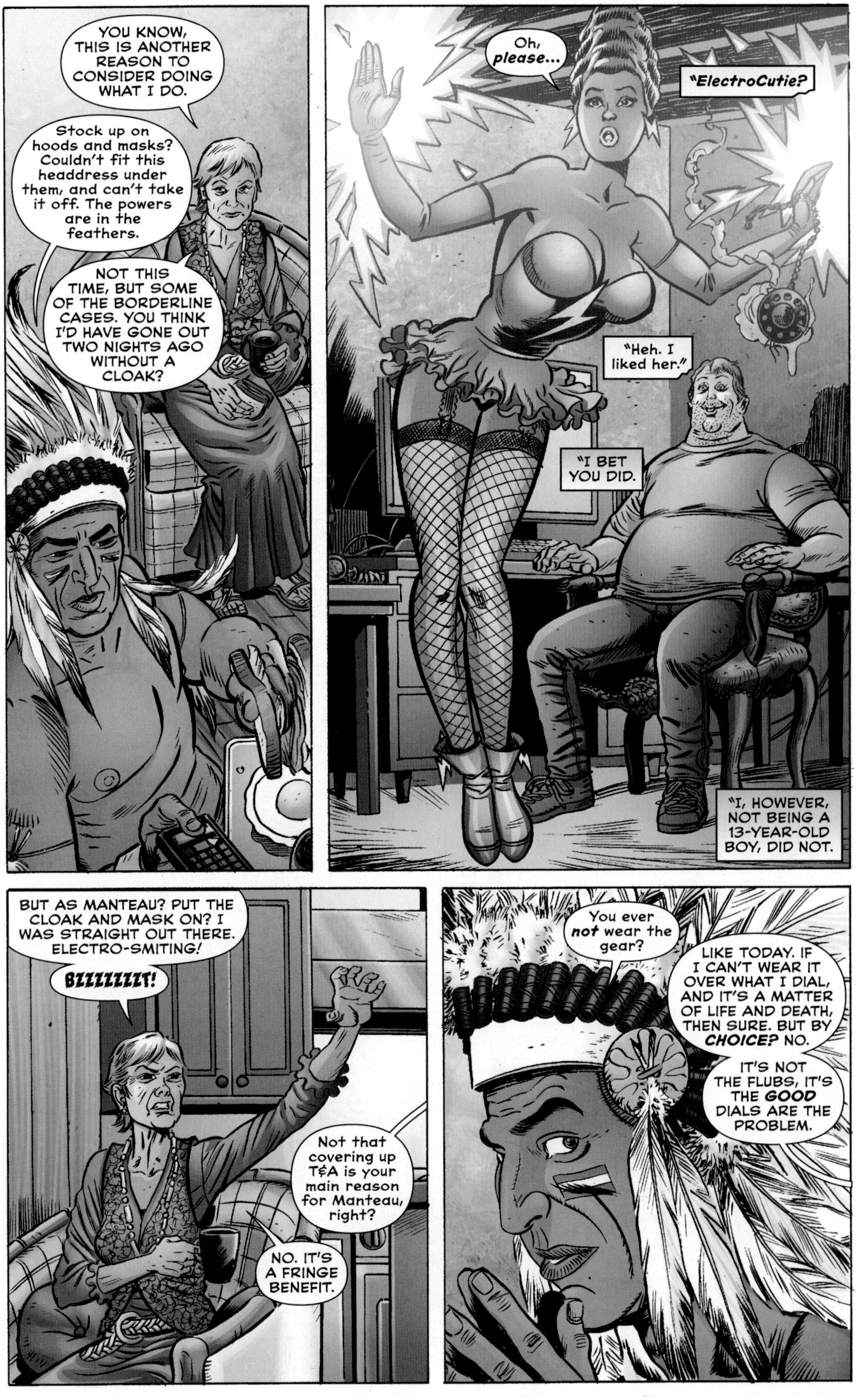
YOU KNOW, THIS IS ANOTHER REASON TO CONSIDER DOING WHAT I DO.
Stock up on hoods and masks? Couldn't fit this headdress under them, and can't take it off. The powers are in the feathers.
NOT THIS TIME, BUT SOME OF THE BORDERLINE CASES. YOU THINK I'D HAVE GONE OUT TWO NIGHTS AGO WITHOUT A CLOAK?
Oh, please...
"ElectroCutie?
"Heh. I liked her."
"I BET YOU DID.
"I, HOWEVER, NOT BEING A 13-YEAR-OLD BOY, DID NOT.
BUT AS MANTEAU? PUT THE CLOAK AND MASK ON? I WAS STRAIGHT OUT THERE. ELECTRO-SMITING!
BZZZZZZZT!
Not that covering up T&A is your main reason for Manteau, right?
NO. IT'S A FRINGE BENEFIT.
You ever not wear the gear?
LIKE TODAY. IF I CAN'T WEAR IT OVER WHAT I DIAL, AND IT'S A MATTER OF LIFE AND DEATH, THEN SURE. BUT BY CHOICE? NO.
IT'S NOT THE FLUBS, IT'S THE GOOD DIALS ARE THE PROBLEM.

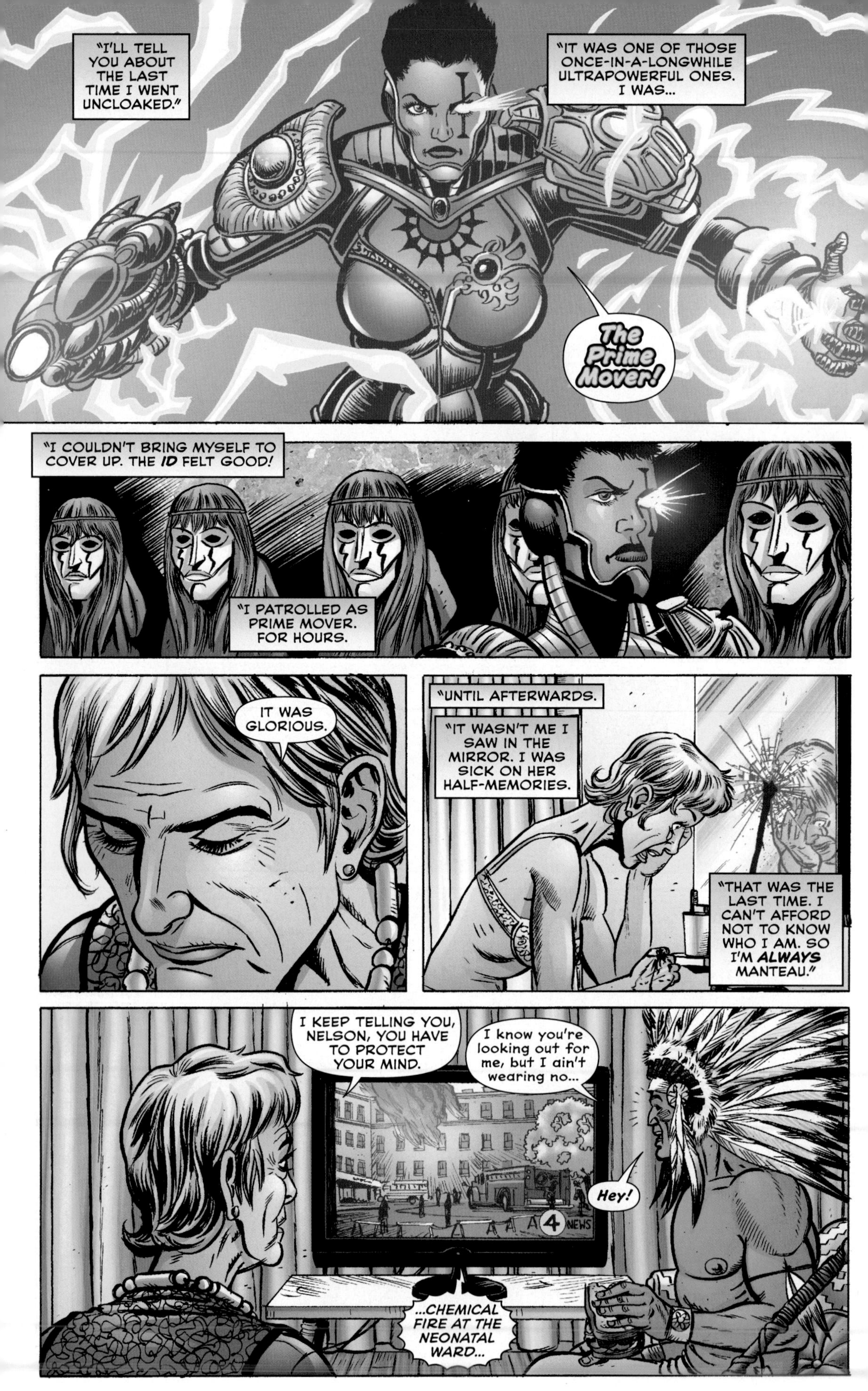
"I'LL TELL YOU ABOUT THE LAST TIME I WENT UNCLOAKED."
"IT WAS ONE OF THOSE ONCE-IN-A-LONGWHILE ULTRAPOWERFUL ONES. I WAS...
The Prime Mover!
"I COULDN'T BRING MYSELF TO COVER UP. THE ID FELT GOOD!
"I PATROLLED AS PRIME MOVER. FOR HOURS.
IT WAS GLORIOUS.
"UNTIL AFTERWARDS.
"IT WASN'T ME I SAW IN THE MIRROR. I WAS SICK ON HER HALF-MEMORIES.
"THAT WAS THE LAST TIME. I CAN'T AFFORD NOT TO KNOW WHO I AM. SO I'M ALWAYS MANTEAU."
I KEEP TELLING YOU, NELSON, YOU HAVE TO PROTECT YOUR MIND.
I know you're looking out for me, but I ain't wearing no...
Hey!
4 NEWS
...CHEMICAL FIRE AT THE NEONATAL WARD...

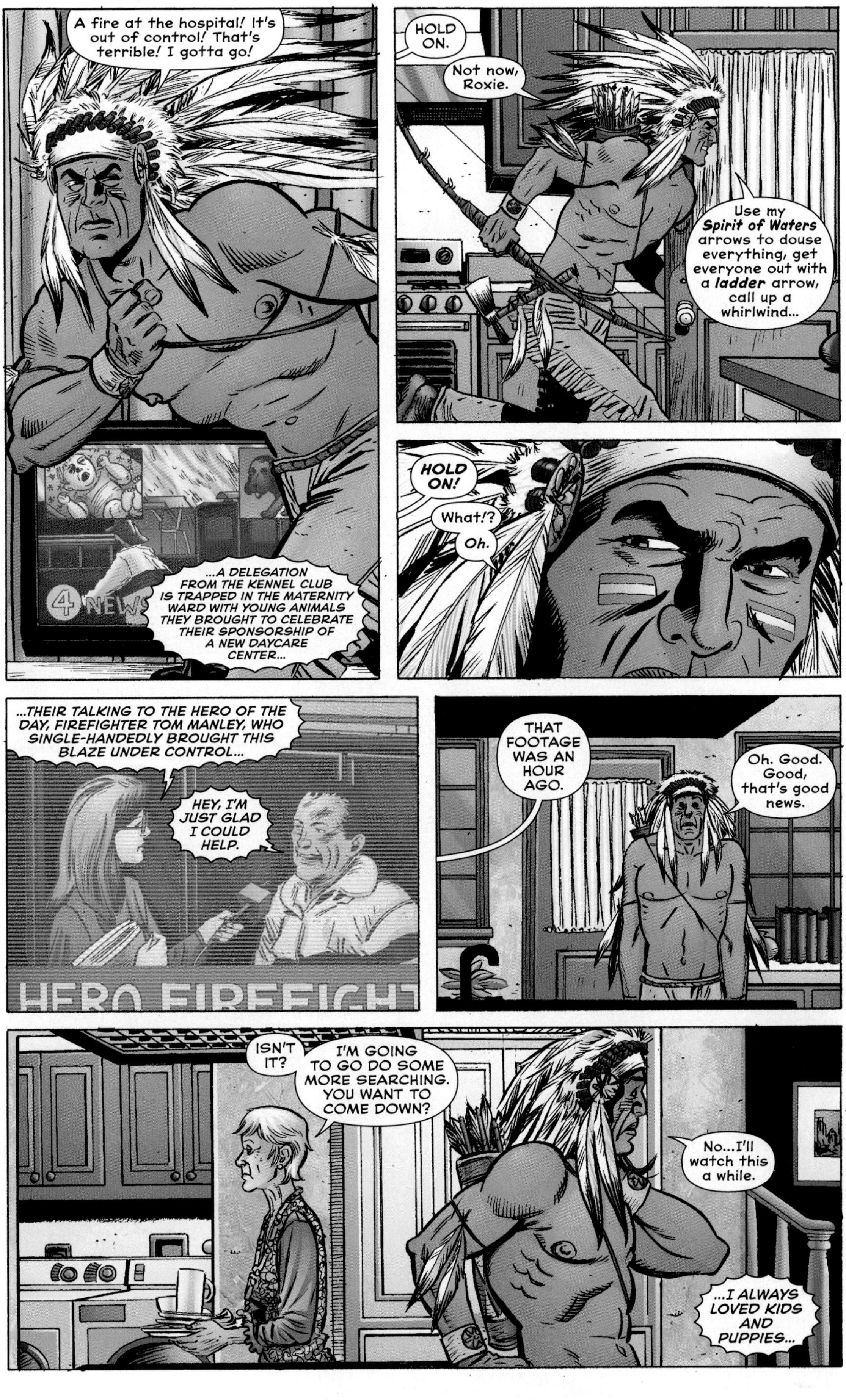
A fire at the hospital! It's out of control! That's terrible! I gotta go!
...A DELEGATION FROM THE KENNEL CLUB IS TRAPPED IN THE MATERNITY WARD WITH YOUNG ANIMALS THEY BROUGHT TO CELEBRATE THEIR SPONSORSHIP OF A NEW DAYCARE CENTER...
4 NEWS
HOLD ON.
Not now, Roxie.
Use my Spirit of Waters arrows to douse everything, get everyone out with a ladder arrow, call up a whirlwind...
HOLD ON!
What!?
Oh.
...THEIR TALKING TO THE HERO OF THE DAY, FIREFIGHTER TOM MANLEY, WHO SINGLE-HANDEDLY BROUGHT THIS BLAZE UNDER CONTROL...
HEY, I'M JUST GLAD I COULD HELP.
HERO FIREFIGHT
THAT FOOTAGE WAS AN HOUR AGO.
Oh. Good. Good, that's good news.
ISN'T IT?
I'M GOING TO GO DO SOME MORE SEARCHING. YOU WANT TO COME DOWN?
No...I'll watch this a while.
...I ALWAYS LOVED KIDS AND PUPPIES...

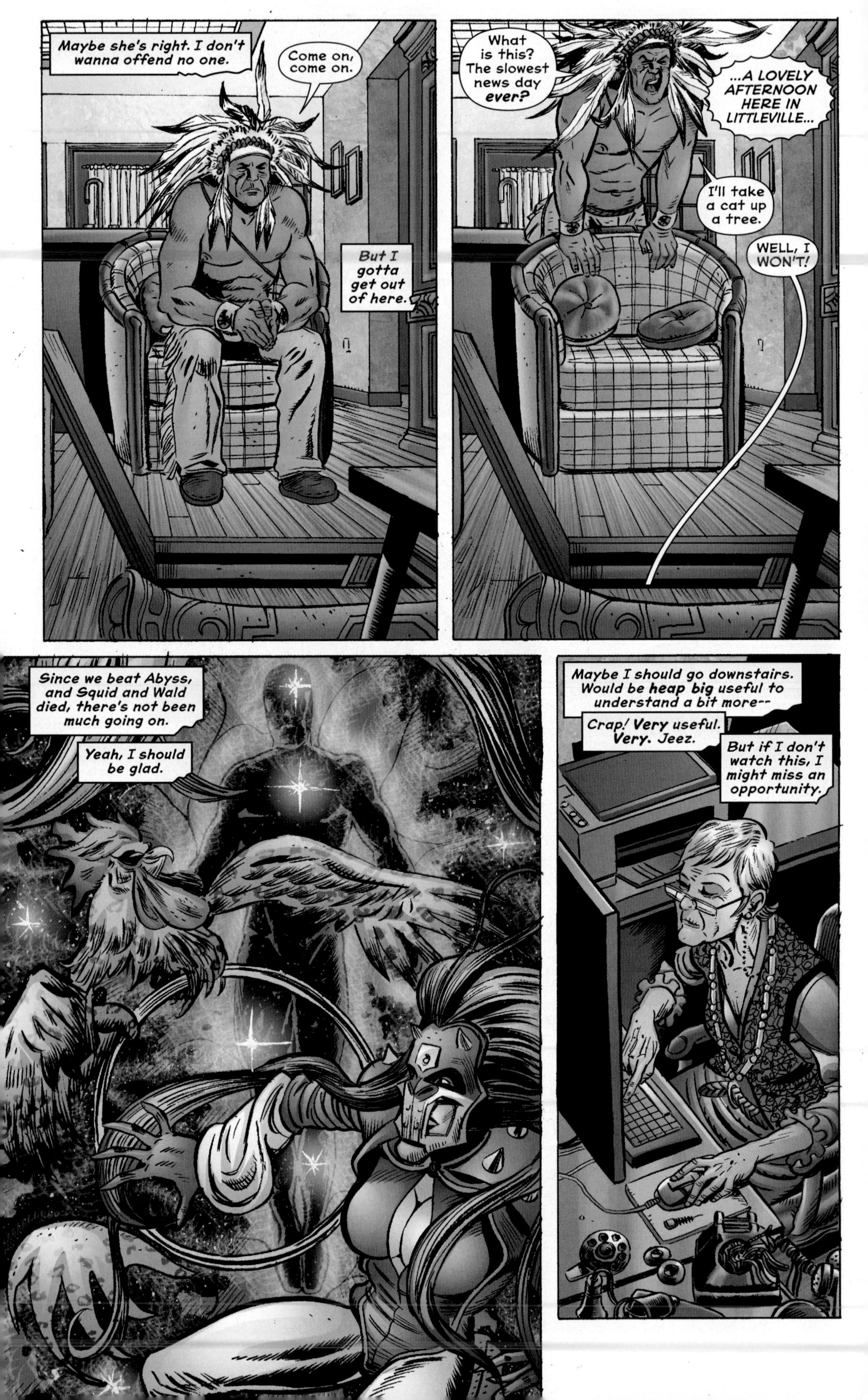

Maybe she's right. I don't wanna offend no one.
Come on, come on.
But I gotta get out of here.
What is this? The slowest news day ever?
...A LOVELY AFTERNOON HERE IN LITTLEVILLE...
I'll take a cat up a tree.
WELL, I WON'T!
Since we beat Abyss, and Squid and Wald died, there's not been much going on.
Yeah, I should be glad.
Maybe I should go downstairs. Would be heap big useful to understand a bit more--
Crap! Very useful. Very. Jeez.
But if I don't watch this, I might miss an opportunity.

Roxie knows more about dials than anyone.

And she don't know much.

She's a historian, as well as an engineer.

The dial we have works as well as it ever did, now, since she finally fixed it.

But at first even she didn't know there was a dial sitting there in that booth. On her doorstep.

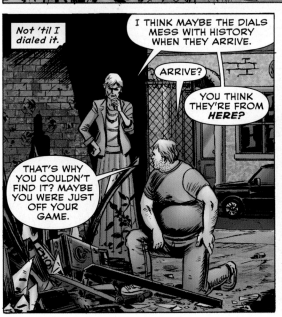

Not 'til I dialed it.

I THINK MAYBE THE DIALS MESS WITH HISTORY WHEN THEY ARRIVE.

ARRIVE?

YOU THINK THEY'RE FROM *HERE?*

THAT'S WHY YOU COULDN'T FIND IT? MAYBE YOU WERE JUST OFF YOUR GAME.

I shouldn't give her a hard time. Like I said, she knows more about this stuff than anyone ever.

'Cept maybe that guy "O" she told me about.

Whoever he was.

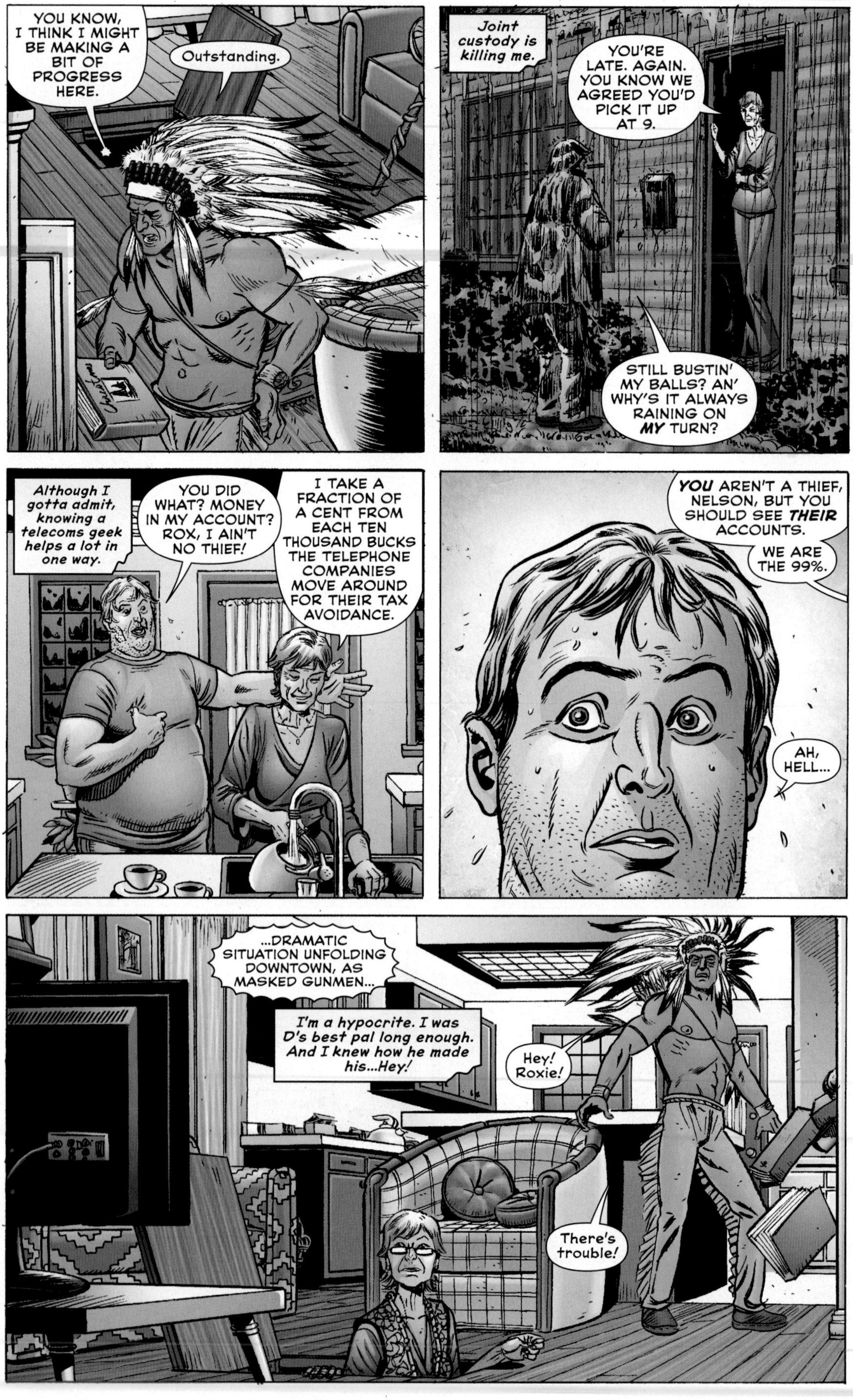

YOU KNOW, I THINK I MIGHT BE MAKING A BIT OF PROGRESS HERE.
Outstanding.
Joint custody is killing me.
YOU'RE LATE. AGAIN. YOU KNOW WE AGREED YOU'D PICK IT UP AT 9.
STILL BUSTIN' MY BALLS? AN' WHY'S IT ALWAYS RAINING ON MY TURN?
Although I gotta admit, knowing a telecoms geek helps a lot in one way.
YOU DID WHAT? MONEY IN MY ACCOUNT? ROX, I AIN'T NO THIEF!
I TAKE A FRACTION OF A CENT FROM EACH TEN THOUSAND BUCKS THE TELEPHONE COMPANIES MOVE AROUND FOR THEIR TAX AVOIDANCE.
YOU AREN'T A THIEF, NELSON, BUT YOU SHOULD SEE THEIR ACCOUNTS.
WE ARE THE 99%.
AH, HELL...
...DRAMATIC SITUATION UNFOLDING DOWNTOWN, AS MASKED GUNMEN...
I'm a hypocrite. I was D's best pal long enough. And I knew how he made his...Hey!
Hey! Roxie!
There's trouble!

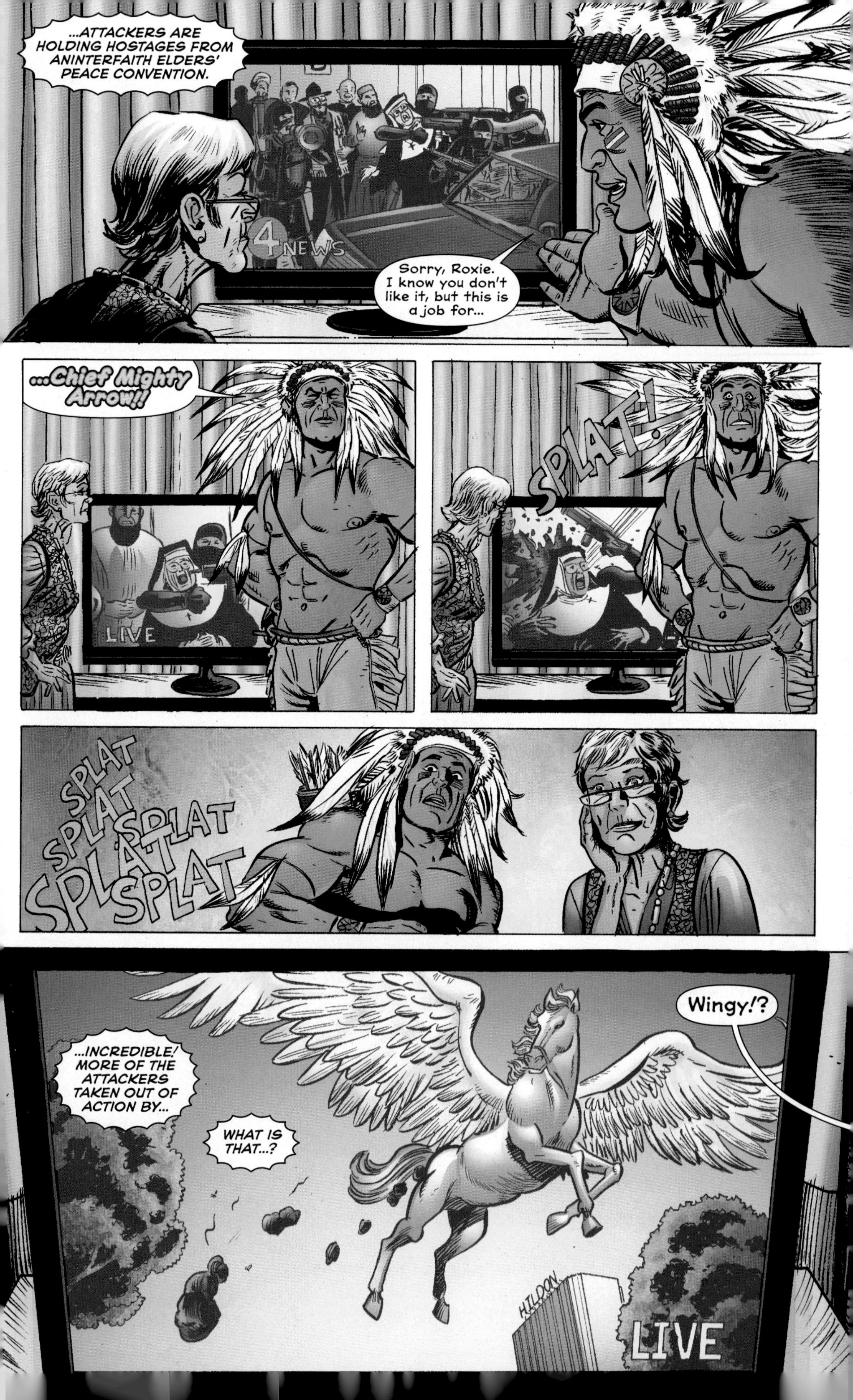
...ATTACKERS ARE HOLDING HOSTAGES FROM ANINTERFAITH ELDERS' PEACE CONVENTION.
4 NEWS
Sorry, Roxie. I know you don't like it, but this is a job for...
...Chief Mighty Arrow!!
LIVE
SPLAT!
SPLAT SPLAT SPLAT SPLAT SPLAT
...INCREDIBLE! MORE OF THE ATTACKERS TAKEN OUT OF ACTION BY...
WHAT IS THAT...?
Wingy!?
HILDON
LIVE

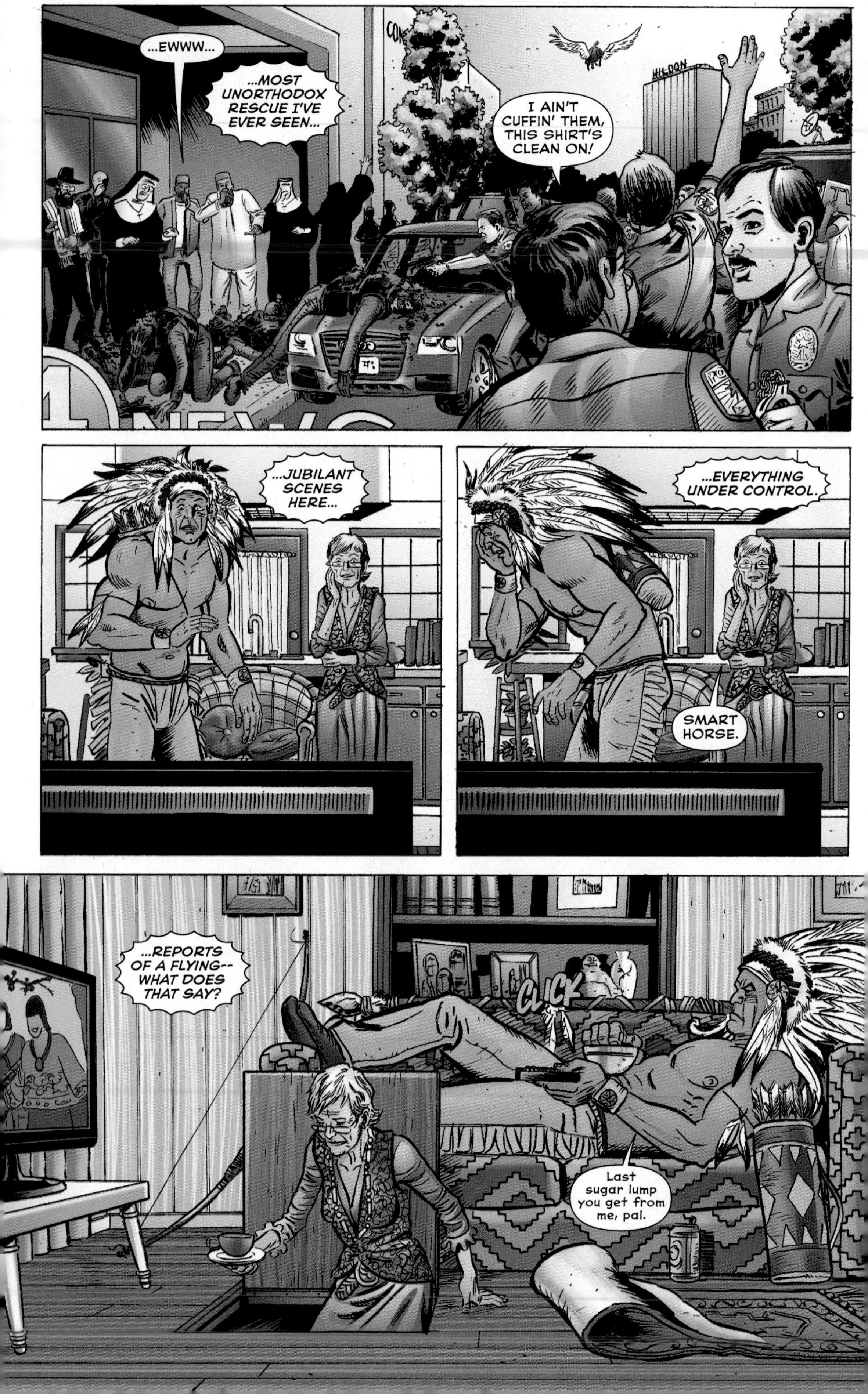
...EWWW...
...MOST UNORTHODOX RESCUE I'VE EVER SEEN...
I AIN'T CUFFIN' THEM, THIS SHIRT'S CLEAN ON!
...JUBILANT SCENES HERE...
...EVERYTHING UNDER CONTROL.
SMART HORSE.
...REPORTS OF A FLYING-- WHAT DOES THAT SAY?
CLICK
Last sugar lump you get from me, pal.

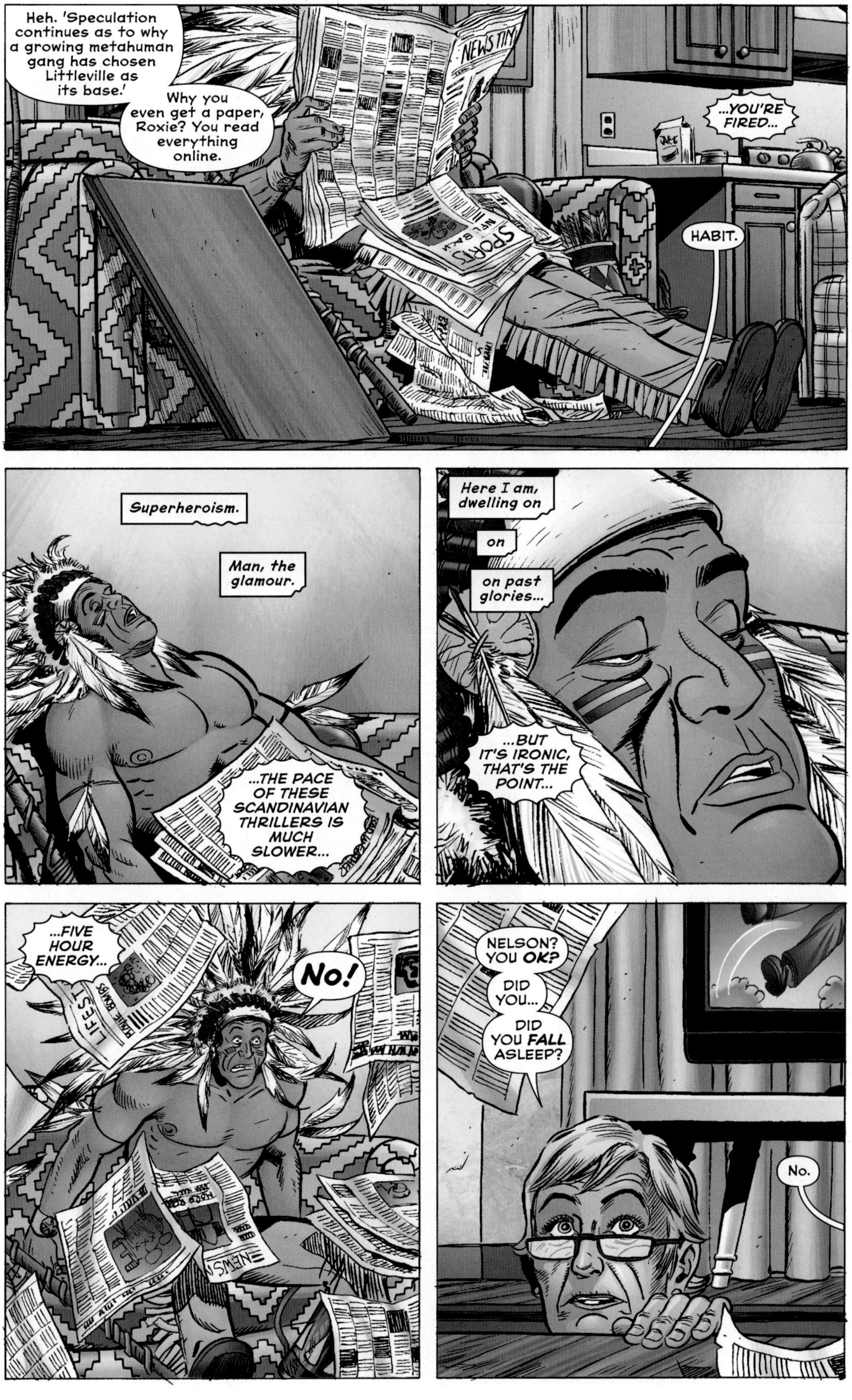

Heh. 'Speculation continues as to why a growing metahuman gang has chosen Littleville as its base.'
Why you even get a paper, Roxie? You read everything online.
HABIT.
...YOU'RE FIRED...
Superheroism.
Man, the glamour.
...THE PACE OF THESE SCANDINAVIAN THRILLERS IS MUCH SLOWER...
Here I am, dwelling on
on
on past glories...
...BUT IT'S IRONIC, THAT'S THE POINT...
...FIVE HOUR ENERGY...
No!
NELSON? YOU OK?
DID YOU...
DID YOU FALL ASLEEP?
No.

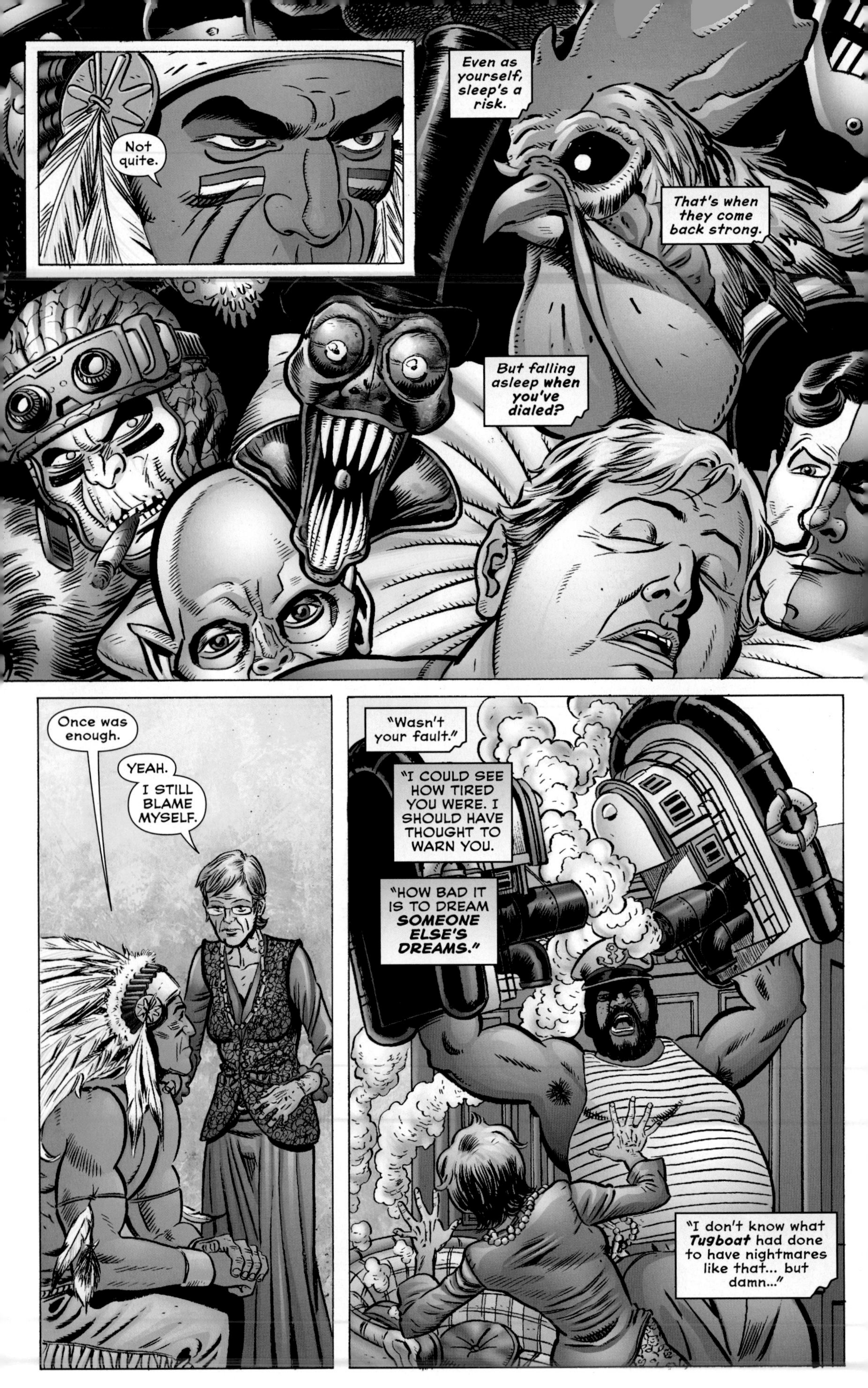
Not quite.
Even as yourself, sleep's a risk.
That's when they come back strong.
But falling asleep when you've dialed?
Once was enough.
YEAH. I STILL BLAME MYSELF.
"Wasn't your fault."
"I COULD SEE HOW TIRED YOU WERE. I SHOULD HAVE THOUGHT TO WARN YOU.
"HOW BAD IT IS TO DREAM SOMEONE ELSE'S DREAMS."
"I don't know what Tugboat had done to have nightmares like that... but damn..."

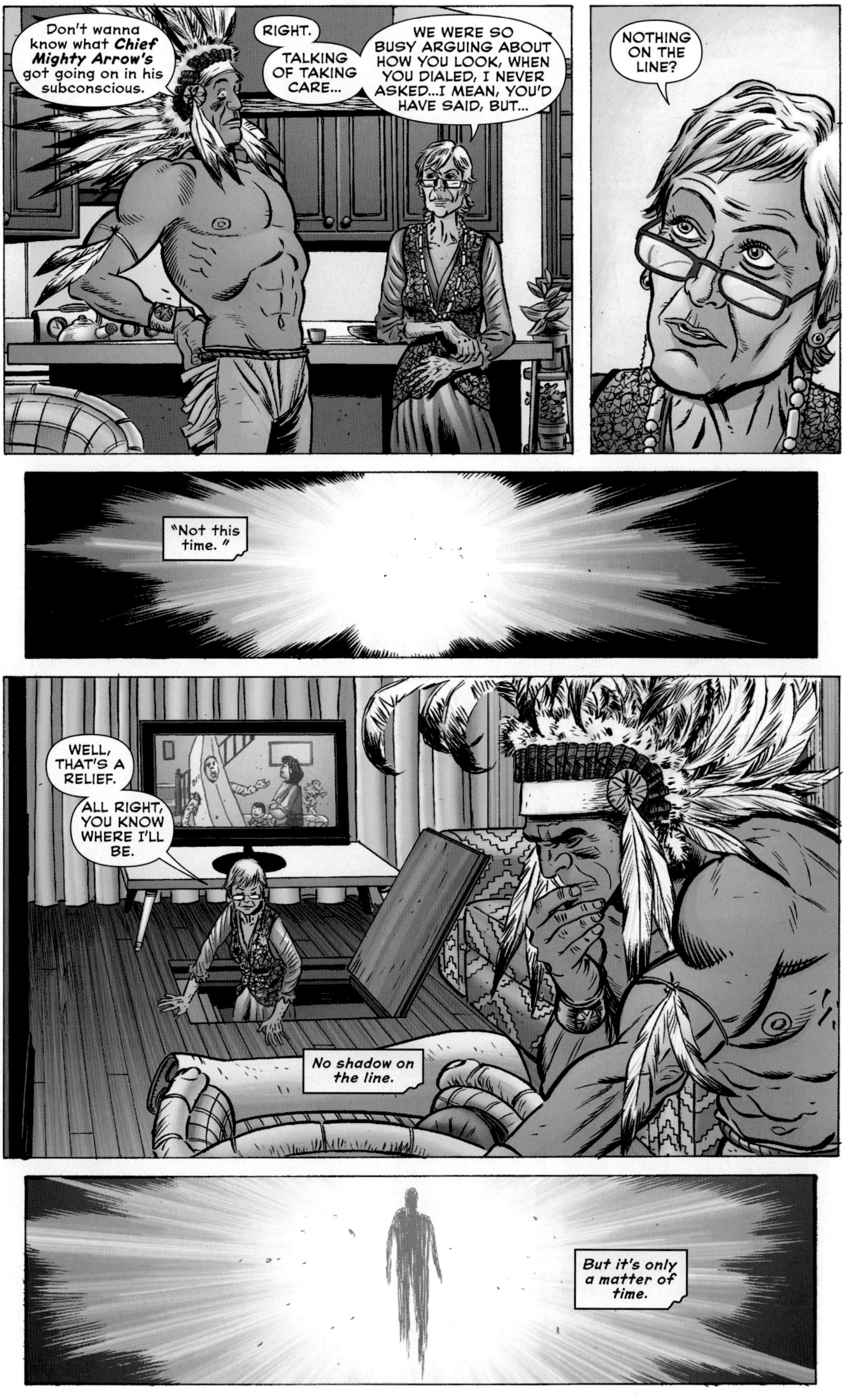
Don't wanna know what *Chief Mighty Arrow's* got going on in his subconscious.
RIGHT.
TALKING OF TAKING CARE...
WE WERE SO BUSY ARGUING ABOUT HOW YOU LOOK, WHEN YOU DIALED, I NEVER ASKED...I MEAN, YOU'D HAVE SAID, BUT...
NOTHING ON THE LINE?
"Not this time."
WELL, THAT'S A RELIEF.
ALL RIGHT, YOU KNOW WHERE I'LL BE.
No shadow on the line.
But it's only a matter of time.

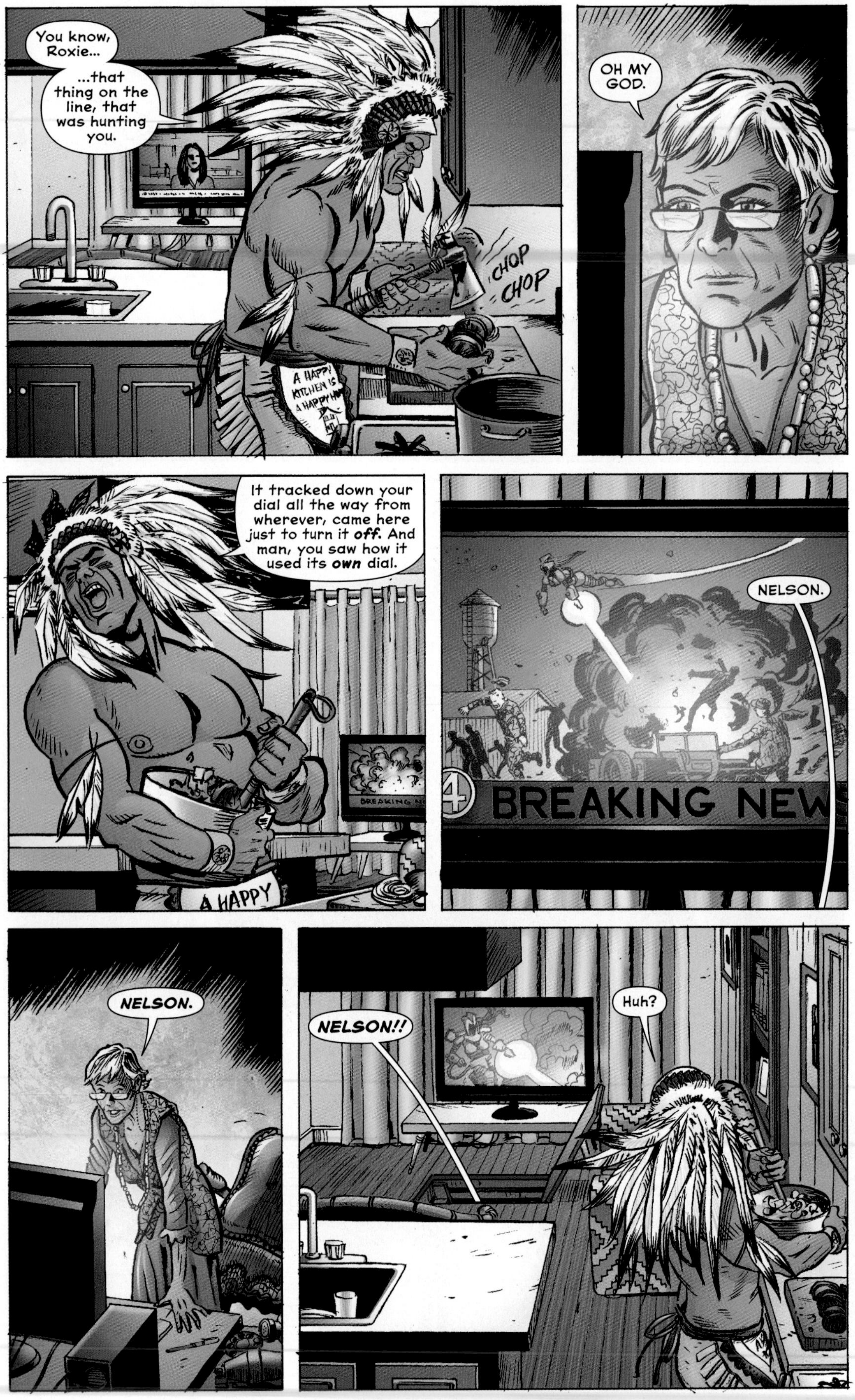
You know, Roxie...
...that thing on the line, that was hunting you.
CHOP CHOP
A HAPPY KITCHEN IS A HAPPY HOME
OH MY GOD.
It tracked down your dial all the way from wherever, came here just to turn it *off*. And man, you saw how it used its *own* dial.
A HAPPY
BREAKING NEWS
NELSON.
NELSON.
NELSON!!
Huh?

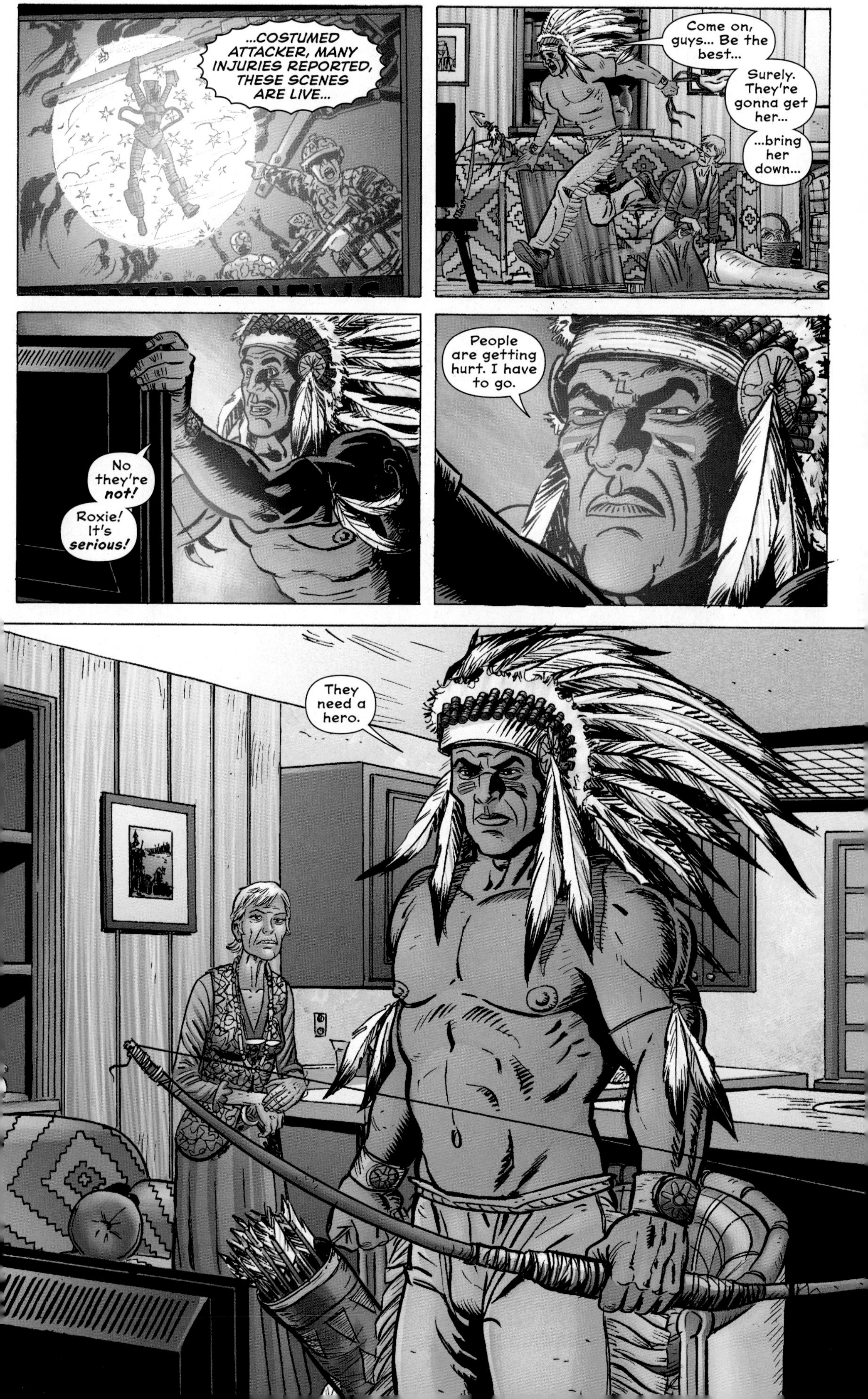
...COSTUMED ATTACKER, MANY INJURIES REPORTED, THESE SCENES ARE LIVE...
Come on, guys... Be the best...
Surely. They're gonna get her...
...bring her down...
No they're *not!*
Roxie! It's *serious!*
People are getting hurt. I have to go.
They need a hero.

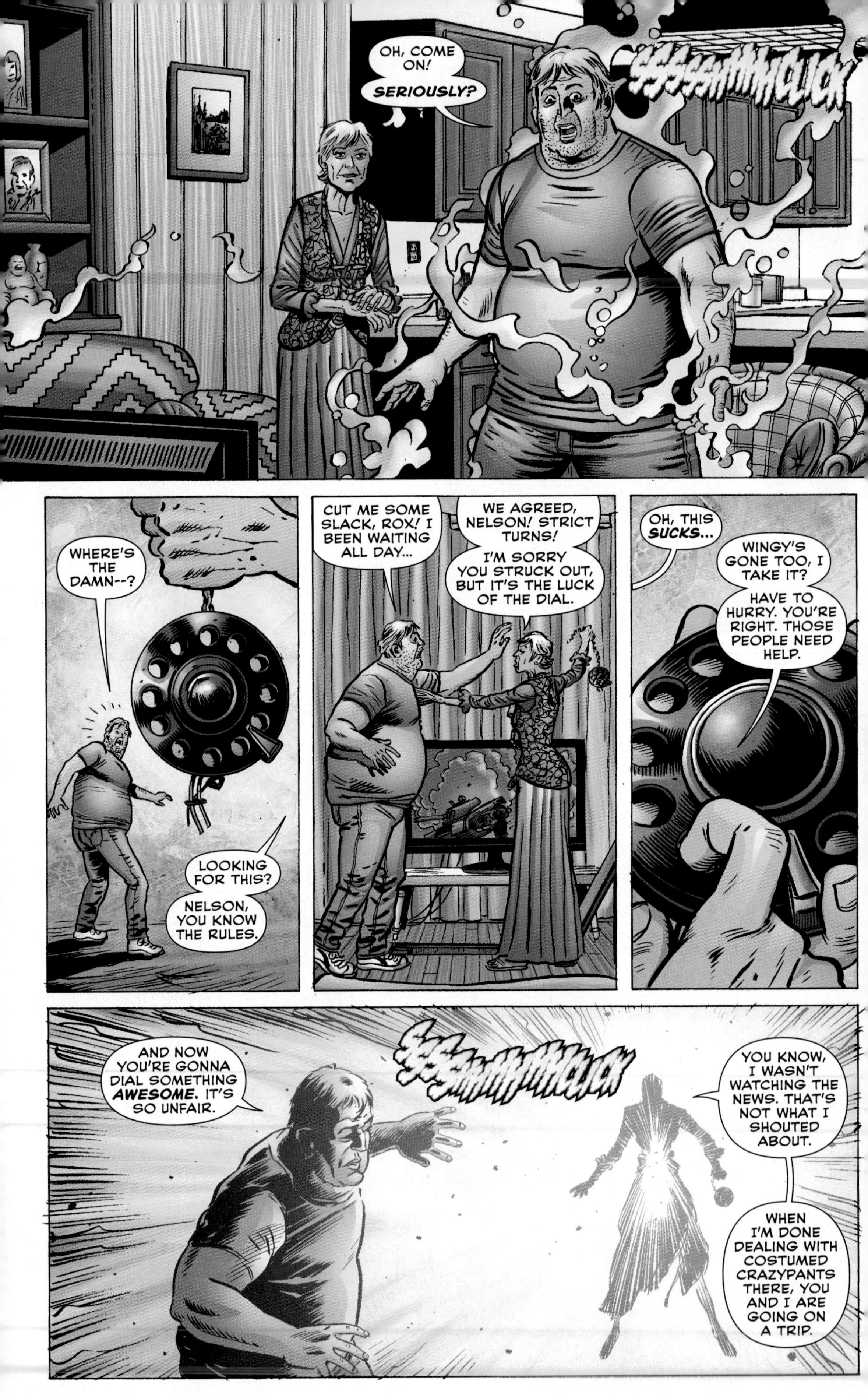
OH, COME ON! SERIOUSLY?
SSSSSHHHMCLICK
WHERE'S THE DAMN--?
LOOKING FOR THIS?
NELSON, YOU KNOW THE RULES.
CUT ME SOME SLACK, ROX! I BEEN WAITING ALL DAY...
WE AGREED, NELSON! STRICT TURNS!
I'M SORRY YOU STRUCK OUT, BUT IT'S THE LUCK OF THE DIAL.
OH, THIS SUCKS...
WINGY'S GONE TOO, I TAKE IT?
HAVE TO HURRY. YOU'RE RIGHT. THOSE PEOPLE NEED HELP.
AND NOW YOU'RE GONNA DIAL SOMETHING AWESOME. IT'S SO UNFAIR.
YOU KNOW, I WASN'T WATCHING THE NEWS. THAT'S NOT WHAT I SHOUTED ABOUT.
WHEN I'M DONE DEALING WITH COSTUMED CRAZYPANTS THERE, YOU AND I ARE GOING ON A TRIP.

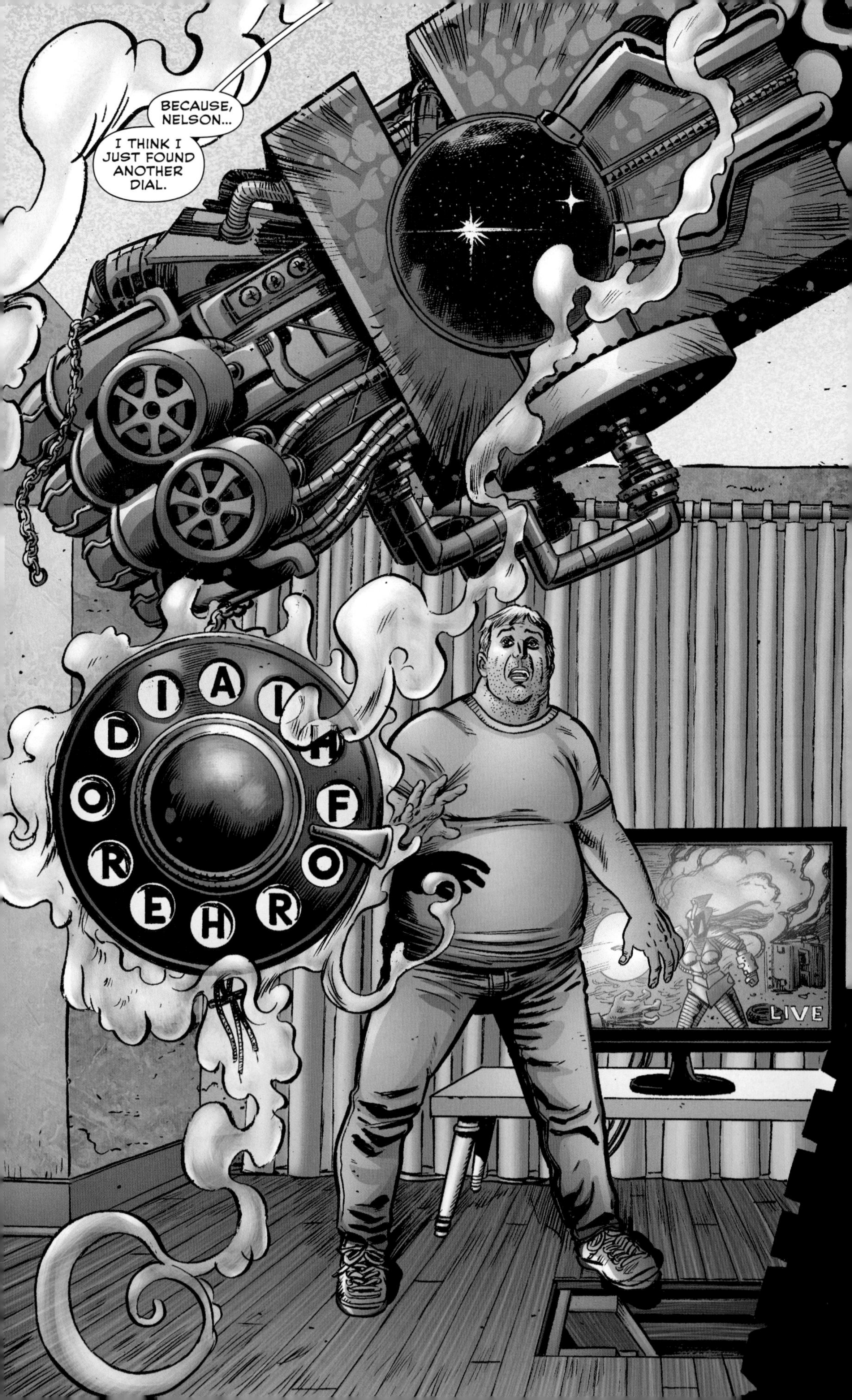
BECAUSE, NELSON...
I THINK I JUST FOUND ANOTHER DIAL.
DIAL H FOR HERO
LIVE

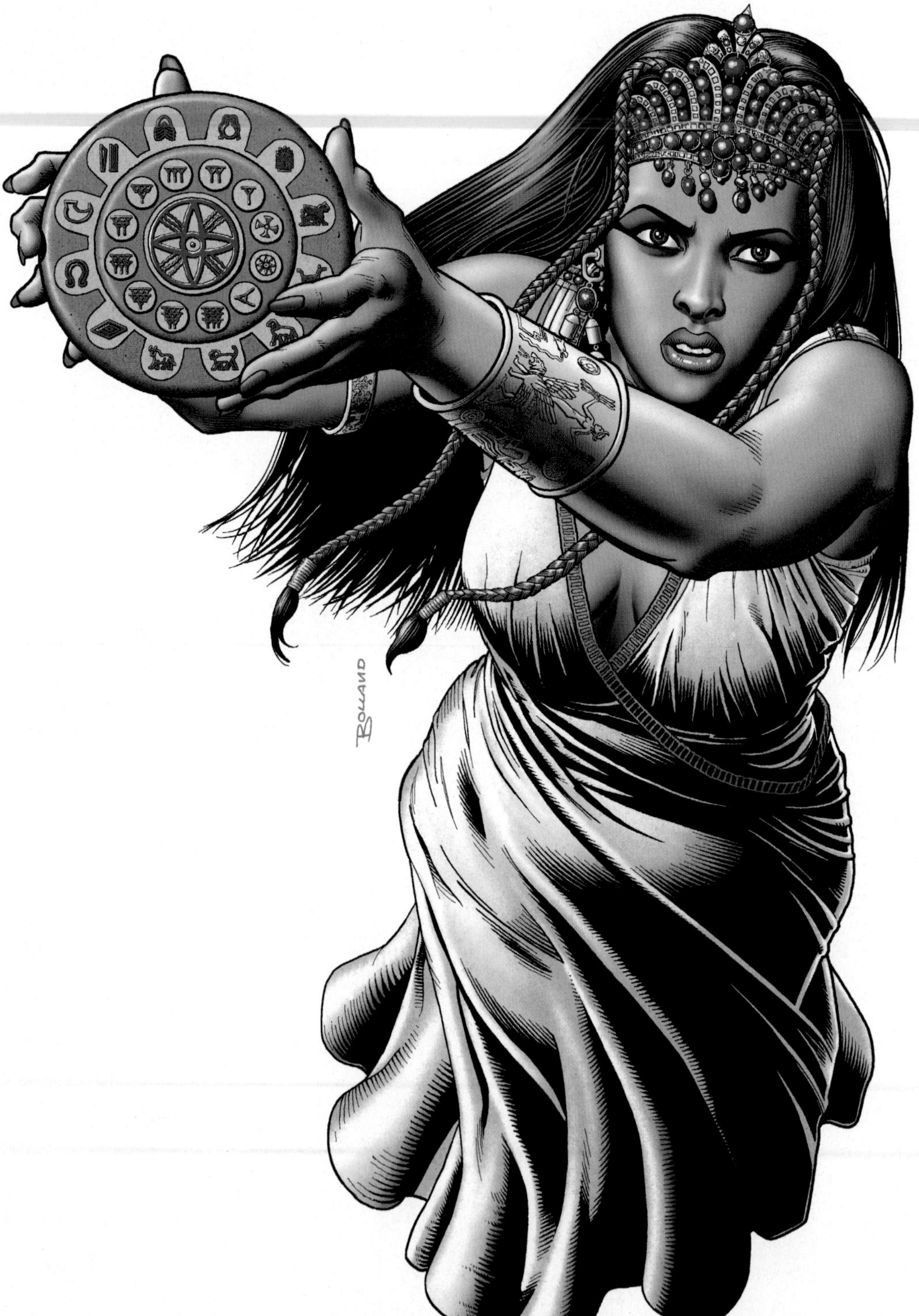
BOLLAND

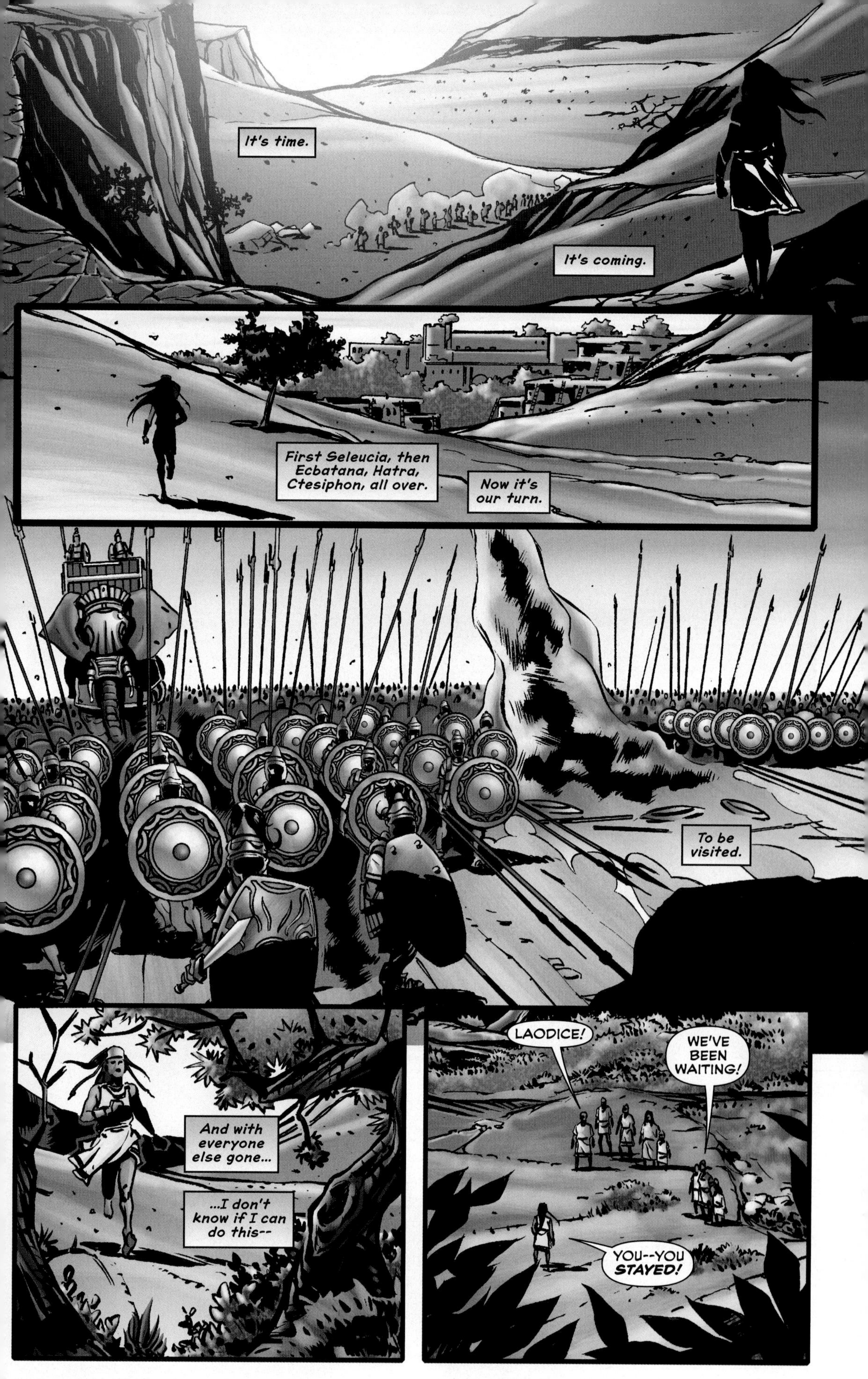
It's time.
It's coming.
First Seleucia, then Ecbatana, Hatra, Ctesiphon, all over.
Now it's our turn.
To be visited.
And with everyone else gone...
...I don't know if I can do this--
LAODICE!
WE'VE BEEN WAITING!
YOU--YOU STAYED!

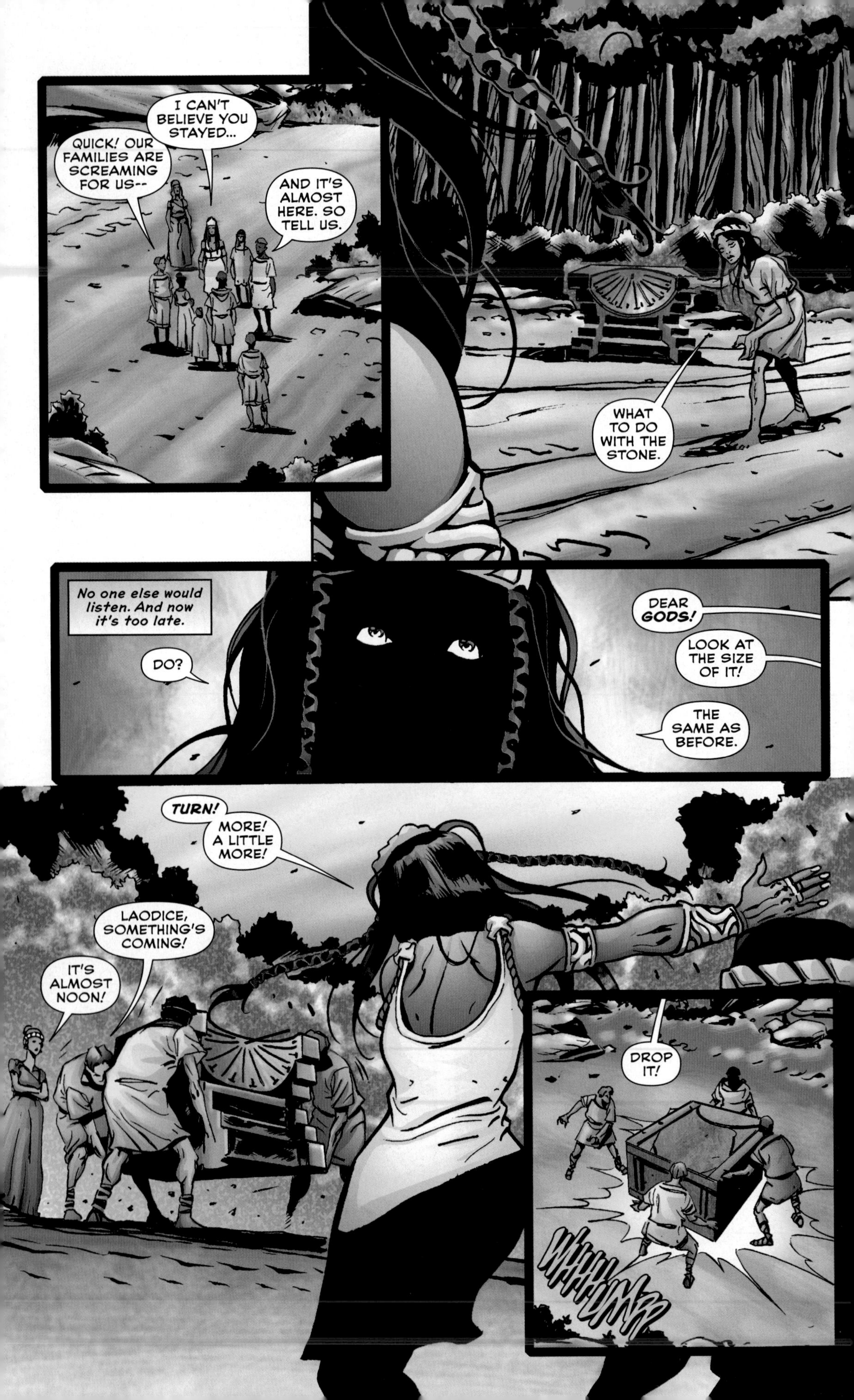

QUICK! OUR FAMILIES ARE SCREAMING FOR US--
I CAN'T BELIEVE YOU STAYED...
AND IT'S ALMOST HERE. SO TELL US.
WHAT TO DO WITH THE STONE.
No one else would listen. And now it's too late.
DO?
DEAR GODS!
LOOK AT THE SIZE OF IT!
THE SAME AS BEFORE.
TURN!
MORE! A LITTLE MORE!
LAODICE, SOMETHING'S COMING!
IT'S ALMOST NOON!
DROP IT!
WHHUMZZ

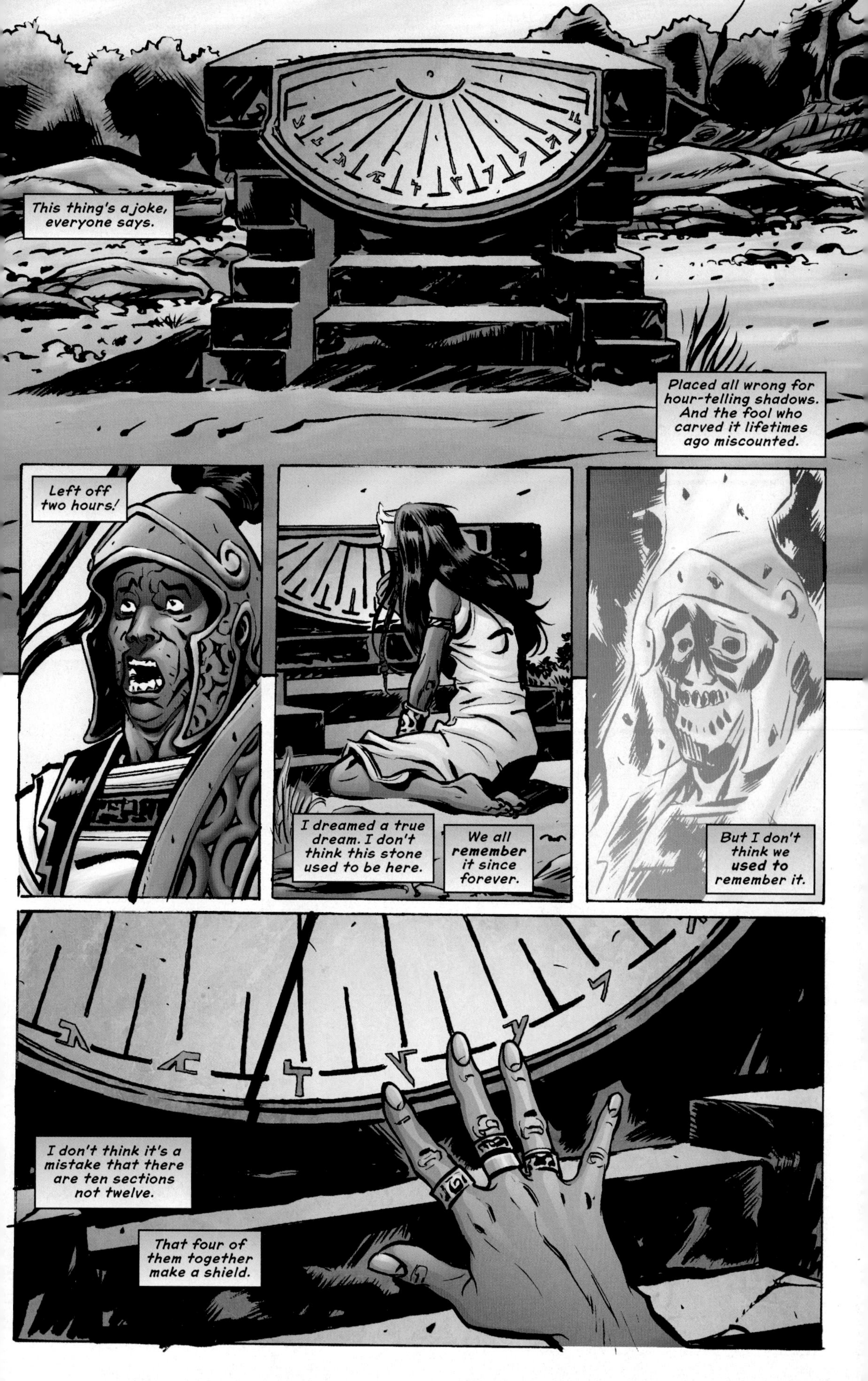
This thing's a joke, everyone says.
Placed all wrong for hour-telling shadows. And the fool who carved it lifetimes ago miscounted.
Left off two hours!
I dreamed a true dream. I don't think this stone used to be here.
We all remember it since forever.
But I don't think we used to remember it.
I don't think it's a mistake that there are ten sections not twelve.
That four of them together make a shield.

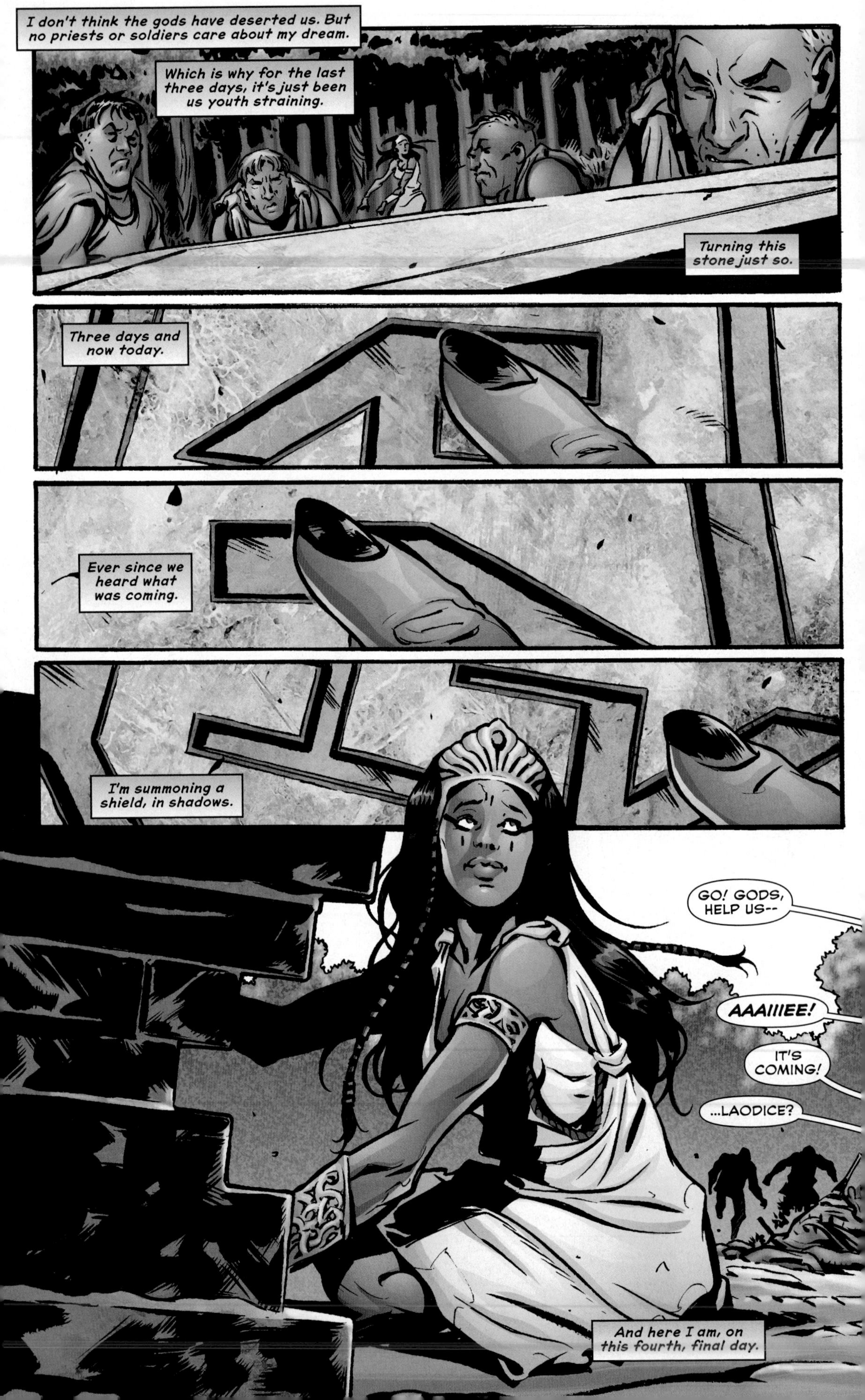
I don't think the gods have deserted us. But no priests or soldiers care about my dream.
Which is why for the last three days, it's just been us youth straining.
Turning this stone just so.
Three days and now today.
Ever since we heard what was coming.
I'm summoning a shield, in shadows.
GO! GODS, HELP US--
AAAIIIEE!
IT'S COMING!
...LAODICE?
And here I am, on this fourth, final day.

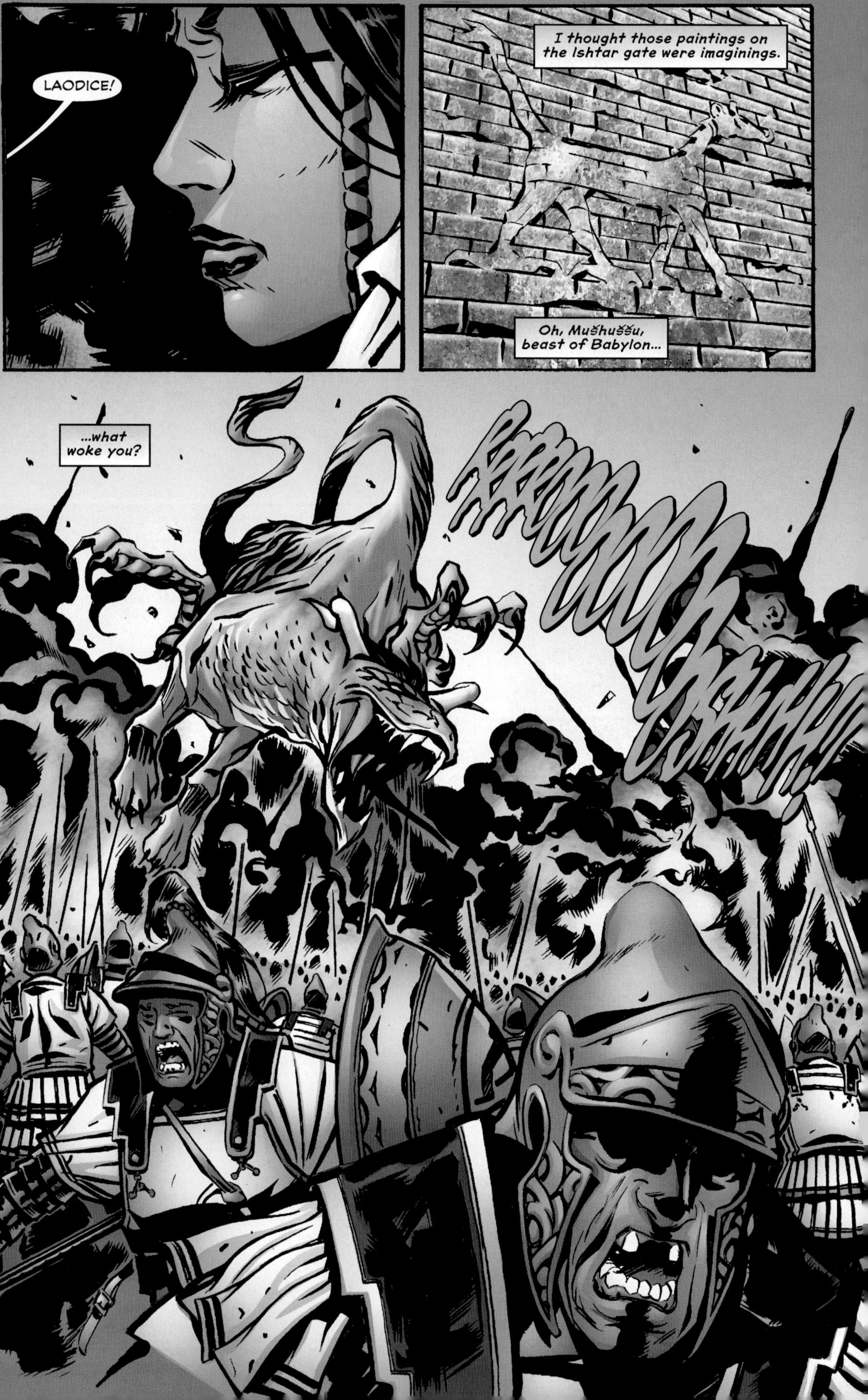
LAODICE!
I thought those paintings on the Ishtar gate were imaginings.
Oh, Mušhuššu, beast of Babylon...
...what woke you?

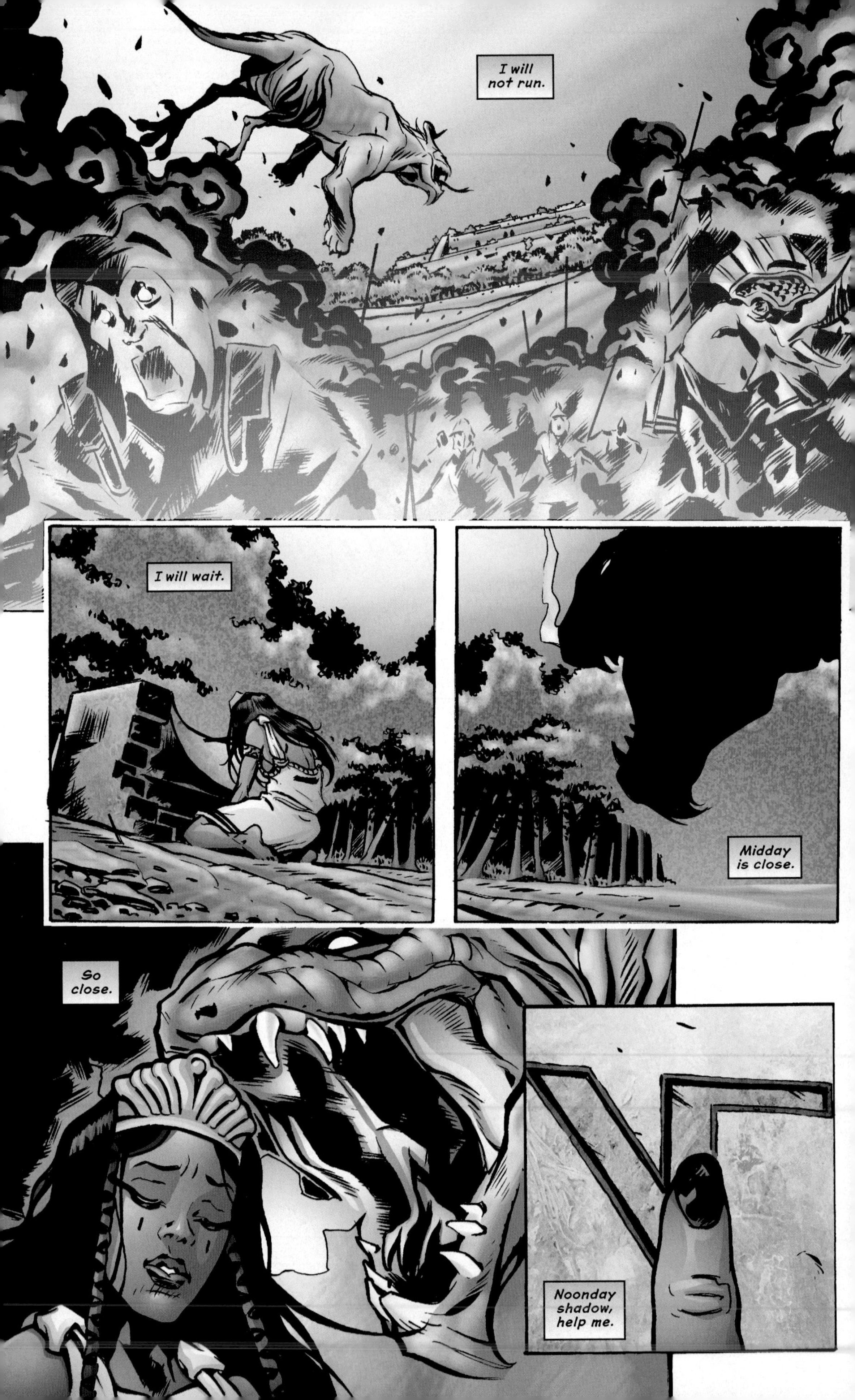
I will not run.
I will wait.
Midday is close.
So close.
Noonday shadow, help me.

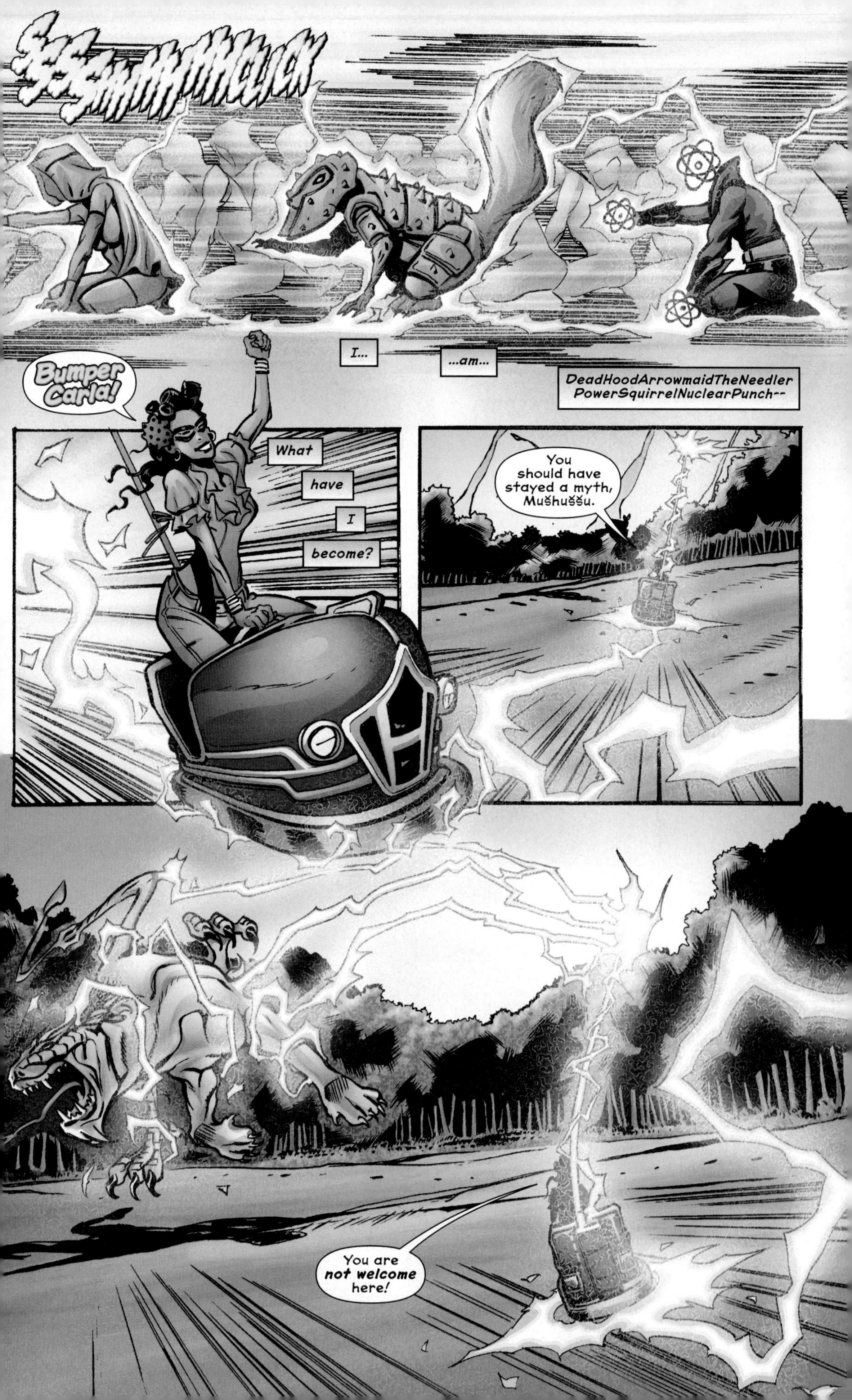
SSSSMMMMMMMCLICK
I...
...am...
DeadHoodArrowmaidTheNeedler
PowerSquirrelNuclearPunch--
Bumper Carla!
What
have
I
become?
You should have stayed a myth, Mušhuššu.
You are *not welcome* here!

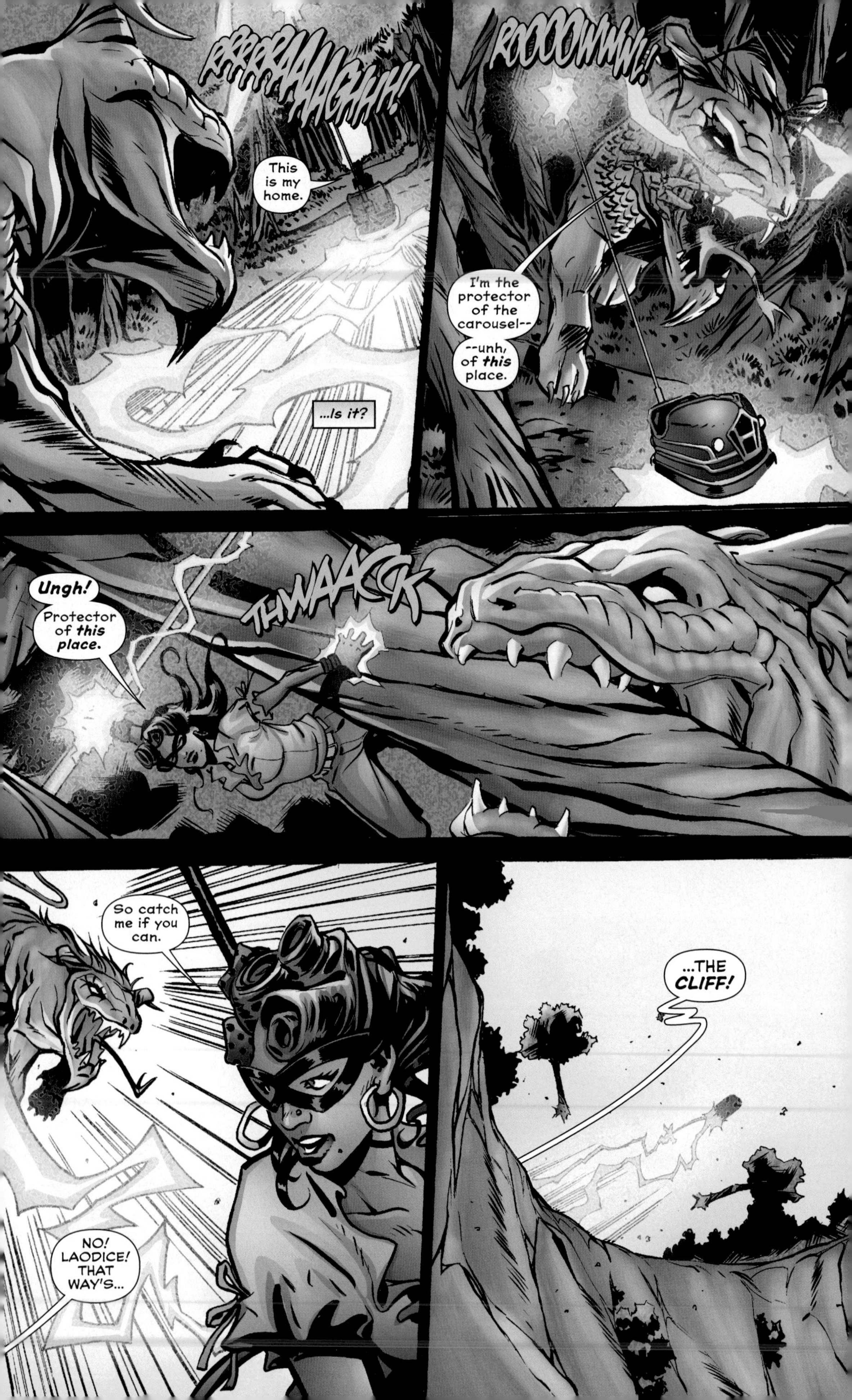

RRRRRAAAAGHHH!
This is my home.
...Is it?
ROOOOWWW!
I'm the protector of the carousel--
--unh, of this place.
Ungh!
Protector of this place.
THWAACCK
So catch me if you can.
NO! LAODICE! THAT WAY'S...
...THE CLIFF!

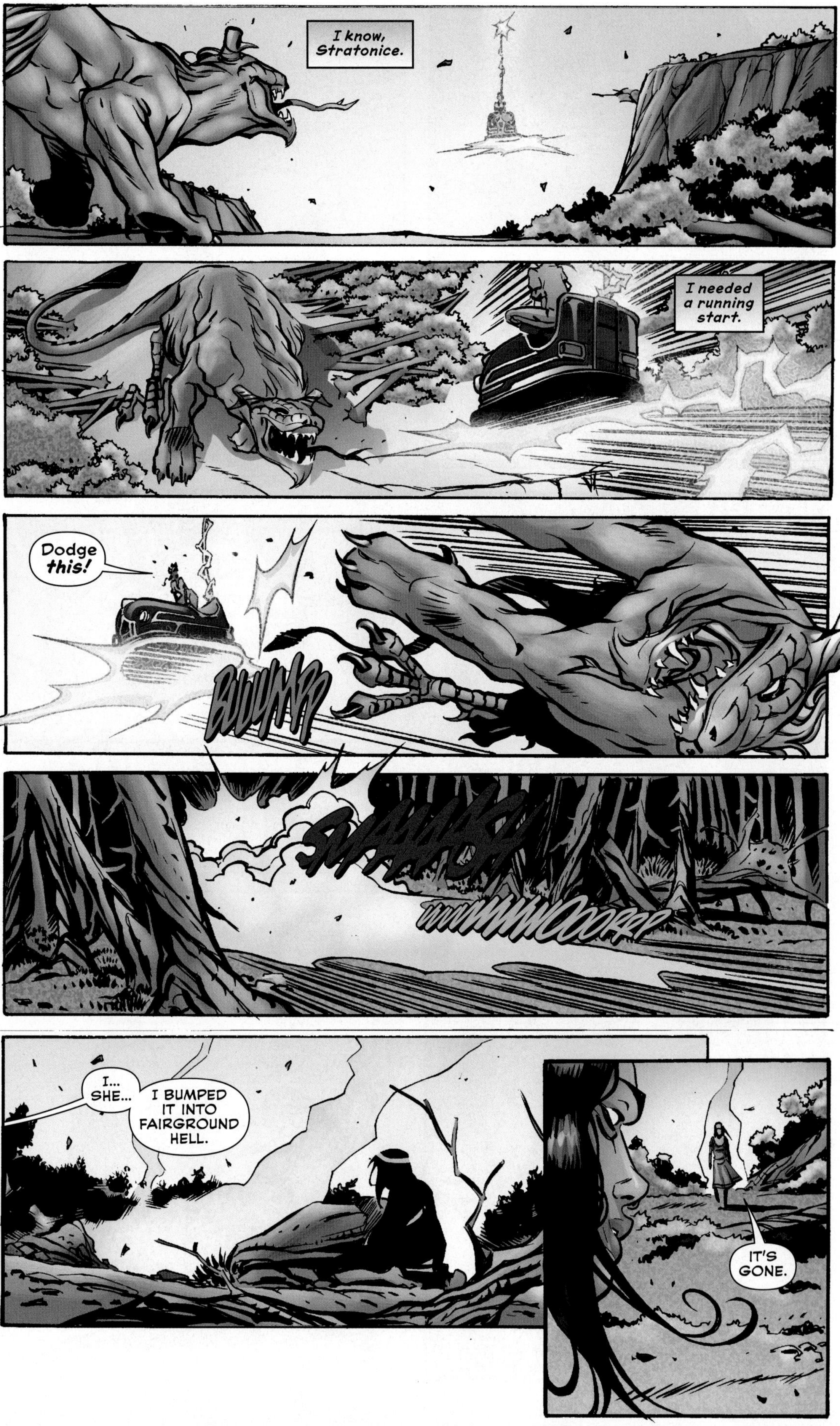
I know, Stratonice.
I needed a running start.
Dodge this!
I... SHE...
I BUMPED IT INTO FAIRGROUND HELL.
IT'S GONE.

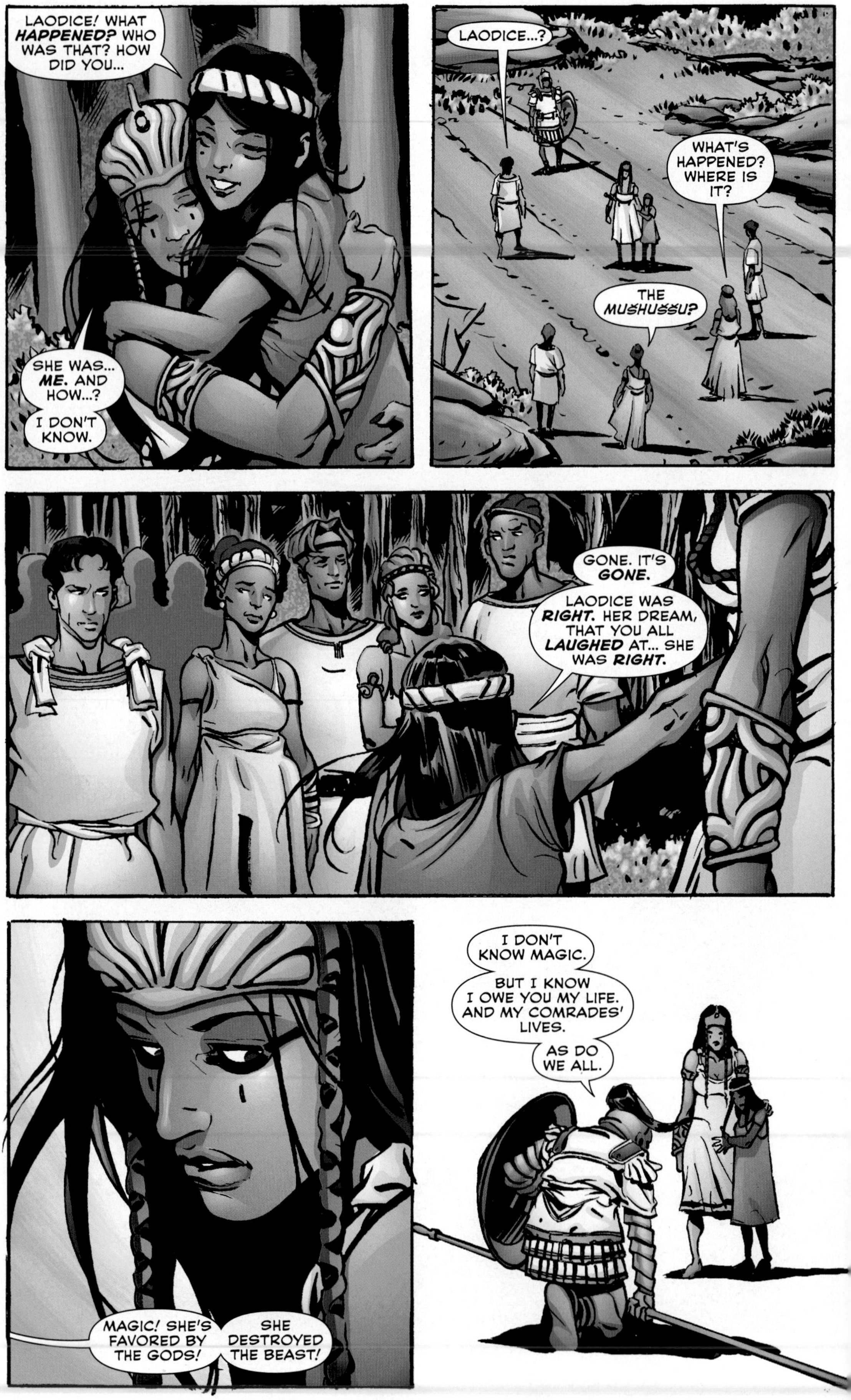
LAODICE! WHAT *HAPPENED?* WHO WAS THAT? HOW DID YOU...
SHE WAS... *ME.* AND HOW...?
I DON'T KNOW.
LAODICE...?
WHAT'S HAPPENED? WHERE IS IT?
THE *MUŠHUŠŠU?*
GONE. IT'S *GONE.*
LAODICE WAS *RIGHT.* HER DREAM, THAT YOU ALL *LAUGHED* AT... SHE WAS *RIGHT.*
MAGIC! SHE'S FAVORED BY THE GODS!
SHE DESTROYED THE BEAST!
I DON'T KNOW MAGIC.
BUT I KNOW I OWE YOU MY LIFE. AND MY COMRADES' LIVES.
AS DO WE ALL.

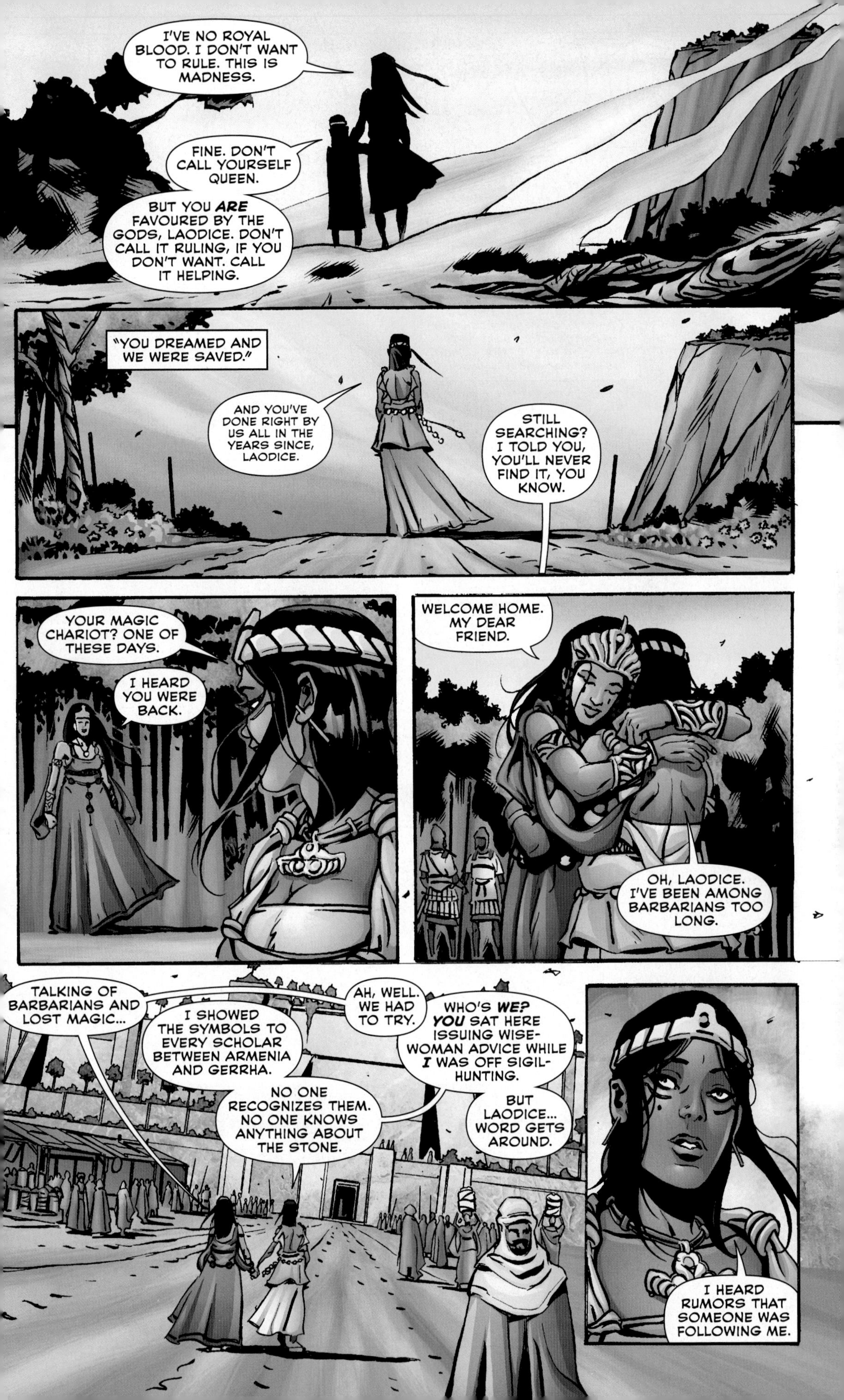
I'VE NO ROYAL BLOOD. I DON'T WANT TO RULE. THIS IS MADNESS.
FINE. DON'T CALL YOURSELF QUEEN.
BUT YOU *ARE* FAVOURED BY THE GODS, LAODICE. DON'T CALL IT RULING, IF YOU DON'T WANT. CALL IT HELPING.
"YOU DREAMED AND WE WERE SAVED."
AND YOU'VE DONE RIGHT BY US ALL IN THE YEARS SINCE, LAODICE.
STILL SEARCHING? I TOLD YOU, YOU'LL NEVER FIND IT, YOU KNOW.
YOUR MAGIC CHARIOT? ONE OF THESE DAYS.
I HEARD YOU WERE BACK.
WELCOME HOME. MY DEAR FRIEND.
OH, LAODICE. I'VE BEEN AMONG BARBARIANS TOO LONG.
TALKING OF BARBARIANS AND LOST MAGIC...
I SHOWED THE SYMBOLS TO EVERY SCHOLAR BETWEEN ARMENIA AND GERRHA.
NO ONE RECOGNIZES THEM. NO ONE KNOWS ANYTHING ABOUT THE STONE.
AH, WELL. WE HAD TO TRY.
WHO'S *WE? YOU* SAT HERE ISSUING WISE-WOMAN ADVICE WHILE *I* WAS OFF SIGIL-HUNTING.
BUT LAODICE... WORD GETS AROUND.
I HEARD RUMORS THAT SOMEONE WAS FOLLOWING ME.

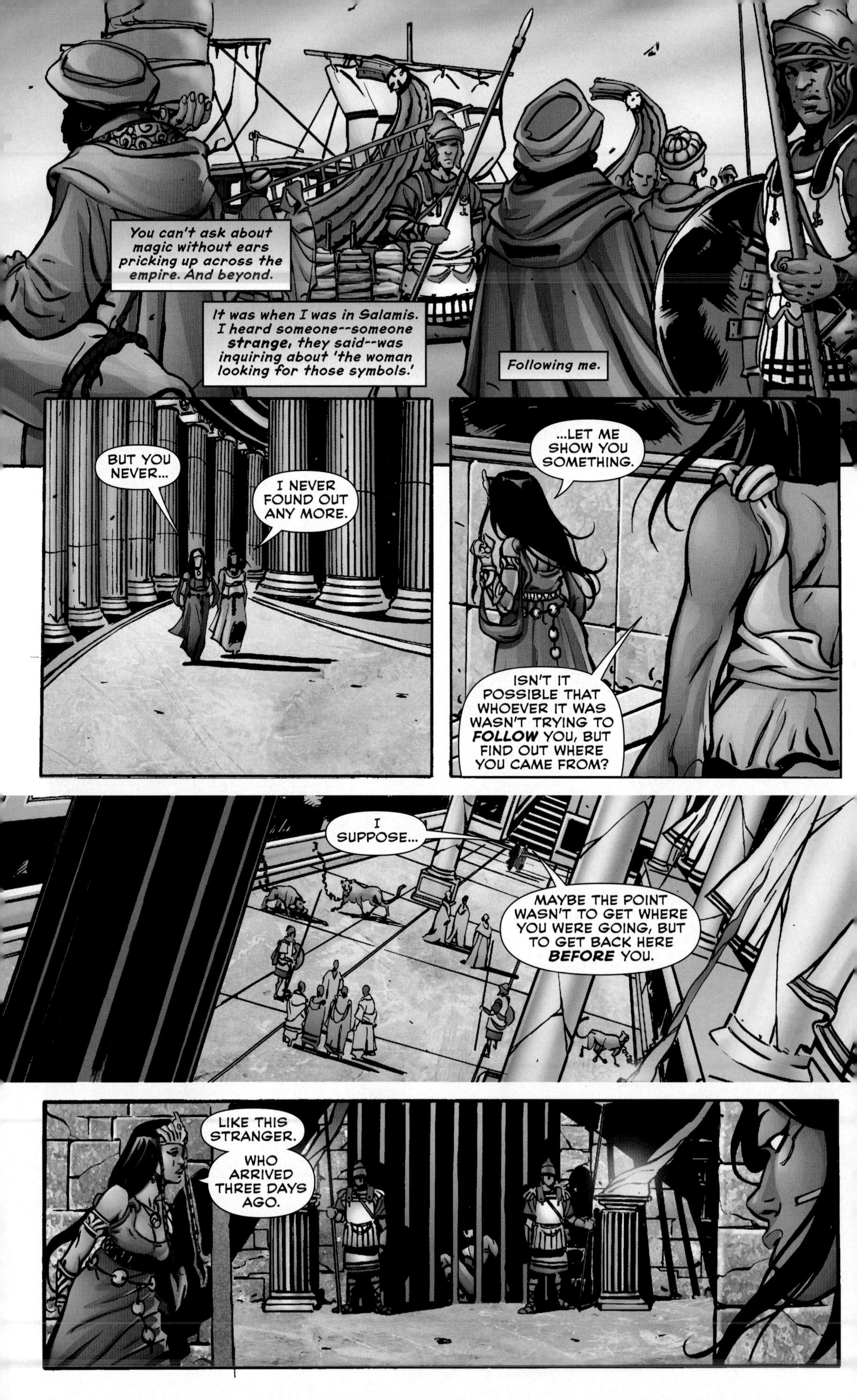
You can't ask about magic without ears pricking up across the empire. And beyond.
It was when I was in Salamis. I heard someone--someone *strange*, they said--was inquiring about 'the woman looking for those symbols.'
Following me.
BUT YOU NEVER...
I NEVER FOUND OUT ANY MORE.
...LET ME SHOW YOU SOMETHING.
ISN'T IT POSSIBLE THAT WHOEVER IT WAS WASN'T TRYING TO **FOLLOW** YOU, BUT FIND OUT WHERE YOU CAME FROM?
I SUPPOSE...
MAYBE THE POINT WASN'T TO GET WHERE YOU WERE GOING, BUT TO GET BACK HERE **BEFORE** YOU.
LIKE THIS STRANGER.
WHO ARRIVED THREE DAYS AGO.

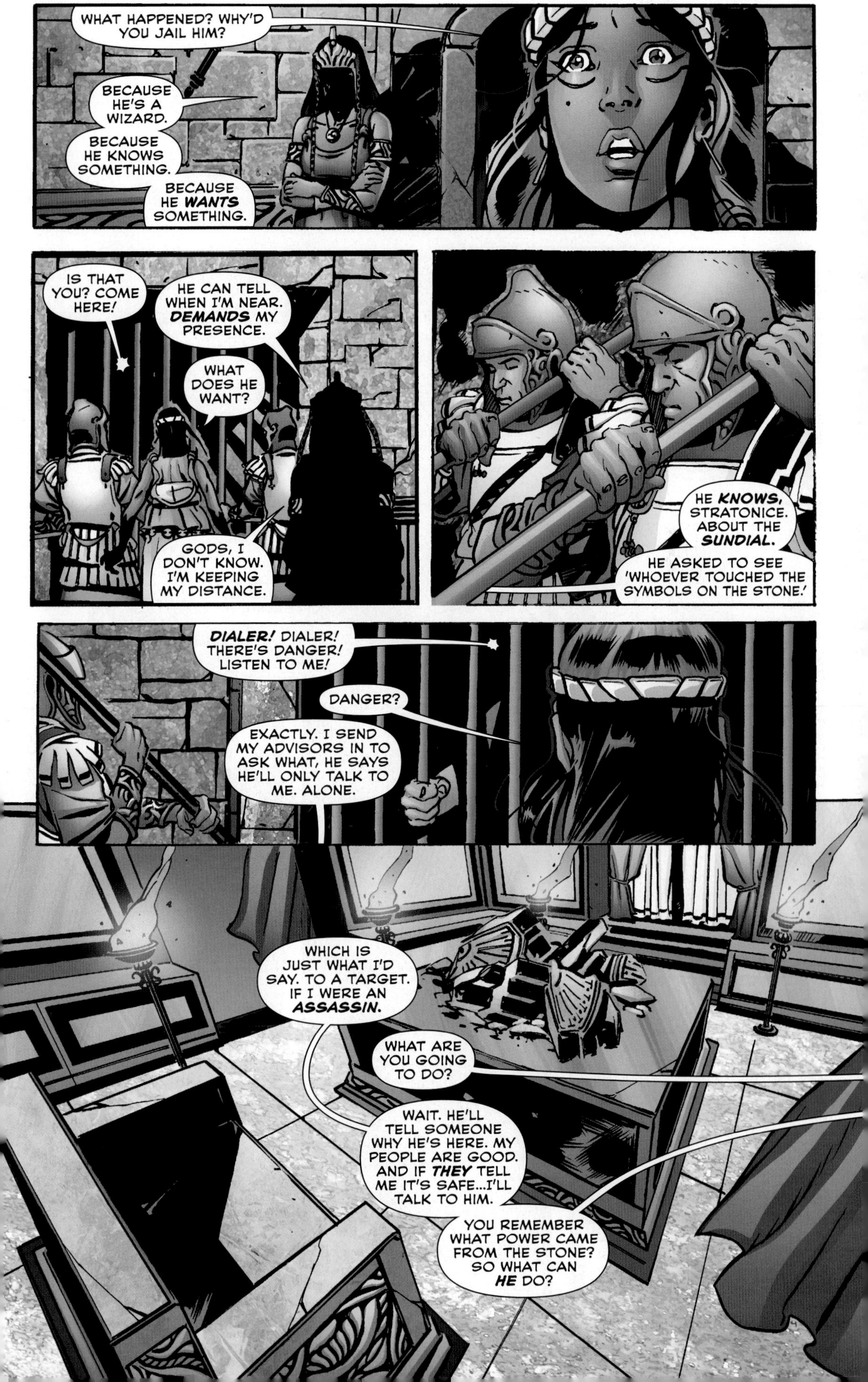
WHAT HAPPENED? WHY'D YOU JAIL HIM?
BECAUSE HE'S A WIZARD.
BECAUSE HE KNOWS SOMETHING.
BECAUSE HE **WANTS** SOMETHING.
IS THAT YOU? COME HERE!
HE CAN TELL WHEN I'M NEAR. **DEMANDS** MY PRESENCE.
WHAT DOES HE WANT?
GODS, I DON'T KNOW. I'M KEEPING MY DISTANCE.
HE **KNOWS,** STRATONICE. ABOUT THE **SUNDIAL.**
HE ASKED TO SEE 'WHOEVER TOUCHED THE SYMBOLS ON THE STONE.'
DIALER! DIALER! THERE'S DANGER! LISTEN TO ME!
DANGER?
EXACTLY. I SEND MY ADVISORS IN TO ASK WHAT, HE SAYS HE'LL ONLY TALK TO ME. ALONE.
WHICH IS JUST WHAT I'D SAY. TO A TARGET. IF I WERE AN **ASSASSIN.**
WHAT ARE YOU GOING TO DO?
WAIT. HE'LL TELL SOMEONE WHY HE'S HERE. MY PEOPLE ARE GOOD. AND IF **THEY** TELL ME IT'S SAFE...I'LL TALK TO HIM.
YOU REMEMBER WHAT POWER CAME FROM THE STONE? SO WHAT CAN **HE** DO?

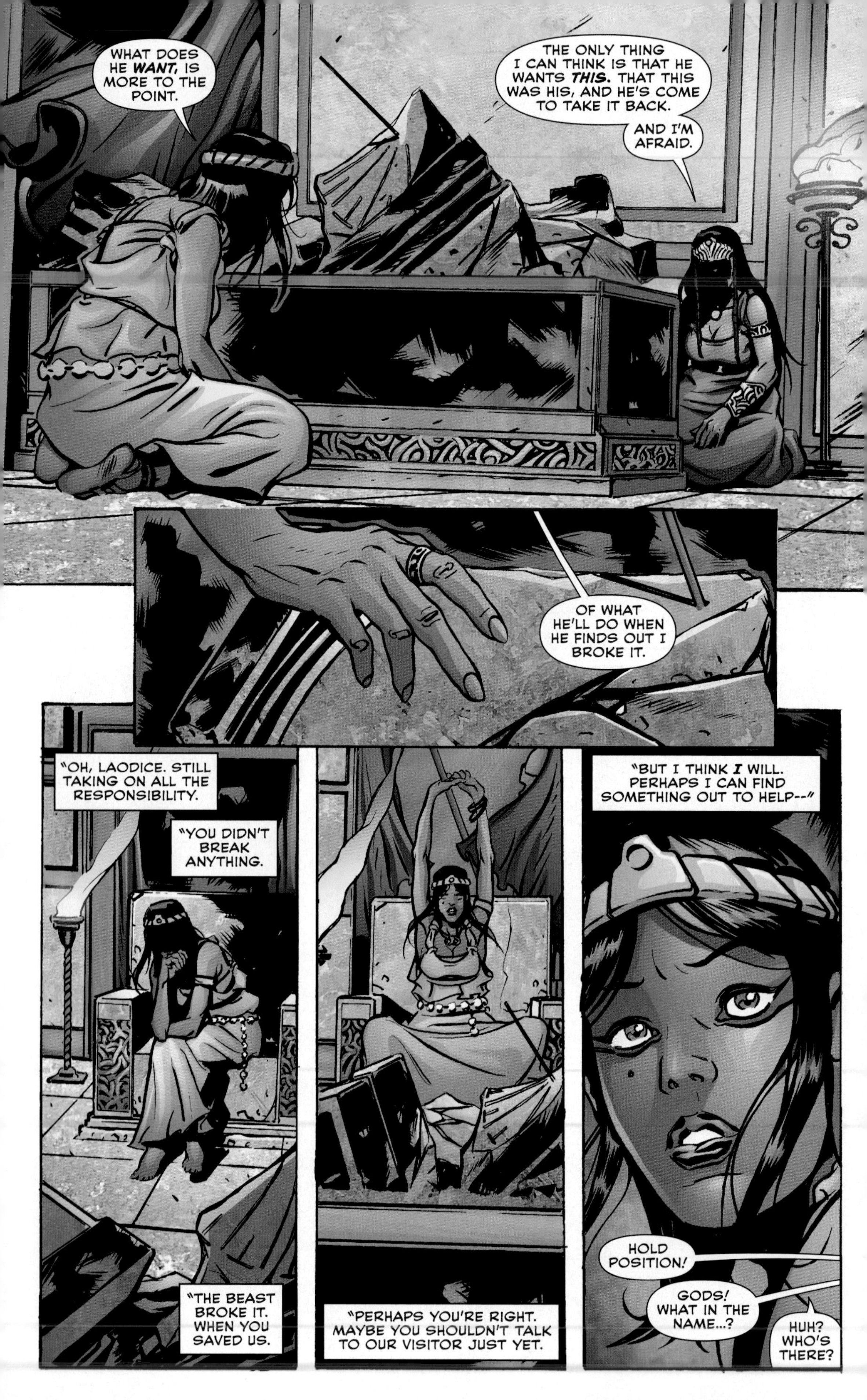
WHAT DOES HE *WANT*, IS MORE TO THE POINT.
THE ONLY THING I CAN THINK IS THAT HE WANTS *THIS*. THAT THIS WAS HIS, AND HE'S COME TO TAKE IT BACK.
AND I'M AFRAID.
OF WHAT HE'LL DO WHEN HE FINDS OUT I BROKE IT.
"OH, LAODICE. STILL TAKING ON ALL THE RESPONSIBILITY.
"YOU DIDN'T BREAK ANYTHING.
"THE BEAST BROKE IT. WHEN YOU SAVED US.
"PERHAPS YOU'RE RIGHT. MAYBE YOU SHOULDN'T TALK TO OUR VISITOR JUST YET.
"BUT I THINK *I* WILL. PERHAPS I CAN FIND SOMETHING OUT TO HELP--"
HOLD POSITION!
GODS! WHAT IN THE NAME...?
HUH? WHO'S THERE?

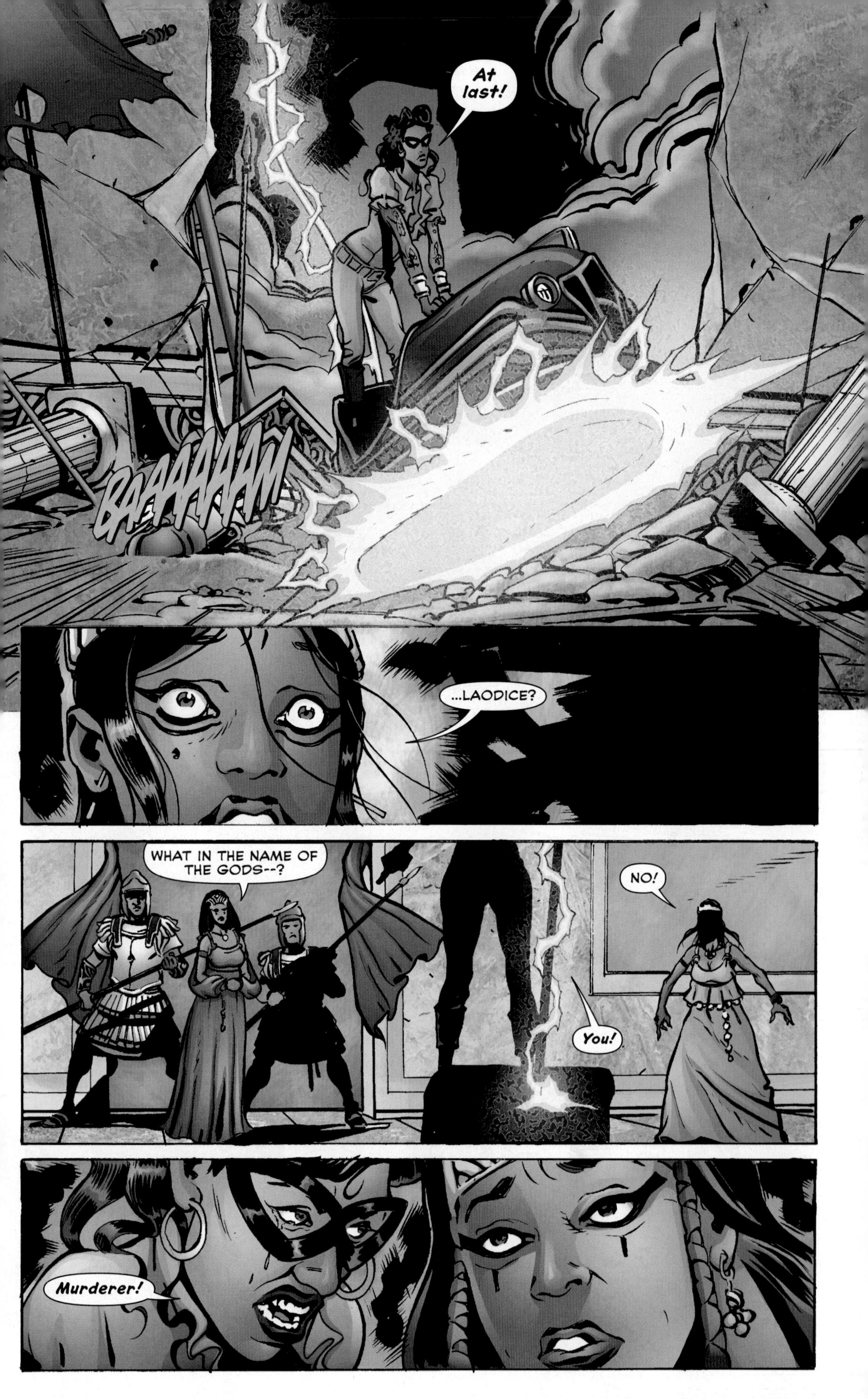
At last!
BAAAAAAM
...LAODICE?
WHAT IN THE NAME OF THE GODS--?
NO!
You!
Murderer!

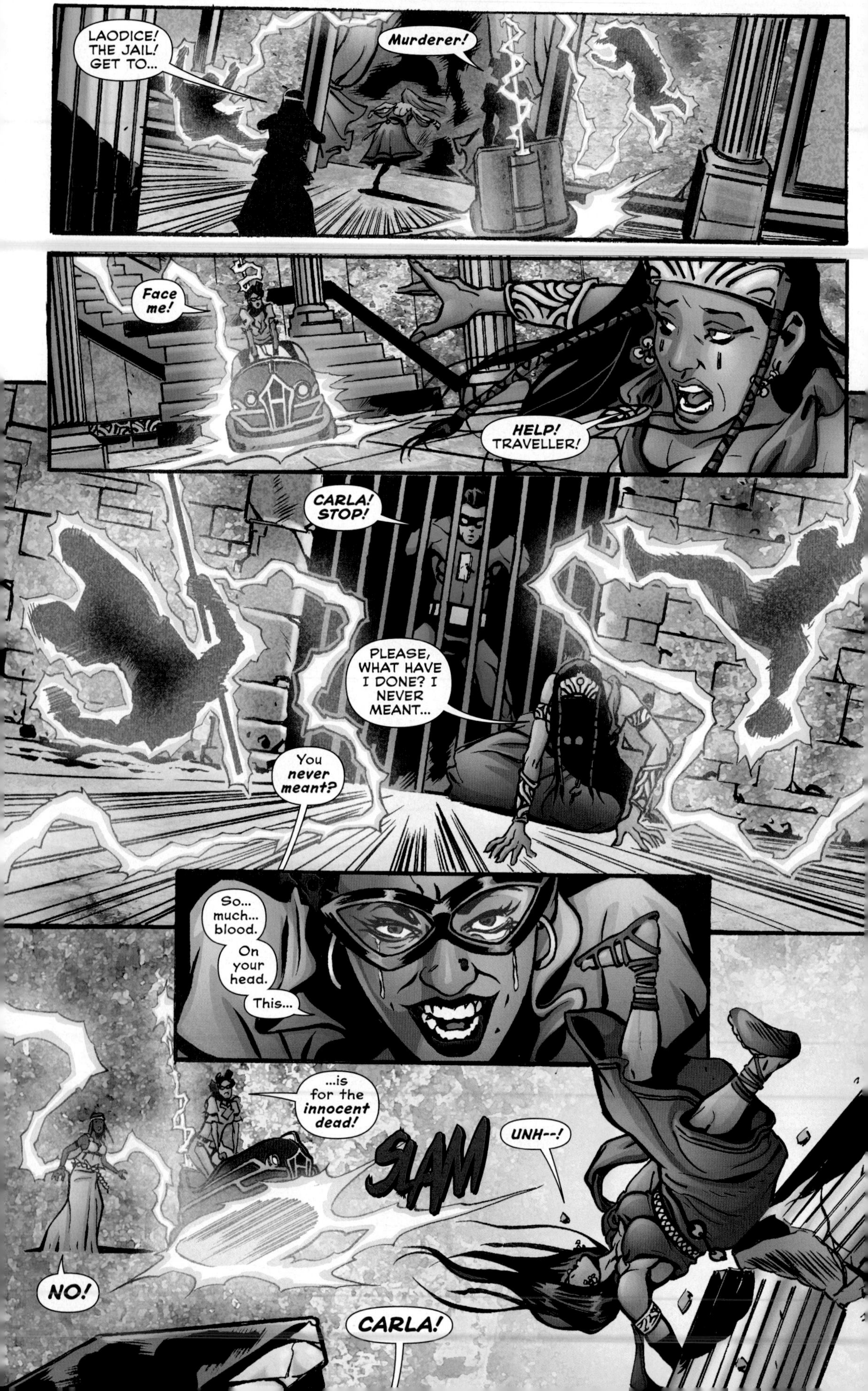
LAODICE! THE JAIL! GET TO...
Murderer!
Face me!
HELP! TRAVELLER!
CARLA! STOP!
PLEASE, WHAT HAVE I DONE? I NEVER MEANT...
You never meant?
So... much... blood.
On your head.
This...
...is for the innocent dead!
SLAM
UNH--!
NO!
CARLA!

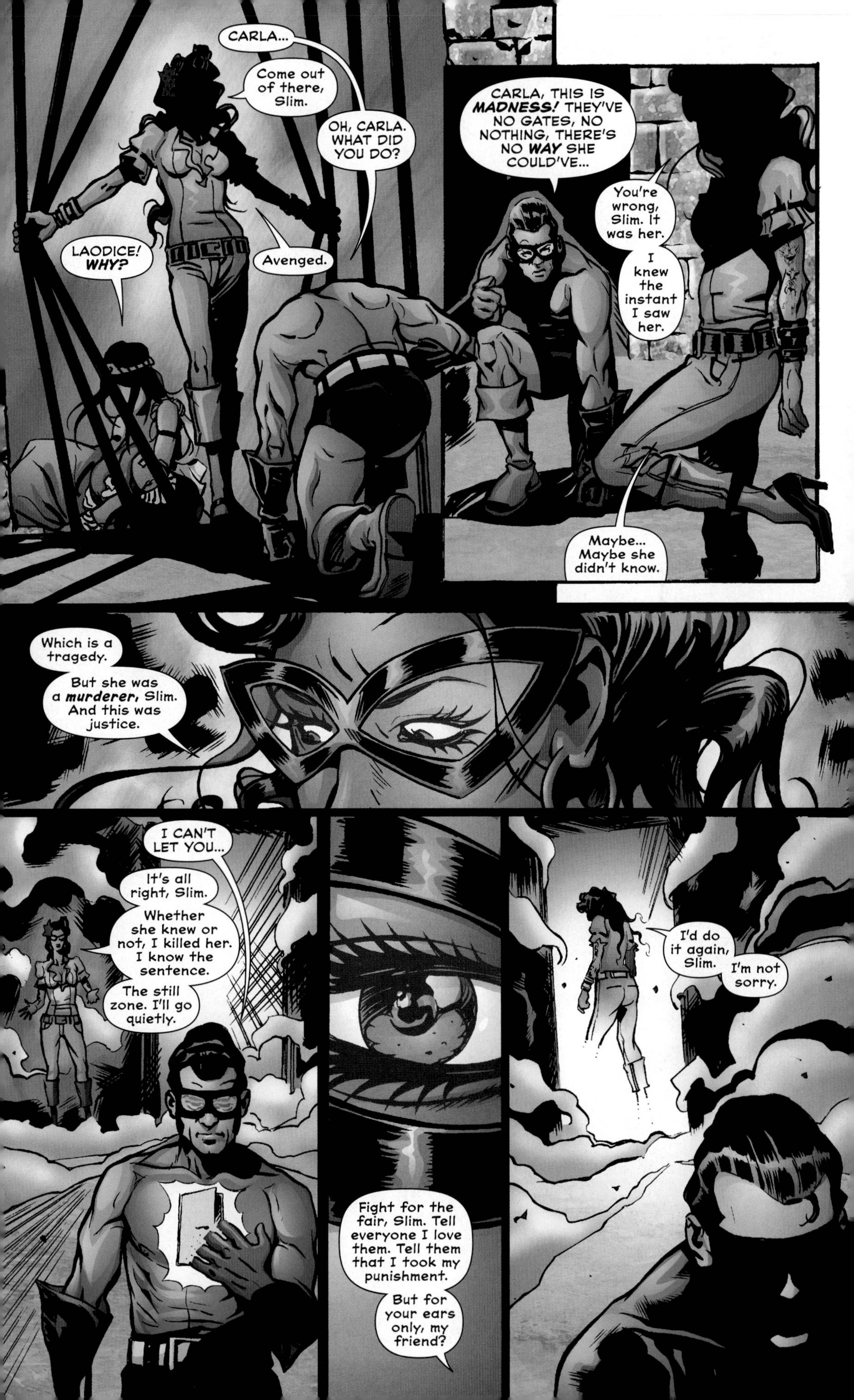
CARLA...
Come out of there, Slim.
LAODICE! WHY?
Avenged.
OH, CARLA. WHAT DID YOU DO?
CARLA, THIS IS MADNESS! THEY'VE NO GATES, NO NOTHING, THERE'S NO WAY SHE COULD'VE...
You're wrong, Slim. It was her.
I knew the instant I saw her.
Maybe... Maybe she didn't know.
Which is a tragedy.
But she was a murderer, Slim. And this was justice.
I CAN'T LET YOU...
It's all right, Slim.
Whether she knew or not, I killed her. I know the sentence.
The still zone. I'll go quietly.
Fight for the fair, Slim. Tell everyone I love them. Tell them that I took my punishment.
But for your ears only, my friend?
I'd do it again, Slim.
I'm not sorry.

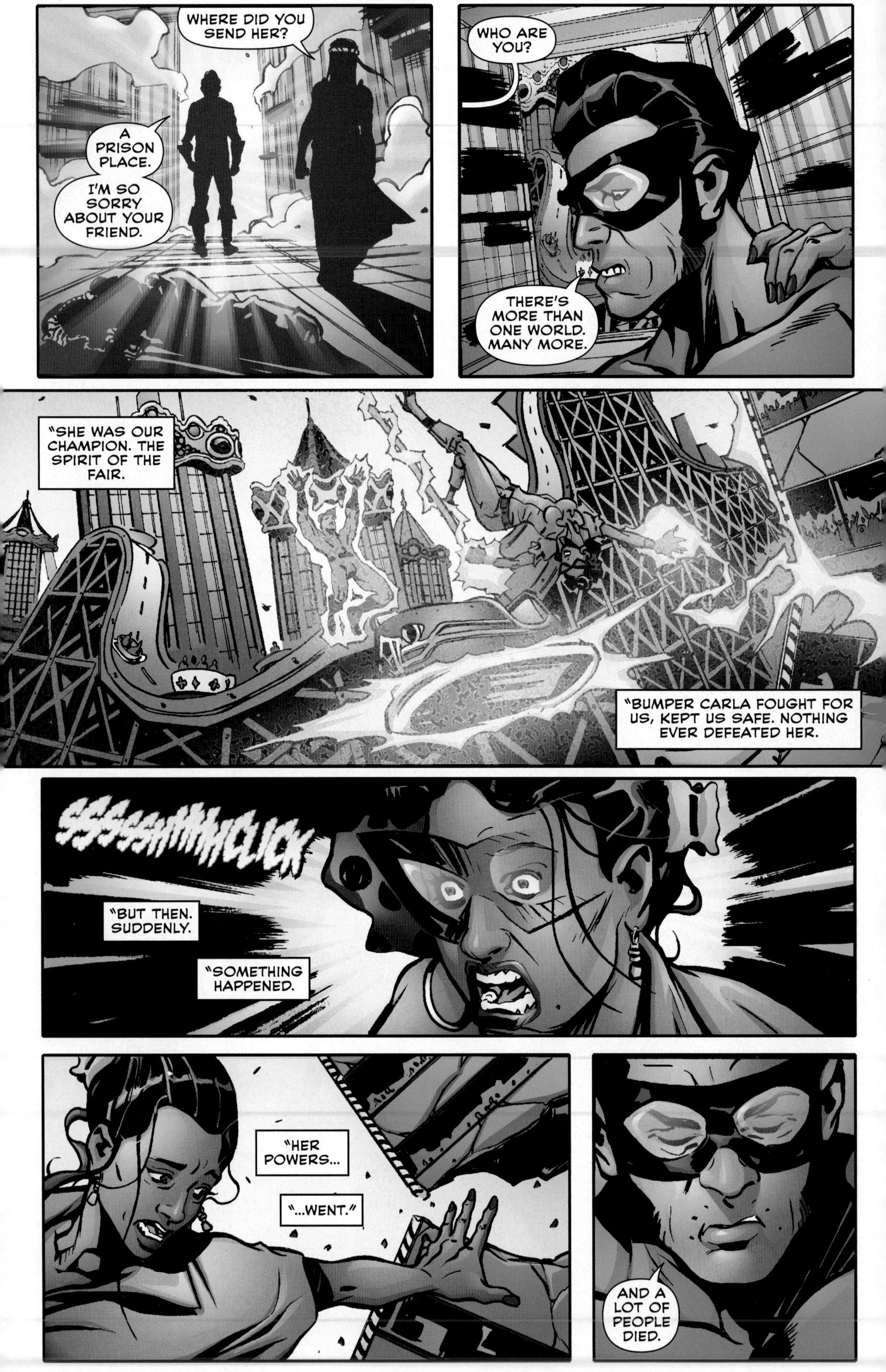
WHERE DID YOU SEND HER?
A PRISON PLACE.
I'M SO SORRY ABOUT YOUR FRIEND.
WHO ARE YOU?
THERE'S MORE THAN ONE WORLD. MANY MORE.
"SHE WAS OUR CHAMPION. THE SPIRIT OF THE FAIR.
"BUMPER CARLA FOUGHT FOR US, KEPT US SAFE. NOTHING EVER DEFEATED HER.
SSSSSHHHHCLICK
"BUT THEN. SUDDENLY.
"SOMETHING HAPPENED.
"HER POWERS...
"...WENT."
AND A LOT OF PEOPLE DIED.

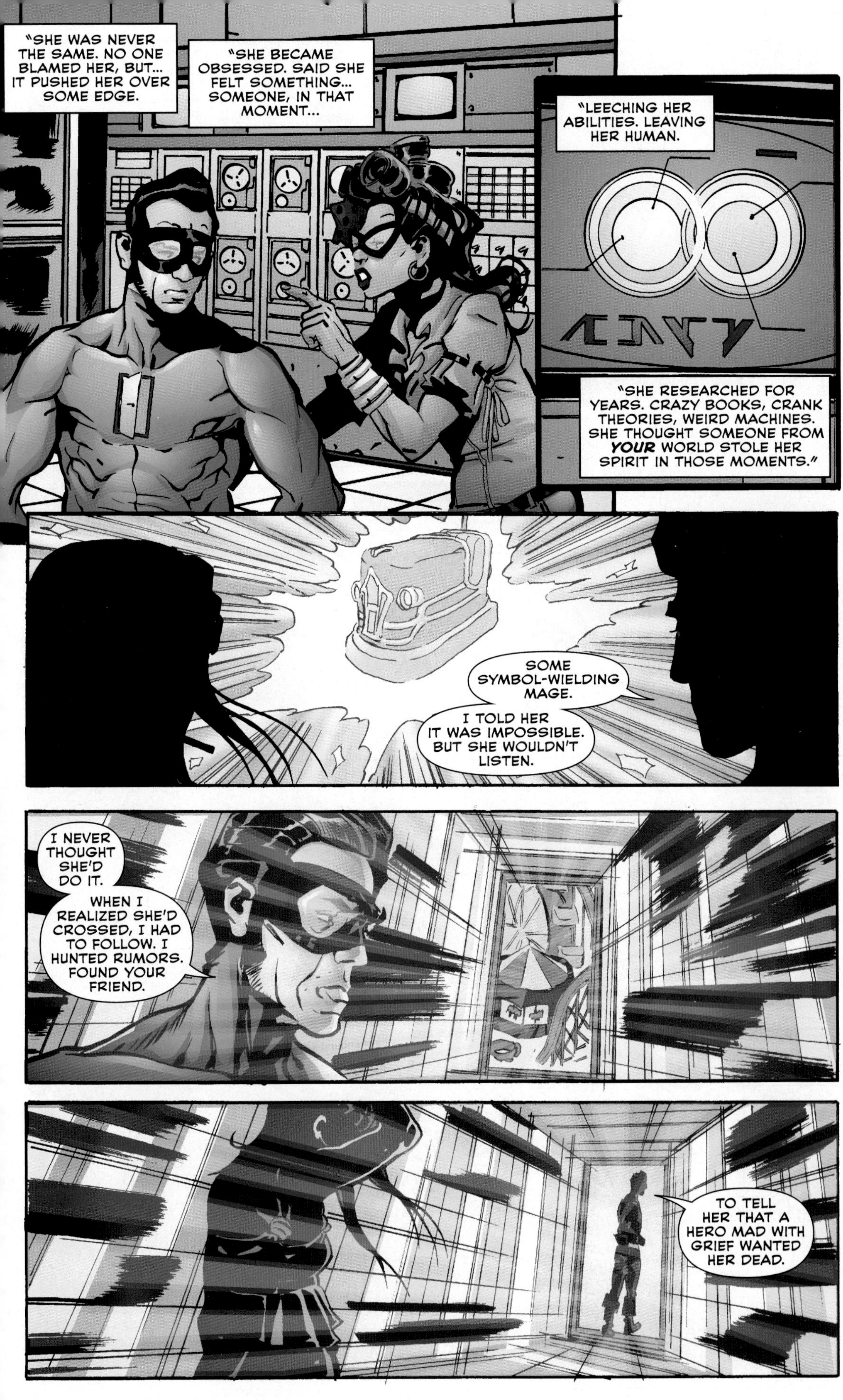
"SHE WAS NEVER THE SAME. NO ONE BLAMED HER, BUT... IT PUSHED HER OVER SOME EDGE.
"SHE BECAME OBSESSED. SAID SHE FELT SOMETHING... SOMEONE, IN THAT MOMENT...
"LEECHING HER ABILITIES. LEAVING HER HUMAN.
"SHE RESEARCHED FOR YEARS. CRAZY BOOKS, CRANK THEORIES, WEIRD MACHINES. SHE THOUGHT SOMEONE FROM ***YOUR*** WORLD STOLE HER SPIRIT IN THOSE MOMENTS."
SOME SYMBOL-WIELDING MAGE.
I TOLD HER IT WAS IMPOSSIBLE. BUT SHE WOULDN'T LISTEN.
I NEVER THOUGHT SHE'D DO IT.
WHEN I REALIZED SHE'D CROSSED, I HAD TO FOLLOW. I HUNTED RUMORS. FOUND YOUR FRIEND.
TO TELL HER THAT A HERO MAD WITH GRIEF WANTED HER DEAD.

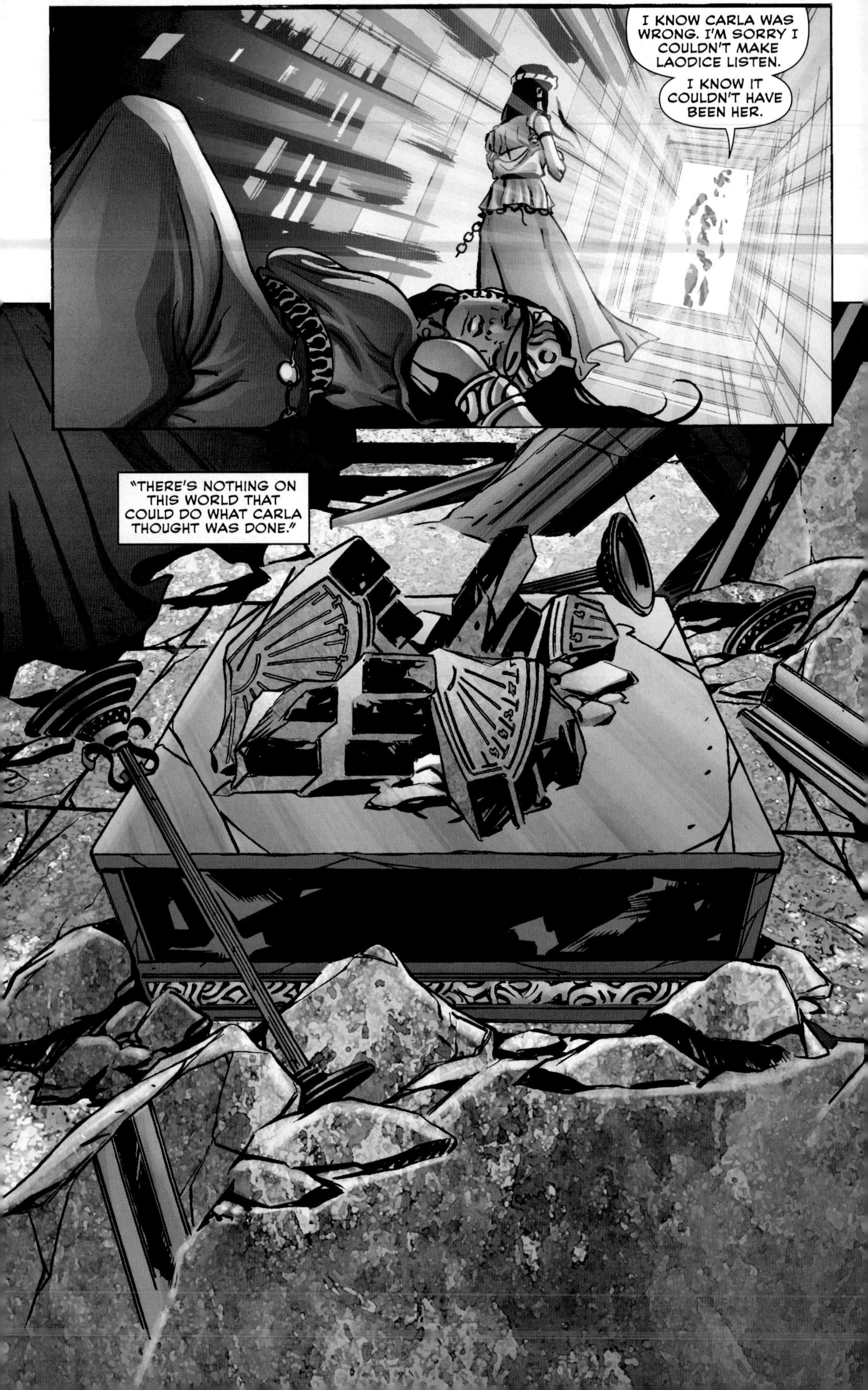
I KNOW CARLA WAS WRONG. I'M SORRY I COULDN'T MAKE LAODICE LISTEN.
I KNOW IT COULDN'T HAVE BEEN HER.
"THERE'S NOTHING ON THIS WORLD THAT COULD DO WHAT CARLA THOUGHT WAS DONE."

WHO'S WHO IN THE NEW 52!

A MOST UNLIKELY HERO

DIAL H

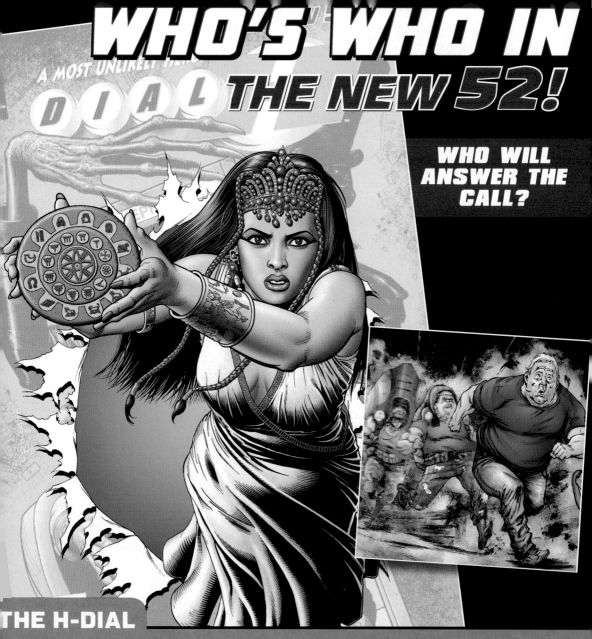

WHO WILL ANSWER THE CALL?

THE H-DIAL

First Appearance:
Dial H #1 (2012)

Base of Operations:
Littleville

Powers:
Whoever uses an H-Dial has the ability to tap or "dial" into a force that overlay the powers --and sometimes memories--of a seemingly random superhero onto the user. These power sets can be extremely strong, extremely bizarre and also extremely dangerous.

Heroes Dialed:
Boy Chimney, Captain Lachrymose Iron Snail, Bumper Carla Control-alt-delete, Baroness Resin

History:

The H-Dial is one of the greatest mysteries of the universe. It is an artifact that combines strange magic and the interdimensional technology of something known only as "The Exchange." The effects of H-Dial use are as diverse as the powers that can be bestowed on the user--ranging from the creation of telephone technology in our world to possibly catastrophic disasters in certain other dimensions. While it is understood that H-Dials have existed throughout time, it may never be uncovered how they were designed--or by whom.

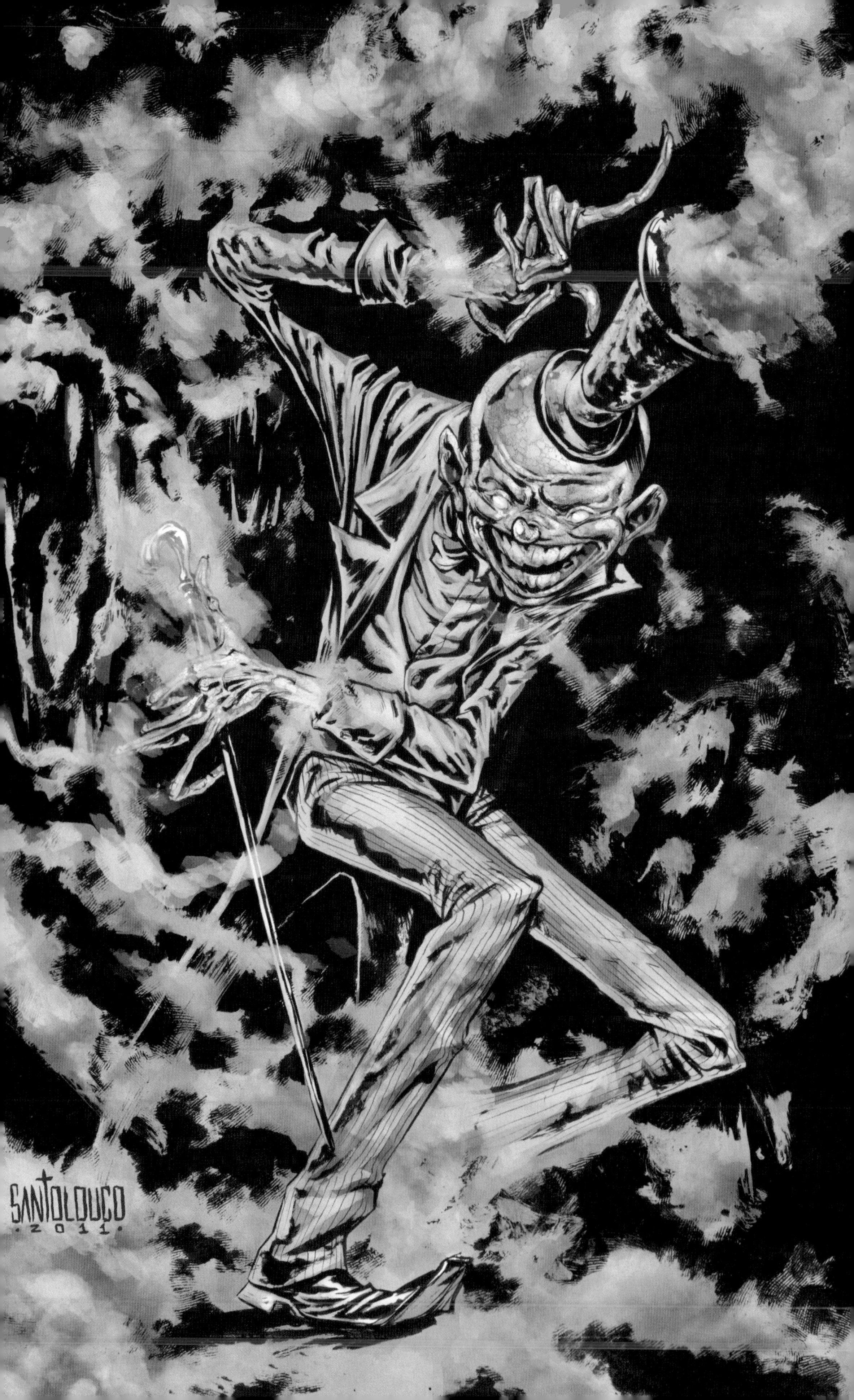
SANTOLOUCO
·2011·

DIAL H
character sketches by **MATEUS SANTOLOUCO**

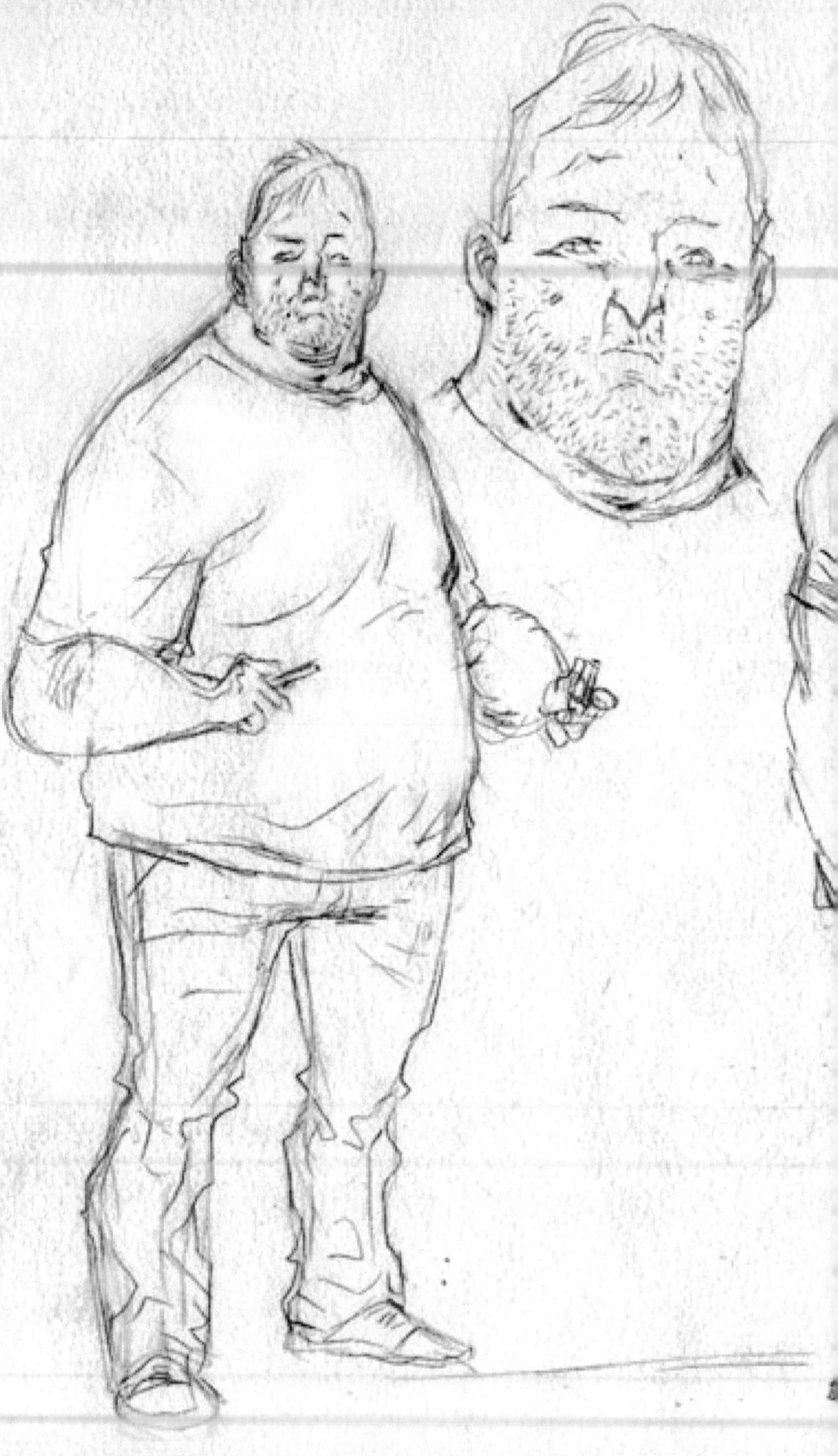

Artist Mateus Santolouco's character designs, which feature two opposing takes on Nelson Jent. An earlier, more bug-eyed portrayal of Boy Chimney makes a guest appearance.

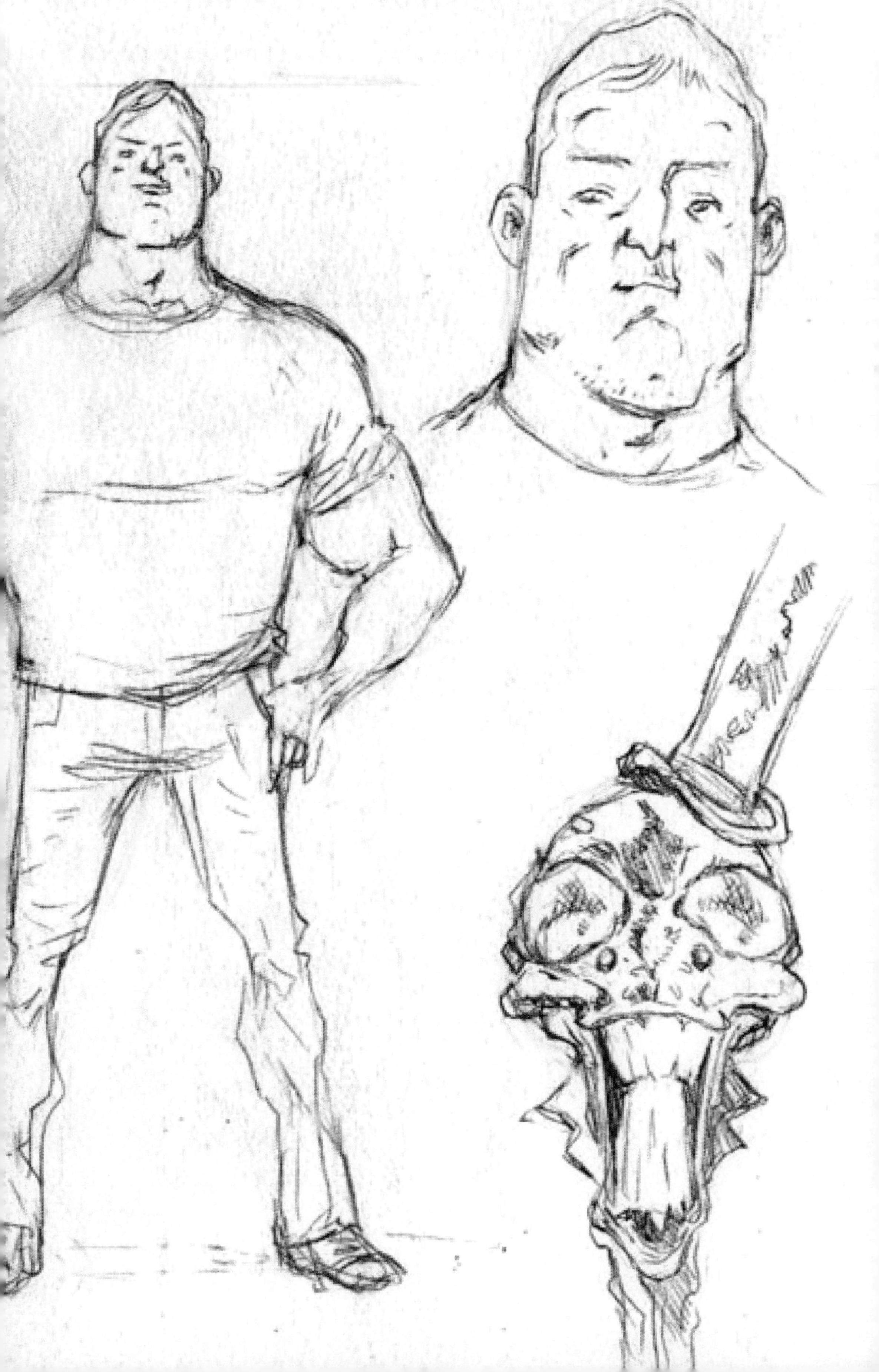

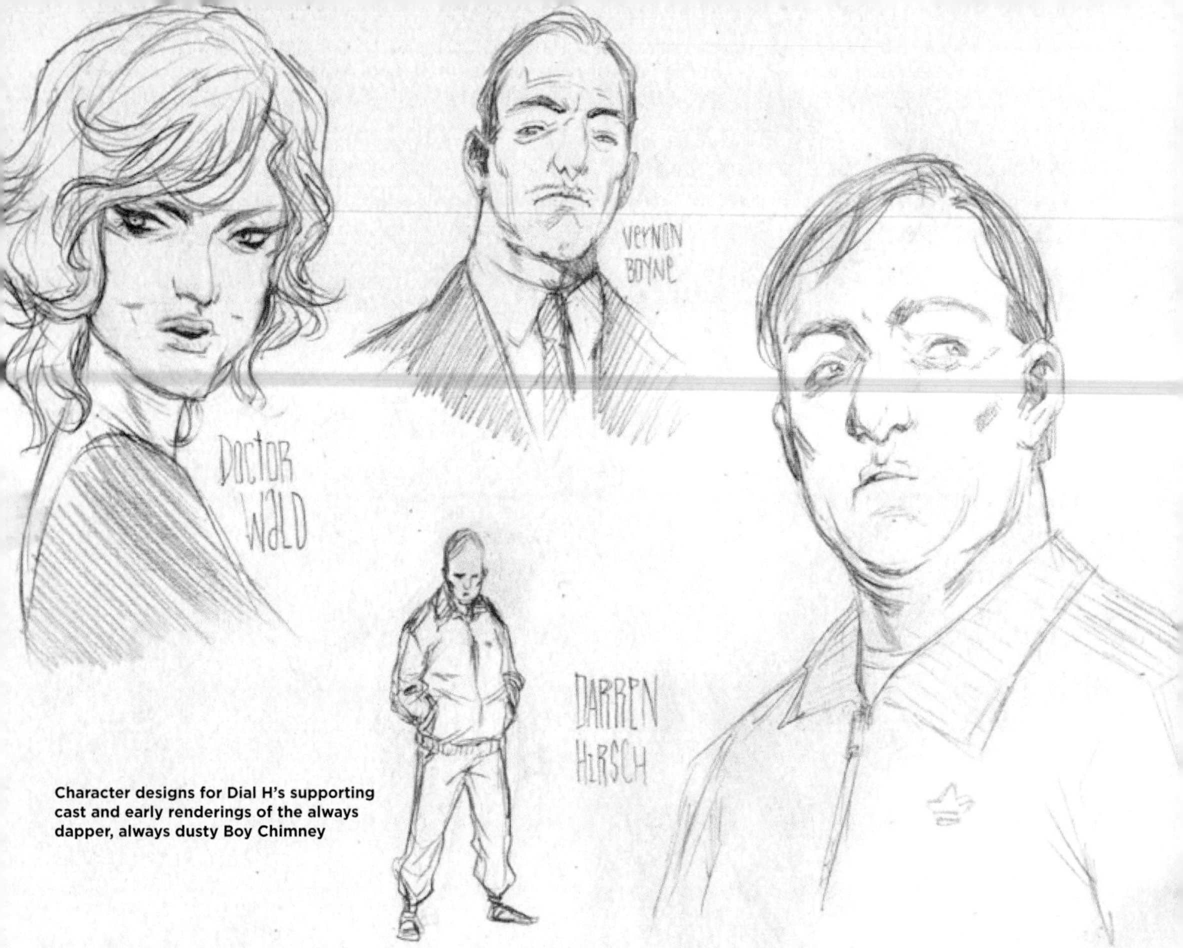

VERNON BOYNE
DOCTOR WALD
DARREN HIRSCH

Character designs for Dial H's supporting cast and early renderings of the always dapper, always dusty Boy Chimney

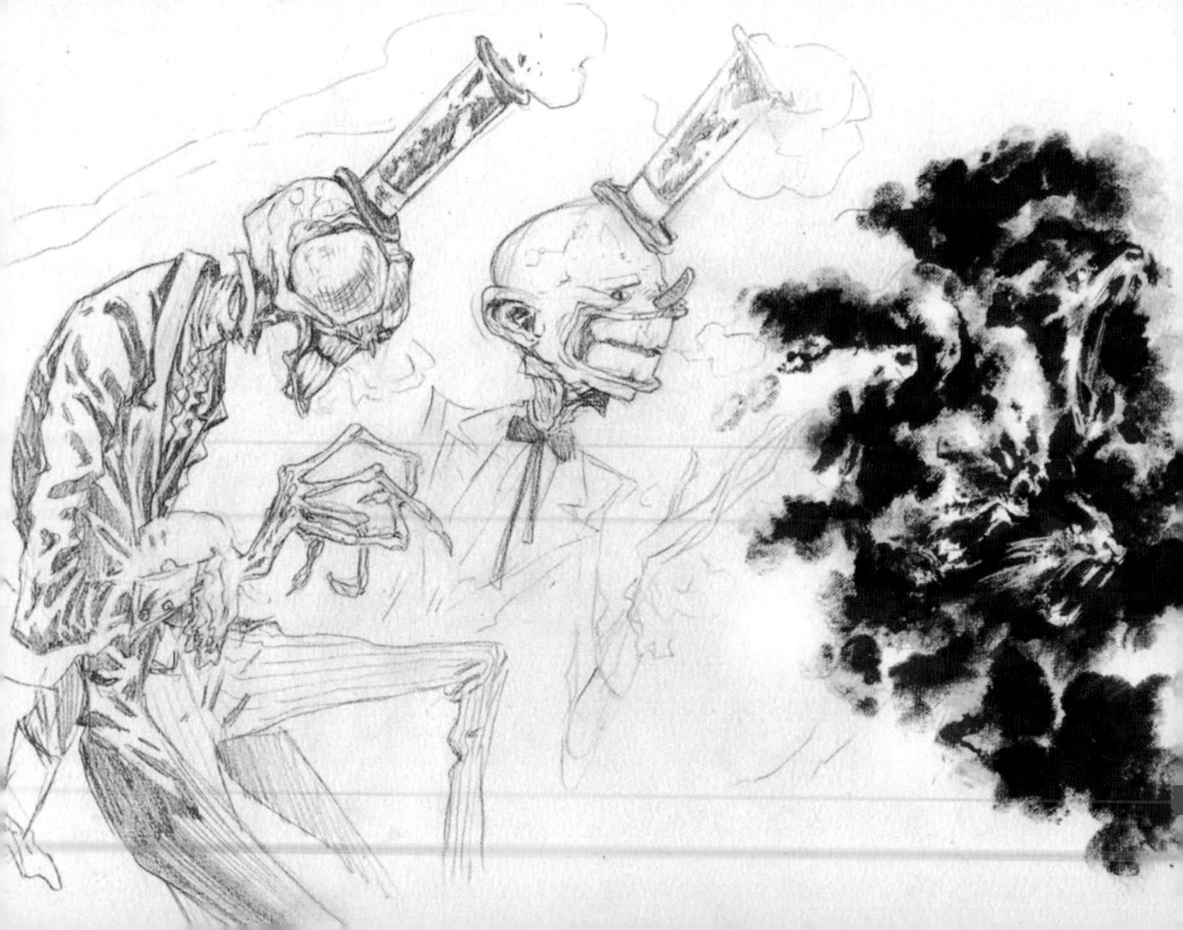

The blackline of issue #1, page 7. The first appearance of Boy Chimney, and Nelson's first activation of the H Dial.

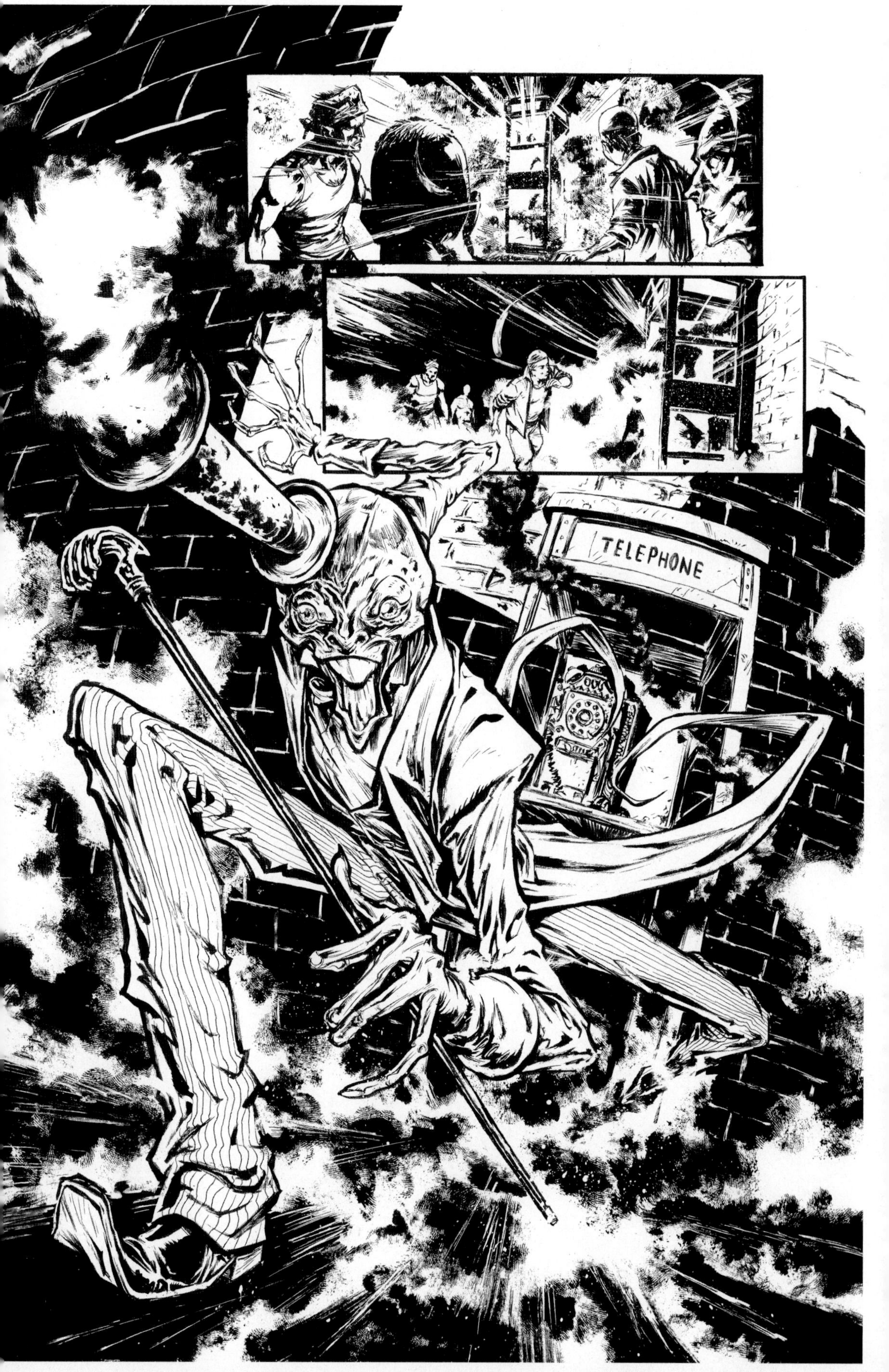
TELEPHONE

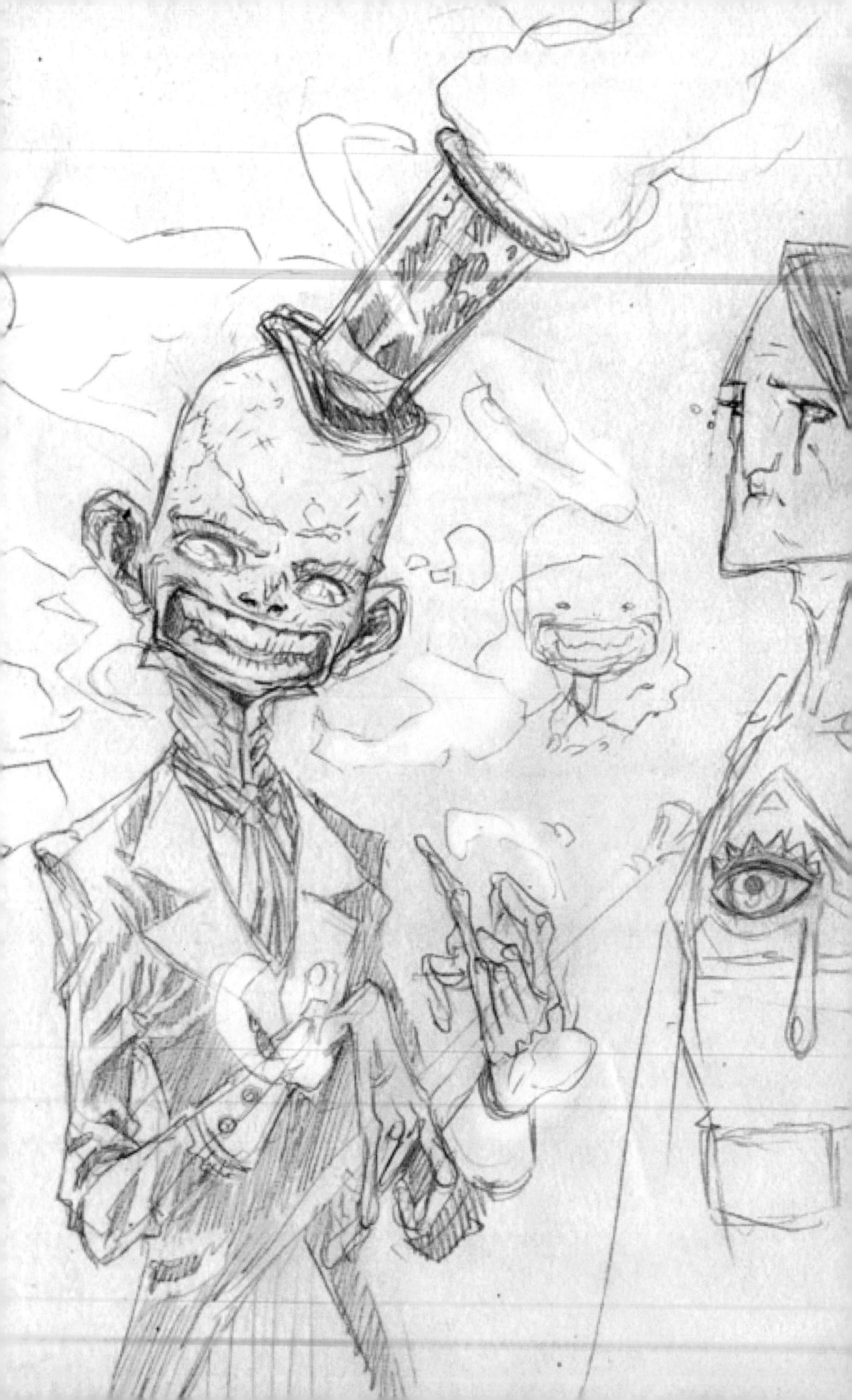

CAPTAIN LACHRYMOSE CHARACTER DESIGN BY MATEUS SANTOLOUCO

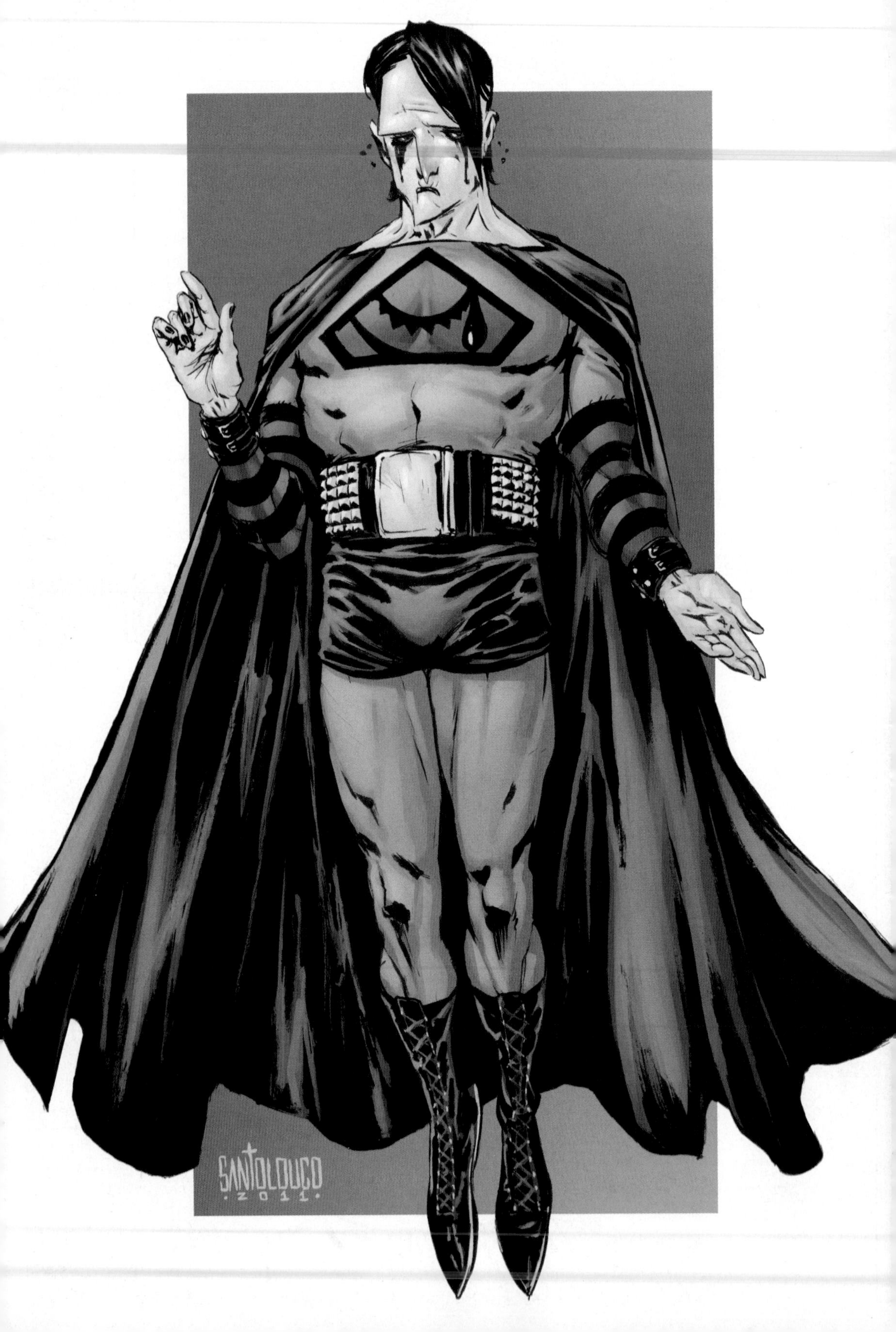
SANTOLOUCO
2011

The blackline of issue #1, page 18. The "emo"-tive Captain Lachrymose crashes the party

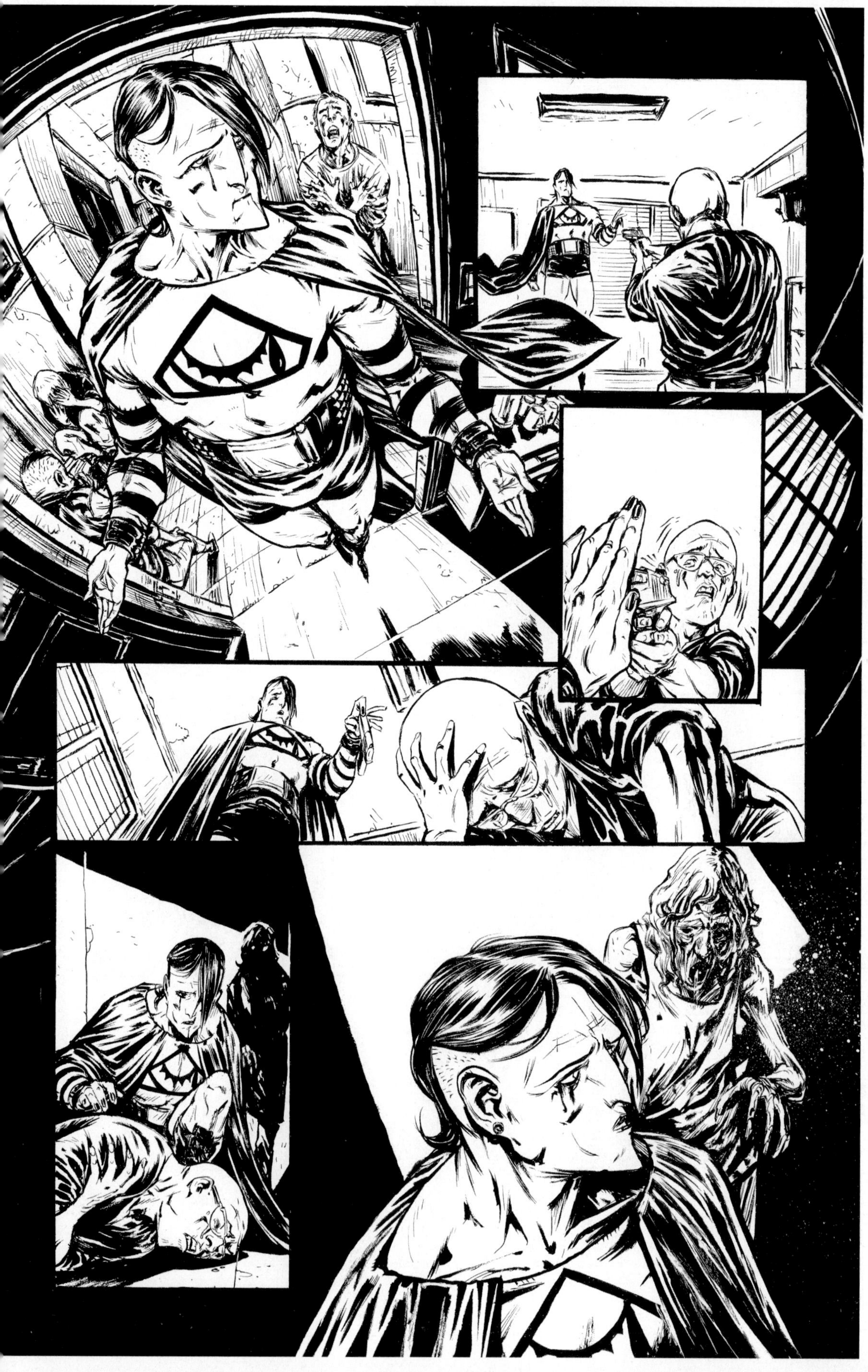

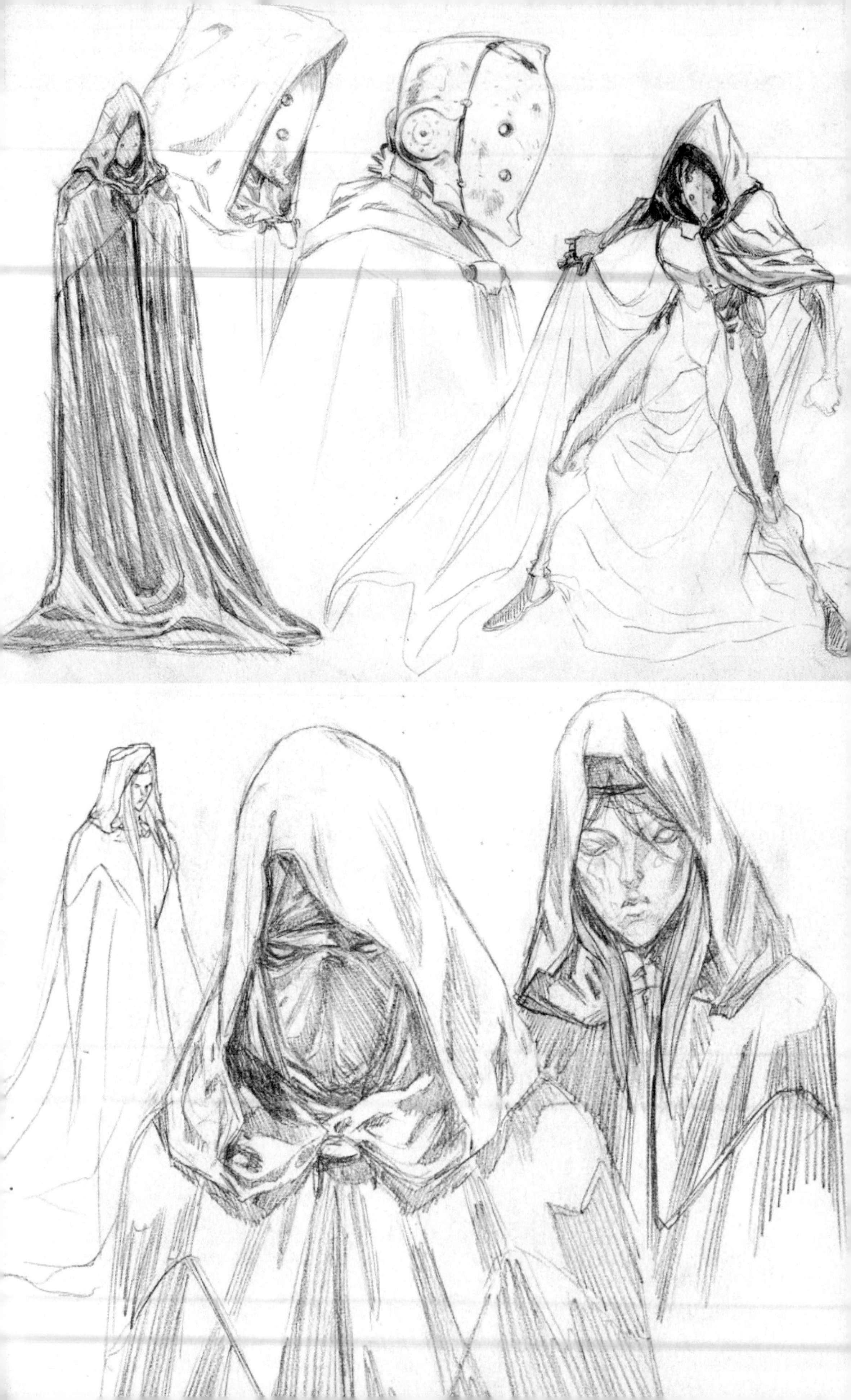

MANTEAU CHARACTER DESIGN BY MATEUS SANTOLOUCO

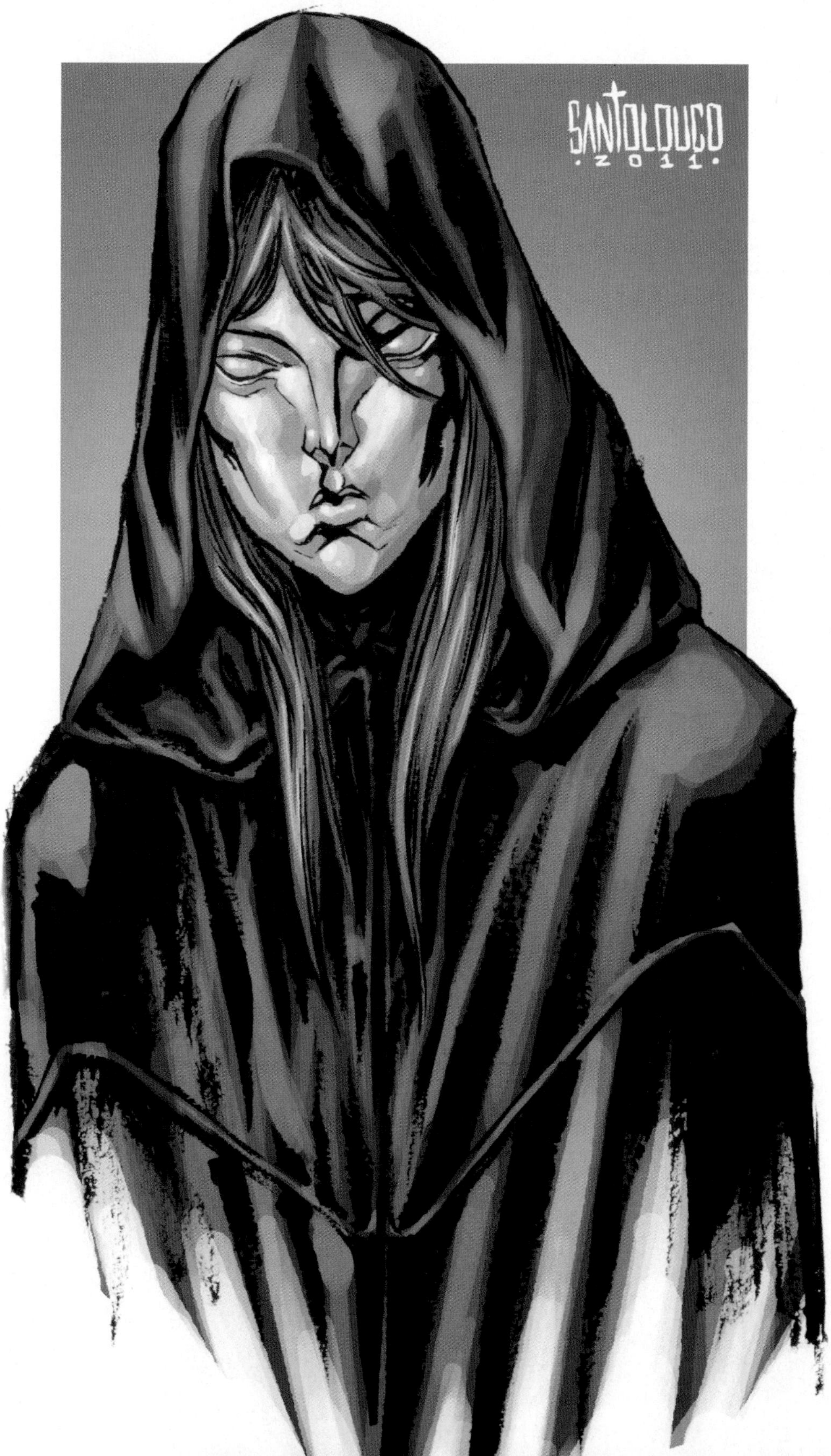
SANTOLOUCO
·2011·

DIAL H

ABYSS AND SQUID CHARACTER DESIGNS BY MATEUS SANTOLOUCO

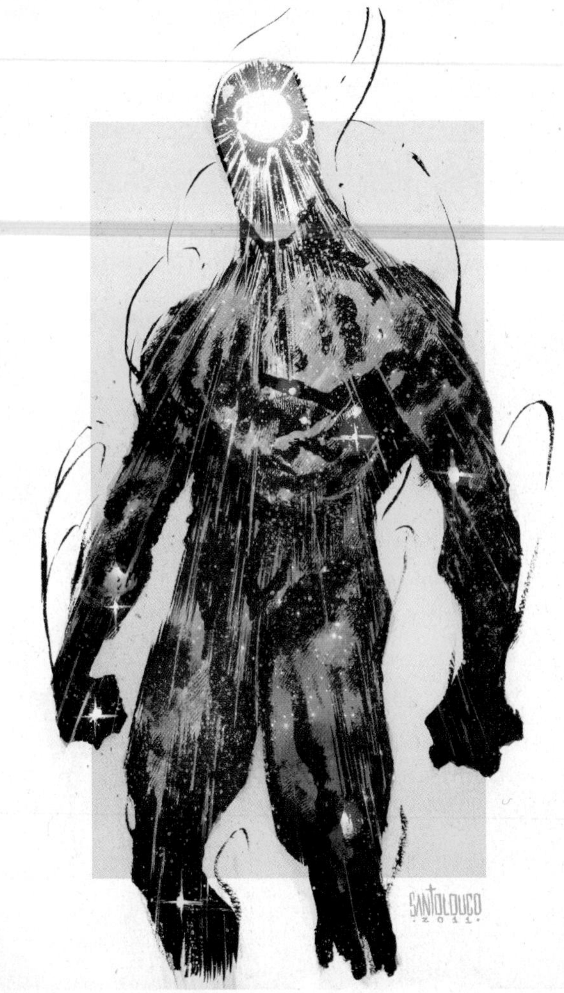
SANTOLOUCO
2011

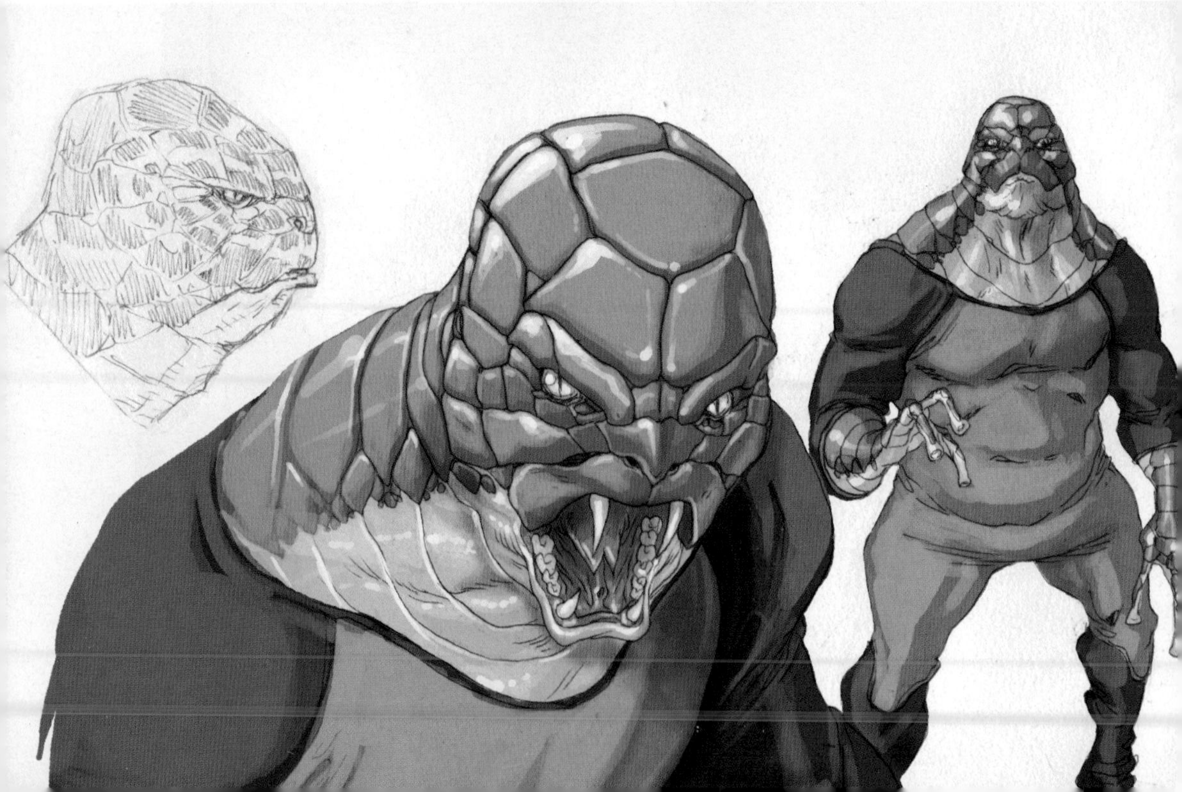